T0197945

Get the eBooks FREE!

(PDF, ePub, Kindle, and liveBook all included)

We believe that once you buy a book from us, you should be able to read it in any format we have available. To get electronic versions of this book at no additional cost to you, purchase and then register this book at the Manning website.

Go to https://www.manning.com/freebook and follow the instructions to complete your pBook registration.

That's it!
Thanks from Manning!

OpenCL in Action

OpenCL in Action

HOW TO ACCELERATE GRAPHICS AND COMPUTATION

MATTHEW SCARPINO

MANNING
SHELTER ISLAND

For online information and ordering of this and other Manning books, please visit
www.manning.com. The publisher offers discounts on this book when ordered in quantity.
For more information, please contact

Special Sales Department
Manning Publications Co.
20 Baldwin Road
PO Box 261
Shelter Island, NY 11964
Email: orders@manning.com

Manning Publications Co.   Development editor: Maria Townsley
20 Baldwin Road   Copyeditor: Andy Carroll
PO Box 261   Proofreader: Maureen Spencer
Shelter Island, NY 11964   Typesetter: Gordan Salinovic
                                   Cover designer: Marija Tudor

ISBN 9781617290176
Printed in the United States of America
6 7 8 9 10 – SP – 20 19

brief contents

contents

4 Kernel programming: data types and device memory   68

5 Kernel programming: operators and functions   94

PART 2   CODING PRACTICAL ALGORITHMS IN OPENCL.......235

preface

In the summer of 1997, I was terrified. Instead of working as an intern in my major (microelectronic engineering), the best job I could find was at a research laboratory devoted to high-speed signal processing. My job was to program the two-dimensional fast Fourier transform (FFT) using C and the Message Passing Interface (MPI), and get it running as quickly as possible. The good news was that the lab had sixteen brand new SPARCstations. The bad news was that I knew absolutely nothing about MPI or the FFT.

Thanks to books purchased from a strange new site called Amazon.com, I managed to understand the basics of MPI: the application deploys one set of instructions to multiple computers, and each processor accesses data according to its ID. As each processor finishes its task, it sends its output to the processor whose ID equals 0.

It took me time to grasp the finer details of MPI (blocking versus nonblocking data transfer, synchronous versus asynchronous communication), but as I worked more with the language, I fell in love with distributed computing. I loved the fact that I could get sixteen monstrous computers to process data in lockstep, working together like athletes on a playing field. I felt like a choreographer arranging a dance or a composer writing a symphony for an orchestra. By the end of the internship, I coded multiple versions of the 2-D FFT in MPI, but the lab's researchers decided that network latency made the computation impractical.

Since that summer, I've always gravitated toward high-performance computing, and I've had the pleasure of working with digital signal processors, field-programmable gate arrays, and the Cell processor, which serves as the brain of Sony's PlayStation 3. But nothing beats programming graphics processing units (GPUs) with OpenCL. As today's supercomputers have shown, no CPU provides the same number-crunching power per watt as a GPU. And no language can target as wide a range of devices as OpenCL.

When AMD released its OpenCL development tools in 2009, I fell in love again. Not only does OpenCL provide new vector types and a wealth of math functions, but it also resembles MPI in many respects. Both toolsets are freely available and their routines can be called in C or C++. In both cases, applications deliver instructions to multiple devices whose processing units rely on IDs to determine which data they should access. MPI and OpenCL also make it possible to send data using similar types of blocking/non-blocking transfers and synchronous/asynchronous communication.

OpenCL is still new in the world of high-performance computing, and many programmers don't know it exists. To help spread the word about this incredible language, I decided to write *OpenCL in Action*. I've enjoyed working on this book a great deal, and I hope it helps newcomers take advantage of the power of OpenCL and distributed computing in general.

As I write this in the summer of 2011, I feel as though I've come full circle. Last night, I put the finishing touches on the FFT application presented in chapter 14. It brought back many pleasant memories of my work with MPI, but I'm amazed by how much the technology has changed. In 1997, the sixteen SPARCstations in my lab took nearly a minute to perform a 32k FFT. In 2011, my $300 graphics card can perform an FFT on millions of data points in seconds.

The technology changes, but the enjoyment remains the same. The learning curve can be steep in the world of distributed computing, but the rewards more than make up for the effort expended.

acknowledgments

I started writing my first book for Manning Publications in 2003, and though much has changed, they are still as devoted to publishing high-quality books now as they were then. I'd like to thank all of Manning's professionals for their hard work and dedication, but I'd like to acknowledge the following folks in particular:

First, I'd like to thank Maria Townsley, who worked as developmental editor. Maria is one of the most hands-on editors I've worked with, and she went beyond the call of duty in recommending ways to improve the book's organization and clarity. I bristled and whined, but in the end, she turned out to be absolutely right. In addition, despite my frequent rewriting of the table of contents, her pleasant disposition never flagged for a moment.

I'd like to extend my deep gratitude to the entire Manning production team. In particular, I'd like to thank Andy Carroll for going above and beyond the call of duty in copyediting this book. His comments and insight have not only dramatically improved the polish of the text, but his technical expertise has made the content more accessible. Similarly, I'd like to thank Maureen Spencer and Katie Tennant for their eagle-eyed proofreading of the final copy and Gordan Salinovic for his painstaking labor in dealing with the book's images and layout. I'd also like to thank Mary Piergies for masterminding the production process and making sure the final product lives up to Manning's high standards.

Jörn Dinkla is, simply put, the best technical editor I've ever worked with. I tested the book's example code on Linux and Mac OS, but he went further and tested the code with software development kits from Linux, AMD, and Nvidia. Not only did he catch quite a few errors I missed, but in many cases, he took the time to find out why the error had occurred. I shudder to think what would have happened without his assistance, and I'm beyond grateful for the work he put into improving the quality of this book's code.

I'd like to thank Candace Gilhooley for spreading the word about the book's publication. Given OpenCL's youth, the audience isn't as easy to reach as the audience for Manning's many Java books. But between setting up web articles, presentations, and conference attendance, Candace has done an exemplary job in marketing *OpenCL in Action*.

One of Manning's greatest strengths is its reliance on constant feedback. During development and production, Karen Tegtmeyer and Ozren Harlovic sought out reviewers for this book and organized a number of review cycles. Thanks to the feedback from the following reviewers, this book includes a number of important subjects that I wouldn't otherwise have considered: Olivier Chafik, Martin Beckett, Benjamin Ducke, Alan Commike, Nathan Levesque, David Strong, Seth Price, John J. Ryan III, and John Griffin.

Last but not least, I'd like to thank Jan Bednarczuk of Jandex Indexing for her meticulous work in indexing the content of this book. She not only created a thorough, professional index in a short amount of time, but she also caught quite a few typos in the process. Thanks again.

about this book

OpenCL is a complex subject. To code even the simplest of applications, a developer needs to understand host programming, device programming, and the mechanisms that transfer data between the host and device. The goal of this book is to show how these tasks are accomplished and how to put them to use in practical applications.

The format of this book is tutorial-based. That is, each new concept is followed by example code that demonstrates how the theory is used in an application. Many of the early applications are trivially basic, and some do nothing more than obtain information about devices and data structures. But as the book progresses, the code becomes more involved and makes fuller use of both the host and the target device. In the later chapters, the focus shifts from learning how OpenCL works to putting OpenCL to use in processing vast amounts of data at high speed.

Audience

In writing this book, I've assumed that readers have never heard of OpenCL and know nothing about distributed computing or high-performance computing. I've done my best to present concepts like task-parallelism and SIMD (single instruction, multiple data) development as simply and as straightforwardly as possible.

But because the OpenCL API is based on C, this book presumes that the reader has a solid understanding of C fundamentals. Readers should be intimately familiar with pointers, arrays, and memory access functions like `malloc` and `free`. It also helps to be cognizant of the C functions declared in the common math library, as most of the kernel functions have similar names and usages.

OpenCL applications can run on many different types of devices, but one of its chief advantages is that it can be used to program graphics processing units (GPUs). Therefore, to get the most out of this book, it helps to have a graphics card attached to your computer or a hybrid CPU-GPU device such as AMD's Fusion.

Roadmap

This book is divided into three parts. The first part, which consists of chapters 1–10, focuses on exploring the OpenCL language and its capabilities. The second part, which consists of chapters 11–14, shows how OpenCL can be used to perform large-scale tasks commonly encountered in the field of high-performance computing. The last part, which consists of chapters 15 and 16, shows how OpenCL can be used to accelerate OpenGL applications.

The chapters of part 1 have been structured to serve the needs of a programmer who has never coded a line of OpenCL. Chapter 1 introduces the topic of OpenCL, explaining what it is, where it came from, and the basics of its operation. Chapters 2 and 3 explain how to code applications that run on the host, and chapters 4 and 5 show how to code kernels that run on compliant devices. Chapters 6 and 7 explore advanced topics that involve both host programming and kernel coding. Specifically, chapter 6 presents image processing and chapter 7 discusses the important topics of event processing and synchronization.

Chapters 8 and 9 discuss the concepts first presented in chapters 2 through 5, but using languages other than C. Chapter 8 discusses host/kernel coding in C++, and chapter 9 explains how to build OpenCL applications in Java and Python. If you aren't obligated to program in C, I recommend that you use one of the toolsets discussed in these chapters.

Chapter 10 serves as a bridge between parts 1 and 2. It demonstrates how to take full advantage of OpenCL's parallelism by implementing a simple reduction algorithm that adds together one million data points. It also presents helpful guidelines for coding practical OpenCL applications.

Chapters 11–14 get into the heavy-duty usage of OpenCL, where applications commonly operate on millions of data points. Chapter 11 discusses the implementation of MapReduce and two sorting algorithms: the bitonic sort and the radix sort. Chapter 12 covers operations on dense matrices, and chapter 13 explores operations on sparse matrices. Chapter 14 explains how OpenCL can be used to implement the fast Fourier transform (FFT).

Chapters 15 and 16 are my personal favorites. One of OpenCL's great strengths is that it can be used to accelerate three-dimensional rendering, a topic of central interest in game development and scientific visualization. Chapter 15 introduces the topic of OpenCL-OpenGL interoperability and shows how the two toolsets can share data corresponding to vertex attributes. Chapter 16 expands on this and shows how OpenCL can accelerate OpenGL texture processing. These chapters require an understanding of OpenGL 3.3 and shader development, and both of these topics are explored in appendix B.

At the end of the book, the appendixes provide helpful information related to OpenCL, but the material isn't directly used in common OpenCL development. Appendix A discusses the all-important topic of software development kits (SDKs), and explains how to install the SDKs provided by AMD and Nvidia. Appendix B discusses the basics of OpenGL and shader development. Appendix C explains how to install and use the Minimalist GNU for Windows (MinGW), which provides a GNU-like environment for building executables on the Windows operating system. Lastly, appendix D discusses the specification for embedded OpenCL.

Obtaining and compiling the example code

In the end, it's the code that matters. This book contains working code for over 60 OpenCL applications, and you can download the source code from the publisher's website at www.manning.com/OpenCLinAction or www.manning.com/scarpino2/.

The download site provides a link pointing to an archive that contains code intended to be compiled with GNU-based build tools. This archive contains one folder for each chapter/appendix of the book, and each top-level folder has subfolders for example projects. For example, if you look in the Ch5/shuffle_test directory, you'll find the source code for Chapter 5's shuffle_test project.

As far as dependencies go, every project requires that the OpenCL library (OpenCL.lib on Windows, libOpenCL.so on *nix systems) be available on the development system. Appendix A discusses how to obtain this library by installing an appropriate software development kit (SDK).

In addition, chapters 6 and 16 discuss images, and the source code in these chapters makes use of the open-source PNG library. Chapter 6 explains how to obtain this library for different systems. Appendix B and chapters 15 and 16 all require access to OpenGL, and appendix B explains how to obtain and install this toolset.

Code conventions

As lazy as this may sound, I prefer to copy and paste working code into my applications rather than write code from scratch. This not only saves time, but also reduces the likelihood of producing bugs through typographical errors. All the code in this book is public domain, so you're free to download and copy and paste portions of it into your applications. But before you do, it's a good idea to understand the conventions I've used:

- Host data structures are named after their data type. That is, each `cl_platform_id` structure is called `platform`, each `cl_device_id` structure is called `device`, each `cl_context` structure is called `context`, and so on.
- In the host applications, the `main` function calls on two functions: `create_device` returns a `cl_device`, and `build_program` creates and compiles a `cl_program`. Note that `create_device` searches for a GPU associated with the first available platform. If it can't find a GPU, it searches for the first compliant CPU.

- Host applications identify the program file and the kernel function using macros declared at the start of the source file. Specifically, the `PROGRAM_FILE` macro identifies the program file and `KERNEL_FUNC` identifies the kernel function.
- All my program files end with the .cl suffix. If the program file only contains one kernel function, that function has the same name as the file.
- For GNU code, every makefile assumes that libraries and header files can be found at locations identified by environment variables. Specifically, the makefile searches for `AMDAPPSDKROOT` on AMD platforms and `CUDA` on Nvidia platforms.

Author Online

Nobody's perfect. If I failed to convey my subject material clearly or (gasp) made a mistake, feel free to add a comment through Manning's Author Online system. You can find the Author Online forum for this book by going to www.manning.com/OpenCLinAction and clicking the Author Online link.

Simple questions and concerns get rapid responses. In contrast, if you're unhappy with line 402 of my bitonic sort implementation, it may take me some time to get back to you. I'm always happy to discuss general issues related to OpenCL, but if you're looking for something complex and specific, such as help debugging a custom FFT, I will have to recommend that you find a professional consultant.

About the cover illustration

The figure on the cover of *OpenCL in Action* is captioned a "Kranjac," or an inhabitant of the Carniola region in the Slovenian Alps. This illustration is taken from a recent reprint of Balthasar Hacquet's *Images and Descriptions of Southwestern and Eastern Wenda, Illyrians, and Slavs* published by the Ethnographic Museum in Split, Croatia, in 2008. Hacquet (1739–1815) was an Austrian physician and scientist who spent many years studying the botany, geology, and ethnography of the Julian Alps, the mountain range that stretches from northeastern Italy to Slovenia and that is named after Julius Caesar. Hand drawn illustrations accompany the many scientific papers and books that Hacquet published.

The rich diversity of the drawings in Hacquet's publications speaks vividly of the uniqueness and individuality of the eastern Alpine regions just 200 years ago. This was a time when the dress codes of two villages separated by a few miles identified people uniquely as belonging to one or the other, and when members of a social class or trade could be easily distinguished by what they were wearing. Dress codes have changed since then and the diversity by region, so rich at the time, has faded away. It is now often hard to tell the inhabitant of one continent from another and today the inhabitants of the picturesque towns and villages in the Slovenian Alps are not readily distinguishable from the residents of other parts of Slovenia or the rest of Europe.

We at Manning celebrate the inventiveness, the initiative, and the fun of the computer business with book covers based on costumes from two centuries ago brought back to life by illustrations such as this one.

Part 1

Foundations of OpenCL programming

Part 1 presents the OpenCL language. We'll explore OpenCL's data structures and functions in detail and look at example applications that demonstrate their usage in code.

Chapter 1 introduces OpenCL, explaining what it's used for and how it works. Chapters 2 and 3 explain how host applications are coded, and chapters 4 and 5 discuss kernel coding. Chapters 6 and 7 explore the advanced topics of image processing and event handling.

Chapters 8 and 9 discuss how OpenCL is coded in languages other than C, such as C++, Java, and Python. Chapter 10 explains how OpenCL's capabilities can be used to develop large-scale applications.

Introducing OpenCL

1

This chapter covers

- Understanding the purpose and benefits of OpenCL
- Introducing OpenCL operation: hosts and kernels
- Implementing an OpenCL application in code

In October 2010, a revolution took place in the world of high-performance computing. The Tianhe-1A, constructed by China's National Supercomputing Center in Tianjin, came from total obscurity to seize the leading position among the world's best performing supercomputers. With a maximum recorded computing speed of 2,566 TFLOPS (trillion floating-point operations per second), it performs nearly 50 percent faster than the second-place finisher, Cray's Jaguar supercomputer. Table 1.1 lists the top three supercomputers.

What's so revolutionary is the presence of GPUs (graphics processing units) in both the Tianhe-1A and Nebulae? In 2009, none of the top three supercomputers had GPUs, and only one system in the top 20 had any GPUs at all. As the table makes clear, the two systems with GPUs provide not only excellent performance, but also impressive power efficiency.

Using GPUs to perform nongraphical routines is called *general-purpose GPU computing*, or GPGPU computing. Before 2010, GPGPU computing was considered a novelty in the world of high-performance computing and not worthy of serious

Table 1.1   Top three supercomputers of 2010 (source: www.top500.org)

Supercomputer	Max speed (TFLOPS)	Processors	Power (kW)
Tianhe-1A	2,566	14,336 Intel Xeon CPUs, 7,168 Nvidia Tesla GPUs	4040.00
Jaguar	1,759	224,256 AMD Opteron CPUs	6950.60
Nebulae	1,271	9,280 Intel Xeon CPUs, 4,640 Nvidia Tesla GPUs	2580.00

attention. But today, engineers and academics are reaching the conclusion that CPU/GPU systems represent the future of supercomputing.

Now an important question arises: how can you program these new hybrid devices? Traditional C and C++ only target traditional CPUs. The same holds true for Cray's proprietary Chapel language and the Cray Assembly Language (CAL). Nvidia's CUDA (Compute Unified Device Architecture) can be used to program Nvidia's GPUs, but not CPUs.

The answer is OpenCL (Open Computing Language). OpenCL routines can be executed on GPUs and CPUs from major manufacturers like AMD, Nvidia, and Intel, and will even run on Sony's PlayStation 3. OpenCL is *nonproprietary*—it's based on a public standard, and you can freely download all the development tools you need. When you code routines in OpenCL, you don't have to worry about which company designed the processor or how many cores it contains. Your code will compile and execute on AMD's latest Fusion processors, Intel's Core processors, Nvidia's Fermi processors, and IBM's Cell Broadband Engine.

The goal of this book is to explain how to program these cross-platform applications and take maximum benefit from the underlying hardware. But the goal of this chapter is to provide a basic overview of the OpenCL language. The discussion will start by focusing on OpenCL's advantages and operation, and then proceed to describing a complete application. But first, it's important to understand OpenCL's origin. Corporations have spent a great deal of time developing this language, and once you see why, you'll have a better idea why learning about OpenCL is worth your own.

1.1   The dawn of OpenCL

The x86 architecture enjoys a dominant position in the world of personal computing, but there is no prevailing architecture in the fields of graphical and high-performance computing. Despite their common purpose, there is little similarity between Nvidia's line of Fermi processors, AMD's line of Evergreen processors, and IBM's Cell Broadband Engine. Each of these devices has its own instruction set, and before OpenCL, if you wanted to program them, you had to learn three different languages.

Enter Apple. For those of you who have been living as recluses, Apple Inc. produces an insanely popular line of consumer electronic products: the iPhone, the iPad, the iPod, and the Mac line of personal computers. But Apple doesn't make processors for the Mac computers. Instead, it selects devices from other companies. If Apple chooses a graphics processor from Company A for its new gadget, then Company A will see a tremendous rise in market share and developer interest. This is why everyone is *so* nice to Apple.

Important events in OpenCL and multicore computing history

2001—IBM releases POWER4, the first multicore processor.

2005—First multicore processors for desktop computers released: AMD's Athlon 64 X2 and Intel's Pentium D.

June 2008—The OpenCL Working Group forms as part of the Khronos Group.

December 2008—The OpenCL Working Group releases version 1.0 of the OpenCL specification.

April 2009—Nvidia releases OpenCL SDK for Nvidia graphics cards.

August 2009—ATI (now AMD) releases OpenCL SDK for ATI graphics cards. Apple includes OpenCL support in its Mac OS 10.6 (Snow Leopard) release.

June 2010—The OpenCL Working Group releases version 1.1 of the OpenCL specification.

In 2008, Apple turned to its vendors and asked, "Why don't we make a common interface so that developers can program your devices without having to learn multiple languages?" If anyone else had raised this question, cutthroat competitors like Nvidia, AMD, Intel, and IBM might have laughed. But no one laughs at Apple. It took time, but everyone put their heads together, and they produced the first draft of OpenCL later that year.

To manage OpenCL's progress and development, Apple and its friends formed the OpenCL Working Group. This is one of many working groups in the Khronos Group, a consortium of companies whose aim is to advance graphics and graphical media. Since its formation, the OpenCL Working Group has released two formal specifications: OpenCL version 1.0 was released in 2008, and OpenCL version 1.1 was released in 2010. OpenCL 2.0 is planned for 2012.

This section has explained why businesses think highly of OpenCL, but I wouldn't be surprised if you're still sitting on the fence. The next section, however, explains the technical merits of OpenCL in greater depth. As you read, I hope you'll better understand the advantages of OpenCL as compared to traditional programming languages.

1.2 Why OpenCL?

You may hear OpenCL referred to as its own separate language, but this isn't accurate. The OpenCL standard defines a set of data types, data structures, and functions that augment C and C++. Developers have created OpenCL ports for Java and Python, but the standard only requires that OpenCL frameworks provide libraries in C and C++.

Here's the million-dollar question: what can you do with OpenCL that you can't do with regular C and C++? It will take this entire book to answer this question in full, but for now, let's look at three of OpenCL's chief advantages: portability, standardized vector processing, and parallel programming.

1.2.1   Portability

Java is one of the most popular programming languages in the world, and it owes a large part of its success to its motto: "Write once, run everywhere." With Java, you don't have to rewrite your code for different operating systems. As long as the operating system supports a compliant Java Virtual Machine (JVM), your code will run.

OpenCL adopts a similar philosophy, but a more suitable motto might be, "Write once, run on anything." Every vendor that provides OpenCL-compliant hardware also provides the tools that compile OpenCL code to run on the hardware. This means you can write your OpenCL routines once and compile them for any compliant device, whether it's a multicore processor or a graphics card. This is a great advantage over regular high-performance computing, in which you have to learn vendor-specific languages to program vendor-specific hardware.

There's more to this advantage than just running on any type of compliant hardware. OpenCL applications can target multiple devices at once, and these devices don't have to have the same architecture or even the same vendor. As long as all the devices are OpenCL-compliant, the functions will run. This is impossible with regular C/C++ programming, in which an executable can only target one device at a time.

Here's a concrete example. Suppose you have a multicore processor from AMD, a graphics card from Nvidia, and a PCI-connected accelerator from IBM. Normally, you'd never be able to build an application that targets all three systems at once because each requires a separate compiler and linker. But a single OpenCL program can deploy executable code to all three devices. This means you can unify your hardware to perform a common task with a single program. If you connect more compliant devices, you'll have to rebuild the program, but you won't have to rewrite your code.

1.2.2   Standardized vector processing

Standardized vector processing is one of the greatest advantages of OpenCL, but before I explain why, I need to define precisely what I'm talking about. The term *vector* is going to get a lot of mileage in this book, and it may be used in one of three different (though essentially similar) ways:

- *Physical or geometric vector*—An entity with a magnitude and direction. This is used frequently in physics to identify force, velocity, heat transfer, and so on. In graphics, vectors are employed to identify directions.
- *Mathematical vector*—An ordered, one-dimensional collection of elements. This is distinguished from a two-dimensional collection of elements, called a *matrix*.
- *Computational vector*—A data structure that contains multiple elements of the same data type. During a vector operation, each element (called a *component*) is operated upon in the same clock cycle.

This last usage is important to OpenCL because high-performance processors operate on multiple values at once. If you've heard the terms *superscalar processor* or *vector processor*, this is the type of device being referred to. Nearly all modern processors are capable of processing vectors, but ANSI C/C++ doesn't define any basic vector data types. This may seem odd, but there's a clear problem: vector instructions are usually vendor-specific. Intel processors use SSE extensions, Nvidia devices require PTX instructions, and IBM devices rely on AltiVec instructions to process vectors. These instruction sets have nothing in common.

But with OpenCL, you can code your vector routines once and run them on any compliant processor. When you compile your application, Nvidia's OpenCL compiler will produce PTX instructions. An IBM compiler for OpenCL will produce AltiVec instructions. Clearly, if you intend to make your high-performance application available on multiple platforms, coding with OpenCL will save you a great deal of time. Chapter 4 discusses OpenCL's vector data types and chapter 5 presents the functions available to operate on vectors.

1.2.3 *Parallel programming*

If you've ever coded large-scale applications, you're probably familiar with the concept of *concurrency*, in which a single processing element shares its resources among processes and threads. OpenCL includes aspects of concurrency, but one of its great advantages is that it enables *parallel programming*. Parallel programming assigns computational tasks to *multiple* processing elements to be performed at the same time.

In OpenCL parlance, these tasks are called *kernels*. A kernel is a specially coded function that's intended to be executed by one or more OpenCL-compliant devices. Kernels are sent to their intended device or devices by *host applications*. A host application is a regular C/C++ application running on the user's development system, which we'll call the host. For many developers, the host dispatches kernels to a single device: the GPU on the computer's graphics card. But kernels can also be executed by the same CPU on which the host application is running.

Hosts applications manage their connected devices using a container called a *context*. Figure 1.1 shows how hosts interact with kernels and devices.

To create a kernel, the host selects a function from a kernel container called a *program*. Then it associates the kernel with argument data and dispatches it to a structure called a *command queue*. The command queue is the mechanism through which the host tells devices what to do, and when a kernel is enqueued, the device will execute the corresponding function.

An OpenCL application can configure different devices to perform different tasks, and each task can operate on different data. In other words, OpenCL provides full *task-parallelism*. This is an important advantage over many other parallel-programming toolsets, which only enable *data-parallelism*. In a data-parallel system, each device receives the same instructions but operates on different sets of data.

Figure 1.1 depicts how OpenCL accomplishes task-parallelism between devices, but it doesn't show what's happening inside each device. Most OpenCL-compliant

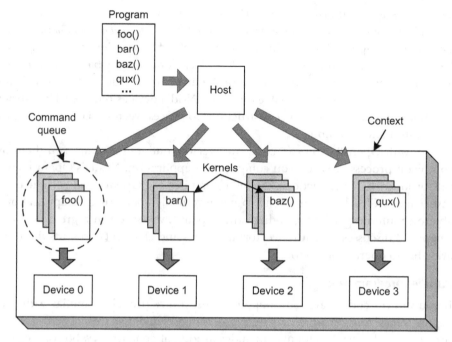

Figure 1.1   Kernel distribution among OpenCL-compliant devices

devices consist of more than one processing element, which means there's an additional level of parallelism internal to each device. Chapter 3 explains more about this parallelism and how to partition data to take the best advantage of a device's internal processing.

Portability, vector processing, and parallel programming make OpenCL more powerful than regular C and C++, but with this greater power comes greater complexity. In any practical OpenCL application, you have to create a number of different data structures and coordinate their operation. It can be hard to keep everything straight, but the next section presents an analogy that I hope will give you a clearer perspective.

1.3   *Analogy: OpenCL processing and a game of cards*

When I first started learning OpenCL, I was overwhelmed by all the strange data structures: platforms, contexts, devices, programs, kernels, and command queues. I found it hard to remember what they do and how they interact, so I came up with an analogy: the operation of an OpenCL application is like a game of poker. This may seem odd at first, but please allow me to explain.

In a poker game, the dealer sits at a table with one or more players and deals a set of cards to each. The players analyze their cards and decide what further actions to take. These players don't interact with each other. Instead, they make requests to the dealer for additional cards or an increase in the stakes. The dealer handles each request in turn, and once the game is over, the dealer takes control.

In this analogy, the dealer represents an OpenCL host, each player represents a device, the card table represents a context, and each card represents a kernel. Each player's hand represents a command queue. Table 1.2 clarifies how the steps of a card game resemble the operation of an OpenCL application.

Table 1.2 Comparison of OpenCL operation to a card game

Card game	OpenCL application
The dealer sits at a card table and determines who the players are.	The host selects devices and places them in a context.
The dealer selects cards from a deck and deals them to each player. Each player's cards form a hand.	The host selects kernels from a program. It adds kernels to each device's command queue.
Each player looks at their hand and decides what actions to take.	Each device processes the kernels that are sent through the command queue.
The dealer responds to players' requests during the game.	The host receives events from the devices and invokes event-handling routines.
The game ends, and the dealer looks at each player's hand to determine who won.	Once the devices are finished, the host receives and processes the output data.

In case the analogy seems hard to understand, figure 1.2 depicts a card game with four players, each of whom receives a hand with four cards. If you compare figures 1.1 and 1.2, I hope the analogy will become clearer.

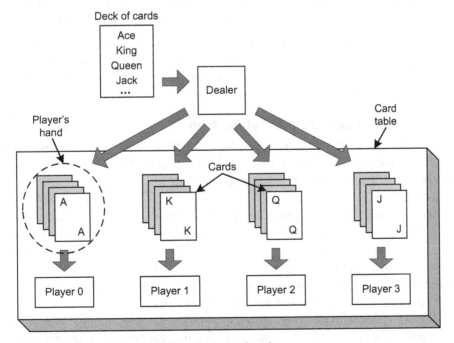

Figure 1.2 Pictorial representation of a game of cards

This analogy will be revisited and enhanced throughout the next few chapters. It provides an intuitive understanding of OpenCL, but it has a number of flaws. These are six of the most significant flaws:

- The analogy doesn't mention *platforms*. A platform is a data structure that identifies a vendor's implementation of OpenCL. Platforms provide one way to access devices. For example, you can access an Nvidia device through the Nvidia platform.

- A card dealer doesn't choose which players sit at the table, but an OpenCL host selects which devices should be placed in a context.

- A card dealer can't deal the same card to multiple players, but an OpenCL host can dispatch the same kernel to multiple devices through their command queues.

- The analogy doesn't mention data or how it's partitioned for OpenCL devices. OpenCL devices usually contain multiple processing elements, and each element may process a subset of the input data. The host sets the dimensionality of the data and identifies the number of work items into which the computation will be partitioned.

- In a card game, the dealer distributes cards to the players, and each player arranges the cards to form a hand. In OpenCL, the host places kernel-execution commands into a command queue, and, by default, each device executes the kernels in the order in which the host enqueues them.

- In card games, dealers commonly deal cards in a round-robin fashion. OpenCL sets no constraints on how kernels are distributed to multiple devices.

If you're still nervous about OpenCL's terminology, don't be concerned. Chapter 2 will explain these data structures further and show how they're accessed in code. After all, code is the primary goal. The next section will give you a first taste of what OpenCL code looks like.

1.4   *A first look at an OpenCL application*

At this point, you should have a good idea of what OpenCL is intended to accomplish. I hope you also have a basic understanding of how an OpenCL application works. But if you want to know anything substantive about OpenCL, you have to look at source code.

This section will present two OpenCL source files, one intended for a host processor and one intended for a device. Both work together to compute the product of a 4-by-4 matrix and a 4-element vector. This operation is central to graphics processing, where the matrix represents a transformation and the vector represents a color or a point in space. Figure 1.3 shows what this matrix-vector multiplication looks like and then presents the equations that produce the result.

If you open the directory containing this book's example code, you'll find the source files in the Ch1 folder. The first, matvec.c, executes on the host. It creates a kernel and

$$
\begin{vmatrix} 0.0 & 2.0 & 4.0 & 6.0 \\ 8.0 & 10.0 & 12.0 & 14.0 \\ 16.0 & 18.0 & 20.0 & 22.0 \\ 24.0 & 26.0 & 28.0 & 30.0 \end{vmatrix} \begin{vmatrix} 0.0 \\ 3.0 \\ 6.0 \\ 9.0 \end{vmatrix} = \begin{vmatrix} 84.0 \\ 228.0 \\ 372.0 \\ 516.0 \end{vmatrix}
$$

$0.0 \times 0.0 + 2.0 \times 3.0 + 4.0 \times 6.0 + 6.0 \times 9.0 = 84.0$

$8.0 \times 0.0 + 10.0 \times 3.0 + 12.0 \times 6.0 + 14.0 \times 9.0 = 228.0$

$16.0 \times 0.0 + 18.0 \times 3.0 + 20.0 \times 6.0 + 22.0 \times 9.0 = 372.0$

$24.0 \times 0.0 + 26.0 \times 3.0 + 28.0 \times 6.0 + 30.0 \times 9.0 = 516.0$

Figure 1.3 Matrix-vector multiplication

sends it to the first device it finds. The following listing shows what this host code looks like. Notice that the source code is written in the C programming language.

NOTE Error-checking routines have been omitted from this listing, but you'll find them in the matvec.c file in this book's example code.

Listing 1.1 Creating and distributing a matrix-vector multiplication kernel: matvec.c

```c
#define PROGRAM_FILE "matvec.cl"
#define KERNEL_FUNC "matvec_mult"

#include <stdio.h>
#include <stdlib.h>
#include <sys/types.h>

#ifdef MAC
#include <OpenCL/cl.h>
#else
#include <CL/cl.h>
#endif

int main() {
   cl_platform_id platform;
   cl_device_id device;
   cl_context context;
   cl_command_queue queue;
   cl_int i, err;

   cl_program program;
   FILE *program_handle;
   char *program_buffer, *program_log;
   size_t program_size, log_size;
   cl_kernel kernel;
   size_t work_units_per_kernel;

   float mat[16], vec[4], result[4];
   float correct[4] = {0.0f, 0.0f, 0.0f, 0.0f};
   cl_mem mat_buff, vec_buff, res_buff;

   for(i=0; i<16; i++) {
      mat[i] = i * 2.0f;
   }
```

Initialize data

```
for(i=0; i<4; i++) {
   vec[i] = i * 3.0f;
   correct[0] += mat[i]    * vec[i];
   correct[1] += mat[i+4]  * vec[i];
   correct[2] += mat[i+8]  * vec[i];
   correct[3] += mat[i+12] * vec[i];
}
```
Initialize data

```
clGetPlatformIDs(1, &platform, NULL);
clGetDeviceIDs(platform, CL_DEVICE_TYPE_GPU, 1,
   &device, NULL);
context = clCreateContext(NULL, 1, &device, NULL,
   NULL, &err);
```
Set platform/ device/context

```
program_handle = fopen(PROGRAM_FILE, "r");
fseek(program_handle, 0, SEEK_END);
program_size = ftell(program_handle);
rewind(program_handle);
program_buffer = (char*)malloc(program_size + 1);
program_buffer[program_size] = '\0';
fread(program_buffer, sizeof(char), program_size,
   program_handle);
fclose(program_handle);
```
Read program file

```
program = clCreateProgramWithSource(context, 1,
   (const char**)&program_buffer, &program_size, &err);
free(program_buffer);
clBuildProgram(program, 0, NULL, NULL, NULL, NULL);
```
Compile program

```
kernel = clCreateKernel(program, KERNEL_FUNC, &err);
queue = clCreateCommandQueue(context, device, 0, &err);
```
Create kernel/queue

```
mat_buff = clCreateBuffer(context, CL_MEM_READ_ONLY |
   CL_MEM_COPY_HOST_PTR, sizeof(float)*16, mat, &err);
vec_buff = clCreateBuffer(context, CL_MEM_READ_ONLY |
   CL_MEM_COPY_HOST_PTR, sizeof(float)*4, vec, &err);
res_buff = clCreateBuffer(context, CL_MEM_WRITE_ONLY,
   sizeof(float)*4, NULL, &err);
clSetKernelArg(kernel, 0, sizeof(cl_mem), &mat_buff);
clSetKernelArg(kernel, 1, sizeof(cl_mem), &vec_buff);
clSetKernelArg(kernel, 2, sizeof(cl_mem), &res_buff);
```
Set kernel arguments

```
work_units_per_kernel = 4;
clEnqueueNDRangeKernel(queue, kernel, 1, NULL,
   &work_units_per_kernel, NULL, 0, NULL, NULL);
```
Execute kernel

```
clEnqueueReadBuffer(queue, res_buff, CL_TRUE, 0,
   sizeof(float)*4, result, 0, NULL, NULL);
if((result[0] == correct[0]) && (result[1] == correct[1])
   && (result[2] == correct[2]) && (result[3] == correct[3])) {
   printf("Matrix-vector multiplication successful.\n");
}
else {
   printf("Matrix-vector multiplication unsuccessful.\n");
}

clReleaseMemObject(mat_buff);
clReleaseMemObject(vec_buff);
```

```
clReleaseMemObject(res_buff);
clReleaseKernel(kernel);
clReleaseCommandQueue(queue);
clReleaseProgram(program);
clReleaseContext(context);

return 0;
}
```

This source file is long but straightforward. Most of the code is devoted to creating OpenCL's data structures, which obey a simple naming convention: the cl_context is called context, the cl_platform_id is called platform, the cl_device_id is called device, and so on. If you follow this convention, you can copy and paste most of your code from one host application to the next.

In contrast, the creation of the cl_program and the cl_kernel structures changes from application to application. In listing 1.1, the application creates a kernel from a function in a file called matvec.cl. More precisely, it reads the characters from mat-vec.cl into a character array, creates a program from the character array, and compiles the program. Then it constructs a kernel from a function called matvec_mult.

The kernel code in matvec.cl is much shorter than the host code in matvec.c. The single function, matvec_mult, performs the entire matrix-vector multiplication algorithm depicted in figure 1.3.

Chapters 2 and 3 discuss how to code host applications like the one presented in listing 1.1. Chapters 4 and 5 explain how to code kernel functions like the one in the following listing.

> **Listing 1.2 Performing the dot-product on the device: matvec.cl**

```
__kernel void matvec_mult(__global float4* matrix,
                          __global float4* vector,
                          __global float* result) {
    int i = get_global_id(0);
    result[i] = dot(matrix[i], vector[0]);
}
```

If you're eager to compile the code in these two listings and test the dot-product, I recommend that you visit appendix A, which explains how to obtain and use OpenCL's development tools. But before you do this, you should have a top-level understanding of the OpenCL standard, which we'll discuss next.

1.5   The OpenCL standard and extensions

If you look through the OpenCL website at www.khronos.org/opencl, you'll find an important file called opencl-1.1.pdf. This contains the OpenCL 1.1 specification, which provides a wealth of information about the language. It defines not only OpenCL's functions and data structures, but also the capabilities required by a vendor's development tools. In addition, it sets the criteria that all devices must meet to be considered compliant.

But compliant software and hardware can provide capabilities beyond those defined in the standard. These additional features are made available to OpenCL applications through *extensions*. There are two main types of extensions: those that relate to a vendor's software package (called a *platform*) and those that relate to specific devices. Chapter 2 explains how to check for platform extensions and device extensions in code.

Every OpenCL extension has a name that depends on the extension's level of acceptance. If an extension has been approved by the OpenCL working group, its name will take the form cl_khr_<name>. If it has been released by a vendor but has not been approved by the working group, the extension's name will be cl_<vendor>_<name>.

For example, on my Linux system, the installed AMD platform supports the extension cl_khr_icd. This extension relates to software. In particular, it makes it possible for build tools to find vendor-specific OpenCL libraries installed on a system. ICD stands for Installable Client Driver, and appendix A explains more about this topic.

1.6   *Frameworks and software development kits (SDKs)*

The code in matvec.c and matvec.cl may look impressive, but the two source files don't serve any purpose until you compile them into an OpenCL application. To do this, you need to access the tools in a compliant framework. As defined in the OpenCL standard, a framework consists of three parts:

- *Platform layer*—Makes it possible to access devices and form contexts
- *Runtime*—Enables host applications to send kernels and command queues to devices in the context
- *Compiler*—Builds programs that contain executable kernels

The OpenCL Working Group doesn't provide any frameworks of its own. Instead, vendors who produce OpenCL-compliant devices release frameworks as part of their software development kits (SDKs). The two most popular OpenCL SDKs are released by Nvidia and AMD. In both cases, the development kits are free and contain the libraries and tools that make it possible to build OpenCL applications. Whether you're targeting Nvidia or AMD devices, installing an SDK is a straightforward process. Appendix A provides step-by-step details and explains how the SDK tools work together to build executables.

1.7   *Summary*

OpenCL is a new, powerful toolset for building parallel programs to run on high-performance processors. With OpenCL, you don't have to learn device-specific languages; you can write your code once and run it on any OpenCL-compliant hardware.

Besides portability, OpenCL provides the advantages of vector processing and parallel programming. In high-performance computing, a vector is a data structure comprising multiple values of the same data type. But unlike other data structures, when a vector is operated upon, each of its values is operated upon at the same time. Parallel programming means that one application controls processing on multiple devices at once. OpenCL can send different tasks to different devices, and this is called task-parallel programming. If used effectively, vector processing and task-parallel programming provide dramatic improvements in computational performance over that of scalar, single-processor systems.

OpenCL code consists of two parts: code that runs on the host and code that runs on one or more devices. Host code is written in regular C or C++ and is responsible for creating the data structures that manage the host-device communication. The host selects functions, called kernels, to be placed in command queues and sent to the devices. Kernel code, unlike host code, uses the high-performance capabilities defined in the OpenCL standard.

With so many new data structures and operations, OpenCL may seem daunting at first. But as you start writing your own code, you'll see that it's not much different from regular C and C++. And once you harness the power of vector-based parallel programming in your own applications, you'll never want to go back to traditional single-core computing.

In the next chapter, we'll start our exploration of OpenCL coding. Specifically, we'll examine the primary data structures that make up the host application.

Host programming: fundamental data structures

This chapter covers

- Understanding the six basic OpenCL data structures
- Creating and examining the data structures in code
- Combining the data structures to send kernels to a device

The first step in programming any OpenCL application is coding the host application. The good news is that you only need regular C and C++. The bad news is that you have to become familiar with six strange data structures: platforms, devices, contexts, programs, kernels, and command queues.

The preceding chapter presented these structures as part of an analogy, but the goal of this chapter is to explain how they're used in code. For each one, we'll look at two types of functions: those that create the structure and those that provide information about the structure after it has been created. We'll also look at

16

examples that demonstrate how these functions are used in applications. These won't be full applications like the matvec example in chapter 1. Instead, these will be short, simple examples that shed light on how these data structures work and work together.

Most of this chapter deals with complex data structures and their functions, but let's start with something easy. OpenCL provides a unique set of primitive data types for host applications, and we'll examine these first.

2.1 Primitive data types

Processors and operating systems vary in how they store basic data. An int may be 32 bits wide on one system and 64 bits wide on another. This isn't a concern if you're writing code for a single platform, but OpenCL code needs to compile on multiple platforms. Therefore, it requires a standard set of primitive data types.

Table 2.1 lists OpenCL's primitive data types. As you can see, these are all similar to their traditional counterparts in C and C++.

Table 2.1 OpenCL primitive data types for host applications

Scalar data type	Bit width	Purpose
cl_char	8	Signed two's complement integer
cl_uchar	8	Unsigned two's complement integer
cl_short	16	Signed two's complement integer
cl_ushort	16	Unsigned two's complement integer
cl_int	32	Signed two's complement integer
cl_uint	32	Unsigned two's complement integer
cl_long	64	Signed two's complement integer
cl_ulong	64	Unsigned two's complement integer
cl_half	16	Half-precision floating-point value
cl_float	32	Single-precision floating-point value
cl_double	64	Double-precision floating-point value

These types are declared in CL/cl_platform.h, and in most cases, they're simply redefinitions of the corresponding C/C++ types. For example, cl_float is defined as follows:

```
#if (defined (_WIN32) && defined(_MSC_VER))
...
typedef float cl_float;
...
#else
...
```

```
typedef float cl_float _attribute__((aligned(4)));
...
#endif
```

These types can be operated upon just like their C/C++ counterparts, so you can add and subtract cl_ints just as you would ints. You can invoke printf with a cl_char using the same formatting symbol (%c) as you would with an ordinary char. We'll rely on the data types in table 2.1 throughout this book and the example code.

2.2   Accessing platforms

When you build an OpenCL application, you don't have to know anything about the underlying hardware. But let's say your computer has two graphics cards—one from AMD and one from Nvidia—and you've installed AMD's SDK and Nvidia's SDK. In this situation, you may want to select which GPU should process your data. To make this possible, you need to identify a specific vendor's OpenCL implementation in code.

Alternatively, you may want to sell your OpenCL application. In this case, you have no idea what hardware your customers are using. Instead of checking for a particular vendor, you may want to count how many OpenCL devices are available for each implementation and distribute tasks evenly between them.

OpenCL handles both scenarios by providing the cl_platform_id data structure. This section explains why these structures are important and how to access them in code.

> **NOTE**   The following discussion will make more sense if you've installed an SDK on your development system. Appendix A explains just about everything you may want to know about SDKs.

2.2.1   Creating platform structures

Each cl_platform_id structure represents a different OpenCL implementation (called a *platform*) installed on the host. If you've installed two SDKs, you'll have two platforms installed, and your code will detect two cl_platform_id structures.

In code, working with platforms is a two-step process. First you need to allocate memory for one or more cl_platform_id structures. Then you need to call clGetPlatformIDs to initialize these structures. This is usually one of the first functions you'll call in your OpenCL code. Its signature, consisting of its function name and parameter list, is given as follows:

```
cl_int clGetPlatformIDs(cl_uint num_entries,
    cl_platform_id *platforms, cl_uint *num_platforms)
```

There are three points to note about this function. First, despite the name, this function doesn't return cl_platform_id structures. Instead, it places cl_platform_id structures in the memory referenced by platforms. It places the number of available platforms in the memory referenced by num_platforms. The return value is an integer that identifies whether the function successfully detected one or more platforms. A value of 0 indicates success. A negative value indicates failure.

Second, it's important to distinguish between num_entries and num_platforms. num_entries identifies the maximum number of platforms you're interested in detecting. This will be the maximum number of cl_platform_id structures that will be placed in the platforms array. If you set this to 0, the function will return an error. num_platforms, on the other hand, is the number of platforms detected on the host. This value is set by the function during its operation.

The num_entries and num_platforms parameters are used frequently in OpenCL functions, and when I first started programming with OpenCL, I found it hard to distinguish between the two. But I learned how to keep them straight by thinking egotistically: What I want (num_entries) comes first. What's available (num_platforms) comes later.

Third, either platforms or num_platforms can be set to NULL. There's a good reason for this. If you want to create a cl_platform_id structure for every platform on your system, you have to know in advance how many platforms are installed. For this purpose, call clGetPlatformIDs with platforms set to NULL and use num_platforms to store the number of installed platforms. Then allocate your array and call clGetPlatformIDs a second time to initialize the cl_platform_id structures. The following code shows how this is accomplished:

```
cl_platform_id *platforms;
cl_uint num_platforms;

clGetPlatformIDs(5, NULL, &num_platforms);

platforms = (cl_platform_id*)
    malloc(sizeof(cl_platform_id) * num_platforms);

clGetPlatformIDs(num_platforms, platforms, NULL);
```

This code calls clGetPlatformIDs twice. The first time, it places the number of platforms in the num_platforms variable. The second time, it places the cl_platform_id structures in the platforms array. We'll employ this function-allocation-function procedure for many other data structures as well.

2.2.2 Obtaining platform information

The clGetPlatformIDs function provides an array of cl_platform_id structures, but it doesn't tell you anything about the platforms themselves. If you want to know what OpenCL version a platform supports or which vendor created it, you need to call a second function called clGetPlatformInfo. The signature for this function is as follows:

```
cl_int clGetPlatformInfo(cl_platform_id platform,
    cl_platform_info param_name, size_t param_value_size,
    void *param_value, size_t *param_value_size_ret)
```

The second argument, param_name, identifies the nature of the information that you're looking for. Its data type is cl_platform_info, an enumerated type whose values are listed in table 2.2.

In each case, the function returns the desired data in a char array whose full length in bytes is given by the last argument, param_value_size_ret. The third

Table 2.2 Platform information parameters

Parameter name	Purpose
CL_PLATFORM_NAME	Returns the name associated with the platform
CL_PLATFORM_VENDOR	Identifies the vendor associated with the platform
CL_PLATFORM_VERSION	Returns the maximum version of OpenCL supported by the platform
CL_PLATFORM_PROFILE	Identifies whether the platform supports the full OpenCL standard (FULL_PROFILE) or the embedded standard (EMBEDDED_PROFILE)
CL_PLATFORM_EXTENSIONS	Returns a list of extensions supported by the platform

argument, param_value_size, tells the function how many bytes you want to store. This is shown in the following code, which reads the data about the platform's vendor into a char array with 40 elements:

```
char pform_vendor[40];

clGetPlatformInfo(platforms[0], CL_PLATFORM_VENDOR, sizeof(pform_vendor),
    &pform_vendor, NULL);
```

This code allocates the char array first and calls clGetPlatformInfo second. This poses no problem, because a vendor's name is unlikely to exceed 40 characters. But if you're trying to find out what extensions a platform supports, you may have no idea how many characters you'll need. In this case, you should call clGetPlatformInfo twice—once to determine the size of the data and once to read the data. The next subsection shows how this is accomplished in code.

2.2.3 Code example: testing platform extensions

As explained in chapter 1, an OpenCL extension defines features that go beyond those defined in the standard. Each extension is identified by a string, and if an extension has been approved by the OpenCL working group, its name will start with cl_khr_. Vendors can add their own extensions to a platform, and these names start with cl_<vendor>_.

Let's say you're providing an application to customers, but it will only work if one of the installed platforms supports a given extension. The following code listing iterates through each installed platform and checks for a specific extension (cl_khr_icd). The first platform that supports the extension is made the active platform.

Listing 2.1 Testing platform extensions: platform_ext_test.c

```
#include <stdio.h>
#include <stdlib.h>
#include <string.h>

#ifdef MAC
#include <OpenCL/cl.h>
#else
```

```
#include <CL/cl.h>
#endif

int main() {

   cl_platform_id *platforms;
   cl_uint num_platforms;
   cl_int i, err, platform_index = -1;

   char* ext_data;
   size_t ext_size;
   const char icd_ext[] = "cl_khr_icd";          ⎤ Find number
                                              ◄──⎦ of platforms
   err = clGetPlatformIDs(1, NULL, &num_platforms);
   if(err < 0) {
      perror("Couldn't find any platforms.");
      exit(1);
   }

   platforms = (cl_platform_id*)                    ⎤ Allocate
      malloc(sizeof(cl_platform_id) * num_platforms); ⎦ platform array
   clGetPlatformIDs(num_platforms, platforms, NULL); ◄──⎤ Initialize
                                                        ⎦ platform array
   for(i=0; i<num_platforms; i++) {
                                                   ⎤ Find size of
      err = clGetPlatformInfo(platforms[i],        ⎦ extension data
         CL_PLATFORM_EXTENSIONS, 0, NULL, &ext_size);
      if(err < 0) {
         perror("Couldn't read extension data.");
         exit(1);
      }

      ext_data = (char*)malloc(ext_size);          ⎤ Read extension
      clGetPlatformInfo(platforms[i],              ⎦ data
            CL_PLATFORM_EXTENSIONS,
            ext_size, ext_data, NULL);
      printf("Platform %d supports extensions: %s\n",
            i, ext_data);

      if(strstr(ext_data, icd_ext) != NULL) {
         free(ext_data);
         platform_index = i;
         break;
      }
      free(ext_data);
   }

   if(platform_index > -1)
      printf("Platform %d supports the %s extension.\n",
            platform_index, icd_ext);
   else
      printf("No platforms support the %s extension.\n", icd_ext);

   free(platforms);
   return 0;
}
```

Here, the for loop iterates through the installed platforms and prints the supported extensions of each one. If a platform supports the cl_khr_icd extension, the loop terminates and the application identifies the platform by its index. On my system, the application produces the following output:

```
Platform 0 supports extensions: cl_khr_icd amd_event_callback
Platform 0 supports the cl_khr_icd extension.
```

Throughout this book's example code, the first step in every host application is to access a cl_platform_id. But these structures are mainly useful because they allow us to access the platform's devices. The next section explains how OpenCL devices are represented in code.

2.3   Accessing installed devices

Once you've accessed a vendor's platform, you can access every connected device provided by the vendor. Returning to the card game analogy, devices are the players that receive cards from the dealer. In an OpenCL application, devices receive tasks and data from the host.

In code, devices are represented by cl_device_id structures. These are easy to work with, and the functions that relate to devices are very similar to those we looked at in the preceding section. This section presents the two OpenCL device functions, clGetDeviceIDs and clGetDeviceInfo, and shows how they're used in code.

2.3.1   Creating device structures

Before you can send a kernel to a device, you need to construct a cl_device_id to represent the device. The clGetDeviceIDs function makes this possible. It populates a cl_device_id array with structures corresponding to OpenCL devices. Its signature is as follows:

```
cl_int clGetDeviceIDs(cl_platform_id platform,
    cl_device_type device_type, cl_uint num_entries,
    cl_device_id *devices, cl_uint *num_devices)
```

This works like the clGetPlatformIDs function discussed in the preceding section. By setting either of the last two arguments to NULL, this can be used to determine the number of connected devices or to populate an cl_device_id array.

The first two arguments constrain which devices should be placed in the devices array. The first identifies the cl_platform_id structure representing the platform of interest. The second identifies a device type, which can be set to any of the values listed in table 2.3.

As an example, the following code populates an array (devs) with a maximum of three GPU-based devices. Each device must be associated with the plat platform:

```
clGetDeviceIDs(plat, CL_DEVICE_TYPE_GPU, 3, devs, NULL);
```

As a second example, suppose you want to know how many accelerator-type devices (such as blade servers containing Cell processors) are associated with the plat platform. In this situation, you could use code similar to the following:

```
cl_uint num_devices;
clGetDeviceIDs(plat, CL_DEVICE_TYPE_ACCELERATOR, 1, NULL, &num_devices);
```

Table 2.3   OpenCL device types

Device type	Meaning
CL_DEVICE_TYPE_ALL	Identifies all devices associated with the platform
CL_DEVICE_TYPE_DEFAULT	Identifies devices associated with the platform's default type
CL_DEVICE_TYPE_CPU	Identifies the host processor
CL_DEVICE_TYPE_GPU	Identifies a device containing a graphics processor unit (GPU)
CL_DEVICE_TYPE_ACCELERATOR	Identifies an external device used to accelerate computation

2.3.2   *Obtaining device information*

The second OpenCL function that accesses devices is clGetDeviceInfo. As its name implies, this function accepts a cl_device_id and provides information about the corresponding device. Its signature is given as follows:

```
cl_int clGetDeviceInfo(cl_device_id device,
    cl_device_info param_name, size_t param_value_size,
    void *param_value, size_t *param_value_size_ret)
```

This operates in exactly the same way that clGetPlatformInfo does. Identify the type of information you're looking for, and the function will place the data in the memory region referenced by param_value. The only difference is that the cl_device_info enumerated type is markedly different from cl_platform_info. It takes over 50 different values, many of which relate to the device's internal architecture, such as its byte order, memory size, and cache structure. Chapter 4 explains many of these concepts in detail and relies on clGetDeviceInfo to a large extent.

Table 2.4 lists eight of the many cl_device_info parameters. Unlike the cl_platform_info parameters, not all of them return char arrays.

Table 2.4   Device information parameters (an abbreviated list)

Parameter name	Output type	Purpose
CL_DEVICE_NAME	char[]	Returns the name of the device
CL_DEVICE_VENDOR	char[]	Returns the device's vendor
CL_DEVICE_EXTENSIONS	char[]	Returns the device's supported OpenCL extensions
CL_DEVICE_GLOBAL_MEM_SIZE	cl_ulong	Returns the size of the device's global memory
CL_DEVICE_ADDRESS_BITS	cl_uint	Returns the size of the device's address space
CL_DEVICE_AVAILABLE	cl_bool	Returns whether the device is available
CL_DEVICE_COMPILER_AVAILABLE	cl_bool	Returns whether the implementation provides a compiler for the device

Note that device extensions (identified in the table by CL_DEVICE_EXTENSIONS) aren't the same thing as platform extensions. Device extensions tell you about the types of operations a device can perform and the data it can process.

Next, we'll look at an example application that reads and displays these extensions.

2.3.3   *Code example: testing device extensions*

Different devices provide different capabilities, and before you send a complex kernel to an OpenCL device, you should be certain that the device has the resources needed to execute it. The code in this listing shows how this works. It accesses the first platform it can find and iterates through each device, printing the device's name, address width, and supported extensions.

Listing 2.2   Testing device extensions: device_ext_test.c

```c
#include <stdio.h>
#include <stdlib.h>
#include <string.h>

#ifdef MAC
#include <OpenCL/cl.h>
#else
#include <CL/cl.h>
#endif

int main() {

   cl_platform_id platform;
   cl_device_id *devices;
   cl_uint num_devices, addr_data;
   cl_int i, err;
   char name_data[48], ext_data[4096];

   err = clGetPlatformIDs(1, &platform, NULL);          ◁─┐ Access first
   if(err < 0) {                                           │ platform
      perror("Couldn't find any platforms");
      exit(1);
   }

   err = clGetDeviceIDs(platform, CL_DEVICE_TYPE_ALL,    │ Determine number
         1, NULL, &num_devices);                         │ of devices
   if(err < 0) {
      perror("Couldn't find any devices");
      exit(1);
   }

   devices = (cl_device_id*)                             │ Allocate device
         malloc(sizeof(cl_device_id) * num_devices);     │ memory
   clGetDeviceIDs(platform, CL_DEVICE_TYPE_ALL,          │ Populate
         num_devices, devices, NULL);                    │ device memory

   for(i=0; i<num_devices; i++) {

      err = clGetDeviceInfo(devices[i], CL_DEVICE_NAME,    │ Get device
            sizeof(name_data), name_data, NULL);           │ name
```

```
      if(err < 0) {
         perror("Couldn't read extension data");
         exit(1);
      }
      clGetDeviceInfo(devices[i], CL_DEVICE_ADDRESS_BITS,      Get device
            sizeof(ext_data), &addr_data, NULL);                address width

      clGetDeviceInfo(devices[i], CL_DEVICE_EXTENSIONS,        Get device
            sizeof(ext_data), ext_data, NULL);                  extensions

      printf("NAME: %s\nADDRESS_WIDTH: %u\nEXTENSIONS: %s",
            name_data, addr_data, ext_data);
   }

   free(devices);
   return 0;
}
```

My MacBook has one platform, and when I run the application, the result is as follows:

```
NAME: GeForce 9400M
ADDRESS_WIDTH: 32
EXTENSIONS: cl_khr_byte_addressable_store cl_khr_global_int32_base_atomics
      cl_khr_global_int32_extended_atomics cl_APPLE_gl_sharing
      cl_APPLE_SetMemObjectDestructor cl_APPLE_ContextLoggingFunctions
```

These extensions may look strange, but later chapters will have a great deal more to say about them—particularly those that deal with device memory and atomic operations. For now, let's examine the context data structure, which provides a way to manage devices as a group.

2.4 *Managing devices with contexts*

The card game analogy likens an OpenCL context to a card table. A card table doesn't seat all the players in the casino—only those involved in a particular game. It provides the foundation through which dealers can distribute cards to players.

In OpenCL, a context identifies a set of devices—not every possible device, but only those selected to work together. Contexts make it possible to create *command queues*, the structures that allow hosts to send kernels to devices. Section 2.7 discusses command queues in detail.

At the time of this writing, the devices in a context must be provided by the same platform. That is, you can't create a context containing both AMD and Nvidia devices—you have to create a different context for each platform. But a host application can manage devices using more than one context, and it can even create multiple contexts from devices in a single platform. This is shown in figure 2.1.

This figure creates three contexts from the devices in two platforms. Two contexts are created from the devices in platform A, and device 1 can be placed in both context 1 and context 2.

Devices from different platforms can't be placed in the same context, but a host application can still utilize multiple contexts during its processing. For example, a

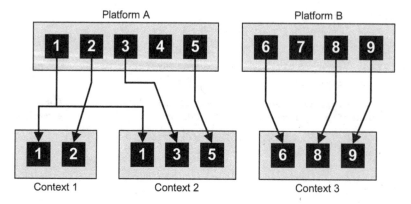

Figure 2.1   Platforms, devices, and contexts

host application can send kernels and other commands to Nvidia and AMD devices, but the devices can't share the resources associated with contexts.

Contexts also become particularly important when you use OpenCL to process graphics. This section will touch upon this topic briefly, and chapter 15 will explain OpenGL-OpenCL interoperability in greater detail.

2.4.1   *Creating contexts*

OpenCL contexts are represented by `cl_context` data structures, and you can create them using one of two functions: `clCreateContext` or `clCreateContextFromType`. Their signatures have a lot in common:

```
cl_context clCreateContext(const cl_context_properties *properties,
    cl_uint num_devices, const cl_device_id *devices,
    (void CL_CALLBACK *notify_func)(...),
    void *user_data, cl_int *error)

cl_context clCreateContextFromType(
    const cl_context_properties *properties,
    cl_device_type device_type,
    (void CL_CALLBACK *notify_func)(...),
    void *user_data, cl_int *error)
```

The primary difference between these functions is that the first creates a context by explicitly identifying devices. The second, `clCreateContextFromType`, forms a context containing all devices of a given type. The possible device types are listed in table 2.3. This function is helpful when you want to create a context without accessing platforms or devices.

Both functions accept a `cl_context_properties` pointer and a `void` pointer that identifies user data. It's important to distinguish between these two parameters. The `user_data` argument can point to any data you like, and its purpose is to provide information when an error occurs. In contrast, the `properties` pointer must identify an array of names and values whose last element must be 0. Both arguments can be set to NULL.

Table 2.5 lists the different names available when setting a context's properties. The nature of the value depends on which property name is used.

Table 2.5   Context property parameters

Property name	Property value	Meaning
CL_CONTEXT_PLATFORM	cl_context_id	Associates the context with the given platform
CL_CONTEXT_D3D10_DEVICE_KHR	ID3D10Device*	Associates the context with the Direct3D device
CL_GL_CONTEXT_KHR	OS-Dependent	Identifies an OpenGL context
CL_EGL_DISPLAY_KHR	EGLDisplay	Displays the OpenGL-ES context on embedded devices
CL_GLX_DISPLAY_KHR	GLXContext	Displays the OpenGL context on Linux
CL_WGL_HDC_KHR	HDC	Serves as the device context for the OpenGL context on Windows
CL_CGL_SHAREGROUP_KHR	CGLShareGroupObj	Serves as the share group for the OpenGL context on Mac OS

The first property in the table identifies the current platform. The other properties relate to graphics and are only functional if specific extensions are installed. If the cl_khr_d3d10_sharing extension is enabled, you can interface OpenCL with Direct3D by providing a pointer to an ID3D10Device defined by Microsoft's Direct3D API.

If the cl_khr_gl_sharing extension is supported, you need to provide two objects: the OpenGL context and the display/device used to display the context. Because OpenGL can run on multiple operating systems, the precise nature of these objects is OS-specific, but all of them must be cast to cl_context_properties.

The following code declares and initializes a cl_context_properties structure that will enable OpenCL-OpenGL interoperability. Remember that the last element must be 0:

```
cl_context_properties context_props[] = {
  CL_CONTEXT_PLATFORM, (cl_context_properties)platforms[0],
  CL_GL_CONTEXT_KHR, (cl_context_properties)glXGetCurrentContext(),
  CL_GLX_DISPLAY_KHR, (cl_context_properties)glXGetCurrentDisplay(),
  0};
```

Don't be concerned if this looks foreign. The cl_context_properties parameter is set to NULL in most of this book's example code. I'll discuss the topic of OpenCL-based graphics in later chapters. Specifically, appendix B discusses OpenGL, and chapter 15 explains how OpenGL relates to OpenCL.

Both clCreateContext and clCreateContextFromType accept a callback function as an argument. This function is invoked whenever an error occurs during the context's operation.

The last two parameters are easy to understand. The user_data parameter can point to any data type, from a char to an int to a table of environment variables. This data is accessed by the callback function when an error occurs. The error parameter identifies an integer that will hold the function's error code. If the cl_context is created successfully, this will be set to 0.

The following code creates a context containing only GPU-based devices. This uses the context_props array discussed earlier:

```
cl_context context = clCreateContextFromType(context_props,
    CL_DEVICE_TYPE_GPU, NULL, NULL, &err);
```

2.4.2 Obtaining context information

The clGetContextInfo function provides information about a context, and it's similar to the clGetPlatformInfo and clGetDeviceInfo functions we looked at earlier. Its signature is as follows:

```
clGetContextInfo(cl_context context, cl_context_info param_name,
    size_t param_value_size, void* param_value,
    size_t *param_value_size_ret)
```

In this case, param_name must take one of the values defined by the cl_context_info enumerated type. Table 2.6 lists the options available.

Table 2.6 Context information parameters

Parameter name	Output type	Purpose
CL_CONTEXT_NUM_DEVICES	cl_uint	Returns the number of devices in the context
CL_CONTEXT_DEVICES	cl_device_id[]	Returns the devices in the context
CL_CONTEXT_PROPERTIES	cl_context_ properties[]	Returns the property array associated with the context
CL_CONTEXT_REFERENCE_ COUNT	cl_uint	Returns the reference count of the context
CL_CONTEXT_D3D10_PREFER_ SHARED_RESOURCES_KHR	cl_bool	Returns whether Direct3D shared resources will be accelerated more than unshared resources

All of these are straightforward except for CL_CONTEXT_REFERENCE_COUNT. Traditional C/C++ applications don't let you keep track of how many times a data structure is accessed, but Mac OS programmers use this capability on a regular basis. The next subsection explains how OpenCL processes these reference counts.

2.4.3 Contexts and the reference count

Unlike functions that create platforms and devices, clCreateContextFromType and clCreateContext return cl_contexts instead of error codes. This means you don't have to allocate and deallocate memory for the structure. If the cl_context is declared as a local variable, its memory will be automatically freed when the enclosing function terminates.

But you may not want the structure to be deallocated. External routines, such as those in a third-party library, might need to continue accessing the cl_context after its enclosing function terminates. For this reason, OpenCL keeps track of how many times cl_context structures are accessed. This number is called the retain count or the *reference count*. It's set to 1 when the structure is created, and when the count equals 0, the structure is deallocated.

You can change this reference count in one of two ways. clRetainContext increments the count and clReleaseContext decrements the count. If you're coding an external function that accesses a pre-existing context, be sure to call clRetainContext before the processing starts and clReleaseContext afterward. If you're coding a function that creates a cl_context, decrement the reference count by calling clRelease-Context before the function completes.

2.4.4 *Code example: checking a context's reference count*

Many OpenCL data structures have associated reference counts, and there are many functions similar to clRetainContext and clReleaseContext. For this reason, it's a good idea to see how they work in code.

The following listing presents an abbreviated portion of the code in Ch2/context_count.c. This creates a context with a single device and updates its reference count with the clRetainContext and clReleaseContext functions. After each update, the code reads the new count with clGetContextInfo.

Listing 2.3   Checking a context's reference count: context_count.c

```
...
cl_context context;
cl_uint ref_count;
...
context = clCreateContext(NULL, 1, &device,            Create
                          NULL, NULL, &err);           context
if(err < 0) {
   perror("Couldn't create a context");
   exit(1);
}

err = clGetContextInfo(context,                        Read initial
      CL_CONTEXT_REFERENCE_COUNT,                      reference count
      sizeof(ref_count), &ref_count, NULL);
if(err < 0) {
   perror("Couldn't read the reference count.");
   exit(1);
}
printf("Initial reference count: %u\n", ref_count);

clRetainContext(context);                              Update and
clGetContextInfo(context, CL_CONTEXT_REFERENCE_COUNT,  print count
      sizeof(ref_count), &ref_count, NULL);
```

```
printf("Reference count: %u\n", ref_count);

clReleaseContext(context);
clGetContextInfo(context, CL_CONTEXT_REFERENCE_COUNT,
    sizeof(ref_count), &ref_count, NULL);
printf("Reference count: %u\n", ref_count);

clReleaseContext(context);
...
```

Update and
print count

Set count
to 0

On my system, the results are as follows:

```
Initial reference count: 1
Reference count: 2
Reference count: 1
```

Many OpenCL data structures can only be created if a context is available. For example, you need a valid context in order to construct a program, and you need a program if you're going to send kernels to your devices (which, honestly, is the whole point of OpenCL programming). The next section explains how programs work.

2.5   *Storing device code in programs*

When I started learning OpenCL, I found it hard to distinguish programs from kernels. They both store executable code, but a kernel represents a single function to be executed on a device. In contrast, a program is a container of kernels. Returning to the card-game analogy, a program is a deck of cards and a kernel is a single card.

In OpenCL, a program is represented by a cl_program data structure. This section explains how to create and build a cl_program so that its kernels can be deployed to devices. This section also discusses how to obtain information about a program and its build process.

2.5.1   *Creating programs*

OpenCL provides two functions that create new programs: clCreateProgramWith-Source and clCreateProgramWithBinary. Both convert code into a cl_program, but neither accepts filenames or file handles. Therefore, if your kernel code is contained in a file, you'll have to read the file's content into a buffer before you can call either function. If you want to create a program from code in multiple files, you'll need to create an array of buffers.

The clCreateProgramWithSource function expects the buffers to contain code in text form. Its signature is as follows:

```
clCreateProgramWithSource(cl_context context, cl_uint src_num,
    const char **src_strings, const size_t *src_sizes,
    cl_int *err_code)
```

To create a program from multiple text files, the content of each file must be placed in an array of strings (char**). The src_num parameter tells the function how many strings to expect, and src_sizes identifies the size of each string.

NOTE Every host application I've encountered either reads source code from a separate text file (*.cl) or initializes a string inside the host application. The example code in this book will rely exclusively on the first method. It's somewhat more involved, but it allows you to keep your host and device code separate.

The following listing shows how to create a `cl_program` from a text file. This is a three-step process. First the code determines the size of kernel.cl. Then it reads the file's content into a buffer. Lastly, it uses the buffer to create a `cl_program`.

> **Listing 2.4 Creating a program from a text file**

```
program_handle = fopen("kernel.cl", "r");          Determine size
fseek(program_handle, 0, SEEK_END);                of source file
program_size = ftell(program_handle);
rewind(program_handle);

program_buffer = (char*)malloc(program_size+1);
program_buffer[program_size] = '\0';
fread(program_buffer, sizeof(char),                Read file content
    program_size, program_handle);                 into buffer
fclose(program_handle);

program = clCreateProgramWithSource(context, 1,     Create program
    (const char**)program_buffer, program_size, &err);   from buffer
```

The `clCreateProgramWithBinary` function is like `clCreateProgramWithSource`, but instead of reading strings from text files, it reads bytes from binary files. Its signature is as follows:

```
clCreateProgramWithBinary(cl_context context,
    cl_uint num_devices, const cl_device_id *devices,
    const size_t *bin_sizes, const unsigned char **bins,
    cl_int *bin_status, cl_int *err_code)
```

This function requires information about the devices intended to perform the program's functions. In particular, it needs to know how many devices will be targeted and the array of `cl_device_id` structures. These devices must be contained within the `cl_context` provided by the first parameter.

2.5.2 Building programs

The functions inside a program rely on OpenCL-specific functions and data structures, so every program must be compiled using an OpenCL-specific compiler. At the time of this writing, AMD's framework contains a standalone compiler called clc, and it can be run from a script or a command line. Nvidia, however, doesn't provide a standalone compiler. Nvidia's compiler is strictly a *runtime compiler*, which means it can only be invoked as part of a running application.

The OpenCL standard doesn't impose many requirements on OpenCL compilers, but one provision is crucial: every compiler must be accessible through `clBuildProgram`. This function compiles and links a `cl_program` for devices associated with the platform. It doesn't return a new cl_program, but instead modifies the input data structure. Its signature is as follows:

```
clBuildProgram(cl_program program, cl_uint num_devices,
    const cl_device_id *devices, const char *options,
    (void CL_CALLBACK *notify_func)(...), void *user_data)
```

The fourth parameter sets options for the compiler. Many are similar to those used in popular compilers like gcc, but a large number of them are specific to OpenCL. Table 2.7 lists a number of the available options.

Table 2.7 Program compilation options

Parameter name	Purpose
-cl-std=VERSION	Tells the compiler which version of OpenCL to use
-DNAME	Sets the macro NAME equal to 1
-DNAME=VALUE	Sets the macro NAME equal to VALUE
-Idir	Identifies a directory containing header files
-w	Suppresses warnings
-Werror	Responds to all warnings as if they were errors
-cl-single-precision-constant	Processes all double-precision floating-point constants as single-precision constants
-cl-denorms-are-zero	Treats all numbers less than the smallest representable number as 0
-cl-opt-disable	Disables all optimizations
-cl-mad-enable	Processes operations involving multiplication and addition (a*b + x) as atomic multiply-and-add (MAD) operations; this may cause a reduction in accuracy
-cl-no-signed-zero	Prevents usage of the positive/negative 0 values defined by IEEE-754
-cl-unsafe-math-optimizations	Optimizes processing by removing error checking, thereby allowing noncompliant operations to occur
-cl-finite-math-only	Assumes that all results and arguments are finite—no operation will accept or produce infinite values or NaN (not a number) values
-cl-fast-relaxed-math	Combines the -cl-unsafe-math-optimizations and -cl-finite-math-only options

The math-related options may seem strange, but the IEEE-754 standard defines many floating-point values that don't correspond to valid numbers (denormals, NaNs, and infinite values). You may improve the performance of your application with options like -cl-finite-math-only, but if errors arise, you won't receive any notification. Chapter 4 discusses the important topic of floating-point processing in detail.

The following two lines of code show how these options are used. Here, program is compiled and linked for a single device (device) using the -cl-std, -cl-mad-enable, and -Werror options:

```
const char options[] = "-cl-std=CL1.1 -cl-mad-enable -Werror";
clBuildProgram(program, 1, &device, options, NULL, NULL);
```

If clBuildProgram fails because of a compile error, the only indication you'll receive is the integer error code. This is helpful, but it doesn't tell you why the compilation failed. If you want details about what happened during the build, you'll need to access the compiler's build log. The following discussion explains how to access this log and other program-related information.

2.5.3 Obtaining program information

Once you've created and compiled a program, you can access information related to it by calling clGetProgramInfo and clGetProgramBuildInfo. The first function provides information about data structures associated with the program, such as its context and target devices. The second function provides information about how the program was built.

The signature of clGetProgramInfo is like that of clGetContextInfo and clGetDeviceInfo:

```
clGetProgramInfo(cl_program program, cl_program_info param_name,
    size_t param_value_size, void *param_value,
    size_t *param_value_size_ret)
```

Here, cl_program_info is an enumerated type that identifies the data to be provided. Table 2.8 lists the different values this can take.

Table 2.8 OpenCL program information

Parameter name	Output type	Purpose
CL_PROGRAM_CONTEXT	cl_context	Returns the context used to create the program
CL_PROGRAM_DEVICES	cl_device_id[]	Returns the devices targeted by the program
CL_PROGRAM_NUM_DEVICES	cl_uint	Returns the number of devices targeted by the program
CL_PROGRAM_SOURCE	char[]	Returns the program's source code concatenated into a single string
CL_PROGRAM_BINARIES	unsigned_char**	Returns the array of binary buffers associated with the program
CL_PROGRAM_BINARY_SIZES	size_t[]	Returns the size of each of the program's binary buffers
CL_PROGRAM_REFERENCE_COUNT	cl_uint	Returns the program's reference count

The CL_PROGRAM_SOURCE property is particularly interesting. It concatenates all of the program's source buffers into one string that contains all of the kernel functions. If you receive inexplicable build errors, it's a good idea to examine this string and verify that the program contains your intended functions.

clGetProgramBuildInfo is a *vital* function to know. It's the only way to find out what happened during the program's build process. Its signature is as follows:

```
clGetProgramBuildInfo(cl_program program,
    cl_device_id device,
    cl_program_build_info param_name,
    size_t param_value_size, void *param_value,
    size_t *param_value_size_ret)
```

As with clGetProgramInfo, the function requires a parameter defined by an enumerated type. In this case, the type is called cl_program_build_info. Table 2.9 lists the different types of information available.

Table 2.9   Program build information parameters

Parameter name	Output type	Purpose
CL_PROGRAM_BUILD_STATUS	cl_build_status	Identifies whether the build succeeded, failed, or is continuing
CL_PROGRAM_BUILD_OPTIONS	char[]	Returns the options used to configure the build
CL_PROGRAM_BUILD_LOG	char[]	Returns the build log—the compiler's output

The first property identifies the status of the build, and the returned value is either CL_BUILD_NONE, CL_BUILD_ERROR, CL_BUILD_SUCCESS, or CL_BUILD_IN_PROGRESS. But rather than check this property, it's easier to examine the return value of clBuild-Program. If the value is less than 0, it's likely that the build failed.

To find out why a build failed, you need to invoke clGetProgramBuildInfo with the CL_PROGRAM_BUILD_LOG parameter. This is demonstrated in the following code, which builds program and prints the compiler's output if the build fails:

```
err = clBuildProgram(program, 1, &device, options, NULL, NULL);
if(err < 0) {
    clGetProgramBuildInfo(program, device, CL_PROGRAM_BUILD_LOG,
        0, NULL, &log_size);
    program_log = (char*) calloc(log_size+1, sizeof(char));
    clGetProgramBuildInfo(program, device, CL_PROGRAM_BUILD_LOG,
        log_size+1, program_log, NULL);
    printf("%s\n", program_log);
    free(program_log);
}
```

Note that clGetProgramBuildInfo is called twice. The first time, it sets log_size equal to the size of the build log. The second time, it places the build log characters in the `program_log` buffer. This log can grow quite long depending on the nature of the build error, so it's a good idea to dynamically allocate memory to hold the text.

2.5.4 Code example: building a program from multiple source files

Throughout this book, program code is usually placed in a single *.cl file. But as your OpenCL projects grow in size, you may need to create a program from code located in multiple files. This is demonstrated in the next listing, which constructs and builds a `cl_project` from source code in two files: good.cl and bad.cl.

Listing 2.5   Building a program from multiple source files: program_build.c

```
...
#define NUM_FILES 2
#define PROGRAM_FILE_1 "good.cl"
#define PROGRAM_FILE_2 "bad.cl"
...
cl_program program;
FILE *program_handle;
char *program_buffer[NUM_FILES];
char *program_log;
const char *file_name[] = {PROGRAM_FILE_1, PROGRAM_FILE_2};
const char options[] = "-cl-finite-math-only -cl-no-signed-zeros";
size_t program_size[NUM_FILES];
size_t log_size;
...
for(i=0; i<NUM_FILES; i++) {
   program_handle = fopen(file_name[i], "r");
   if(program_handle == NULL) {
      perror("Couldn't find the program file");
      exit(1);
   }
   fseek(program_handle, 0, SEEK_END);           Find size of
   program_size[i] = ftell(program_handle);      source file
   rewind(program_handle);
   program_buffer[i] = (char*)malloc(program_size[i]+1);
   program_buffer[i][program_size[i]] = '\0';
   fread(program_buffer[i], sizeof(char),        Read source
       program_size[i], program_handle);         text into buffer
   fclose(program_handle);
}

program = clCreateProgramWithSource(context, NUM_FILES,     Create
   (const char**)program_buffer, program_size, &err);       program
if(err < 0) {
   perror("Couldn't create the program");
   exit(1);
}

err = clBuildProgram(program, 1, &device,          Build
                  options, NULL, NULL);            program
if(err < 0) {
```

```
clGetProgramBuildInfo(program, device,
    CL_PROGRAM_BUILD_LOG, 0, NULL, &log_size);
program_log = (char*)malloc(log_size+1);
program_log[log_size] = '\0';
    clGetProgramBuildInfo(program, device,
    CL_PROGRAM_BUILD_LOG,
    log_size+1, program_log, NULL);
printf("%s\n", program_log);
free(program_log);
exit(1);
}

for(i=0; i<NUM_FILES; i++) {
    free(program_buffer[i]);
}
...
```

| Find size of build log |

| Read build log |

When `clBuildProgram` performs the build, the compilation will fail and the function will return a negative value. This is because good.cl and bad.cl both define a kernel function with the same name. After `clBuildProgram` returns a negative value, the `clGetProgramBuildInfo` function will place the compiler's error message in the program_log buffer.

To avoid the error, change the function name in bad.cl to anything other than good. Then, when you run the application, the build log won't contain any text at all. This means the build succeeded and the functions in good.cl and bad.cl can be deployed to devices for processing. But before you can deploy these functions, they must be converted into kernels. This is the topic of the next section.

2.6   *Packaging functions in kernels*

After you've compiled and linked a program, you can package its functions into data structures called kernels. The advantage of using kernels is that they're deployable—kernels can be dispatched to a command queue and sent to a device. In the card game analogy, kernels are the cards, devices are the players, and a command queue is a player's hand.

Each kernel is represented by a cl_kernel data structure, and this section presents three functions related to them. These functions make it possible to create kernels and obtain information about them.

This section will *not* discuss how to configure kernel arguments. This important topic will be fleshed out in chapter 3.

2.6.1   *Creating kernels*

The OpenCL standard defines two functions that construct cl_kernel structures from a cl_program. They're both simple to use, but clCreateKernelsInProgram is the simpler of the two—it creates a kernel for every function in the program. Its signature is as follows:

```
clCreateKernelsInProgram(cl_program program, cl_uint num_kernels,
    cl_kernel *kernels, cl_uint *num_kernels_ret);
```

When the function completes, the new `cl_kernels` are placed in the `kernels` array, and `num_kernels_ret` identifies how many kernels are available. By calling this function twice, you can determine how much memory to allocate and then store the kernels in the allocated memory.

If you'd rather create a single kernel, you can use the `clCreateKernel` function. Unlike `clCreateKernelsInProgram`, this function requires that you know the name of the function from which the kernel is to be created. Its signature is as follows:

```
clCreateKernel(cl_program program, const char *kernel_name, cl_int *error)
```

This function returns a single `cl_kernel`, so if you want to create multiple kernels by name, you'll have to invoke `clCreateKernel` repeatedly. The following code shows how this function is used:

```
char kernel_name[] = "convolve";
kernel = clCreateKernel(program, kernel_name, &error);
```

When this code executes, `clCreateKernel` examines the program to make sure it defines a function called `convolve`. If this doesn't exist, `clCreateKernel` returns NULL, and `error` is set to `CL_INVALID_KERNEL_NAME`.

2.6.2 *Obtaining kernel information*

Once you've created a `cl_kernel`, you may want to know which function it represents and which program it belongs to. `clGetKernelInfo` is the function to use, and its signature is as follows:

```
clGetKernelInfo(cl_kernel kernel, cl_kernel_info param_name,
    size_t param_value_size, void *param_value,
    size_t *param_value_size_ret)
```

The enumerated type `cl_kernel_info` defines the different types of kernel information that can be accessed. Table 2.10 lists these parameter names and their associated data.

Table 2.10 Kernel information parameters

Parameter name	Output type	Purpose
CL_KERNEL_FUNCTION_NAME	char[]	Returns the name of the function from which the kernel was formed
CL_KERNEL_NUM_ARGS	cl_uint	Returns the number of input arguments accepted by the kernel's associated function
CL_KERNEL_REFERENCE_COUNT	cl_uint	Returns the number of times the kernel has been referenced in code
CL_KERNEL_CONTEXT	cl_context	Returns the context associated with the kernel
CL_KERNEL_PROGRAM	cl_program	Returns the program from which the kernel was created

These properties are easy to understand. They're also easy to access in code, and the next discussion will show how this is accomplished.

2.6.3   Code example: obtaining kernel information

The first parameter in table 2.10, CL_KERNEL_FUNCTION_NAME, becomes important when you need to search through an array of kernels to find one that corresponds to a specific function. This is shown in the following code, which creates an array of four kernels and searches for the one whose function is named mult.

Listing 2.6   Searching for a kernel by name: kernel_search.c

```
...
cl_kernel *kernels, found_kernel;
char kernel_name[20];
cl_uint num_kernels;
...
err = clCreateKernelsInProgram(program, 0,            Determine number
        NULL, &num_kernels);                          of kernels
if(err < 0) {
   perror("Couldn't find any kernels");
   exit(1);
}

kernels = (cl_kernel*)malloc(num_kernels*sizeof(cl_kernel));
clCreateKernelsInProgram(program,                     Create
        num_kernels, kernels, NULL);                  kernels

for(i=0; i<num_kernels; i++) {
   clGetKernelInfo(kernels[i], CL_KERNEL_FUNCTION_NAME,
        sizeof(kernel_name), kernel_name, NULL);
   if(strcmp(kernel_name, "mult") == 0) {             Find kernel
      found_kernel = kernels[i];                       called mult
      printf("Found the kernel at index %u.\n", i);
      break;
   }
}

for(int i=0; i<num_kernels; i++)                      Deallocate
    clReleaseKernel(kernels[i]);                      kernels
...
```

This code calls the clCreateKernelsInProgram function twice. The first time, it provides the number of kernels available. The second time, it places the kernels in the array. Once the kernels have been processed, the clReleaseKernel function is used to deallocate them. This operates just like the clReleaseContext and clRelease-Program functions.

Now that you know how to create kernels, you'd probably like to send them to devices for execution. But there's one last step. To enable communication between the host and device, you need to create a command queue. This is the topic of the next section.

2.7   *Collecting kernels in a command queue*

When you create a kernel, you don't have to identify a target device—it can be sent to any device in the context. Instead, you identify the target device when you create a command queue. Then when you deploy kernels to the queue, they will be sent to the device associated with the queue.

This chapter has been focused on kernels, but kernel execution is only one type of *command* that can be dispatched to a command queue. A command is a message sent from the host that tells a device to perform an operation. Besides kernel execution, many OpenCL command operations involve data transfer: reading data from the device to the host, writing data from the host to the device, and copying data between devices. Chapter 3 discusses these commands in detail.

Figure 2.2 shows a host sending commands to three devices. As shown, each device has its own command queue.

Data transfer operations may convey data to or from a device, but commands in a command queue move in one direction only: from the host to a device. The device doesn't send commands to the host.

By default, command queues process commands in the order in which they're received, but you can change this default behavior when you create a command queue. This is the topic of the next discussion.

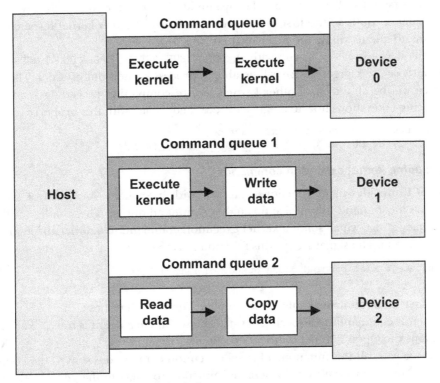

Figure 2.2 Sending commands to devices

2.7.1   Creating command queues

In OpenCL, command queues are represented by `cl_command_queue` structures, which are simple to work with. Unlike the other data structures we've looked at, command queues don't have functions that provide information. Also, there's only one function that creates new queues. It's called `clCreateCommandQueue` and its signature is as follows:

```
clCreateCommandQueue(cl_context context, cl_device_id device,
    cl_command_queue_properties properties, cl_int *err)
```

This returns a `cl_command_queue` whose reference count can be incremented with `clRetainCommandQueue` and decremented with `clReleaseCommandQueue`. The parameters of the signature are easy to understand except for the third parameter. This must identify one of the two values in the `cl_command_queue_properties` enumerated type:

- `CL_QUEUE_PROFILING_ENABLE`—Enables profiling events
- `CL_QUEUE_OUT_OF_ORDER_EXEC_MODE_ENABLE`—Enables out-of-order execution of queue commands

By setting the first property, you can receive timing events as the queue processes its commands. Chapter 7 discusses this topic in detail. The second property relates to how the device processes items in the queue. By default, command queues follow the first-in, first-out (FIFO) principle. For example, if you're the first person in a restaurant queue, you'll be the first to be served. Similarly, the first kernel dispatched to a command queue will be the first executed.

But if you create a queue with the `CL_QUEUE_OUT_OF_ORDER_EXEC_MODE_ENABLE` property set, the target device will be able to process kernels out of order. That is, the device will be able to start other kernels before completing preceding kernels. The following code shows how to create a `cl_command_queue` with this property:

```
clCreateCommandQueue(context, device,
    CL_QUEUE_OUT_OF_ORDER_EXEC_MODE_ENABLE, &err)
```

2.7.2   Enqueuing kernel execution commands

OpenCL provides many functions that start with `clEnqueue`, and each of them dispatches a command to a device through a command queue. The simplest of these is `clEnqueueTask`, which sends a kernel execution command to a device through a command queue. The signature for this function is as follows:

```
clEnqueueTask(cl_command_queue queue, cl_kernel kernel,
    cl_uint num_events, const cl_event *wait_list, cl_event *event)
```

The first two arguments couldn't be simpler. The first identifies a `cl_command_queue` that sends commands to a specific device. The second argument is the `cl_kernel` that contains the OpenCL function to be executed.

Once you call this function, a kernel execution command is sent to the command queue. You don't have to call a separate function to execute the kernel—the device will execute the kernel function when it processes the command.

The following code shows how this works. It creates a command queue and enqueues a command to execute a kernel.

| Listing 2.7   Enqueue a kernel execution command: queue_kernel.c |

```
...
cl_command_queue queue;
...                                                              Create command
queue = clCreateCommandQueue(context, device, 0, &err);    ◁──┘ queue
if(err < 0) {
   perror("Couldn't create the command queue");
   exit(1);
}                                                                Enqueue kernel
err = clEnqueueTask(queue, kernel, 0, NULL, NULL);         ◁──┘ execution
if(err < 0) {
   perror("Couldn't enqueue the kernel execution command");
   exit(1);
}                                                                Deallocate
clReleaseCommandQueue(queue);                              ◁──┘ command queue
...
```

As shown in this listing, command queues are easy to work with in code. But there's a problem: the queue_kernel.c source code compiles, but it may not execute properly. This is because the kernel function doesn't have any arguments. You can see this by looking at the kernel code:

```
kernel void blank() {}
```

Boring, isn't it? Without arguments, the function has no data to process. The next chapter explains how to code host applications to set arguments for kernel functions. Then, in chapter 4, we'll look closely at kernel coding.

2.8   *Summary*

Although I love the English language, I have to admit that its grammar is complicated. You have to deal with clauses, phrases, tenses, moods, and many other syntax elements. OpenCL is similar. I admire the idea of a cross-platform toolkit for high-performance coding, but dealing with OpenCL's data structures can be a harrowing process. Yet there's no getting around it—if you want to build a nontrivial OpenCL application, you need a solid grasp of platforms, devices, contexts, programs, kernels, and command queues.

This chapter has focused on host applications, whose primary function involves sending commands to devices. Host applications usually start by creating one or more `cl_platform_id` data structures, each of which represents a vendor's implementation of OpenCL. Then, using the platform or platforms, the application finds connected devices, which are represented by `cl_device_id` structures. The application can find information about these devices by calling `clGetDeviceInfo`, and once it has determined which devices to target, it combines them within a `cl_context`.

Next, the application reads in source code or binary code that contains specifically marked functions called kernel functions. It uses this code to form a `cl_program` and then builds the program with `clBuildProgram`. This compiles the code for every device in the context, and once the program is built successfully, the host application creates `cl_kernels` for the functions contained inside.

To enable communication with a device, the host application creates a `cl_command_queue`. It dispatches commands into this queue, and each command tells the target device to perform an operation. For example, `clEnqueueTask` sends a kernel function to the device for execution. Other commands tell the device to transfer data to and from the host.

Host development is a complicated topic, and don't be concerned if the discussion doesn't make sense just yet. As you examine more code and start writing your own, dealing with these data structures will become second nature.

This chapter has explained how to write host applications that dispatch kernel functions to devices. But in practical applications, you need to deliver data to the connected devices. It takes an entire chapter to explain OpenCL data transfer and partitioning, and we'll look at this next.

Host programming: data transfer and partitioning

This chapter covers

- Creating memory objects to serve as kernel arguments
- Commands that transfer data between the host and a device
- Partitioning kernel execution using work-items and work-groups

The preceding chapter explained a great deal about host applications, from accessing platforms to creating kernels. But to do their jobs, devices need more than just kernels—they need *data*. If you want a device to perform a nontrivial computing task, you have to provide at least three pieces of information: the instructions to be executed, a buffer containing data to be processed, and a buffer where processed data should be stored.

In regular C/C++ programming, this isn't a big deal. Just set suitable input and output parameters in a function call. But when you're sending functions to another processor, this becomes more complicated. The first part of this chapter is devoted to explaining how to set arguments for OpenCL kernel functions.

After you've assigned data to a kernel, you may want to tell the target devices how to partition the data to improve performance. Different devices have different memory sizes and processing characteristics, so it's a good idea to subdivide the data to take best advantage of the target architecture. This topic is discussed in the second part of this chapter.

Once you've finished reading this chapter, you'll have a solid understanding of how to code host applications, and you'll be able to send functions and data to your devices. But to reach that point, you need to become familiar with kernel arguments. We'll examine this first.

3.1   *Setting kernel arguments*

Chapter 2 explained how to create kernels from functions, but it didn't discuss how to set arguments for the functions. This is accomplished by using `clSetKernelArg`, whose signature is as follows:

```
clSetKernelArg (cl_kernel kernel, cl_uint index, size_t size,
    const void *value)
```

In this signature, the `index` parameter identifies the order of the kernel argument in the kernel function's parameter list. If `index` is set to 0, the argument will come first. If `index` equals 1, the argument will be accessed second.

The last argument of `clSetKernelArg` points to the data that will be transferred to the kernel function. This can take one of the following forms:

- *Pointer to primitive data*—Transfers simple primitives to the device
- *Pointer to a memory object*—Transfers significant or complex data
- *Pointer to a sampler object*—Transfers an object that defines how images are read
- NULL—Transfers no data from the host; the device will just reserve memory in its local address space for the kernel argument

I like to think of the first two options as being similar to an envelope and a cardboard box. Envelopes are great for sending small, regularly shaped packages, but for anything large or complex, you need a cardboard box. Similarly, if you want to send a single `float` or an `int` to the device, make the last argument of `clSetKernelArg` a pointer to the `float` or `int`. But if you need to send a large array or a composite data type, make the last argument a pointer to a memory object.

Let's look at an example. Say you want to send two arguments to a kernel called `proc`: an integer called `num` and memory object called `mem_obj`. You would make the following function calls within your host application:

```
clSetKernelArg(proc, 0, sizeof(num), &num);
clSetKernelArg(proc, 1, sizeof(mem_obj), &mem_obj);
```

Chapter 4 discusses kernel arguments in greater detail and explains why you might set an argument's data to NULL. Chapter 6 discusses samplers and their usage in image processing. This section is devoted to memory objects, which serve as standard packages for transferring data between a host and device.

In OpenCL, memory objects are represented by cl_mem data structures, and they come in two types: buffer objects and image objects. If the memory object is intended to contain pixel data, you should create an image object. In all other circumstances, you should place your data in a buffer object. We'll look at buffer objects first.

3.2   Buffer objects

Buffer objects package any type of data that doesn't involve images. These are created by the clCreateBuffer function, whose signature is as follows:

```
clCreateBuffer(cl_context context, cl_mem_flags options, size_t size,
    void *host_ptr, cl_int *error)
```

This returns a cl_mem that wraps around the data identified by the host_ptr argument. The options parameter configures many of the object's characteristics, such as whether the buffer data is read-only or write-only and the manner in which the data is allocated on the host. Table 3.1 lists the six values of the cl_mem_flags enumerated type.

Table 3.1 Memory object properties (`cl_mem_flags`)

Flag value	Meaning
CL_MEM_READ_WRITE	The memory object can be read from and written to.
CL_MEM_WRITE_ONLY	The memory object can only be written to.
CL_MEM_READ_ONLY	The memory object can only be read from.
CL_MEM_USE_HOST_PTR	The memory object will access the memory region specified by the host pointer.
CL_MEM_COPY_HOST_PTR	The memory object will set the memory region specified by the host pointer.
CL_MEM_ALLOC_HOST_PTR	A region in host-accessible memory will be allocated for use in data transfer.

The first three properties determine the buffer object's accessibility, and they're all easy to understand. The only point to remember is that they constrain the *device*'s access to the buffer object, not the host's. If a device attempts to modify a buffer object created with the CL_MEM_READ_ONLY flag, the operation will produce an undefined result.

The last three properties specify how the buffer object is allocated in host memory. This section will explore this topic and then explain how to create subbuffer objects.

3.2.1   Allocating buffer objects

When you set the second argument of clCreateBuffer, you'll commonly provide a combination of two flags. First, you'll select one of the first three flags in table 3.1 to set the buffer object's accessibility. Then you'll select one or more of the second three to specify where the buffer object should be allocated. As an example, the following function creates a buffer object to package vec, an array of 32 floats:

```
vec_buff = clCreateBuffer(context,
    CL_MEM_READ_ONLY | CL_MEM_COPY_HOST_PTR,
    sizeof(float)*32, vec, &error);
```

In this case, the buffer object vec_buff is created as read-only. Its allocation is controlled by the CL_MEM_COPY_HOST_PTR flag. This buffer packages the data referenced by vec, and because the data is initially allocated on the host, vec is called the *host pointer.*

> **NOTE** The following discussion is based partly on the OpenCL 1.1 standard and partly on my experiments. My conclusions aren't fully supported by the standard, which is unclear on this topic.

Let's say you want to create a buffer object to hold a kernel's *output* data. It's a good idea to make the buffer object write-only so that the device can only write to it. You can do this by setting the CL_MEM_WRITE_ONLY flag in clCreateBuffer. For write-only buffers, the device allocates memory but the host doesn't. Therefore, you can set the host pointer parameter in clCreateBuffer to NULL.

On the other hand, if you're transferring data from the host to the device, the host pointer must not be NULL. In this case, you need to specify where the buffer object's data should be allocated. If you want the buffer object to access the same memory referenced by the host pointer, set CL_MEM_USE_HOST_PTR. This is memory-efficient, but there's a drawback. Data transfer between hosts and devices can be unpredictable, so you may not be able to safely access the host pointer memory after communication starts.

Alternatively, you can tell OpenCL to allocate memory elsewhere and copy the data from the host pointer to this new region. The CL_MEM_COPY_HOST_PTR flag makes this possible. This isn't memory-efficient, but it allows you to modify the host pointer memory even though the host may be transferring the buffer object to and from devices.

The last allocation flag, CL_MEM_ALLOC_HOST_PTR, can only be used in combination with CL_MEM_COPY_HOST_PTR. According to the OpenCL 1.1 standard, it constrains the new memory region to be *host-accessible.* I have read (outside the standard) that host-accessible memory is supposed to mean *pinned memory,* which isn't subject to paging. This implies that performance will be improved because the operating system won't transfer the memory content to and from system memory. However, the standard says nothing about pinned memory.

Based on these observations, we can derive two rules. Set the CL_MEM_USE_HOST_PTR flag if you're running host applications on a memory-limited system or on the same device that you're using to process kernels. Set the CL_MEM_COPY_HOST_PTR flag if low memory isn't an issue but reliable data transfer is.

> **NOTE** In this book, memory objects will always be created with the CL_MEM_COPY_HOST_PTR flag.

Let's look at an example. The following code creates two buffer objects: one containing an input array (read-only) and one containing an output array (write-only). Then it calls clSetKernelArg twice to make the buffer objects into kernel arguments:

```
input_buffer = clCreateBuffer(context,
    CL_MEM_READ_ONLY | CL_MEM_COPY_HOST_PTR,
    sizeof(input_vector), input_vector, &error);

output_buffer = clCreateBuffer(context,
    CL_MEM_WRITE_ONLY, sizeof(input_vector), NULL, &error);

clSetKernelArg(kernel, 0, sizeof(cl_mem), &input_buffer);
clSetKernelArg(kernel, 1, sizeof(cl_mem), &output_buffer);
```

Note that the second call to clCreateBuffer uses only one of the flags in table 3.1: CL_MEM_WRITE_ONLY. This is because output data isn't allocated on the host. Also, remember that write-only buffer objects can use NULL as their host pointers, but you still need to set the size of the memory encapsulated by the buffer object.

3.2.2 Creating subbuffer objects

Just as you can create a substring from a string, you can create a subbuffer object from a buffer object. You may want to do this if one kernel needs a subset of the data required by another kernel. Subbuffer objects are created by clCreateSubBuffer, whose signature is as follows:

```
clCreateSubBuffer(cl_mem buffer,
    cl_mem_flags flags, cl_buffer_create_type type,
    const void *info, cl_int *error)
```

The second argument, flags, takes the same values as those listed in table 3.1. The third argument, type, must be set to CL_BUFFER_CREATE_TYPE_REGION.

The fourth argument is more complicated. Its data type is const void*, but the function expects a pointer to a _cl_buffer_region structure. This is defined as follows:

```
typedef struct _cl_buffer_region {
    size_t origin;
    size_t size;
} cl_buffer_region;
```

The origin field specifies the start of the subbuffer's data inside the buffer. The size field defines the size of the subbuffer. For example, the following code creates a subbuffer containing 40 floats from a buffer object containing 100 floats. The start of the subbuffer data is the 50th float in the main buffer:

```
cl_buffer_region region;
region.size = 40*sizeof(float);
region.origin = 50*sizeof(float);
sub_buffer = clCreateSubBuffer(main_buffer, CL_MEM_READ_ONLY |
    CL_MEM_COPY_HOST_PTR, CL_BUFFER_CREATE_TYPE_REGION, &region, &err);
```

Figure 3.1 shows how the subbuffer data is related to the data inside the main buffer.

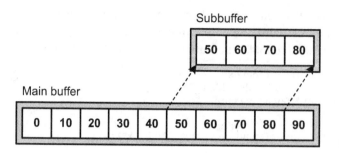

Figure 3.1   Creating a subbuffer

The code in section 3.4 provides another example of how subbuffers are created in code. The next section, however, discusses the second type of memory object, image objects.

3.3   Image objects

Image processing is a major priority in high-performance computing. This is particularly true for OpenCL, which is one of the few languages capable of targeting graphics cards. For this reason, OpenCL provides a specific type of memory object for holding pixel data. The standard refers to them as *image objects*, but there is no separate data structure for them. Like buffer objects, image objects are represented by cl_mem structures.

Much of our discussion of buffer objects applies to image objects as well. Image objects are created with the same configuration flags as those listed in table 3.1, and their allocation properties are exactly the same. Chapter 6 discusses image objects in detail, but this section will explain how to create them in code and examine their properties.

3.3.1   Creating image objects

Image objects come in two types: two-dimensional and three-dimensional. Two-dimensional image objects are created by clCreateImage2D. Three-dimensional image objects, which are essentially successions of two-dimension images, are created with clCreateImage3D. Both functions return a cl_mem structure and their signatures are as follows:

```
clCreateImage2D (cl_context context, cl_mem_flags opts,
    const cl_image_format *format, size_t width, size_t height,
    size_t row_pitch, void *data, cl_int *error)

clCreateImage3D (cl_context context, cl_mem_flags opts,
    const cl_image_format *format, size_t width, size_t height,
    size_t depth, size_t row_pitch, size_t slice_pitch,
    void *data, cl_int *error)
```

The first two arguments are the same as those used to create buffer objects. The third argument identifies the format in which the image data is provided. The rest of the arguments, with the exception of error, identify the dimensions and pitches of the pixels in the image.

IMAGE OBJECT FORMATS

In both functions, the third argument identifies how the image's pixels are stored in memory. The argument's data type is `cl_image_format`, which is defined as follows:

```
typedef struct _cl_image_format {
    cl_channel_order image_channel_order;
    cl_channel_type image_channel_data_type;
} cl_image_format;
```

The first field of the structure has the `cl_channel_order` data type. This defines what channels are present in each pixel and the order in which they're stored. This is an enumerated type, and most of its values involve red, green, blue, and alpha (opacity) channels: `CL_RGB`, `CL_RGBA`, `CL_ARGB`, `CL_BGRA`, `CL_RG`, `CL_RA`, `CL_R`, and `CL_A`. Others add bit padding, represented by x: `CL_RGBx`, `CL_RGx`, and `CL_Rx`. `CL_INTENSITY` measures alpha (opacity) independent of color, and `CL_LUMINANCE` is used for grayscale images.

The second field specifies how an image's channels are represented at the bit level. This includes the numerical format of the channels (floating-point, signed integer, or unsigned integer) and the number of bits per channel (8, 16, or 32). The data type of this field is `cl_channel_type`. This is an enumerated type that can take any of the values listed in table 3.2.

Table 3.2 Image channel types (`cl_channel_type`)

Flag value	Meaning
CL_HALF_FLOAT	Each component is floating-point (16 bits).
CL_FLOAT	Each component is floating-point (32 bits).
CL_UNSIGNED_INT8	Each component is an unsigned integer (8 bits).
CL_UNSIGNED_INT16	Each component is an unsigned integer (16 bits).
CL_UNSIGNED_INT32	Each component is an unsigned integer (32 bits).
CL_SIGNED_INT8	Each component is a signed integer (8 bits).
CL_SIGNED_INT16	Each component is a signed integer (16 bits).
CL_SIGNED_INT32	Each component is a signed integer (32 bits).
CL_UNORM_INT8	Each component is a normalized unsigned integer (8 bits).
CL_UNORM_INT16	Each component is a normalized unsigned integer (16 bits).
CL_SNORM_INT8	Each component is a normalized signed integer (8 bits).
CL_SNORM_INT16	Each component is a normalized signed integer (16 bits).
CL_UNORM_SHORT_565	The RGB components are combined into a normalized 16-bit format (5-6-5).
CL_UNORM_SHORT_555	The xRGB components are combined into a normalized 16-bit format (x-5-5-5).
CL_UNORM_INT_101010	The xRGB components are combined into a normalized 32-bit format (x-10-10-10).

These are easy to understand. The common 24-bit RGB color model is represented by the `CL_UNSIGNED_INT8` format, which uses 8 bits to store each channel. The High-Color format uses `CL_UNORM_SHORT_565`, adding an extra bit for the green channel. The 30-bit Deep Color format is provided for with the `CL_UNORM_INT_101010` flag.

As an example, the following code initializes a `cl_image_format` structure whose pixels are formatted according to the 24-bit RGB format:

```
cl_image_format rgb_format;
rgb_format.image_channel_order = CL_RGB;
rgb_format.image_channel_data_type = CL_UNSIGNED_INT8;
```

IMAGE OBJECT DIMENSIONS AND PITCH

The final arguments in `clCreateImage2D` and `clCreateImage3D` relate to the dimensions of the image object and the number of bytes per dimension, also called *pitch*. Each dimension is given in pixels, and figure 3.2 presents the dimensions of a three-dimensional image object. The individual two-dimensional components are called *slices*.

In most images, you can determine how many bytes are in a row by multiplying bytes-per-pixel by pixels-per-row. But this won't work if the rows contain trailing bits or if the rows need to be aligned on memory boundaries. For this reason, both `clCreateImage2D` and `clCreateImage3D` accept a `row_pitch` argument that identifies how many bytes are in each row. Similarly, `clCreateImage3D` accepts a `slice_pitch` argument that identifies the number of bytes in each two-dimensional image, or slice.

If `row_pitch` is set to 0, OpenCL will assume its value equals `width` * (pixel size). If `slice_pitch` is set to 0, its value will be set to `row_pitch` * `height`. In this book's example code, `row_pitch` and `slice_pitch` will always be set to 0.

Let's look at an example. The following code creates a three-dimensional image object containing four slices, each slice containing 64 * 80 pixels. The image's color format is set equal to the `rgb_format` structure defined earlier:

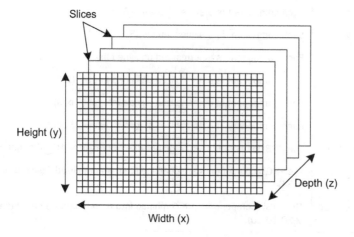

Figure 3.2   Image object dimensions

```
#DEFINE NUM_ROWS 64
#DEFINE NUM_COLS 80
#DEFINE NUM_SLICES 4

unsigned char image_data[NUM_SLICES][NUM_ROWS][NUM_COLS];

cl_mem image_object = clCreateImage3D(context,
    CL_MEM_READ_ONLY | CL_MEM_COPY_HOST_PTR, rgb_format, NUM_COLS,
    NUM_ROWS, NUM_SLICES, NULL, NULL, image_data, &error);
```

This is a read-only image object, but you can create write-only image objects by setting the CL_MEM_WRITE_ONLY flag. In this case, the object data must be set to NULL.

3.3.2 Obtaining information about image objects

This book has presented many data structures whose properties can be examined with functions named get*XX*Info. Image objects are no exception. The getImageInfo function provides information about an image object's dimensions and pixel format, and its signature is as follows:

```
clGetImageInfo (cl_mem image,
    cl_image_info param_name,
    size_t param_value_size, void *param_value,
    size_t *param_value_size_ret)
```

The data type of the fourth argument is cl_image_info. This enumerated type can take any of the values listed in table 3.3.

All of these parameters are straightforward. If you're interested in data regarding pointers, memory sizes, and memory allocation flags, you can examine image objects with clGetMemObjectInfo, which will be discussed next.

Table 3.3 Image object information parameters (`cl_image_info`)

Parameter name	Parameter value	Purpose
CL_IMAGE_ELEMENT_SIZE	size_t	Returns the bit size of the elements (pixels) that make up the image
CL_IMAGE_WIDTH	size_t	Returns the pixel width
CL_IMAGE_HEIGHT	size_t	Returns the pixel height
CL_IMAGE_DEPTH	size_t	Returns the depth of a 3-D image (the number of 2-D components)
CL_IMAGE_ROW_PITCH	size_t	Returns the row pitch (the number of bytes per row)
CL_IMAGE_SLICE_PITCH	size_t	Returns the slice pitch of a 3-D image (the number of bytes per 2-D component)
CL_IMAGE_FORMAT	cl_image_format	Returns the data structure that sets the image's channel/pixel format
CL_IMAGE_D3D10_SUBRESOURCE_KHR	ID3D10 Resource*	Returns a pointer to the Direct3D subresource used to create the image object

3.4   *Obtaining information about buffer objects*

Whereas `clGetImageInfo` provides information about image objects only, you can obtain information about image objects and buffer objects with `clGetMemObjectInfo`. Its signature is as follows:

```
clGetMemObjectInfo (cl_mem object, cl_mem_info param_name,
    size_t param_value_size, void *param_value,
    size_t *param_value_size_ret)
```

These arguments are straightforward. The first three provide input: the memory object, a name that identifies the type of data you're requesting, and the amount of data you're requesting. The last two arguments are output arguments, in which the function returns the data you're requesting and the size of the returned data.

Table 3.4 lists the different types of information that can be accessed with `clGetMemObjectInfo`.

Table 3.4   Memory object information parameters (`cl_mem_info`)

Parameter name	Parameter value	Purpose
CL_MEM_TYPE	cl_mem_object_ type	Returns the type of the memory object (CL_MEM_OBJECT_BUFFER, CL_MEM_OBJECT_IMAGE2D, or CL_MEM_OBJECT_IMAGE3D)
CL_MEM_FLAGS	cl_mem_flags	Returns the flags used to configure the memory object's accessibility and allocation
CL_MEM_HOST_PTR	void*	Returns the host pointer that references the memory object's data
CL_MEM_SIZE	size_t	Returns the size of the memory object's data
CL_MEM_CONTEXT	cl_context	Returns the context associated with the memory object
CL_MEM_ASSOCIATED_ MEMOBJECT	cl_mem	Returns the memory object from which this memory object was created (only valid for subbuffer objects)
CL_MEM_OFFSET	size_t	Returns the offset used to create the subbuffer object (only valid for subbuffer objects)
CL_MEM_REFERENCE COUNT	cl_uint	Returns the memory object's reference count (the number of times the object has been accessed)
CL_MEM_D3D10_ RESOURCE_KHR	ID3D10Resource*	Returns a pointer to the OpenCL-Direct3D interface

These parameters become particularly useful when you want to examine the size and location of a memory object's data. The following code shows how this works. It creates a buffer containing 100 `float` values and a subbuffer containing a 20-element subset of these `float`s. Then it invokes `clGetMemObjectInfo` to examine both buffer objects.

NOTE The following code makes use of subbuffers and therefore will only compile on systems that support the OpenCL 1.1 standard.

Listing 3.1 Buffers and subbuffers: buffer_check.c

```c
...
float main_data[100];
cl_mem main_buffer, sub_buffer;
void *main_buffer_mem = NULL, *sub_buffer_mem = NULL;
size_t main_buffer_size, sub_buffer_size;
cl_buffer_region region;
...
main_buffer = clCreateBuffer(context,                         ┤ Create buffer
      CL_MEM_READ_ONLY | CL_MEM_COPY_HOST_PTR,                   with 100 values
      sizeof(main_data), main_data, &err);
if(err < 0) {
   perror("Couldn't create a buffer");
   exit(1);
}

region.origin = 30*sizeof(float);
region.size = 20*sizeof(float);
sub_buffer = clCreateSubBuffer(main_buffer,                   ┤ Create subbuffer
      CL_MEM_READ_ONLY | CL_MEM_COPY_HOST_PTR,                   with 20 values
      CL_BUFFER_CREATE_TYPE_REGION,
      &region, &err);
if(err < 0) {
   perror("Couldn't create a sub-buffer");
   exit(1);
}

clGetMemObjectInfo(main_buffer, CL_MEM_SIZE,                  ┤ Obtain size
      sizeof(main_buffer_size), &main_buffer_size, NULL);       information
clGetMemObjectInfo(sub_buffer, CL_MEM_SIZE,
      sizeof(sub_buffer_size), &sub_buffer_size, NULL);
printf("Main buffer size: %lu\n", main_buffer_size);
printf("Sub-buffer size:  %lu\n", sub_buffer_size);

clGetMemObjectInfo(main_buffer, CL_MEM_HOST_PTR,             ┤ Obtain host
      sizeof(main_buffer_mem), &main_buffer_mem, NULL);        pointers
clGetMemObjectInfo(sub_buffer, CL_MEM_HOST_PTR,
      sizeof(sub_buffer_mem), &sub_buffer_mem, NULL);
printf("Main buffer memory address: %p\n", main_buffer_mem);
printf("Sub-buffer memory address:  %p\n", sub_buffer_mem);

printf("Main array address: %p\n", main_data);

clReleaseMemObject(main_buffer);                              ┤ Deallocate
clReleaseMemObject(sub_buffer);                                buffer objects
...
```

On my system, the printed results are as follows:

```
Main buffer size: 400
Sub-buffer size:  80
Main buffer data address: 0x972000
Sub-buffer data address:  0x972078
Main array address: 0x7ff60805920
```

The subbuffer doesn't allocate its own memory region to hold data. Instead, it accesses the same memory region used by the main buffer. Because createBuffer is called with the CL_MEM_COPY_HOST_PTR flag, neither buffer accesses data in the original float array.

At this point, you should have a solid understanding of how to create and examine memory objects, whether they're image objects, buffer objects, or subbuffer objects. You can send these objects to a device by making them arguments of a kernel function, but there are other ways to transfer this data. The next section presents commands that convey memory object data from the host to a device, from a device to a host, and between devices.

3.5   *Memory object transfer commands*

Let's review the topic of command queues. A host creates a command queue when it wants to access a device. The host communicates with the device by dispatching commands to the queue. We refer to this process of placing commands in a command queue as *enqueuing*.

So far, we've focused solely on commands that tell the device to execute kernels. However, kernel execution is only one type of command. Other commands tell the device how and where to transfer data, and this section will examine these commands in detail.

OpenCL provides many functions that enqueue data transfer commands, and their names all take the form clEnqueue*XX*. For the sake of convenience, we'll group them into three categories: functions that initiate read/write data transfer, functions that map and unmap memory, and functions that copy data between memory objects.

NOTE These functions don't create new memory objects. They access data from memory objects that have already been transferred to the device as kernel arguments.

3.5.1   *Read/write data transfer*

At this point, you know how to send memory objects to devices using clSetKernelArg. But let's say you've created a write-only buffer object to hold the device's output. After the kernel has completed its processing, how can you get the buffer data back to the host?

To read a buffer object from a device to the host, the simplest function to use is clEnqueueReadBuffer. This is one of the six functions that read and write memory objects. Table 3.5 lists them all, including their arguments and purposes. All of them return an integer error code.

In each of these functions, the two most important arguments are the cl_mem argument, which identifies the memory object on the device, and the void pointer that references host memory. A read operation transfers data from the memory object to host memory. A write operation transfers data from host memory to the memory object.

Table 3.5   Functions that read and write memory objects

Function	Purpose

`clEnqueueReadBuffer(cl_command_queue queue,`
`    cl_mem buffer, cl_bool blocking, size_t offset,`
`    size_t data_size, void *ptr, cl_uint num_events,`
`    const cl_event *wait_list, cl_event *event)`
	Reads data from a buffer object to host memory

`clEnqueueWriteBuffer(cl_command_queue_queue,`
`    cl_mem buffer, cl_bool blocking, size_t offset,`
`    size_t data_size, const void *ptr,`
`    cl_uint num_events, const cl_event *wait_list,`
`    cl_event *event)`
	Writes data from host memory to a buffer object

`clEnqueueReadImage(cl_command_queue queue,`
`    cl_mem image, cl_bool blocking,`
`    const size_t origin[3], const size_t region[3],`
`    size_t row_pitch, size_t slice_pitch,`
`    void *ptr, cl_uint num_events,`
`    const cl_event *wait_list, cl_event *event)`
	Reads data from an image object to host memory

`clEnqueueWriteImage(cl_command_queue queue,`
`    cl_mem image, cl_bool blocking,`
`    const size_t origin[3], const size_t region[3],`
`    size_t row_pitch, size_t slice_pitch,`
`    const void * ptr, cl_uint num_events,`
`    const cl_event *event_wait_list, cl_event *event)`
	Writes data from host memory to an image object

`clEnqueueReadBufferRect(cl_command_queue_queue,`
`    cl_mem buffer, cl_bool blocking,`
`    const size_t buffer_origin[3],`
`    const size_t host_origin[3],`
`    const size_t region[3], size_t buffer_row_pitch,`
`    size_t buffer_slice_pitch, size_t host_row_pitch,`
`    size_t host_slice_pitch, void *ptr,`
`    cl_uint num_events, const cl_event *wait_list,`
`    cl_event *event)`
	Reads a rectangular portion of data from a buffer object to host memory

`clEnqueueWriteBufferRect(cl_command_queue queue,`
`    cl_mem buffer, cl_bool blocking,`
`    const size_t buffer_origin[3],`
`    const size_t host_origin[3],`
`    const size_t region[3], size_t buffer_row_pitch,`
`    size_t buffer_slice_pitch, size_t host_row_pitch,`
`    size_t host_slice_pitch, void *ptr,`
`    cl_uint num_events, const cl_event *wait_list,`
`    cl_event *event)`
	Writes a rectangular portion of data from host memory to a buffer object

Each of these functions also contains a Boolean argument called `blocking`. If this is set to `CL_TRUE`, the function won't return until the read/write operation is finished. If `blocking` is set to `CL_FALSE`, the function will enqueue the read/write command but it won't wait for the data transfer to complete.

Figure 3.3   Transferring buffer object data

Many of the remaining arguments specify what portion of the memory object should be accessed. The `offset` argument in the buffer read/write functions identifies the start of the buffer data to be read or written. The `data_size` argument identifies how much data, starting from `offset`, should be transferred. Figure 3.3 shows how the two main read/write functions work.

The `clEnqueueReadImage` and `clEnqueueWriteImage` functions both accept two arguments that may not make sense at first glance: `origin[3]` and `region[3]`. These arrays specify the rectangular region of image data to be transferred into or out of the image object. `origin` identifies the location of the first pixel to be accessed, and its three `size_t` elements identify the pixel's column, row, and slice, respectively. The `region` argument also contains three `size_t` elements, and they identify the dimensions (width, height, and depth) of the image data to be read or written. If the image object is two-dimensional, the last element of `origin` must be 0 and the last element of `region` must be 1. Figure 3.4 shows how the image read/write functions operate.

The last two functions in table 3.5 transfer data to and from buffer objects, but they access data in rectangular regions similar to those used to transfer image data. As with the image read/write functions, `region` identifies the dimensions of the rectangle to be transferred. `buffer_origin[3]` sets the start of the buffer object data, and `host_origin[3]` sets the start of the data in host memory. You have to specify the row pitch and slice pitch for both the host and buffer objects, but these parameters can be set to 0.

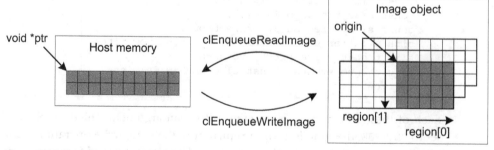

Figure 3.4   Transferring image object data

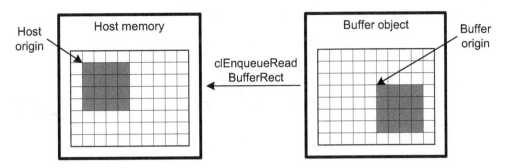

Figure 3.5 Transferring buffer object data in rectangles

The clEnqueueReadBufferRect and clEnqueueWriteBufferRect functions are useful when you want to transfer multidimensional data that isn't image-related. For example, suppose you've stored a matrix in a buffer object, and you want to read a submatrix into host memory. In this case, clEnqueueReadBufferRect is the function to use, and figure 3.5 shows how it works.

Here, region sets the size of the submatrix: [4, 4, 1]. host_origin equals [1, 1, 0] and buffer_origin equals [5, 3, 0]. The following listing shows how this rectangular data transfer is accomplished in code.

NOTE clEnqueueReadBufferRect and clEnqueueWriteBufferRect are only available on platforms that support the OpenCL 1.1 standard. At the time of this writing, Mac OS supports only OpenCL 1.0, so this code won't run properly on Mac OS systems.

Listing 3.2 Reading rectangular buffer data: buffer_test.c

```
...
float full_matrix[80], zero_matrix[80];
const size_t buffer_origin[3] = {5*sizeof(float), 3, 0};
const size_t host_origin[3] = {1*sizeof(float), 1, 0};
const size_t region[3] = {4*sizeof(float), 4, 1};
cl_mem matrix_buffer;
...
matrix_buffer = clCreateBuffer(context,                          Create and
      CL_MEM_READ_WRITE | CL_MEM_COPY_HOST_PTR,                  initialize buffer
      sizeof(full_matrix), full_matrix, &err);
if(err < 0) {
   perror("Couldn't create a buffer object");
   exit(1);
}

err = clSetKernelArg(kernel, 0,                                  Set buffer as
      sizeof(cl_mem), &matrix_buffer);                          kernel argument
if(err < 0) {
   perror("Couldn't set the buffer as the kernel argument");
   exit(1);
}
```

```
err = clEnqueueTask(queue, kernel, 0, NULL, NULL);          ◁──┐  Enqueue kernel
if(err < 0) {                                                   │  command
   perror("Couldn't enqueue the kernel");
   exit(1);
}

err = clEnqueueWriteBuffer(queue, matrix_buffer,               │  Write data
      CL_TRUE, 0, sizeof(full_matrix), full_matrix,            │  to buffer
      0, NULL, NULL);
if(err < 0) {
   perror("Couldn't write to the buffer object");
   exit(1);
}

err = clEnqueueReadBufferRect(queue, matrix_buffer,            │  Read rectangle
      CL_TRUE, buffer_origin, host_origin, region,             │  from buffer
      10*sizeof(float), 0, 10*sizeof(float), 0,
      zero_matrix, 0, NULL, NULL);
if(err < 0) {
   perror("Couldn't read the rectangle from the buffer object");
   exit(1);
}
...
```

This application creates a kernel argument out of a buffer of zeros, writes to the buffer, and then reads a 4x4 rectangle from the buffer at the specified offset. This dispatches three commands to the command queue. The first tells the device to execute the kernel, the second transfers host data to the buffer object, and the third reads a rectangular memory region from the buffer object into host memory.

3.5.2   *Mapping memory objects*

When a regular C/C++ application needs to access a file, it's common to place the file's content in process memory and read or modify it using memory operations. This is referred to as *memory-mapping* or just *mapping* the file. This usually provides improved performance over regular file I/O. For me, it's also simpler because I use memory-related functions more frequently than file-related functions.

OpenCL provides a similar mechanism for accessing memory objects. Instead of using the read/write operations presented earlier, you can map a memory object on a device to a memory region on the host. Once this map is established, you can read or modify the memory object on the host using pointers or other memory operations.

Table 3.6 lists the functions that enqueue commands to map and unmap memory objects. Notice that you don't have to map the entire memory object. For buffer objects, you can access any one-dimensional region. For image objects, you can access a rectangular region.

Most of the arguments in these functions resemble those used for reading and writing, but one significant difference is that the first two functions return a void pointer. This pointer serves two purposes: it identifies the start of the mapped memory on the host, and it identifies the map so that clEnqueueUnmapMemObject knows which region to unmap.

Table 3.6 Functions that map and unmap memory objects

Function	Purpose
```void* clEnqueueMapBuffer(cl_command_queue queue, cl_mem buffer, cl_bool blocking, cl_map_flags map_flags, size_t offset, size_t data_size, cl_uint num_events, const cl_event *wait_list, cl_event *event, cl_int *errcode_ret)```	Maps a region of a buffer object to host memory
```void* clEnqueueMapImage(cl_command_queue queue, cl_mem image, cl_bool blocking, cl_map_flags map_flags, const size_t origin[3], const size_t region[3], size_t *row_pitch, size_t *slice_pitch, cl_uint num_events, const cl_event *wait_list, cl_event *event, cl_int *errcode_ret)```	Maps a rectangular region of an image object to host memory
```int clEnqueueUnmapMemObject(cl_command_queue queue, cl_mem memobj, void *mapped_ptr, cl_uint num_events, const cl_event *wait_list, cl_event *event)```	Unmaps an existing memory object from host memory

A second difference between the map/unmap functions and the read/write functions is the `map_flags` argument used in `clEnqueueMapBuffer` and `clEnqueueMapImage`. This configures the accessibility of the mapped memory on the host. If `map_flags` is set to `CL_MAP_READ`, the mapped memory will be read-only. If the flag is set to `CL_MAP_WRITE`, the mapped memory will be write-only. If `CL_MAP_READ|CL_MAP_WRITE` is used, the memory will be readable and writeable.

Working with memory-mapped data in OpenCL is usually a three-step process. First, enqueue the memory map operation with `clEnqueueMapBuffer` or `clEnqueue-MapImage`. Then transfer data to and from the mapped memory with a function like `memcpy`. Last, unmap the region by calling `clEnqueueUnmapMemObject`.

In my experience, memory mapping provides a significant improvement in performance over regular read/write operations. Chapter 7, which explains timing and profiling, will show you how to test this on your own.

3.5.3 Copying data between memory objects

Up to this point, every data transfer operation we've looked at has been focused on moving data between host memory and a memory object. But OpenCL provides additional functions that transfer data between memory objects. With these functions, you can copy data between two memory objects on a device, or between memory objects on different devices. Table 3.7 lists each data-copying function and its arguments.

The first two functions enqueue commands that copy data between similar memory object types: buffer object to buffer object, image object to image object. The next functions enqueue commands that copy data between different types of

Table 3.7   Functions that copy data between memory objects

Function	Purpose

`clEnqueueCopyBuffer(cl_command_queue queue,`
`    cl_mem src_buffer, cl_mem dst_buffer,`
`    size_t src_offset, size_t dst_offset,`
`    size_t data_size, cl_uint num_events,`
`    const cl_event *wait_list, cl_event *event)`
	Copies data from a source buffer object to a destination buffer object

`clEnqueueCopyImage(cl_command_queue queue,`
`    cl_mem src_image, cl_mem dst_image,`
`    const size_t src_origin[3],`
`    const size_t dst_origin[3],`
`    const size_t region[3], cl_uint num_events,`
`    const cl_event *wait_list, cl_event *event)`
	Copies data from a source image object to a destination image object

`clEnqueueCopyBufferToImage(cl_command_queue queue,`
`    cl_mem src_buffer, cl_mem dst_image,`
`    size_t src_offset, const size_t dst_origin[3],`
`    const size_t region[3], cl_uint num_events,`
`    const cl_event *wait_list, cl_event *event)`
	Copies data from a source buffer object to a destination image object

`clEnqueueCopyImageToBuffer(cl_command_queue queue,`
`    cl_mem src_image, cl_mem  dst_buffer,`
`    const size_t src_origin[3],`
`    const size_t region[3], size_t dst_offset,`
`    cl_uint num_events, const cl_event *wait_list,`
`    cl_event *event)`
	Copies data from a source image object to a destination buffer object

`clEnqueueCopyBufferRect(cl_command_queue queue,`
`    cl_mem src_buffer, cl_mem dst_buffer,`
`    const size_t src_origin[3],`
`    const size_t dst_origin[3],`
`    const size_t region[3], size_t src_row_pitch,`
`    size_t src_slice_pitch, size_t dst_row_pitch,`
`    size_t dst_slice_pitch, cl_uint num_events,`
`    const cl_event *wait_list, cl_event *event)`
	Copies data from a rectangular region in a source buffer object to a rectangular region in a destination buffer object

memory objects: buffer object to image object and image object to buffer object. If you've followed the discussion of the read/write functions, these functions won't present any difficulty.

Let's look at an example that demonstrates how to map and copy memory objects. Figure 3.6 shows the plan. The goal is to create two buffer objects and copy the content of Buffer 1 to Buffer 2 with `clEnqueueCopyBuffer`. Then `clEnqueueMapBuffer` maps the content of Buffer 2 to host memory and `memcpy` transfers the mapped memory to an array.

The following listing shows how this is implemented in code. The `map_copy` application enqueues four commands. The first transfers the kernel and its arguments to the device. The second copies one buffer object to the next. The third command configures the memory map, and the fourth unmaps the memory.

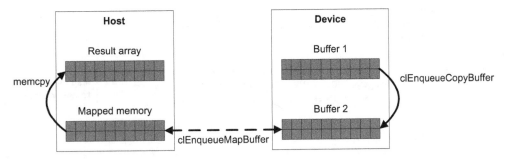

Figure 3.6 Copying and mapping buffer objects

Listing 3.3   Copying and mapping buffer objects: map_copy.c

```
...
float data_one[100], data_two[100], result_array[100];
cl_mem buffer_one, buffer_two;
void* mapped_memory;
...
buffer_one = clCreateBuffer(context,
      CL_MEM_READ_WRITE | CL_MEM_COPY_HOST_PTR,
      sizeof(data_one), data_one, &err);
if(err < 0) {
   perror("Couldn't create a buffer object");
   exit(1);
}
buffer_two = clCreateBuffer(context,
      CL_MEM_READ_WRITE | CL_MEM_COPY_HOST_PTR,
      sizeof(data_two), data_two, &err);

err = clSetKernelArg(kernel, 0, sizeof(cl_mem),
                     &buffer_one);
err |= clSetKernelArg(kernel, 1, sizeof(cl_mem),
                     &buffer_two);
if(err < 0) {
   perror("Couldn't set the buffer as the kernel argument");
   exit(1);
}

queue = clCreateCommandQueue(context, device, 0, &err);
if(err < 0) {
   perror("Couldn't create a command queue");
   exit(1);
};
err = clEnqueueTask(queue, kernel, 0, NULL, NULL);
if(err < 0) {
   perror("Couldn't enqueue the kernel");
   exit(1);
}

err = clEnqueueCopyBuffer(queue, buffer_one,
      buffer_two, 0, 0, sizeof(data_one),
      0, NULL, NULL);
```

Create buffer objects

Set kernel arguments

Enqueue kernel command

Enqueue command to copy buffers

```
if(err < 0) {
   perror("Couldn't perform the buffer copy");
   exit(1);
}
mapped_memory = clEnqueueMapBuffer(queue,
      buffer_two, CL_TRUE, CL_MAP_READ, 0,
      sizeof(data_two), 0, NULL, NULL, &err);
if(err < 0) {
   perror("Couldn't map the buffer to host memory");
   exit(1);
}
memcpy(result_array, mapped_memory, sizeof(data_two));
err = clEnqueueUnmapMemObject(queue, buffer_two,
      mapped_memory, 0, NULL, NULL);
if(err < 0) {
   perror("Couldn't unmap the buffer");
   exit(1);
}
...
```

Map buffer object to host memory

Copy host memory

Unmap buffer object

This code shouldn't present any surprises. As long as the command queue is configured to process commands in order (the default configuration), it will transfer the content of buffer_one to buffer_two and map buffer_two to host memory.

At this point, you should have a thorough understanding of memory objects and the different methods available for transferring data. In the next section, we'll continue our exploration of data, but this time, we'll examine how to distribute data and computational tasks within a single device.

3.6   *Data partitioning*

If you're implementing an algorithm with OpenCL, you probably have a great deal of data to process. This makes data partitioning an important priority—the better you distribute the processing load, the sooner your computational tasks will be finished.

You already know how to divide data among multiple devices, but you can partition your data even further. Most OpenCL devices contain several processing elements, and with the right code, you can control how much data each processing element receives.

There's only one function to know: clEnqueueNDRangeKernel. This is one of the most important functions in the OpenCL API, and it's also one of the most complex. Like clEnqueueTask, this places a kernel in a command queue for execution. But unlike clEnqueueTask, clEnqueueNDRangeKernel allows you to control how the kernel execution is distributed among the device's processing resources. This is shown by its signature, which is as follows:

```
clEnqueueNDRangeKernel(cl_command_queue queue, cl_kernel kernel,
      cl_uint work_dims, const size_t *global_work_offset,
      const size_t *global_work_size, const size_t *local_work_size,
      cl_uint num_events, const cl_event *wait_list, cl_event *event)
```

This is considerably more involved than clEnqueueTask. The difference between the two functions is that clEnqueueNDRangeKernel accepts four additional arguments:

- `work_dims`—The number of dimensions in the data
- `global_work_offset`—The global ID offsets in each dimension
- `global_work_size`—The number of work-items in each dimension
- `local_work_size`—The number of work-items in a work-group, in each dimension

Don't be concerned if these terms don't make sense just yet. The goal of this section is to explain what they mean and how to configure them so that you can take the best advantage of your hardware.

3.6.1 *Loops and work-items*

When you have a great deal of data, it's common to iterate through the data using loops. If you need to process multidimensional data in regular C/C++, you might use a nested loop, such as the following:

```
for(i=0; i<Z; i++) {
    for(j=0; j<Y; j++) {
        for(k=0; k<X; k++) {
            process(point[i][j][k]);
        }
    }
}
```

Loops like this are common but inefficient. The inefficiency arises because each iteration requires a separate comparison and addition. Comparisons are time-consuming on the best of processors, but they're especially slow on dedicated number-crunchers like graphic processor units (GPUs). GPUs excel at performing the same operations over and over again, but they're not good at making decisions. If a GPU has to check a condition and branch, it may take hundreds of cycles before it can get back to crunching numbers at full speed.

One fascinating aspect of OpenCL is that you don't have to configure these loops in your kernel. Instead, your kernel only executes code that would lie inside the innermost loop. We call this individual kernel execution a *work-item*. In the preceding example loop, the work-item consists of the single function call: `process(point[i][j][k])`.

It's important to understand the difference between kernels and work-items. A kernel identifies a set of tasks to be performed on data. A work-item is a single implementation of the kernel on a specific set of data. For every kernel, there can be multiple work-items. In the preceding example, a kernel might be represented by `process(point[i][j][k])`. A specific implementation of this kernel, such as `process(point[1][2][3])`, would be a work-item.

The array {`i`, `j`, `k`} is called the work-item's *global ID*. It uniquely identifies the work-item and allows it to access the data that it's supposed to process. As an example, the following kernel code accesses the elements of the item's ID and processes a point:

```
int i = get_global_id(0);
int j = get_global_id(1);
int k = get_global_id(2);
process(point[i][j][k]);
```

Once this work-item has executed, a new work-item will execute with a different global ID.

The number of elements in a global ID is referred to as the data's *dimensionality*. You configure this by setting the `work_dims` argument of `clEnqueueNDRangeKernel`. The minimum number of dimensions is 1 and the maximum number depends on the device. To find the maximum number of dimensions, call `clGetDeviceInfo` with the `CL_DEVICE_MAX_WORK_ITEM_DIMENSIONS` parameter. In the previous i-j-k loop, you would set `work_dims` equal to 3.

We examined dimensionality earlier when we looked at buffer objects and image objects. Image objects can be two- or three-dimensional, whereas buffer objects are accessed in one dimension only. `clEnqueueNDRangeKernel` doesn't care about this distinction. If you're dealing with image objects, you should probably set `work_dims` equal to 2 or 3. But for buffer objects, you can set whatever dimensionality you think best. For a buffer object containing a two-dimensional matrix, such as that shown in figure 3.5, you might set `work_dims` equal to 2.

3.6.2 *Work sizes and offsets*

The left side of figure 3.7 depicts a processing loop. The right side presents the *index space* corresponding to the loop. The index space contains all the possible combinations of indices. If there are N different indices in a loop, the corresponding index space has N dimensions.

The `global_work_sizes` argument of `clEnqueueNDRangeKernel` identifies how many work-items need to be processed for each dimension. The inner loop starts at $k=3$ and proceeds to $k=11$, so there are 9 work-items to be processed in the k-direction. Similarly, there are 6 work-items to be processed in the j-direction and 4 work-items to be processed in the i-direction. Therefore, you'd set `global_work_sizes` to {4, 6, 9}.

When the first work-item starts its execution, you want it to access data corresponding to the index triple (0, 2, 3) because these are the initial values of i, j, and k. In other words, you want the first work-item's global ID to equal {0, 2, 3}. You specify this in code by setting `global_work_offset` in `clEnqueueNDRangeKernel` to {0, 2, 3}.

NOTE `global_work_offset` is always set to `NULL` in this book's example code.

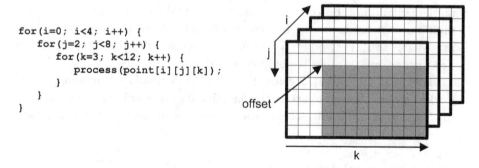

```
for(i=0; i<4; i++) {
    for(j=2; j<8; j++) {
        for(k=3; k<12; k++) {
            process(point[i][j][k]);
        }
    }
}
```

Figure 3.7 A processing loop and its index space

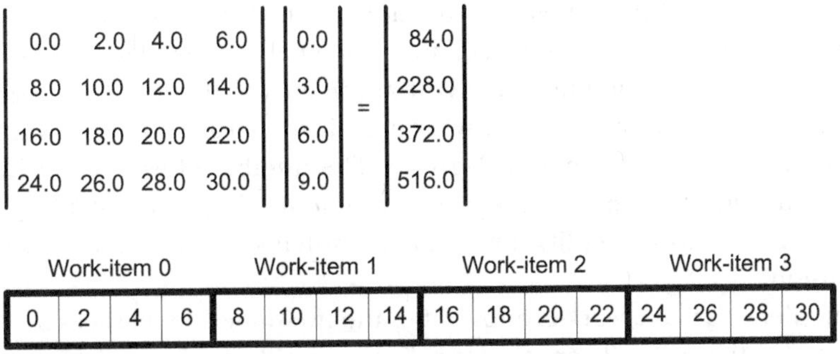

$$\begin{bmatrix} 0.0 & 2.0 & 4.0 & 6.0 \\ 8.0 & 10.0 & 12.0 & 14.0 \\ 16.0 & 18.0 & 20.0 & 22.0 \\ 24.0 & 26.0 & 28.0 & 30.0 \end{bmatrix} \begin{bmatrix} 0.0 \\ 3.0 \\ 6.0 \\ 9.0 \end{bmatrix} = \begin{bmatrix} 84.0 \\ 228.0 \\ 372.0 \\ 516.0 \end{bmatrix}$$

Work-item 0				Work-item 1				Work-item 2				Work-item 3			
0	2	4	6	8	10	12	14	16	18	20	22	24	26	28	30

Figure 3.8 Partitioning data in a matrix-vector multiplication

3.6.3 A simple one-dimensional example

A good way to understand clEnqueueNDRangeKernel is to see how it's used in code. In chapter 1, I did my best to scare you by presenting the code for a complete OpenCL application. This application multiplies a vector by a matrix and produces a vector. Figure 3.8 shows the computation. It also depicts the buffer object containing the matrix data and the manner in which the matrix data is partitioned among four work-items.

The matrix-vector multiplication consists of four dot-products, and I chose to perform the multiplication using four work-items. This is accomplished with the following code:

```
work_items_per_kernel = 4;

clEnqueueNDRangeKernel(queue, kernel, 1, NULL,
    &work_items_per_kernel, NULL, 0, NULL, NULL);
```

This tells OpenCL that the data to be partitioned has a single dimension and that four work-items should be generated to execute the kernel. The global offset is set to 0.

On the kernel side, each work-item checks its global ID and accesses one row of the matrix. It multiplies this row (1-by-4) by the vector (4-by-1) using the dot function, and places the result (1-by-1) in an array position determined by its ID. This is shown in the following code:

```
int i = get_global_id(0);
result[i] = dot(matrix[i], vector[0]);
```

See? No loops. The four work-items operate in parallel with none of the delay associated with for statements or similar constructs.

3.6.4 Work-groups and compute units

A work-group is a combination of work-items that access the same processing resources. When it comes to programming, work-groups provide two main advantages:

- Work-items in a work-group can access the same block of high-speed memory called local memory.
- Work-items in a work-group can be synchronized using fences and barriers.

Chapter 4 explains the different types of memory in an OpenCL device and chapter 7 discusses work-item synchronization. For now, my goal is to explain work-groups in enough depth so that you fully understand the arguments of `clEnqueueNDRangeKernel`.

In addition to the global ID, each work-item has a local ID that distinguishes it from all the other work-items in a work-group. The number of work-items in a work-group is set through the `local_work_size` argument of `clEnqueueNDRangeKernel`. The elements in this array identify how many work-items can fit in the work-group in each dimension.

For example, let's make work-groups out of the two-dimensional slices in the index space depicted in figure 3.7. There are four slices, so we'll have four work-groups. Each group contains 6 work-items in the *j*-direction and 9 work-items in the *k*-direction. Therefore, we'd set `local_work_size` in `clEnqueueNDRangeKernel` equal to {0, 6, 9}.

In OpenCL, a processing resource capable of supporting a work-group is called a *compute unit*. Each work-group executes on a single compute unit, and each compute unit executes only one work-group at a time. Figure 3.9 shows this relationship graphically.

You don't have to create work-groups. If you set `local_work_size` equal to NULL, OpenCL will decide how best to distribute work-items among a device's processing elements.

NOTE Don't be concerned if you're still not comfortable with the topics of work-groups, work-group IDs, compute units, and local IDs. These abstract but important concepts will be discussed throughout this book.

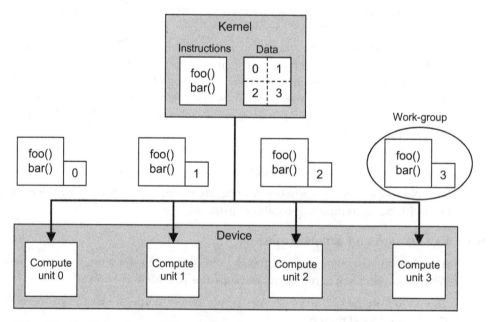

Figure 3.9 Sending work-groups to compute units

3.7   *Summary*

It's crucial to know how to code and enqueue kernels, but kernels are useless without data to process. The goal of this chapter has been to show how OpenCL packages and partitions data to be processed by devices.

OpenCL provides a memory object (cl_mem) data structure as a standard mechanism for transferring data between a host and a device. The process of transferring memory objects is simple: create a memory object from existing data, and call clSetKernelArg to make the object into a kernel argument. When the kernel executes, the kernel will be able to access its data as a regular function parameter. Then, as the host sends further commands, the device may transfer data to the host or copy the data to another buffer object.

There are two types of memory objects. Buffer objects store general data in a single dimension, and image objects store formatted pixel data in two or three dimensions. For both types, OpenCL provides functions that enqueue data transfer commands. Read/write functions transfer data between a memory object and a host, but you can usually improve performance by mapping the memory object's memory to host memory.

The last part of this chapter discussed data partitioning, which is crucial for any OpenCL application that demands high performance. The basic unit of work is the work-item, which corresponds to the code executed within a traditional C/C++ loop. Each work-item receives a global ID that allows it to access data specifically intended for it. If work-items require synchronization, they can be placed into work-groups. Each work-group executes on a single compute unit on the device.

This chapter, in conjunction with chapter 2, has explained almost everything you need to know about host applications. The only topics that remain to be covered are synchronization, event-processing, and threads, which will be discussed in chapter 7. In the next chapter, we'll depart from host programming and launch our discussion of kernel development.

Kernel programming: data types and device memory

This chapter covers

- Introducing a simple OpenCL kernel
- Using OpenCL's scalar and vector data types
- Understanding the OpenCL device model

In this chapter, we're going to put aside the scaffolding that creates and deploys kernels, and start coding the kernels themselves. We'll examine the data types available in OpenCL kernels, and that means we'll finally get to discuss *vectors*. When you process data with vectors, you put aside boring, decades-old data types like `char`, `float`, and `int`, and use new, exciting data types like `char16`, `int3`, and `float4`. Now we're cooking!

I didn't learn about vector programming until after I left college, but I've always enjoyed it since. It doesn't matter whether it's Intel's Streaming SIMD Extensions (SSE), Motorola's AltiVec, or the odd language IBM devised to program the

Synergistic Processor Units (SPUs) on a Cell processor. I just find it gratifying to crunch several numbers with a single command, and my enjoyment increases when I crunch numbers on several cores at once. What more could anyone ask?

After examining different types of data, we'll look at how and where this data is stored. OpenCL has a model for devices that includes four different address spaces. The final sections of this chapter will discuss these spaces and how to configure data storage in code.

But before getting into the details of data and memory storage, it's important to understand the basic structure of a kernel function. We'll discuss this first.

4.1 Introducing kernel coding

Chapter 2 explained how host applications send kernels to devices, and chapter 3 explained how to set arguments for kernels. Now, at long last, we're ready to look at an actual kernel. The following listing presents an OpenCL equivalent for the venerable Hello World! function so common in C programming literature.

Listing 4.1 A basic kernel: hello_kernel.cl

```
__kernel void hello_kernel(__global char16 *msg) {

   *msg = (char16)('H', 'e', 'l', 'l', 'o', ' ',
      'k', 'e', 'r', 'n', 'e', 'l', '!', '!', '!', '\0');
}
```

If you look at the overall structure of this function, you'll see that it resembles a regular C function: a function name, arguments in parentheses, and executable statements inside curly brackets. But there are three main differences between an OpenCL kernel and a regular C function:

- Every kernel declaration must start with __kernel.
- Every kernel function must return void.
- Some platforms won't compile kernels without arguments.

Every example project in this book stores kernel functions in *.cl files, but this suffix isn't necessary. In fact, kernels don't have to be stored in separate files at all. But every kernel function must be preceded by the __kernel keyword. If __kernel is present, the compiler will know that the function is intended to be run on a device, not the host.

The clSetKernelArg function sets arguments for kernels, but there are no functions that access a kernel's return value. This is because kernels don't have return values—every kernel function returns void. For this reason, every kernel in this book has the same basic structure:

```
__kernel void func_name(args) {

   ...
}
```

The ... section is the hard part, and it will take many chapters to discuss this. For now, let's look at the arguments. A kernel function can only access and return data through its arguments, and if you attempt to compile a kernel without arguments, some compilers will give you an error.

As with regular C functions, kernel functions accept arguments by value or by reference. When you pass data by value, you provide actual data such as a char, an int, or a float. Kernel functions *do not* support composite structures. If you pass data by reference, you provide a pointer that references data in device memory (commonly a memory object). In listing 4.1, the msg argument references a 16-byte buffer object that the host application will read after the kernel is executed.

Now we come to an important point: *all pointers passed to a kernel must be preceded by an address space qualifier.* This tells the device what address space the argument should be stored in. Section 4.5 discusses this topic in depth, but for now, keep in mind that there are four possible qualifiers: __global, __constant, __local, and __private. In listing 4.1, the function declaration states that the msg argument should be stored in the device's global address space.

Before continuing, let's review how the host application creates kernel arguments from memory objects. In hello_kernel.c, this is accomplished with the following lines of code:

```
char msg[16];
cl_mem msg_buffer;

msg_buffer = clCreateBuffer(context, CL_MEM_WRITE_ONLY,
      sizeof(msg), NULL, &err);

clSetKernelArg(kernel, 0, sizeof(cl_mem), &msg_buffer);
```

After the kernel is enqueued and the device executes the function, the host application accesses the buffer data using clEnqueueReadBuffer. This is shown here:

```
clEnqueueReadBuffer(queue, msg_buffer, CL_TRUE, 0,
      sizeof(msg), &msg, 0, NULL, NULL);
```

Note that the host declares msg as a char[16] and the kernel declares msg as char16. These are different data types, but because the data is passed to the kernel by reference, it doesn't make any difference to the compiler.

The char16 data type is one of OpenCL's vector data types, and section 4.3 will discuss these types in detail. The kernel code in this book will rely on vectors whenever possible, but before we look at vectors, we need to examine OpenCL's support for traditional data types such as ints and floats. In contrast to vector types, these are called *scalar data types*, and they'll be discussed in the next section.

4.2   Scalar data types

The terms *scalar* and *vector* have different meanings depending on whether you talk to a mathematician, scientist, or programmer. In vector computing, a scalar is a data type in which each data representation contains a single value. In OpenCL, a scalar is any of the data types listed in table 4.1.

Table 4.1 OpenCL scalar data types (required minimum)

Scalar data type	Purpose
bool	A Boolean condition: true (1) or false (0)
char	Signed two's complement 8-bit integer
unsigned char/uchar	Unsigned two's complement 8-bit integer
short	Signed two's complement 16-bit integer
unsigned short/ushort	Unsigned two's complement 16-bit integer
int	Signed two's complement 32-bit integer
unsigned int/uint	Unsigned two's complement 32-bit integer
long	Signed two's complement 64-bit integer
unsigned long/ulong	Unsigned two's complement 64-bit integer
half	16-bit floating-point value, IEEE-754-2008 conformant
float	32-bit floating-point value, IEEE-754 conformant
intptr_t	Signed integer to which a void pointer can be converted
uintptr_t	Unsigned integer to which a void pointer can be converted
ptrdiff_t	Signed integer produced by pointer subtraction
size_t	Unsigned integer produced by the size of operator
void	Untyped data

These data types are straightforward and function like their C/C++ counterparts. But when I first read this list, one prominent question came to mind: where's double? I prefer to use 64-bit floating-point values for nongraphic applications. Are doubles available in OpenCL? The answer is maybe.

4.2.1 Accessing the double data type

The double data type can be accessed if the target device supports the cl_khr_fp64 extension. From the host, you can determine whether this extension is available by calling clGetDeviceInfo, a function explained in chapter 2. If the extension is supported, you can enable its capability in the kernel with the following pragma statement:

```
#pragma OPENCL EXTENSION cl_khr_fp64 : enable
```

When this is present, you can declare double variables and operate on them normally. If you want to enable every supported extension, replace cl_khr_fp64 with all. To disable an extension, replace enable with disable.

In the Ch4/double_test project, the kernel uses the double type if it's supported and uses the float type if it's not. This is shown in the following listing.

Listing 4.2   Checking for the double data type: double_test.cl

```
#ifdef FP_64
#pragma OPENCL EXTENSION cl_khr_fp64: enable          ←┐ Enable extension
#endif                                                 │ if available

__kernel void double_test(__global float* a,
                          __global float* b,
                          __global float* out) {
#ifdef FP_64
   double c = (double)(*a / *b);                      ←┐ Compute with
   *out = (float)c;                                    │ doubles if available
#else
   *out = *a * *b;
#endif
}
```

The host application calls `clGetDeviceInfo` to obtain the extensions supported by the device. If `cl_khr_fp64` is one of them, the host adds the option `-DFP_64` to `clBuild-Program`. As shown in listing 4.2, this option tells the kernel to enable the `cl_khr_fp64` extension. Once this extension is enabled, the kernel can declare `double` values and operate on them.

The host code also checks the address width of the target device. This becomes important if you deal with the `size_t` and `ptrdiff_t` types at a bit level. The `size_t` and `ptrdiff_t` types will be 64 bits wide on a 64-bit system and 32 bits wide on a 32-bit system.

4.2.2   Byte order

Table 4.1 tells you how many bytes are in a data type, but it doesn't say anything about how the bytes are ordered. Neither does the OpenCL standard. The reason for this is that different devices and operating systems order bytes differently.

Therefore, if you're going to perform an operation that involves byte order, such as accessing data with pointers, you need to determine the *endianness* of the target device. This tells you whether bytes become more or less significant as memory addresses run from low to high. Figure 4.1 depicts this graphically.

`unsigned int x = 0x01020304`

Storage on a little-endian device:

Storage on a big-endian device:

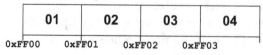

Figure 4.1   Byte order in little-endian and big-endian devices

I find it easy to distinguish between the two by remembering that big-endianness is more intuitive to me (I'd rather have $43.21 in my pocket than $12.34). But little-endianness is more prevalent because x86 devices are little-endian. The most common big-endian processors are IBM's POWER and PowerPC architectures.

There are two ways to determine whether a device is little-endian or big-endian. From the host, you can call clGetDeviceInfo with CL_DEVICE_ENDIAN_LITTLE as the parameter. If this returns CL_TRUE, the device is little-endian. If it returns CL_FALSE, the device is big-endian.

Within the kernel, you can use #ifdef to determine whether the __ENDIAN_LITTLE__ macro is defined. If this macro is defined, the device is little-endian. If not, the device is big-endian.

We'll discuss endianness further when we look at vectors. But before we leave the subject of scalars, we need to examine how OpenCL processes floating-point values.

4.3 Floating-point computing

Computers don't process *numbers*—they manipulate electrical signals whose values we interpret numerically. No matter how large the processor, these digital signals can never represent more than a tiny portion of the set of real numbers. There is an infinite number of numbers that are too small to be processed by a computer and an infinite number of numbers that are too large.

But we do our best. The IEEE-754 standard, formed by the Institute of Electrical and Electronics Engineers, defines three methods of representing real numbers in computer memory. They're embodied in the float, double, and half data types. OpenCL only requires the float type, but the other two types may be available if the target device supports them. OpenCL requires compliant devices to follow many of the provisions in the IEEE-754 standard, *but not all of them*. If you intend to use OpenCL for mission-critical floating-point computing, you should be aware of the differences between OpenCL's requirements and those of IEEE-754.

4.3.1 The float data type

At the time of this writing, most graphics cards process graphics using only 32 bits. Therefore, it makes sense that the only floating-point data type required by OpenCL is the 32-bit float. Figure 4.2 shows how the bits in a float are organized.

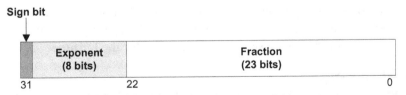

Sign bit

| Exponent (8 bits) | Fraction (23 bits) |

31   22   0

Smallest positive value (normal): $2^{-126} \approx 1.18 \times 10^{-38}$

Largest positive value: $2^{127} \times (2 - 2^{-23}) \approx 3.4 \times 10^{38}$

Figure 4.2   IEEE-754 format for single-precision floating-point values

According to the IEEE standard, the value contained within a `float` can fall into one of four categories:

- *Normal numbers*—Numbers that can be fully represented by the dynamic range supported by the `float` format
- *Denormalized numbers*—Numbers smaller in magnitude than the smallest possible normal number
- *Infinite numbers*—Numbers whose magnitude is larger than the largest possible normal number
- *Not a number*—Values produced by impossible operations such as 0/0 or taking the square root or logarithm of a negative number

OpenCL requires that devices support numbers in the third (`INF`) and fourth (`NaN`) categories, but not denormalized numbers. Denormalized numbers commonly take more cycles to process than normal numbers, and you can improve performance by setting the `-cl-denorms-are-zero` flag in `clBuildProgram`. But denormalized numbers serve a useful purpose; if they're supported, an operation that subtracts two close numbers will produce a denormalized number instead of 0. Then, if the denormalized difference is used in division, the result will be valid. If the difference is 0, the result will be `NaN`.

When it comes to rounding `float`s, the IEEE-754 standard defines four modes:

- *Round to nearest even*—Rounds a `float` to the nearest representable value. If the `float` lies exactly between two numbers, it rounds to the one whose lowest-order digit is even (0).
- *Round toward +infinity*—Always rounds toward the value that's closer to +infinity
- *Round toward –infinity*—Always rounds toward the value that's closer to –infinity
- *Round toward zero*—Always rounds toward the value that's closer to zero (truncation)

A device may support all of these modes, but OpenCL only requires the first. In addition, OpenCL doesn't require devices to enable mode-switching at runtime. Therefore, it's safe to assume that the target device will always round `float`s according to the first mode.

IEEE-754 defines a series of runtime exceptions that raise status flags. These arise when an operation divides by zero, takes the square root of a negative number, or produces a result that's too high (overflow) or too low (underflow) to be represented by a `float`. OpenCL doesn't require any exception-checking, so if you want to check for these conditions, you'll have to write code specifically for the purpose.

4.3.2   *The double data type*

The `double` data type uses 64 bits to represent floating-point values. Figure 4.3 depicts the structure of a `double` at the bit level.

As explained in section 4.2, OpenCL-compliant devices aren't required to support the `double` data type. But you can determine whether a device supports this type by

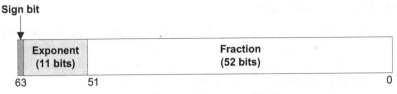

Smallest positive value (normal): $2^{-1022} \approx 1 \times 10^{-323.3}$

Largest positive value: $2^{1023} \times (2 - 2^{-52}) \approx 1 \times 10^{308.3}$

Figure 4.3   IEEE-754 format for double-precision floating-point values

calling clGetDeviceInfo with the CL_DEVICE_EXTENSIONS parameter and checking whether cl_khr_fp64 is one of the supported extensions.

It may seem odd, but if a device supports doubles, OpenCL places *more* requirements on double processing than it places on float processing. First, a device that supports doubles must support denormalized numbers—they can't simply be set equal to 0. Second, the device must support all of the rounding modes described earlier, not just rounding to the nearest even value.

Finally, a device that supports doubles must support an operation called floating-point multiply-and-add, or FMA. This computes the product and sum of three doubles (a*b + c) as a single operation. This operation must execute as fast as or faster than the multiplication and addition operations performed separately.

4.3.3   The half data type

The half type uses 16 bits to represent a floating-point value. This is smaller than the more-common float type and it's much newer. It was first defined by Nvidia as part of its Cg language, but it has since been adopted by OpenGL and Direct3D. Figure 4.4 shows how these 16 bits are used to represent a floating-point number.

OpenCL doesn't require compliant devices to support the half data type, but you can test whether a device does by calling clGetDeviceInfo with the CL_DEVICE_ EXTENSIONS parameter. If cl_khr_fp16 is one of the supported extensions, then the device supports the half data type.

For devices that support halfs, OpenCL makes few requirements. Devices have to support INF and NaN values, but they don't have to support denormalized numbers or FMA operations. For rounding, devices have to support rounding toward +/– infinity or rounding toward the nearest even value, but they don't have to support both.

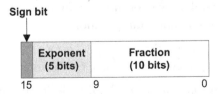

Smallest positive value (normal): $2^{-14} \approx 6.10 \times 10^{-5}$

Largest positive value: $2^{15} \times (2 - 2^{-10}) = 65504$

Figure 4.4   IEEE-754 format for half-precision floating-point values

4.3.4   *Checking IEEE-754 compliance*

This section has described many of the floating-point processing features required by IEEE-754, such as rounding modes and denormalized numbers. OpenCL doesn't require all of these for each of the floating-point data types, but it does provide a way to find out what capabilities are available for the target device.

clGetDeviceInfo is the function to call, but you have to understand what data parameters to set and how to interpret the result. Three parameters tell clGetDeviceInfo to provide information about supported IEEE-754 features:

- CL_DEVICE_SINGLE_FP_CONFIG—Identifies features for processing floats
- CL_DEVICE_DOUBLE_FP_CONFIG—Identifies features for processing doubles
- CL_DEVICE_HALF_FP_CONFIG—Identifies features for processing halfs

NOTE   At the time of this writing, both Nvidia and AMD comment out the CL_DEVICE_DOUBLE_FP_CONFIG and CL_DEVICE_HALF_FP_CONFIG constants in their cl.h header files. Therefore, you can only test a device's support for processing floats.

Using these parameters, the information returned by clGetDeviceInfo takes the form of an enumerated type called a cl_device_fp_config. Table 4.2 lists the possible values for this type.

Table 4.2   Floating-point configuration parameters (cl_device_fp_config)

Parameter	Float	Double	Half
CL_FP_INF_NAN	Required	Required	Required
CL_FP_DENORM	Not required	Required	Not required
CL_FP_ROUND_TO_NEAREST	Required	Required	Not required
CL_FP_ROUND_TO_INF	Not required	Required	Alternate
CL_FP_ROUND_TO_ZERO	Not required	Required	Alternate
CL_FP_FMA	Not required	Required	Not required
CL_FP_SOFT_FLOAT	Not required	Not required	Not required

After the preceding discussion of floats, doubles, and halfs, most of these floating-point parameters should make sense. But the last one is new. CL_FP_SOFT_FLOAT identifies whether basic processing of the given data type occurs in software. In this case, basic processing refers to addition, subtraction, and multiplication.

NOTE   At the time of this writing, CL_FP_SOFT_FLOAT isn't supported on Mac OS systems. It isn't defined in the OpenCL.framework/Headers/cl.h header file.

The host application in the float_config project accesses the first device it finds and determines which features it supports for processing floats. The following listing shows the relevant code needed to accomplish this.

Listing 4.3   Testing a device's floating-point features: float_config.c

```
...
cl_device_fp_config flag;                                          Obtain device
err = clGetDeviceInfo(device, CL_DEVICE_SINGLE_FP_CONFIG,          information
      sizeof(flag), &flag, NULL);
if(err < 0) {
   perror("Couldn't read device information");
   exit(1);
}
printf("Float Processing Features:\n");
if(flag & CL_FP_INF_NAN)
   printf("INF and NaN values supported.\n");
if(flag & CL_FP_DENORM)
   printf("Denormalized numbers supported.\n");
if(flag & CL_FP_ROUND_TO_NEAREST)
   printf("Round To Nearest Even mode supported.\n");
if(flag & CL_FP_ROUND_TO_INF)                                     Check processing
   printf("Round To Infinity mode supported.\n");                 features
if(flag & CL_FP_ROUND_TO_ZERO)
   printf("Round To Zero mode supported.\n");
if(flag & CL_FP_FMA)
   printf("Floating-point multiply-and-add operation
      supported.\n");

#ifndef MAC
   if(flag | CL_FP_SOFT_FLOAT)
      printf("Basic floating-point processing performed in software.\n");
#endif
...
```

On my Mac OS system, the printed output is as follows:

```
Float Processing Features:
INF and NaN values supported.
Round To Nearest Even mode supported.
```

As shown in table 4.2, these are the minimum features required by OpenCL for processing floats. If your application depends on denormalized numbers, you'll have to specifically check for small values in code and process them accordingly.

This section has discussed floats, doubles, and halfs at length, but from this point onward, we'll use these data types sparingly in example code. For the most part, we'll rely on vectors that contain multiple floating-point values: float*n*, double*n*, and half*n*, where *n* identifies how many scalar elements are contained in the vector. The next section explains these new data types in full.

4.4   *Vector data types*

Vectors resemble arrays in that they contain multiple elements of the same type. But there are two important differences. First, a vector of a given type can only contain a specific number of elements. Second, when a vector is operated upon, every element is operated upon *at the same time.*

An example will make this distinction clear. Suppose you want to compute four sums of floating-point values. That is, a and b are arrays of four floats each, and you want c to hold the sums of the corresponding elements in a and b. You could try using code similar to the following:

```
float a[4], b[4], c[4];
for(int i=0; i<4; i++) {
    c[i] = a[i] + b[i];
}
```

Now suppose a, b, and c are vectors, and each vector contains four floats. In this case, you could perform the same addition with code that looks like this:

```
float4 a, b, c;
c = a + b;
```

Processing vectors isn't just simpler than processing data with arrays, it's faster. And pay attention to the new data type: float4. As you might guess, any variable declared with this type can hold four floats. Elements within a vector are commonly called *components*, and we'll use this term throughout this book.

OpenCL provides vector types that contain most, but not all, of the scalar types in table 4.1. Table 4.3 lists each vector type and the nature of its components.

Table 4.3   OpenCL vector data types

Vector data type	Purpose
char*n*	Vector containing n 8-bit signed two's complement integers
uchar*n*	Vector containing n 8-bit unsigned two's complement integers
short*n*	Vector containing n 16-bit signed two's complement integers
ushort*n*	Vector containing n 16-bit unsigned two's complement integers
int*n*	Vector containing n 32-bit signed two's complement integers
uint*n*	Vector containing n 32-bit unsigned two's complement integers
long*n*	Vector containing n 64-bit signed two's complement integers
ulong*n*	Vector containing n 64-bit unsigned two's complement integers
float*n*	Vector containing n 32-bit single-precision floating-point values

In addition to those listed, OpenCL optionally supports vector types that contain double-precision and half-precision floating-point values: double*n* and half*n*. These are only available if the corresponding scalars are available, and the previous two sections explain the double and half types in full.

In table 4.3, *n* represents a number, and OpenCL accepts 2, 3, 4, 8, and 16 as valid values of *n*. But not every compliant device can process large vectors without assistance. For example, the graphics card in my MacBook can't possibly operate directly on a float16, which is a $16 * 32 = 512$ bit vector containing 16 floats.

For this reason, the OpenCL standard requires that device compilers know the limitations of the target device and divide large vectors into sizes the device can operate on. Still, it can be helpful to know in advance what vector sizes a device can process without assistance. This is called a device's *preferred vector width,* and it will be discussed next.

4.4.1 Preferred vector widths

Chapter 2 introduced clGetDeviceInfo and explained how it provides device-related information. Section 4.2 showed how to use this function to determine a device's support for floating-point processing. Now we're going to see how clGetDeviceInfo can tell us a device's preferred vector width for a given data type.

clGetDeviceInfo accepts a parameter that identifies what information is being sought. OpenCL provides a series of parameters that reference vector widths, and they all have the same format: CL_DEVICE_PREFERRED_VECTOR_WIDTH_*TYPE*. The result is a cl_uint that identifies how many scalars of the given type can be placed in a vector. Here, *TYPE* can be set to CHAR, SHORT, INT, LONG, or FLOAT. It can also be set to HALF or DOUBLE, but if those data types aren't supported, the result will be 0.

Let's look at an example. The following code determines the vector width of a device in terms of chars:

```
cl_uint char_width;
clGetDeviceInfo(device, CL_DEVICE_PREFERRED_VECTOR_WIDTH_CHAR,
    sizeof(char_width), &char_width, NULL);
```

The vector_width project uses code like this to print the vector widths of a device for each scalar type. On my system, the output is as follows:

```
Preferred vector width in chars:    16
Preferred vector width in shorts:   8
Preferred vector width in ints:     4
Preferred vector width in longs:    2
Preferred vector width in floats:   4
Preferred vector width in doubles:  0
Preferred vector width in halfs:    0
```

This target device prefers 128-bit (16-byte) vectors, and each vector can hold 16 chars, 8 shorts, 4 ints, 2 longs, or 4 floats. At the time of this writing, 128 bits is a common vector size, and you'll see a great deal of example code that uses 128-bit types like char16 and float4.

Suppose you want to tailor your kernel to support the preferred vector width of your user's device, but you don't know what it is. How should you decide on the data types in the kernel? You can't change a float2 to a float4 at runtime, but there are at least two options available. First, you can find the target device's preferred width using clGetDeviceInfo and use it to set options for clBuildProgram such as -DVECTOR_SIZE_128 or -DVECTOR_SIZE_256. Then, inside the kernel code, you can insert lines such as the following:

```
#ifdef VECTOR_SIZE_128
#define FLOATS_PER_VECTOR 4
float4 data[N/FLOATS_PER_VECTOR];
...
#endif

#ifdef VECTOR_SIZE_256
#define FLOATS_PER_VECTOR 8
float8 data[N/FLOATS_PER_VECTOR];
...
#endif
```

This works well if your algorithm doesn't depend on vector width. But if that's not possible, the second option involves creating multiple versions of your kernel source code, each relying on a different vector width. You might have one function called convolution_128 and another called convolution_256. Then, once the host determines the preferred vector width, it will create kernels from functions that support the given width.

4.4.2   Initializing vectors

Once you've decided how wide a vector should be, you can initialize its components. This is similar to initializing the elements of an array, but vector components must be placed in parentheses instead of curly brackets, and set of values must be cast to the vector type. For example, the following code initializes data_vec with four floats:

```
float4 data_vec = (float4)(1.0, 1.0, 1.0, 1.0);
```

In this case, the components have the same value, so you can use the following code instead:

```
float4 data_vec = (float4)(1.0);
```

You're not limited to scalars. You can initialize a vector using smaller vectors, as shown here:

```
float2 a_vector = (float2)(1.0, 1.0);
float2 b_vector = (float2)(2.0, 2.0);
float4 c_vector = (float4)(a_vector, b_vector);
```

Finally, you can create a vector with a combination of scalars and smaller vectors:

```
float3 rgb = (float3)(0.25, 0.5, 0.75);
float4 rgba = (float4)(rgb, 1.0);
```

4.4.3   Reading and modifying vector components

OpenCL provides three simple ways to select the components of a vector: number-indexing, letter-indexing, and hi/lo/even/odd. Number-indexing is useful for accessing components of vectors in general applications, whereas letter-indexing is more suitable for vectors in graphics applications. The hi, lo, even, and odd suffixes become helpful when you want to access half of a vector's components at a time. Each method uses a dot-notation similar to that used to access the fields of a composite data structure.

NUMBER-INDEXING

With numeric indices, you can access elements of a vector just as easily as you can access elements of an array. But instead of using square brackets, the vector name is followed by .s*N* or .S*N*, where *N* is the position of the element in the vector. The code in table 4.4 shows how to access components of the following vector:

```
char16 msg = (char16)('H', 'e', 'l', 'l', 'o', 'P', 'r', 'o', 'g', 'r',
    'a', 'm', 'm', 'e', 'r', '!');
```

Code	Result
char a = msg.s0;	Sets a to 'H'
char b = msg.s4	Sets b to 'o'
char c = msg.s8;	Sets c to 'g'
char d = msg.sC;	Sets d to 'm'

Table 4.4 **Accessing individual elements of a vector using numbers**

The last entry accesses the vector's thirteenth component using the hexadecimal value for twelve: 0xC. Because 16 is the maximum number of components in an OpenCL vector, the use of hexadecimal guarantees that every possible index will only require one digit.

You can access multiple components of a vector by specifying multiple indices. They don't have to be in numeric order, and you can repeat an index multiple times. In this manner, you can create a subvector or a vector of the same size with the components rearranged. The code in table 4.5 shows how to create subvectors from the following vector:

```
char16 msg = (char16)('H', 'e', 'l', 'l', 'o', 'P', 'r', 'o', 'g', 'r',
    'a', 'm', 'm', 'e', 'r', '!');
```

Table 4.5 **Accessing multiple elements of a vector using numbers**

Code	Result
char8 e = msg.s01234567;	Sets e to 'HelloPro'
char4 f = msg.s5431;	Sets f to 'Pole'
char16 h = msg.sFEDCBA9876543210;	Sets h to '!remmargorPolleH'
char8 g = (char8)(msg.0ABB, msg.sE9, msg.sE9);	Sets g to 'Hammerer'

In addition to accessing components of a vector, you can use these indices to modify the components' values. The code in table 4.6 shows how to modify components in the following vector:

```
char16 msg = (char16)('H', 'e', 'l', 'l', 'o', 'P', 'r', 'o', 'g', 'r',
    'a', 'm', 'm', 'e', 'r', '!');
```

Table 4.6   Modifying elements of a vector using numbers

Code	Result
`msg.s5 = 'O';`	Sets sixth character to `'O'`
`msg.sB986 = (char4)('c', 'C', 'n', 'P');`	Sets characters to `'c'`, `'C'`, `'n'`, and `'P'`
`msg.s7E = (char2)(msg.s1);`	Sets eighth, sixteenth characters to `'e'`
`msg.sACDF = (char4)((char2)('L', 'o'), (char2)('d', 'r'));`	Sets characters to `'L'`, `'o'`, `'d'`, and `'r'`

These assignments are easy to understand, and I recommend that you experiment with them in code.

LETTER-INDEXING

Graphics processing frequently uses homogeneous coordinates, which contain x, y, and z values and a scaling factor. To make this coding simpler, OpenCL allows you to access vector components using the letters x, y, z, and w. These serve identical purposes to the numeric indices .s0, .s1, .s2, and .s3.

You can use all four letters if a vector contains four components. Otherwise, you can only use the first *N* letters to access components of an *N*-component vector. The code in table 4.7 shows how to use letters to access components of the following vector:

```
float4 coord = (float4)(3.0, 5.0, 7.0, 9.0);
```

Code	Result
`float a = coord.x;`	Sets a to `3.0`
`float b = coord.y;`	Sets b to `5.0`
`float c = coord.z;`	Sets c to `7.0`
`float d = coord.w;`	Sets d to `9.0`

Table 4.7   Accessing components of a vector using letters

To create subvectors of a vector, follow the dot with multiple letters. These letters can be provided in any order and can be repeated. The code in table 4.8 shows how to create subvectors of following vector:

```
float4 coord = (float4)(5.0, 7.0, 9.0, 11.0);
```

Table 4.8   Creating subvectors from a vector using letters

Code	Result
`float2 e = coord.xy;`	Sets e to `(5.0, 7.0)`
`float2 f = coord.zx;`	Sets f to `(9.0, 5.0)`
`float3 g = coord.yyx;`	Sets g to `(7.0, 7.0, 5.0)`
`float4 h = coord.wwwx;`	Sets h to `(11.0, 11.0, 11.0, 5.0)`

You can modify vector components using x, y, z, and w just as you can using numerical indices. The code in table 4.9 shows how to modify components of the following vector:

```
float4 coord = (float4)(7.0, 9.0, 11.0, 13.0);
```

Table 4.9 Modifying elements of a vector using letters

Code	Result
`coord.x = 2.0;`	Sets first element to `2.0`
`coord.zy = (float2)(4.0, 3.0);`	Sets third, second elements to `(4.0, 3.0)`
`coord.wzx = (float3)((float2)(4.0,3.0),2.0);`	Sets fourth, first, second elements to `(4.0, 3.0, 2.0)`
`coord.wzyx = coord.s3210`	Leaves the vector unchanged

The last line uses letter-indexing and number-indexing in a single assignment. OpenCL has no problem with this, but you can't use letters and numbers in the same index. Expressions like `vec.xy12` will produce an error.

HI, LO, EVEN, ODD

The last method of accessing components uses the suffixes `.hi`, `.lo`, `.even`, and `.odd`. Each identifies half of a vector's components, and they're defined as follows:

- `.hi`—Components in the upper half (indices equal to $N/2$, $N/2 + 1$ ... $N-1$)
- `.lo`—Components in the lower half (indices equal to $0, 1, ... N/2-1$)
- `.even`—Even elements
- `.odd`—Odd elements

For vectors with an even number of elements, these are all straightforward. Vectors with three elements are treated like four-component vectors with an undefined fourth component. Therefore, in a three-component vector, the middle component is considered part of the lower half.

The `.hi`, `.lo`, `.even`, and `.odd` suffixes can be used to both access and modify components inside a vector. The code in table 4.10 shows how this works for the following vector:

```
ushort8 shorts = (ushort8)(0, 10, 20, 30, 40, 50, 60, 70);
```

Table 4.10 Accessing and modifying elements of a vector using hi, lo, even, odd

Code	Result
`ushort4 a = shorts.hi;`	Sets a to `(40, 50, 60, 70)`
`ushort4 b = shorts.lo;`	Sets b to `(0, 10, 20, 30)`
`ushort4 c = shorts.even;`	Sets c to `(0, 20, 40, 60)`

Table 4.10 Accessing and modifying elements of a vector using hi, lo, even, odd *(continued)*

Code	Result
ushort4 d = shorts.odd;	Sets d to (10, 30, 50, 70)
ushort8 e = (ushort8)(a, b);	Sets e to (40, 50, 60, 70, 0, 10, 20, 30)
shorts.odd = (ushort4)(shorts.s2);	Sets odd elements to 20
shorts.hi = (ushort4)(5, 15, 25, 35);	Sets upper half to (5, 15, 25, 35)
shorts.even = shorts.odd;	Sets even elements to odd elements

With these suffixes, you can easily code routines that rearrange values, such as matrix transposes and sorting routines. Further, because each suffix always affects half of a vector, you can apply the same routines to vectors of different types and widths.

4.4.4 Endianness and memory access

In section 4.2, we examined how bytes are ordered within a scalar. If a device is little-endian, the most-significant byte will have a higher memory address than the least-significant byte. If a device is big-endian, the reverse is true.

Vector storage follows a similar methodology. Figure 4.5 shows how data inside a uint4 is stored on little-endian and big-endian devices.

If you access vector components using the indexing methods described earlier, endianness won't make a difference. But if you access vector data using memory operations, the results will change depending on whether the device is big-endian or little-endian.

This is shown in the following listing, which initializes a uint4 and uses memory operations to place its bytes into a uchar16.

```
uint4 vec = (vec4)(0x00010203, 0x04050607,
                   0x08090A0B, 0x0C0D0E0F);
```

Storage on a little-endian device:

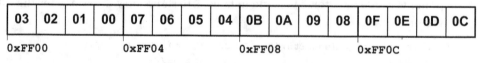

Storage on a big-endian device:

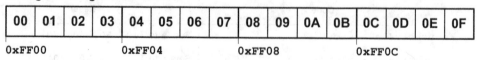

Figure 4.5 Vector storage on little-endian and big-endian systems

Listing 4.4 Displaying bytes of a vector: vector_bytes.cl

```
__kernel void vector_bytes(__global uchar16 *test) {

    uint4 vec = (global uint4)(0x00010203, 0x04050607,
        0x08090A0B, 0x0C0D0E0F);

    uchar *p = &vec;
    *test = (uchar16)(*p, *(p+1), *(p+2), *(p+3), *(p+4), *(p+5),
        *(p+6), *(p+7), *(p+8), *(p+9), *(p+10), *(p+11), *(p+12),
        *(p+13), *(p+14), *(p+15));
}
```

On my little-endian system, the output of the `vector_bytes` application is as follows:

```
0x3, 0x2, 0x1, 0x0, 0x7, 0x6, 0x5, 0x4, 0xB, 0xA, 0x9, 0x8, 0xF, 0xE, 0xD, 0xC
```

Because of the different data storage on big-endian and little-endian devices, it's important to know how to test a device's endianness. As discussed earlier, if a device is little-endian, OpenCL defines a macro called `__ENDIAN_LITTLE__`. This macro is undefined for kernels running on big-endian devices.

Now that you know *how* scalars and vectors are stored in device memory, it's time to look at *where* these data structures are stored. The next section will discuss OpenCL's device memory model and the different ways you can constrain the storage of kernel data.

4.5 *The OpenCL device model*

In our example kernel from section 4.1, the `__global` modifier precedes the data types of the function's parameters. This modifier serves a purpose similar to the `automatic` modifier in ANSI C—both specify where the data should be stored. In OpenCL, `__global` is called an *address space modifier* because any pointer it modifies will be stored in the global address space, also known as global memory. Every kernel argument that references memory must have an address space modifier.

This section discusses OpenCL address spaces in detail, placing emphasis on how they're accessed in code. But first, it's important to see how this memory is used by the work-items and work-groups introduced in the preceding chapter. The relationship between work-items, work-groups, and memory is one of the hardest aspects of OpenCL to comprehend, but it's absolutely essential to understand. Therefore, before we get into technical details, I'd like to present an analogy of how OpenCL devices process kernels.

4.5.1 *Device model analogy part 1: math students in school*

To grasp my analogy, you need to understand what my math classes were like in middle school. My math teacher would assign thirty problems to her thirty students *every day*, but she didn't check all 900 answers. Instead, she assigned a number to each of us, and we'd go to the front of the class and copy our work from our notebook to the blackboard. The teacher would look over our solutions, and if she liked what she saw, we'd get a good grade. Clever, huh?

Here's the analogy: an OpenCL device is like a school composed of classrooms like mine. Each classroom contains students performing math problems. Each student has their own notebook, and every student in a class shares the blackboard. Students in the same class can work together at their blackboard, but students in different classes can't work together.

Here's where it gets tricky: none of these classrooms has a teacher. Also, every student in the school works on the same math problem, but with different values. For example, if the problem involves adding two numbers, one student might add 1 + 2, another might add 3 + 4, and another might add 5 + 6. When all the students in a classroom complete their processing, they can leave. Then the blackboard will be erased and a new class of students will come in and work on the same problem as the preceding class, but with different values.

Each student entering a class automatically knows what problem they'll be solving, but they have no idea what values they'll be working with. The blackboard in each classroom is initially blank, so the students need to go to a central blackboard that contains values for the entire school. This central blackboard is much larger than the blackboards in the classrooms, but because of the long hallway, it takes quite a bit of time for students to read its values. Figure 4.6 depicts the relationship between classes, classrooms, students, notebooks, and blackboards.

For most math problems, each student will go to the central blackboard only twice—once to read the values for their problem and once to jot down their final

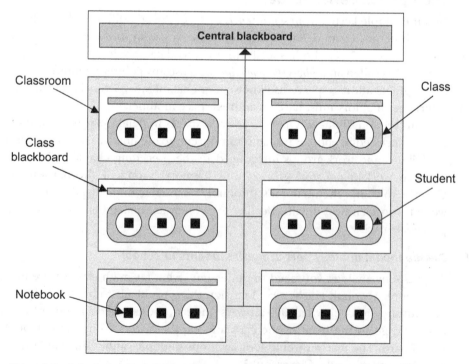

Figure 4.6   School of math students in OpenCL device analogy

answer. Because the central blackboard is so far away, students do their actual solving using their notebooks and classroom blackboards. Once all of the final answers are on the central blackboard, the school day is over.

Students in different classes can't talk to one another, so the students in Class 1 won't know when the students in Class 2 have finished. The only way to be certain that a class has finished is when the school day ends.

It's important to make the distinction between a classroom and a class. A classroom is a physical area with a blackboard. A class is a group of students that occupy a classroom. As one class leaves a classroom, another can enter.

To keep things organized, each class has an identifier that distinguishes it from every other class. Each student has two identifiers: one that distinguishes it from every other student in the class, and one that distinguishes it from every other student in the school. As an example, a student may have a Class ID of 12 and a School ID of 638.

4.5.2 Device model analogy part 2: work-items in a device

In my analogy, the school corresponds to an OpenCL device and the math problem represents the kernel. Each classroom corresponds to a compute unit (processing core), and just as each classroom can be occupied by a class, each compute unit can be occupied by a work-group. That is, classes correspond to work-groups and students correspond to work-items. Figure 4.7 depicts this graphically.

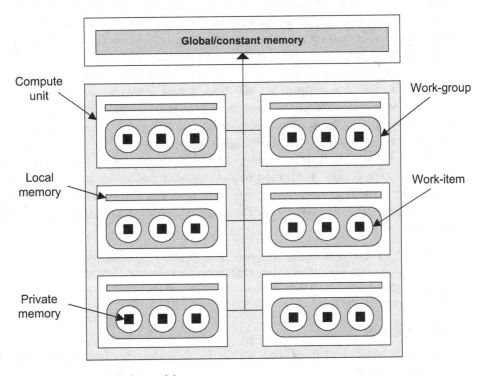

Figure 4.7   OpenCL device model

Now let's talk about memory. The OpenCL device model identifies four address spaces:

- *Global memory*—Stores data for the entire device and can be read from and written to
- *Constant memory*—Similar to global memory, but is read-only
- *Local memory*—Stores data for the work-items in a work-group
- *Private memory*—Stores data for an individual work-item

Some devices provide memory specifically for constant data, but in many cases, the constant address space is the same memory region as the global address space. For this reason, these two address spaces are frequently lumped together.

In my analogy, the central blackboard corresponds to global/constant memory, which can be read from and written to by both the host and the device. When the host application transfers a buffer object to the device, the buffer's data is stored in global/constant memory. When the host reads a buffer object from a device, the data comes from the device's global memory. Global/constant memory is commonly the largest memory region on an OpenCL-compliant device, but it's also the slowest for work-items to access.

Work-items can access local memory much faster (~100x) than they can access global/constant memory, and this corresponds to the blackboards in each classroom. Local memory isn't nearly as large as global/constant memory, but because of the access speed, it's a good place for a work-item to store intermediate results during its execution of a kernel. Just as students in the same class can work together on the blackboard, work-items in the same work-group can access the same block of local memory. Work-items in different classes can never access the same local memory.

The private memory in an OpenCL device corresponds to the notebook each student uses to solve a math problem. Each work-item has exclusive access to its private memory, and it can access this memory faster than it can access local memory or global/constant memory. But this address space is much smaller than any other address space, so it's important not to use too much of it.

When I first started using OpenCL, I wondered how many work-items could be generated for a kernel. As I hope this analogy has made clear, you can generate however many work-items and work-groups you like. But if the device only contains M compute units and N work-items per work-group, only MN work-items will execute the kernel at any given time.

> **NOTE** You can determine the size of a device's address spaces by calling `clGetDeviceInfo` with `CL_DEVICE_GLOBAL_MEM_SIZE`, `CL_DEVICE_GLOBAL_MEM_CACHE_SIZE`, `CL_DEVICE_MAX_CONSTANT_BUFFER_SIZE`, or `CL_DEVICE_LOCAL_MEM_SIZE`.

4.5.3   *Address spaces in code*

Every kernel argument must have a qualifier that identifies its address space. These are the four qualifiers:

- __global—The argument's data will be placed in global memory
- __constant—The argument's data will be stored in global, read-only memory (if available)
- __local—The argument's data will be stored in local memory
- __private—The argument's data will be stored in private memory (default)

These qualifiers are important to understand, and not just because of memory access speed. If you don't use them properly, your code won't compile. For example, if two pointers reference memory stored in different address spaces, they can't be cast to one another. We'll look at each of these address spaces in turn.

THE __GLOBAL QUALIFIER

Every kernel argument in this chapter's example code has been stored in global memory with the __global qualifier. In our earlier code examples, the types of the vector arguments are __global char16* and __global uchar16*. This __global qualifier can be used for all kernel arguments, not just pointers.

In addition to arguments, __global can qualify pointer variables declared within a kernel. This is shown in the following code:

```
__kernel void kernel_func(__global float *f) {

    __global uint *x = 5;
    f = (global float*)x;
}
```

Here, the cast from x to f is only possible because both pointers reference global memory. If *x was declared as __local, the cast would not be possible. Also, if x wasn't a pointer, this code couldn't compile. Inside a kernel, the __global qualifier can only be used with pointer variables.

THE __CONSTANT QUALIFIER

It may seem odd to have a separate qualifier for read-only data, but a number of devices, such as AMD's Evergreen GPUs, have cache registers dedicated to holding constants. Kernel arguments and variables declared within a kernel can be qualified with __constant. String literals are stored as constants and any attempt to modify constant data produces an error.

The __constant qualifier makes data available to every work-item processing a kernel. In addition, constant data is global to the entire *program*, not just a single kernel. It must be initialized before use.

THE __LOCAL QUALIFIER

If data needs to be shared among work-items in a work-group, but not shared with other work-groups, it should be declared with the __local qualifier. This data will be allocated once for each work-group processing the kernel. It's deallocated as each work-group completes its processing.

The __local qualifier can be used for kernel arguments and variables declared within a kernel, but local variables in a kernel can't be directly initialized, either by the host or the device. For example, the following code inside a kernel function will produce an error:

```
__local float x = 4.0;
```

The following code will work instead:

```
__local float x;
x = 4.0;
```

THE __PRIVATE QUALIFIER

If a kernel argument or variable doesn't have an address space qualifier, it's stored in private memory. This includes all variables and arguments of non-kernel functions. Private data is allocated for each work-item processing a kernel.

If a pointer variable doesn't have a qualifier, it will be set to reference private memory. But `image2d_t` and `image3d_t` pointers are always global. We'll examine these data structures in chapter 6, which presents the topic of OpenCL image processing.

4.5.4 *Memory alignment*

If you've ever looked at the memory addresses of your data, you may notice that your 32-bit structures, such as `ints` and `floats`, are always stored at memory addresses that are multiples of 0x4, such as 0xFFF0, 0xFFF4, 0xFFF8, and 0xFFFC. For this reason, we say that 32-bit structures are aligned on 4-byte boundaries. 64-bit structures, such as `longs` and `doubles`, are stored at addresses that are multiples of 0x8. We say that 64-bit structures are aligned on 8-byte boundaries.

There's an algorithm for this: when a data structure is stored, its memory alignment is set to the smallest power of two that's greater than or equal to the data's size. For example, a `float3` contains 12 bytes. This vector will be stored on a 16-byte boundary because 16 is the smallest power of 2 greater than or equal to 12.

You can control data alignment with the `aligned` attribute, which can only be used when the data is declared. The `aligned` keyword must be preceded by `__attribute__`, and the following declaration shows how this works:

```
short x __attribute__ ((aligned(4)));
```

This states that x, which would normally be aligned on a 2-byte boundary, should instead be aligned on a 4-byte boundary. The alignment factor must be a power of 2.

Now that you understand OpenCL's device model and its address spaces, you're ready to learn how to configure kernel arguments that lie outside the global/constant address space. That's the topic of the next section.

4.6 *Local and private kernel arguments*

Every kernel argument we've dealt with has been declared as `__global` and has been transferred from the host as a memory object. But you don't have to rely on memory objects to form kernel arguments. You can configure arguments in a device's local and private spaces by configuring `clSetKernelArg` correctly. This function is central to the discussion in this section, so let's review its signature:

```
clSetKernelArg (cl_kernel kernel, cl_uint index, size_t size,
    const void *value)
```

The last parameter, value, identifies the data that will be sent to the device as a kernel argument. So far, the example code has always set this to point to a memory object, and the corresponding kernel argument must be declared as __global or __constant. Data in the global and constant spaces is easy to work with, but compared to local or private data, the memory bandwidth is much slower.

For this reason, it's important to know how to configure kernel arguments in the local and private address spaces. This section explains both procedures.

4.6.1 Local arguments

If you transfer data to a kernel using a memory object, you can't set the kernel argument's specifier to __local. If you attempt this, you'll receive a runtime error whose code is –50: CL_INVALID_ARG_VALUE. As it turns out, the host can't directly access a device's local memory. That is, a host application can neither read nor write data in local memory space.

But a host application can tell the device to allocate local memory for a kernel argument. To configure this in code, set the last argument of clSetKernelArg to NULL. For example, the following code, executed by the host, configures a local argument to occupy space sufficient to hold 16 floats:

```
clSetKernelArg(kernel, 0, 16*sizeof(float), NULL);
```

Now you can have __local arguments in your kernel. For example, given the preceding code, your kernel function could look like this:

```
__kernel void proc_data(__local float* nums, ...) {
   ...
}
```

Work-items can access local memory faster than global memory, so it's a good idea to have them read global memory into local memory and process the data there. Then, when the work-items have finished processing the local data, they can write the results to global memory, which can be transferred back to the host. The code examples in Chapters 10 through 14 demonstrate how local memory is used in practical computation.

Besides speed, local memory also has the advantage of being available to every work-item in a work-group. This means you can have multiple work-items processing the same data, thereby improving performance. Synchronization is an important priority in many applications, and chapter 7 discusses work-item synchronization in detail.

4.6.2 Private arguments

Private memory can only be accessed by a single work-item, and this memory access is even faster than local memory access. But private memory is usually small compared to local and global memory.

Unlike local data, a kernel's private data can be initialized by a host application. To configure this in code, the host needs to make the last parameter of clSetKernelArg a pointer to primitive data: an int*, float*, char*, and so on.

For example, suppose you want each work-item to be able to access its own copy of an int called num_iterations, and you want the initial value to be 4. You can specify this in the host application with the following code:

```
int num_iterations = 4;
clSetKernelArg(kernel, 0, sizeof(num_iterations), &num_iterations);
```

Then your kernel function should look similar to the following:

```
__kernel void proc_data(int num_iters, ...) {
    ...
}
```

There are two points to note about this function's argument. First, it has no address space specifier like __global or __local. This means that num_iters will be stored in the device's private address space and each work-item will have its own copy. Second, unlike every other kernel argument we've seen, num_iters isn't a pointer. Private kernel arguments can't be references—they must be simple primitives like int and float.

If you're familiar with the distinction between pass-by-value data and pass-by-reference data in regular C, it should be clear that global/constant data is passed to kernels by reference and private data is passed to kernels by value. If the host sends data to the kernel as part of a memory object, it can read back the modified data. If the host sends data as a simple primitive, it can't read that data back.

Private kernel arguments must be primitives, but they don't have to be scalars. You can also send data that the kernel should interpret as a vector type. For example, let's say you want to send four floats to the kernel, and you want the floats to be placed in the device's private address space so they can be accessed quickly. Then, in the host application, you could add code such as the following:

```
float nums[4] = {0.0f, 1.0f, 2.0f, 3.0f};
clSetKernelArg(kernel, 0, sizeof(nums), nums);
```

The kernel can't access the private data as a four-element array because private arguments can't be pointers. But the data can be accessed as a float4 vector, as shown in the following kernel function:

```
__kernel void proc_data(float4 values, ...) {
    ...
}
```

The relationship between clSetKernelArg and the arguments of a kernel function is one of the most important but least understood aspects of OpenCL. Global/constant data and memory objects are simple to work with, but when you need high performance, you're better off making sure work-items process data in local and private memory. You'll see this again in chapter 10 and later chapters, where we'll use OpenCL to perform practical, time-critical tasks.

4.7   *Summary*

Programming an OpenCL kernel is a lot like programming a regular C function, but there are a few important differences. First, each kernel must be identified with __kernel and the function must return void. Second, OpenCL doesn't support all of the old data types, but it does provide new ones. Finally, OpenCL models devices in such a way that you can constrain which address space is used to store kernel data.

OpenCL's scalar data types present only a couple of complications. You can still code with chars, shorts, ints, floats, and longs, but you can only declare doubles and halfs if they're supported on the device. When it comes to floating-point processing, OpenCL supports many aspects of the IEEE-754 standard, but not all of them. If you intend to port code to OpenCL, you should know which capabilities are available and which aren't.

Of all the vector data types I've dealt with, OpenCL's vectors are the simplest to work with. The data type that holds four floats is simply called float4. Initializing a vector's content is like initializing an array, and accessing the components of a vector is easy—you can use numbers (.s0, .s1, .s2, ...sF), letters (x, y, z, and w), and suffixes that return half of the vector's components (.hi, .lo, .even, and .odd).

OpenCL's memory model may seem frightening at first glance, but once you understand the operation of work-groups and work-items, you'll see why the different address spaces are necessary. The global address space stores data for the entire device, the constant address space stores read-only data, the local address space stores data for a specific work-group, and the private address space stores data for a specific work-item. OpenCL provides qualifiers that allow you to specify which address space a variable or function argument should be stored in.

The last part of this chapter discussed the different ways you can configure kernel arguments in OpenCL. If you invoke clSetKernelArg with a pointer to a memory object, then the corresponding kernel argument must be a pointer declared as __global or __constant. If you invoke clSetKernelArg with NULL, the corresponding kernel argument must be a pointer declared as __local. If you invoke clSetKernelArg with a pointer to primitive data, the kernel argument won't be a pointer and it won't have any address space specifier.

This chapter has covered OpenCL data in detail, but there's been no discussion of all the different ways you can operate on this data. The next chapter will discuss OpenCL's operators and functions in detail, and we'll put these vector types to work.

Kernel programming: operators and functions

This chapter covers

- Operators for scalar and vector types
- OpenCL's built-in functions and their usage in code

Chapter 4 discussed data types and emphasized the different types of vectors available. Vectors can dramatically improve an application's performance by making it possible to operate on multiple values at once. But before you can use them in a practical application, you need to know what operators and functions are available to process them. The goal of this chapter is to explain these operators and functions, and to provide example code to demonstrate their usage.

Most of these operators and functions relate to mathematics, and the OpenCL working group has wisely kept to the naming conventions set by math.h. For example, you can call sqrt to compute the square root of a floating-point vector and pow to compute x^y. But OpenCL also provides new functions like mad_sat and mad_hi, which make it possible to perform math operations quickly and accurately.

The bulk of this chapter discusses OpenCL's *built-in* functions. They're called built-in because you don't need to link additional libraries or include any special header files. There are many built-in functions available, so I've divided them into seven categories:

- *Work-item and work-group functions*—For identifying the dimensionality of data, determining work-group participation, obtaining IDs of work-items and work-groups
- *Data transfer functions*—For loading and storing data between memory regions
- *Floating-point functions*—For arithmetic and rounding, comparing components, exponential and logarithmic operations, trigonometric operations, and miscellaneous operations
- *Integer functions*—For arithmetic and comparison of integer vectors
- *Shuffle and select functions*—For creating vectors with bits or components of other vectors
- *Vector test/comparison functions*—For testing and comparing components inside vectors
- *Geometric functions*—For dot products, cross products, lengths, and normalization

Multiple implementations of a function are often available for different types of arguments. For example, the second argument of the `min` and `max` functions can be a `float` vector or a single `float`. In addition, many functions accept pointers to memory, but only pointers that reference specific address spaces. For example, the `vloadn` function can store data to global memory, local memory, and private memory, but not constant memory.

Rather than list every implementation of a function, this chapter will adopt the following conventions to identify the different usages of a function:

- `type/n`—The slash indicates that the argument can be either the scalar type `type` or the vector type `typen`, where *n* can be 2, 3, 4, 8, and 16.
- `__(g|c|l|p)`—This states that the pointer can reference memory in the global (g), constant (c), local (l), and private (p) address spaces.
- `all`—This argument can be any scalar or vector type
- `integer`—This argument can be any integer type: `uchar`, `char`, `ushort`, `short`, `uint`, `int`, `ulong`, and `long`
- `uinteger`—This argument can be any unsigned integer type: `uchar`, `ushort`, `uint`, `int`, and `ulong`

But before we delve into the different functions, let's take a brief look at OpenCL's operators. These are exactly like the operators used in traditional C, but they apply to vectors as well as scalars.

5.1 Operators

One of the most convenient aspects of OpenCL is that you can perform basic vector operations using regular C operators. Let's say you want to add two `float4` vectors, a and b. If you were programming with SSE, you'd call _mm_addps(a, b). If you were programming with AltiVec, you'd call vec_add(a, b). But with OpenCL, you don't have to remember any function names—just use a + b as though the arguments were scalars.

Table 5.1 lists all of the OpenCL operators that operate on bits, numbers, and logical expressions. Of those that accept multiple arguments, each of them can operate on all-scalar and all-vector arguments. Many of them can also operate on mixed-type arguments.

Table 5.1   OpenCL operators

Operator	Purpose	Operator	Purpose	Operator	Purpose
+	Addition	==	Equal to	!	Logical NOT
−	Subtraction	!=	Not equal to	&	Bitwise AND
*	Multiplication	>	Greater than	|	Bitwise OR
/	Division (quotient)	>=	Greater than or equal to	^	Bitwise XOR
%	Division (modulus)	<	Less than	~	Bitwise NOT
++	Increment	<=	Less than or equal to	>>	Right-shift
--	Decrement	&&	Logical AND	<<	Left-shift
		||	Logical OR	?:	Ternary selection

The usual rules apply. For the arithmetic operators, if the operands have the same type, the result will have the same type as the operands. If an operation involves a vector containing integers and a vector containing floating-point values, the resulting vector will contain floating-point values. You can't use bitwise operators on floating-point values or vectors containing floating-point values.

In many cases, you can perform an operation on a vector and a scalar. For example, the following code adds 5 to every component in a short8 vector:

```
short8 s = (short8)(1, 2, 3, 4, 5, 6, 7, 8);
s = s + 5;
```

In the second line, s = s + 5 can be replaced with s += 5. This is called an *addition assignment operator* because it adds a value to the operand's value and assigns the new value to the operand. The other supported assignment operators are -=, *=, /=, %=, <<=, >>=, &=, |=, and ^=.

The code in the following listing presents a number of different ways these operators can be used.

Listing 5.1   Operator usage: op_test.cl

```
__kernel void op_test(__global int4 *output) {

   int4 vec = (int4)(1, 2, 3, 4);

   vec += 4;                                          Add 4 to every
                                                      element
```

```
    if(vec.s2 == 7)                              Set 3rd
        vec &= (int4)(-1, -1, 0, -1);            element to 0

    vec.s01 = vec.s23 < 7;                       Set lst, 2nd
                                                 elements to -l, 0
    while(vec.s3 > 7 && (vec.s0 < 16 || (vec.s1 < 16))
        vec.s3 >>= 1;                            Shift 4th
                                                 element right
    *output = vec;
}
```

The arithmetic operators are easy to understand, but the relational operators, such as <, >, and ==, need explanation. When used with scalars, these operators return a 1 if the relation is true and 0 if false. They're commonly used in if and while statements, and if x equals 3, the operation x > 2 returns 1 and you can test the relation with if(x > 2).

But if x is a vector, the usage changes. The operation tests all the components of a vector, and the components of the resulting vector identify whether the corresponding test returned true or false. For vector components, truth is represented by all 1s (0xFF, 0xFFFF, 0xFFFFFFFF, and so on). OpenCL represents signed integers using their two's complement, so the signed value for true is -1, not 1. The value for false is 0. This is shown in listing 5.1, which contains the following line of code:

```
vec.s01 = vec.s23 < 7;
```

The < operator tests the third and fourth components of vec. The first test returns true because vec.s2 is less than 7, so the first element (vec.s0) is set to 0xFFFFFFFF, or -1. The second test returns false, so the second element (vec.s1) is set to 0.

This isn't the only difference between scalar and vector relations. Unlike scalar relations, vector relations can't be used directly in if and while statements. For example, if x is a vector, statements like while(x > 2) and if(x > 2) will produce compiler errors. Instead, you can test the elements individually with code such as the following:

```
while(x.s0 > 2 && x.s1 > 2 && x.s2 > 2 && x.s3 > 2)
```

Alternatively, you can use the all or any functions. The all function tests the most significant bits (MSBs) of every component and returns 1 if they're all set to 1. In contrast, any returns 1 if any of the MSBs are set to 1. Therefore, you can test all the components of a vector with code like the following:

```
while(all(x > 2))
```

Section 5.7 discusses the all and any functions, along with other vector test functions. But the most important OpenCL functions to know are those that relate to work-items and work-groups. We'll discuss these next.

5.2 Work-item and work-group functions

Let's briefly review the topic of data partitioning, which chapter 3 discussed in detail. A host application can call clEnqueueNDRangeKernel with arguments that define the number of dimensions in the kernel data, the number of work-items per dimension, and the number of work-items in a work-group per dimension.

For a work-item to execute its job, it must be able to access data specifically intended for it. This means it needs to know its ID among all other work-items executing the kernel. If the work-item is part of a work-group, it may also need to know its ID among all other work-items in the work-group.

In this section, we'll look at the functions that provide this information. In many kernel functions, these are the first functions to be invoked.

5.2.1 Dimensions and work-items

The number of dimensions needed for a work-item's ID usually equals the number of indices you'd use to access an element of an array containing the work-item's data. For example, suppose your input data is stored in an array called point. If you'd normally access the data with point[x][y], the number of dimensions is two. If you'd access the data with point[x][y][z], the number of dimensions is three.

A work-item is a single implementation of a kernel, and each work-item has an identifier that distinguishes it from every other work-item that processes the kernel. This identifier, called the global ID, is an array of unsigned integers—one for each dimension in the data.

A work-item obtains its global ID using the get_global_id function. Table 5.2 lists this function along with others that provide information related to dimensions and work-items.

Table 5.2 Functions related to work-items

Function	Purpose
uint get_work_dim()	Returns the number of dimensions in the kernel's index space
size_t get_global_size(uint dim)	Returns the number of work-items for a given dimension
size_t get_global_id(uint dim)	Returns the element of the work-item's global ID for a given dimension
size_t get_global_offset(uint dim)	Returns the initial offset used to compute global IDs

NOTE The get_global_offset function is new in OpenCL 1.1 and won't compile on systems that don't support the new standard.

An example will help make these functions clear. Let's say you want to process a portion of the data in a 9 * 9 image. Without OpenCL, you might use a nested for loop similar to the following:

```
for(i = 3; i < 9; i++) {
   for(j = 5; j < 9; j++) {
      process(data(i, j));
   }
}
```

Figure 5.1 shows the index space corresponding to this nested loop. Inside the inner loop, the first iteration receives index pair $(3, 5)$.

In OpenCL, the loop iterations correspond to work-items and the loop indices correspond to a work-item's global ID. A work-item can obtain its ID by calling `get_global_id(0)` and `get_global_id(1)`. It can also find out how many work-items will be executed per dimension using `get_global_size(0)` and `get_global_size(1)`.

In the nested loop, the index pair of the first iteration is $(3, 5)$. This corresponds to OpenCL's global offset, which is the first global ID given to a work-item. A work-item can access this by calling `get_global_offset(0)` and `get_global_offset(1)`.

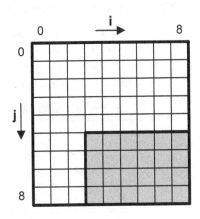

Figure 5.1 Index space for a two-dimensional kernel

5.2.2 *Work-groups*

Work-groups become important when work-items need to synchronize their execution. Chapter 7 will explain OpenCL's implementation of synchronization, but for now, you should know that OpenCL provides functions that tell you about work-groups, and they work just like the functions that tell you about work-items.

The functions in table 5.3 provide *local* information, whereas the functions in table 5.2 provide *global* information. It's important to understand the difference. `get_global_id` identifies a work-item among all other work-items executing the kernel. But `get_local_id` identifies the work-item only among work-items in the same work-group. If two work-items execute the same kernel in different work-groups, they might have the same local ID, but they'll never have the same global ID.

Table 5.3 Functions related to work-groups

Function	Purpose
`size_t get_num_groups(uint dim)`	Returns the number of work-groups for a given dimension
`size_t get_group_id(uint dim)`	Returns the ID of the work-item's work-group for a given dimension
`size_t get_local_id(uint dim)`	Returns the ID of the work-item within its work-group for a given dimension
`size_t get_local_size(uint dim)`	Returns the number of work-items in the work-group for a given dimension

Similarly, `get_global_size` tells you how many work-items are executing the same kernel. `get_local_size` tells you how many work-items are in the same work-group as the calling work-item.

5.2.3 *An example application*

The clEnqueueNDRangeKernel function is complicated, and it's hard to verify that it will create work-items and work-groups as you've intended. The code in the next listing can help. Each work-item accesses global and local information, combines the data into a float, and stores the float in an array.

> **Listing 5.2 Testing work-item/work-group IDs: id_check.cl**

```
__kernel void id_check(__global float *output) {
    size_t global_id_0 = get_global_id(0);
    size_t global_id_1 = get_global_id(1);
    size_t global_size_0 = get_global_size(0);        Access item/
    size_t offset_0 = get_global_offset(0);           group info
    size_t offset_1 = get_global_offset(1);
    size_t local_id_0 = get_local_id(0);
    size_t local_id_1 = get_local_id(1);

    int index_0 = global_id_0 - offset_0;             Determine
    int index_1 = global_id_1 - offset_1;             array index
    int index = index_1 * global_size_0 + index_0;

    float f = global_id_0 * 10.0f + global_id_1 * 1.0f;   Set float
    f += local_id_0 * 0.1f + local_id_1 * 0.01f;          data

    output[index] = f;
}
```

The host application, presented in id_check.c, configures processing for the task depicted in figure 5.1. That is, the first global ID is {3, 5} and the global size is {6, 4}. It also configures four work-groups by setting a local size equal to {3, 2}. The relevant code is as follows:

```
size_t dim = 2;
size_t global_offset[] = {3, 5};
size_t global_size[] = {6, 4};
size_t local_size[] = {3, 2};

err = clEnqueueNDRangeKernel(queue, kernel, dim, global_offset,
    global_size, local_size, 0, NULL, NULL);
```

When the application is run for this example, it prints each work-item's identification data as a float. The two digits before the decimal point correspond to the global ID, and the two digits after the decimal point correspond to the local ID. On my system, the output results are as follows:

```
35.00    45.10    55.20    65.00    75.10    85.20
36.01    46.11    56.21    66.01    76.11    86.21
37.00    47.10    57.20    67.00    77.10    87.20
38.01    48.11    58.21    68.01    78.11    88.21
```

This example clarifies how clEnqueueNDRangeKernel configures the local and global IDs for a work-item. This is a complex topic, and if you're still not comfortable with it, I recommend that you experiment with the code in the id_check project until the results are clear.

Thankfully, accessing vector memory is much simpler to understand than configuring work-groups and work-items. We'll discuss this next.

5.3 Data transfer operations

The preceding chapter explained the different address spaces available in an OpenCL kernel and why it's so important to be able to transfer data from one region to another. The code required to transfer a block of data depends on whether the data has the same type on the sending and receiving ends. For example, if you need to load a `float4` from one memory region into a `float4` in another region, you'd use different code than if you need to load a `float4` from a `float` array. This section will discuss how to transfer data of the same type, how to load vectors from a scalar array, and how to store vectors to a scalar array.

5.3.1 Loading and storing data of the same type

If you want to transfer data of the same type, such as loading an `int4` from an `int4`, there's only one symbol to know: `=`. In addition to assigning values to variables, the equals sign transfers data from one memory region to another. For example, suppose you want a kernel to load data from global memory into local memory, process the data, and then store the data in global memory. Your code might look similar to the following:

```
__kernel void test(__global int4 *in_data, __global int4 *out_data) {
    __local int4 local_data;
    int id = get_local_id(0);
    local_data = in_data[id];
    ...process data in local memory...
    out_data[id] = local_data;
}
```

In this code, the `=` operator is used twice to transfer data between global memory and local memory. The data doesn't have to be vector-based; the code will work just as well if `int4` is changed to `int`. Similarly, to change from local memory to private memory, remove the `__local` specifier in the data declaration. The default specifier is `__private`, so the compiler will store variables without specifiers in private memory.

5.3.2 Loading vectors from a scalar array

In many cases, you may want to process data using vector operations, but the input is given as a scalar array. The `=` won't work, and you can't cast data in one address space to data in another. Thankfully, OpenCL provides `vloadn` for loading scalar data into vectors. Its signature is as follows:

```
vector vloadn(size_t offset, const __(g|c|l|p) scalar *mem)
```

In this signature, *n* identifies the number of components in the returned vector, and it must be set to 2, 3, 4, 8, or 16. `vector` can be any vector type, and `scalar` must have the same data type as that of the components inside `vector`. The memory containing `vector` and `scalar` can be located in different address spaces.

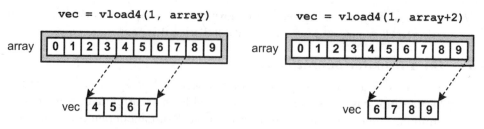

Figure 5.2 Loading vectors from a scalar array

For example, suppose `float_vec` is a `float4` vector and `float_array` is an array of `floats`. The following code loads the first four `floats` of `float_array` into `float_vec`:

```
float_vec = vload4(0, float_array);
```

The `offset` argument determines which elements of the array are placed in the vector. This is given in terms of the size of the *vector*, not the size of its scalar components. In the preceding example, if the first argument of `vload4` is 1, `float_vec` will contain the fifth through eighth elements of `float_array`. This is depicted on the left side of figure 5.2.

The right side of figure 5.2 shows how pointer operations make it possible to load unaligned data from a scalar array into a vector. Note that unaligned data transfer may cause memory access delays.

5.3.3 *Storing vectors to a scalar array*

Just as `vloadn` transfers data from a scalar array to a vector, `vstoren` transfers data from a vector to a scalar array. The signature of this function is as follows:

```
void vstoren(vector vec, size_t offset, __(g|l|p) scalar *mem)
```

This function stores the vector `vec` in the scalar array identified by `mem` at the location determined by `offset`. As with `vloadn`, *n* must equal the number of components in `vec`, and it can be set to 2, 3, 4, 8, or 16. But unlike `vloadn`, the scalar array can't be stored in the constant address space.

As an example, the following code stores the `int4` vector `int_vec` at the start of an array of integers called `int_array`:

```
vstore4(int_vec, 0, int_array);
```

By changing the `offset` argument, you can store the vector at different vector-sized offsets inside the array. With pointer arithmetic, you can store the vector at unaligned offsets inside the array.

> **NOTE** The OpenCL standard also provides functions that load floating-point vectors from half-precision data (`vload_halfn`) and functions that store floating-point vectors to half-precision data (`vstore_halfn`). See section 6.11.7 of the OpenCL 1.1 specification for more information.

Now that you know how to transfer data, it's time to look into the primary use of OpenCL kernels: number crunching. The next section discusses functions that operate on floating-point scalars and vectors.

5.4 Floating-point functions

If you need to process real-world quantities like temperature or pressure values, you're probably going to model your data using floating-point values. Section 5.1 presented the basic operators available for floating-point processing, but now we're going to look at functions. This section divides OpenCL's floating-point functions into five categories: arithmetic and rounding, comparison, exponential and logarithmic, trigonometric, and miscellaneous.

5.4.1 Arithmetic and rounding functions

Table 5.4 lists the OpenCL functions that perform arithmetic and rounding operations on floating-point values. These are all simple to use and understand. Most of the math functions compute products, quotients, and remainders, and most of the rounding functions accept `float`s and return `float`s whose fractional part equals 0.

Table 5.4 Arithmetic and rounding functions

Function	Purpose
`floatn fabs(floatn x)`	Returns the absolute value of the argument, $\lvert x \rvert$
`floatn fma(floatn a, floatn b, floatn c)`	Returns `a * b + c`, where the multiplication is performed with precision
`floatn fmod(floatn x, floatn y)`	Returns the modulus of x and y: `x - (y * trunc(y/x))`
`floatn mad(floatn a, floatn b, floatn c)`	Returns `a * b + c`
`floatn remainder(floatn x, floatn y)`	Returns the remainder of x and y: `x - n * y`, where n is the integer closest to x/y
`floatn remquo(floatn x, floatn y, __(g|l|p) *quo)`	Returns the remainder of x and y: `x - n * y`, where n is the integer closest to x/y; places the signed lowest seven bits of the quotient (x/y) in `quo`
`floatn rint(floatn x)`	Returns the closest integer as a `float`—if two integers are equally close, it returns the even integer as a `float`
`floatn round(floatn x)`	Returns the integer closest to x—if two integers are equally close, it returns the one farther from 0
`floatn ceil(floatn x)`	Returns the closest integer larger than x
`floatn floor(floatn x)`	Returns the closest integer smaller than x
`floatn trunc(floatn x)`	Removes the fractional part of x and returns the integer

This table contains two functions that perform the same operation. The mad and fma (Fused Multiply and Add) functions both compute a * b + c. According to the OpenCL 1.1 standard, "mad is intended to be used where speed is preferred over accuracy." In contrast, fma provides greater precision by rounding only the final result and not the intermediate multiplication.

Some devices can process fma operations in hardware, providing improved speed and accuracy. This is defined in the IEEE-754 standard but it's not required by OpenCL. To test whether a device supports this capability, call clGetDeviceInfo with the parameter CL_DEVICE_SINGLE_FP_CONFIG. Then test the result to see whether the CL_FP_FMA flag is set. Chapter 4 explains OpenCL's floating-point support in detail.

The / operator (division) is available for integers and floating-point values, but the % operator (modulus) is only available for integers. Instead, you can compute a floating-point modulus by calling fmod, which returns x - (y * trunc(y/x)). The remainder function serves a similar purpose but computes x - n * y, where n is the integer closest to x/y.

When it comes to the rounding functions, there's only one point to remember: rint rounds to the nearest even but round doesn't. round returns the closest integer, and in the event that the two closest integers are equally close, it returns the one further from 0. The following listing shows how fmod and remainder are used in code and also demonstrates the usage of each of the five rounding functions.

Listing 5.3 Division and rounding: mod_round.cl

```
__kernel void mod_round(__global float *mod_input,
                        __global float *mod_output,
                        __global float4 *round_input,
                        __global float4 *round_output) {

    mod_output[0] = fmod(mod_input[0], mod_input[1]);
    mod_output[1] = remainder(mod_input[0], mod_input[1]);

    round_output[0] = rint(*round_input);
    round_output[1] = round(*round_input);
    round_output[2] = ceil(*round_input);
    round_output[3] = floor(*round_input);
    round_output[4] = trunc(*round_input);
}
```

These functions are easy to understand. On my system, the printed results are as follows:

```
fmod(317.0, 23.0)      = 18.0
remainder(317.0, 23.0) = -5.0

Rounding input: -6.5 -3.5 3.5 6.5
rint:  -6.0, -4.0, 4.0, 6.0
round: -7.0, -4.0, 4.0, 7.0
ceil:  -6.0, -3.0, 4.0, 7.0
floor: -7.0, -4.0, 3.0, 6.0
trunc: -6.0, -3.0, 3.0, 6.0
```

Notice that round(-6.5) returns -7.0 instead of -6.0. This is because it rounds away from 0. You can think of round as the opposite of trunc.

5.4.2 Comparison functions

OpenCL provides a number of functions that compare the components of two floating-point vectors. Table 5.5 lists them all. Some functions return the maximum of the two inputs and others return the minimum. Other functions clamp or smooth the components of an input according to thresholds.

Table 5.5 Comparison functions

Function	Purpose
floatn clamp(floatn x, float/n min, float/n max)	Returns min if x < min; returns max if x > max; otherwise returns x
floatn fdim(floatn x, floatn y)	Returns x - y if x > y; returns 0 if x <= y
floatn fmax(floatn x, float/n y)	Returns x if x >= y; returns y if y > x
floatn fmin(floatn x, float/n y)	Returns x if x <= y; returns y if y < x
floatn max(floatn x, float/n y)	Returns x if x >= y; returns y if y > x
floatn min(floatn x, float/n y)	Returns x if x <= y; returns y if y < x
floatn mix(floatn x, floatn y, float/n a)	Interpolates between x and y using the equation x + (y - x) * a, where 0.0 < a < 1.0
floatn maxmag(floatn x, floatn y)	Returns x if |x| >= |y|; returns y if |y| > |x|
floatn minmag(floatn x, floatn y)	Returns x if |x| <= |y|; returns y if |y| < |x|
floatn step(float/n edge, floatn x)	Returns 0.0 if x < edge; returns 1.0 if x >= edge
floatn smoothstep(float/n edge1, float/n edge2, floatn x)	Returns 0.0 if x <= edge1; returns 1.0 if x >= edge1; uses smooth interpolation if edge0 < x < edge1

These functions are easy to understand, but two functions—clamp and smoothstep—deserve attention. Both functions compare an input vector to a minimum and maximum threshold, which can be given in scalar or vector form. If the input components are larger than the maximum, clamp sets the output components to the maximum value and smoothstep sets the output components to 1.0. If components of the input vector are smaller than the minimum threshold, clamp sets the output components to the minimum value and smoothstep sets the output components to 0.0. If the input components lie between the thresholds, smoothstep interpolates the value using Hermitian interpolation.

5.4.3 *Exponential and logarithmic functions*

The functions in table 5.6 compute exponents and logarithms of the components in a floating-point vector. These closely resemble their counterparts in math.h, so if you're familiar with pow, exp, log, and sqrt, these won't present any difficulty.

Table 5.6 Exponential and logarithmic functions

Function	Purpose
floatn pow(floatn x, floatn y)	Returns xy
floatn pown(floatn x, intn y)	Returns xy, where y is an integer
floatn powr(floatn x, floatn y)	Returns xy, where x is greater than or equal to 0
floatn exp/expm1(floatn x)	Returns ex and ex − 1
floatn exp2/exp10(floatn x)	Returns 2x and 10x
floatn ldexp(floatn x, intn n))	Returns x * 2n
floatn rootn(floatn x, floatn y)	Returns x1/y
floatn sqrt/cbrt(floatn x)	Returns the square root/cube root of x
floatn rsqrt(floatn x)	Returns the inverse square root of x
floatn log/log1p(floatn x)	Returns ln(x) and ln(1.0 + x)
floatn log2/log10(floatn x)	Returns log2 x and log10 x
floatn logb(floatn x)	Returns the integral part of log2 x
floatn erf/erfc(floatn x)	Returns the error function and the complementary error function
floatn tgamma/lgamma(floatn x)	Returns the gamma function and the log gamma function
floatn lgamma_r(floatn x, __(g|l|p) intn *mem)	Returns the log gamma function and places the sign in the memory referenced by mem

The names of these functions can be confusing. Keep in mind that expm1 (exp minus 1) computes $e^x − 1$ and that exp10 computes 10^x. Also, log1p computes $\ln(1.0 + x)$, whereas log10 computes $\log_{10}x$.

5.4.4 *Trigonometric functions*

OpenCL provides many more trigonometric functions than those in math.h. These include hyperbolic trigonometric functions, inverse trigonometric functions, and functions that multiply the input by π. Table 5.7 lists all of them.

The sincos function computes sines and cosines, returning the sine values and storing the cosine values in the memory referenced by the second argument. This function is ideal for converting polar coordinates (r, θ) into rectilinear components

Table 5.7 Trigonometric functions

Function	Purpose
`floatn sin/cos/tan(floatn)`	Returns the sine, cosine, and tangent
`floatn sinpi/cospi/tanpi(floatn x)`	Returns the sine, cosine, and tangent of πx
`floatn asin/acos/atan(floatn)`	Returns the arcsine, arccosine, and arctangent
`floatn asinpi/acospi/atanpi` `  (floatn x)`	Returns the arcsine, arccosine, and arctangent of πx
`floatn sinh/cosh/tanh(floatn)`	Returns the hyperbolic sine, cosine, and tangent
`floatn asinh/acosh/atanh(floatn)`	Returns the hyperbolic arcsine, arccosine, and arctangent
`floatn sincos(floatn x,` `  __(g|l|p) floatn *mem)`	Returns the sine of x and places the cosine in the memory referenced by mem
`floatn atan2/atan2pi(floatn x)`	Returns the sine, cosine, and tangent of πx

(x, y). Figure 5.3 shows four points on a unit circle and presents their coordinates in polar and rectilinear form.

In polar_rect.c, the host sends four radius values and four angular values to the device. The kernel computes the corresponding rectilinear coordinates.

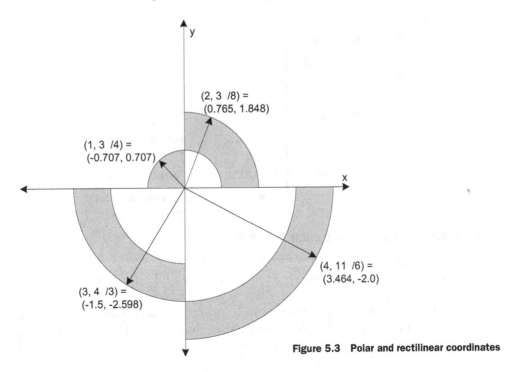

Figure 5.3 Polar and rectilinear coordinates

Listing 5.4   Rectilinear to polar coordinates: polar_rect.cl

```
__kernel void polar_rect(__global float4 *r_vals,
                         __global float4 *angles,
                         __global float4 *x_coords,
                         __global float4 *y_coords) {      Compute
                                                           coordinates
    *y_coords = sincos(*angles, x_coords);                 on unit circle
    *x_coords *= *r_vals;            Compute coordinates
    *y_coords *= *r_vals;           for different radii
}
```

The printed results are as follows:

```
( 0.765,  1.848)
(-0.707,  0.707)
(-1.500, -2.598)
( 3.464, -2.000)
```

The host application defines angular values using the M_PI constant defined in math.h. This header isn't supported in kernel coding, but the M_PI_F constant is. Table 5.8 lists all the floating-point constants provided by OpenCL.

Table 5.8   Floating-point constants

Constant	Content	Constant	Content
M_E_F	Value of e	M_1_PI_F	Value of $1/\pi$
M_LOG2E_F	Value of log2e	M_2_PI_F	Value of $2/\pi$
M_LOG10E_F	Value of log10e	M_2_SQRTPI_F	Value of 2/sqrt (π)
M_LN2_F	Value of loge2	M_SQRT2_F	Value of sqrt (2)
M_LN10_F	Value of loge10	M_SQRT1_2_F	Value of 1/sqrt (2)
M_PI_F	Value of π	MAXFLOAT	Maximum float value
M_PI_2_F	Value of $\pi/2$	HUGE_VALF	Positive floating-point infinity
M_PI_4_F	Value of $\pi/4$	INFINITY	Unsigned infinity
		NAN	Not-a-Number value

5.4.5   *Miscellaneous floating-point functions*

Table 5.9 presents the last set of floating-point functions we'll examine in this section. These can't be grouped into a simple category, so I'll refer to them as miscellaneous functions.

A number of these functions provide information about the float components in the input vector. An example will make their usages clear. If x equals –93.64, then the following functions can be called:

Table 5.9 Miscellaneous floating-point functions

Function	Purpose
`floatn copysign(floatn x, floatn y)`	Returns x with the sign of y
`intn ilogb(floatn x)`	Returns the integer part of $\log2 \|x\|$
`floatn fract(floatn x, __(g|l|p) floatn *mem)`	Returns `fmin(x - floor (x), 0x1.fffffep-1f )`, places `floor(x)` in mem
`floatn frexp(floatn x, __(g|l|p) intn *mem)`	Expresses x as the product of $2\exp$ and a value between 0.5 and 1; returns the value and places the exponent in mem
`floatn modf(floatn x, __(g|l|p) floatn *mem)`	Returns the fractional part, and places the integer part in mem; both keep the same sign as x
`floatn nan(uintn nancode)`	Returns a NaN with a given `nancode` that doesn't raise exceptions
`floatn nextafter(floatn x, floatn y)`	If y > x, returns the next floating-point value greater than x; if y < x, returns the next floating-point value less than x
`floatn sign(floatn x)`	Returns –1.0 if x < 0; returns 1.0 if x > 0; returns 0.0 if x is NaN; otherwise returns x

- `sign(x)` $= -1.0$
- `modf(x, mem)` returns –0.639999, stores –93 in mem
- `frexp(x, mem)` returns –0.731562, stores 7 in mem
- `ilogb(x)` $= 6$

The last two functions, `frexp` and `ilogb`, provide information about the input's binary representation. Because –93.64 equals –0.731562 * 2^7, the `frexp` function returns –0.731562 and stores 7 in memory. The binary logarithm of |–93.64| equals $\log_2 93.64 = 6.549$, so `ilogb` returns `trunc(6.549) = 6`.

Now that you've seen OpenCL's floating-point functions, let's switch gears and look at functions that operate on integers. The next section discusses them in detail.

5.5   *Integer functions*

Many fields, such as cryptography and bioinformatics, model data using integers. OpenCL provides a wide range of integer operations, and this section divides them into three categories: addition and subtraction, multiplication, and miscellaneous. In each case, the `integer` data type refers to all signed and unsigned integers: `uchar`, `char`, `ushort`, `short`, `uint`, `int`, `ulong`, and `long`. The `uinteger` type refers to only unsigned integers: `uchar`, `ushort`, `uint`, and `ulong`.

5.5.1 Adding and subtracting integers

OpenCL provides the + and - operators for addition and subtraction, but these may not be sufficient for all cases. Table 5.10 lists the OpenCL functions that add and subtract integers.

Table 5.10 Integer addition functions

Function	Purpose
integern add_sat(integern x, integern y)	Returns x + y with saturation
integern hadd(integern x, integern y)	Returns x + y, shifted right by 1 to prevent overflow
integern rhadd(integern x, integern y)	Returns x + y + 1, shifted right by 1 to prevent overflow
integern sub_sat(integern x, integern y)	Returns x - y, saturating the result

When performing integer arithmetic, the fundamental question is what to do when a result requires more memory than either of the operands. This condition is called *arithmetic overflow*. In the case of addition, overflow occurs when the sum of two integers exceeds the maximum value for the data type or falls below the minimum value. In subtraction, this occurs when the operands have different signs, and the subtraction produces a value that exceeds the maximum or falls below the minimum.

Some devices set a flag when an overflow condition occurs, but OpenCL doesn't require this. Regular addition and subtraction, performed by the + and - operators, simply ignore the possibility of overflow. If you add two positive signed numbers and the sum exceeds the maximum value for a positive number, overflow will cause the result to be negative.

But the add_sat and sub_sat functions saturate the result in the event of overflow. This sets the result to its maximum value. In the case of a 32-bit int, the maximum value is 0x7FFFFFFF.

To make this clear, let's look at some examples. Suppose x, y, and z are signed integers such that x = 1,968,526,677 (0x75555555), y = 1,914,839,586 (0x72222222), and z = −1,932,735,283 (−0x73333333). The correct value of x + y is 3,883,366,263 (0xE7777777) and the correct value of x - z is 3,901,261,960 (0xE8888888). But the results produced by OpenCL's operators and functions are quite different:

- x + y = −411,601,033 (0xE7777777 in two's complement)
- add_sat(x, y) = 2,147,483,647 (0x7FFFFFFF)
- x - z = −393,705,336 (0xE8888888 in two's complement)
- sub_sat(x, z) = 2,147,483,647 (0x7FFFFFFF)

The functions hadd and rhadd take a different approach to dealing with overflow. Instead of saturating the result, they shift the result right by one bit and place the carry bit in the most significant position. This produces a result that's close to the correct value, but divided by two. The difference between hadd and rhadd is that rhadd adds 1 before right-shifting the sum.

Let's return to our previous example. If x equals 1,968,526,677 (0x75555555) and y equals 1,914,839,586 (0x72222222), then calling hadd and rhadd produces the following results:

- hadd(x, y) = 1,941,683,131 (0x73BBBBBB)
- rhadd(x, y) = 1,941,683,132 (0x73BBBBBC)

Dividing the correct sum by 2 produces 1,941,683,131.5, which lies exactly between the values returned by hadd and rhadd. These two functions will help if saturation is a concern, but remember that the actual sum is twice the result.

5.5.2 Multiplication

Like addition and subtraction, integer multiplication can produce a result that requires more memory than either operand. In the worst case, the product may need twice as much memory to store. The functions in table 5.11 take this into account.

Table 5.11 Integer multiplication functions

Function	Purpose
integern mad_hi(integern a, integern b, integern c)	Returns mul_hi(a, b) + c
integern mad_sat(integern a, integern b, integern c)	Returns a * b + c, saturating the result
u/intn mad24(u/intn a, u/intn b, u/intn c)	Returns mul24(a, b) + c
integern mul_hi(integern x, integern y)	Multiplies x and y and returns the upper half of the product
u/intn mul24(u/intn x, u/intn y)	Multiplies the low 24 bits of x and y

To obtain a full product, you need to combine the results of the mul_hi function in table 5.11 and the * operator in table 5.1. mul_hi returns the upper half of the product and * returns the lower half. Let's look at an example. If x equals 0x71111111 and y equals 0x72222222, their correct product is given by 0x3268ACF11ECA8642. You can compute this exact value in OpenCL by making the following function calls:

- mul_hi(x,y) = 0x3268ACF1
- x * y = 0x1ECA8642

The `mul24` function is useful when speed is a priority and precision isn't. This only operates on `int`s and `uint`s, and only on the low 24 bits of the operands. Therefore, if x and y are `int`s, their values should lie between -2^{23} and $2^{23} - 1$. If x and y are unsigned, their values should lie between 0 and $2^{24} - 1$.

Like the `*` operator, `mul24` returns only the lower 32 bits of the product. The difference is that it computes the result faster because it only takes the lower 24 bits into account. For example, suppose x and y are `int`s such that x equals 0x00711111 and y equals 0x00722222. Their full product is 0x3268ACDA8642, which requires 46 bits to store. The returned value of `mul24(x,y)` will be 0xACDA8642.

The first three functions in table 5.11 perform multiplication and addition. Each performs the multiplication in a different manner. `mad_sat` relies on the `*` operator and saturates the result, setting it to the maximum value in the event of overflow. `mad_hi` computes the upper half of the result using `mul_hi` to multiply the first two inputs. Then it adds the third input without saturation. `mad24` is similar to `mad_hi`, but it computes the lower half of the result using `mul24`.

The code in the following listing shows how to combine `mad_hi` and `mad24` to multiply and add large numbers. `mad_hi` computes the upper half of the result and `mad24` computes the lower half.

> **Listing 5.5   Multiply-and-add large numbers: mad_test.cl**

```
__kernel void mad_test(__global uint *result) {

    uint a = 0x123456;
    uint b = 0x112233;
    uint c = 0x111111;

    result[0] = mad24(a, b, c);
    result[1] = mad_hi(a, b, c);
}
```

The imprecision of `mad24` keeps the result from matching perfectly (0x111248E85AEA33 versus 0x111248E849D922), but you can't replace `mad24` with `mad_sat` in this code. Why? Because `mad_sat` doesn't understand upper halves and lower halves. It assumes that it's performing the entire operation, and if the result is larger than the maximum storable value, it saturates the result.

5.5.3 *Miscellaneous integer functions*

The functions in table 5.12 closely resemble those we've looked at in previous sections, but they only operate on integer values. They don't fit suitably in any single group, so we'll refer to them as miscellaneous integer functions.

It's important to see the difference between the `rotate` function and the left-shift operator, `<<`. Both shift the input bits to the left, but as each bit is shifted, the `<<` operator places a 0 in the rightmost position whereas `rotate` places the shifted bit in the rightmost position. But if the input value is unsigned, `rotate` places a 0 in the rightmost position.

Table 5.12 Miscellaneous integer functions

Function	Purpose
`uintegern abs(integern x)`	Returns the absolute value of x, |x|
`uintegern abs_diff(integern x, integern y)`	Returns the absolute value of x – y, |x – y|
`integern clamp(integern x, integer/n min, integer/n max)`	Returns min if x < min; returns max if x > max; otherwise returns x
`integern max(integern x, integern y)`	Returns x if x >= y; otherwise returns y
`integern min(integern x, integern y)`	Returns y if x > y; otherwise returns x
`integern rotate(integern x, integern y)`	Components of x are shifted left by the components of y; returns the shifted bits on the right
`u/shortn upsample(u/charn high, ucharn low)`	Forms a u/short by concatenating the components of high and low
`u/intn upsample(u/shortn high, ushortn low)`	Forms a u/int by concatenating the components of high and low
`u/longn upsample(u/intn high, uintn low)`	Forms a u/long by concatenating the components of high and low

Two examples will make this clear. If x is a uchar with a value of 252 (11111100), rotate(x,3) will return 224 (11100000). This is the same result as x << 3. But if x is a signed char equal to –4 (11111100), rotate(x,3) returns –25 (11100111), whereas x << 3 equals –32 (11100000).

The upsample function concatenates its input arguments to produce a value whose data type is twice that of either input. If the first input is signed, the result will be signed. The second input must always be unsigned. This is shown in the following examples:

- If x is a char that equals 0x95 and y is a uchar equal to 0x31, upsample(x, y) will return a short that equals 0x9531.
- If x is a ushort that equals 0x7654 and y is a ushort that equals 0x3210, upsample(x, y) will return an uint that equals 0x76543210.
- If x is a uint that equals 0x79ABCDEF and y is a uint that equals 0x12345678, upsample(x, y) will return a ulong that equals –0x79ABCDEF12345678 if 64-bit values are supported.

The upsample function isn't the only way to create vectors from the content of other vectors. Using a mask vector, you can use the shuffle and select functions to choose which input bits or input components should be placed in the output. The next section discusses these functions in detail.

5.6   Shuffle and select functions

Chapter 4 presented different ways of accessing and modifying a vector's components. With suffixes like .s*N*, .x, .y, .hi, and .lo, you can easily assign the components of one vector equal to the components of other vectors. But you can make similar assignments using values inside a vector called a *mask vector*. For this purpose, OpenCL provides shuffle and select functions. The two shuffle functions rely on index values inside the mask vector to create the output, and the two select functions rely on bits inside the mask vector.

5.6.1   Shuffle functions

OpenCL's shuffle functions accept one or two input vectors and create an output vector that contains the components of the inputs. Table 5.13 lists the signatures of both shuffle functions.

NOTE   These functions are new in OpenCL 1.1 and won't compile on systems that don't support this standard.

Table 5.13   Shuffle functions

Function	Purpose
`allm shuffle(alln x, uintegerm mask);`	Creates a vector containing the components of x in the order prescribed by `mask`
`allm shuffle2(alln x, alln y,` `    uintegerm mask);`	Creates a vector containing the components of x and y in the order prescribed by `mask`

The shuffle function creates a vector whose components are taken from those in the input x vector. shuffle2 creates a vector from components in x and y. The last argument of both functions is the mask vector. This vector determines which input components are placed in the output and the order in which they're placed.

The size of the components of the mask vector must be the same size as those of the returned vector. But the data type of the mask components must be an unsigned integer type (uchar, ushort, uint, or ulong). The returned vector will contain the same number of components as the mask vector, but the data type of the returned components will be the same as that of the components of the input vector or vectors.

To make matters more confusing, only a select number of bits in the mask vector's components are important. The k least significant bits (LSBs) in each mask component select which input component is placed in the corresponding position in the returned vector. The value of k depends on the number of components in the input vector. If the input vector has n components, then $k = \log_2 n$ for the shuffle function, and $n = 2^k$. For shuffle2, $k = \log_2 2n$, and $n = 2^{k-1}$.

An example will help make this clear. Suppose you want to use shuffle to create a float8 vector from components of a float4. There are eight components in the returned vector, so the mask must contain eight components. Each component in the

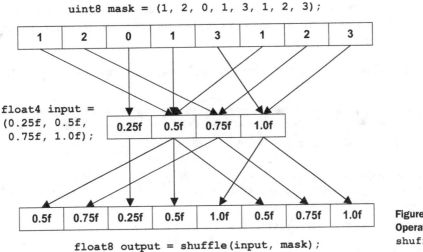

Figure 5.4
Operation of the
shuffle **function**

output is 32 bits wide, so each element of the mask vector must be 32 bits. Therefore, the mask vector must be a uint8.

Because there are four components in the input vector, only the 2 LSBs ($\log_2 4 = 2$) in each of the mask's components are important. Each LSB pair selects one of the four input components and places it in the corresponding position in the returned vector. Figure 5.4 presents this operation graphically.

shuffle2 is similar to shuffle, but instead of accepting only one input, it accepts two. For example, suppose you want to select characters from two input char8 vectors and place them in a char16. In this case, the mask must contain 16 components and each mask component must be 1 byte. Therefore, the mask vector must be a uchar16.

In each component, the 4 LSBs ($\log_2 16 = 4$) determine which input chars are placed in the output and where they're placed. Figure 5.5 shows this operation graphically.

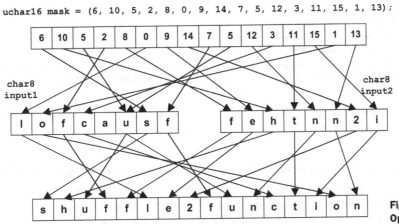

Figure 5.5
Operation of the
shuffle2 **function**

The code in the next listing shows how shuffle and shuffle2 are used in a kernel. The host application creates write-only buffers for the shuffled data, reads them from the device, and prints out the results.

NOTE This code only compiles on platforms that support the OpenCL 1.1 standard.

Listing 5.6 Shuffling vector components: shuffle_test.cl

```
__kernel void shuffle_test(__global float8 *s1,
                           __global char16 *s2) {
    uint8 mask1 = (uint8)(1, 2, 0, 1, 3, 1, 2, 3);
    float4 input = (float4)(0.25f, 0.5f, 0.75f, 1.0f);          shuffle
    *s1 = shuffle(input, mask1);                                usage

    uchar16 mask2 = (uchar16)(6, 10, 5, 2, 8, 0, 9, 14,
                              7, 5, 12, 3, 11, 15, 1, 13);
    char8 input1 = (char8)('l', 'o', 'f', 'c', 'a', 'u', 's', 'f');
    char8 input2 = (char8)('f', 'e', 'h', 't', 'n', 'n', '2', 'i');   shuffle2
    *s2 = shuffle2(input1, input2, mask2);                            usage
}
```

When you need to create vectors from components of other vectors, shuffle and shuffle2 are the best functions to use. It takes practice to construct the mask vectors, but once you see how the mask bits are used to select components, using the functions becomes simple.

5.6.2 Select functions

The two functions in table 5.14, bitselect and select, are similar to shuffle2. They both create an output vector from the contents of two input vectors. The difference is that select and bitselect rely on individual bits inside the mask vector instead of component indices. This means you don't have to worry about how many LSBs should be in each mask component.

Table 5.14 Select functions

Function	Purpose
alln bitselect(alln a, alln b, u/integern mask)	Selects bits from a and b according to the bits in mask
alln select(alln a, alln b, u/integern mask)	Selects components from a and b according to the most-significant bits in mask

Unlike the mask vectors in shuffle and shuffle2, the mask vectors in bitselect and select can contain signed or unsigned integer values. In the case of select, only the most significant bit in each vector matters. If the MSB of one mask component is 0, the corresponding component of the output vector will be set equal to the component in

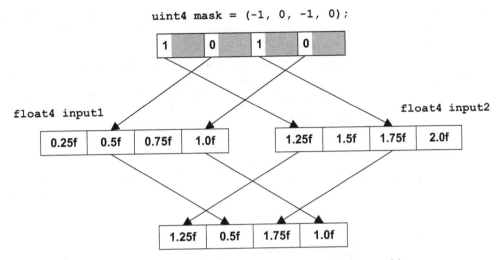

Figure 5.6 Operation of the select function

the first input vector. If the MSB equals 1, the output component will be taken from the second input vector.

Figure 5.6 depicts an example of how select is used. In this case, the MSBs of the mask vector select floats from input vectors. Notice that the mask must have the same number of elements as the inputs. Also, because the first and third mask values are set to –1, the corresponding representation contains all ones: 0xFFFFFFFF.

With bitselect, every bit of the mask vector plays a part. If the mask bit equals 0, the corresponding bit of the first input is placed in the output. If the bit equals 1, the corresponding bit of the second input is placed in the output. Figure 5.7 shows an example of how bitselect is used.

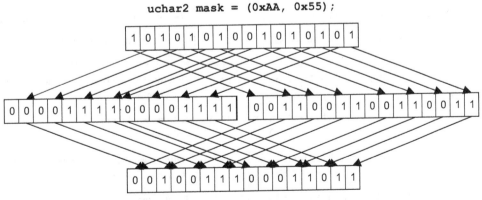

Figure 5.7 Operation of the bitselect function

In this case, the distinction between components in the mask isn't important. All that matters is the order of bits. This is similarly true for the bits in the output vector.

The code in the following listing demonstrates the usage of select and bitselect. This code performs the operations depicted in figures 5.6 and 5.7.

Listing 5.7   Selecting component content: select_test.cl

```
__kernel void select_test(__global float4 *s1,
                          __global uchar2 *s2) {

   int4 mask1 = (int4)(-1, 0, -1, 0);
   float4 input1 = (float4)(0.25f, 0.5f, 0.75f, 1.0f);
   float4 input2 = (float4)(1.25f, 1.5f, 1.75f, 2.0f);       select
   *s1 = select(input1, input2, mask1);                      usage

   uchar2 mask2 = (uchar2)(0xAA, 0x55);
   uchar2 input3 = (uchar2)(0x0F, 0x0F);
   uchar2 input4 = (uchar2)(0x33, 0x33);                     bitselect
   *s2 = bitselect(input3, input4, mask2);                   usage
}
```

Mask vectors for select and bitselect can be created easily using the vector relational operators, such as <, >, and ==. You can also use OpenCL's vector test functions, described in the next section.

5.7   *Vector test functions*

The functions in table 5.15 analyze the content of vectors and return information about their components. Some functions are specific to floats and others analyze integer data types. One function, vec_step, can be used with vectors of all data types.

Table 5.15   Vector test and comparison functions

Function	Purpose
int any(integern x)	Returns 1 if the MSB of any component is set
int all(integern x)	Returns 1 if the MSB of all components are set
integern clz(integern x)	Returns the number of leading 0's in each component of x
intn isequal(floatn x, floatn y)	Returns whether each component of x equals each component of y
intn isnotequal(floatn x, floatn y)	Returns whether each component of x doesn't equal each component of y
intn isgreater(floatn x, floatn y)	Returns whether each component of x is greater than each component of y
intn isgreaterequal(floatn x, floatn y)	Returns whether each component of x is greater than or equal to each component of y

Table 5.15 Vector test and comparison functions *(continued)*

Function	Purpose
`intn isless(floatn x, floatn y)`	Returns whether each component of x is less than each component of y
`intn islessequal(floatn x, floatn y)`	Returns whether each component of x is less than or equal to each component of y
`intn islessgreater(floatn x, floatn y)`	Returns whether each component of x is less than or greater than each component of y
`intn isfinite(floatn x)`	Returns whether each component of x is finite
`intn isinf(floatn x)`	Returns whether each component of x is infinite
`intn isnan(floatn x)`	Returns whether each component of x is NaN
`intn isnormal(floatn x)`	Returns whether each component of x is normal (not 0, denormalized, infinite, or NaN)
`intn isordered(floatn x, floatn y)`	Returns whether the components of x and y are ordered
`intn isunordered(floatn x, floatn y)`	Returns whether the components of x and y are unordered
`intn signbit(floatn x)`	If sign bit is set, returns 1 for scalars and –1 for vectors; otherwise 0
`int vec_step(alln)`	Returns the number of elements in a vector; returns 4 if there are 3 elements

Section 5.1 briefly mentioned the any and all functions, which can be used to determine if any or all of a vector's components have nonzero MSBs. Similarly, clz tells you how many leading zeroes are in each component of the input. This can be helpful when you need to gauge the sign and approximate magnitude of a vector's components.

If you write your code to support vectors of different lengths, you'll find vec_step useful. This identifies the number of components in a vector. But if a vector contains 3 components, vec_step will return 4.

Most of the functions in the table analyze floats and vectors containing floats. These are easy to understand, and they're similar to their counterparts in the math.h header. The following examples show how they're used:

- `isgreater(5.5f, 4.5f)` returns 1
- `islessequal(2.3f, -2.3f)` returns 0
- `isnan(nan(0))` returns 1
- `signbit(-10.0)` returns 1
- `isnormal((float3)(rsqrt(2.0), rsqrt(2.0), 0.0))` returns $(-1, -1, 0)$

The last function, isnormal, identifies whether each component of the input vector is normal (not 0, denormalized, infinite, or NaN). Note that, for vectors, the comparison operations represent truth with –1 instead of 1. Because the two's complement of –1 is all ones, this makes the result ideal for vector bitmasks.

When it comes to vectors and the isnormal function, I tend to get confused. I always assume the function will return true if the vector is perpendicular to a surface. But this is the *geometric* sense of the word normal, not the mathematical sense. The next section will explain the geometrical sense of the word normal and other concepts related to OpenCL's geometric functions.

5.8   *Geometric functions*

In physics, engineering, and graphics, the term *vector* takes on a different meaning than a simple collection of scalars. It identifies an entity with a magnitude (length) and a direction. The functions in table 5.16 perform operations related to vectors used in this sense.

Table 5.16   Geometric functions

Function	Purpose
float3 cross(float3 x, float3 y) float4 cross(float4 x, float4 y)	Returns the cross product of x and y
float dot(floatn x, floatn y)	Returns the dot-product of x and y
float distance(floatn x, floatn y)	Returns the Euclidean distance between x and y
float hypot(floatn x, floatn y)	Returns the square root of $x^2 + y^2$
float length(floatn x)	Returns the length of x
floatn normalize(floatn x)	Returns x with a length of 1
float fast_distance(floatn x, floatn y)	Computes fast_length(x - y)
float fast_length(floatn x)	Returns the length of C using half_sqrt
floatn fast_normalize(floatn x)	Returns x with a length of 1 using half_rsqrt

The components of a geometrical vector represent dimensions. In a Euclidean space, coordinates are specified by (x, y, z), and a vector's components identify its length in the x, y, and z directions. The total length can be obtained using the Pythagorean Theorem. That is, the square of the length equals the sum of the squares of its components. If d is a two-dimensional vector, its length is denoted by $|d|$, which can be computed through the following equation: $|d|^2 = (d.x)^2 + (d.y)^2$. For vectors in three dimensions, $|d|^2 = (d.x)^2 + (d.y)^2 + (d.z)^2$. This is shown in figure 5.8.

The `length` function in table 5.16 computes the length of a vector containing *x*, *y*, and *z* components. The `normalize` function returns a vector that points in the same direction as the input vector, but changes its components so that the length equals 1. The following code shows how `length` and `normalize` work:

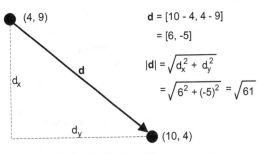

Figure 5.8   Vectors and length

```
float3 vec = (float3)(6, -5, 0);
float vec_length = length(vec);

float3 norm = normalize(vec);
float norm_length = length(norm);
```

As depicted in figure 5.8, the first `length` function will return the square root of 61. The `norm` vector will have the same direction as `vec`, but the `normalize` function will set its length equal to 1. Therefore, the second `length` function will return 1.

The dot product of two vectors returns a scalar that tells you about how closely the vectors' directions resemble one another. If the dot product is positive, they point in similar directions. If the product is 0, the two vectors are perpendicular, and if the product is negative, they point in approximately opposite directions.

The dot product is computed by multiplying the corresponding components of both vectors and adding the products. For example, if vector *p* has components (*p.x*, *p.y*, *p.z*) and vector *q* has components (*q.x*, *q.y*, *q.z*), then the dot product of the two vectors is as follows:

$$p \bullet q = (p.x * q.x) + (p.y * q.y) + (p.z * q.z)$$

The `dot` function computes the dot product, and not just in three dimensions. It computes the product of every component pair in the two input vectors and returns the sum of the products.

The cross product differs from the dot product in a number of ways. Instead of returning a scalar, it returns a vector. The computation is more involved, and if *r* equals the cross-product of *p* and *q* (denoted $r = p \times q$), then the components of *r* are computed as follows:

- $r.x = p.y * q.z - p.z * q.y$
- $r.y = p.z * q.x - p.x * q.z$
- $r.z = p.x * q.y - p.y * q.x$

The vector computed by a cross product has a direction perpendicular to the plane containing the two input vectors. We say that this vector is *normal* to the plane, and we call the vector a *normal vector*. In graphics, normal vectors are important because they're needed to calculate how light reflects from a surface.

The cross function computes the cross product of two vectors, whose data types must be both float3 or both float4. If the input vectors are both float4s, the fourth component of the result will be 0.0. The following code shows how this works:

```
float3 p = (float3)(3.5, 8.2, 2.4);
float3 q = (float3)(2.9, 5.5, 6.8);
float3 r = cross(p, q);
```

The components of the result equal (−42.56, −16.84, −4.53). If you compute the dot product of this vector with either of the input vectors, the result will be 0. This is because the direction of the resulting vector is perpendicular to that of both input vectors.

5.9   Summary

A major strength of OpenCL is that its operators and functions closely resemble those of traditional C and C++. OpenCL's arithmetic and logical operators are the same, the math functions generally have the same names, and pointers are referenced and dereferenced in the same way.

One significant difference, however, is that OpenCL's operators and functions accept both scalars and vectors. By calling functions that operate on vectors, you can dramatically reduce the amount of time needed to process data. This chapter has explained a large number of these functions and has provided examples of their use.

Number-crunching is the ultimate goal, but the most important OpenCL functions aren't math-based. Instead, they access information related to work-items and work-groups. These are usually the first functions called in a kernel function because they obtain the work-item's global and local IDs. The global ID distinguishes the work-item from all other work-items executing the kernel. The local ID distinguishes the work-item from all others in the same work-group.

A large portion of this chapter has dealt with floating-point and integer functions. These generally have the same names and roles as the functions defined in math.h. But when adding and multiplying integers, traditional operators won't be sufficient. OpenCL doesn't require carry flags or overflow flags, so it's vital to understand details like which functions saturate the result in the event of overflow. And if you want to obtain a full product of two integers, be sure to combine the results of mul_hi and the * operator.

Three sections of this chapter have discussed vector-specific functions: those that load and store vector data, those that shuffle and select vector contents, and those that test vector components. These may seem difficult if you're used to scalar processing. However, the more you code, the more you'll appreciate their advantages when it comes to high-performance computing.

This chapter has discussed the basics of OpenCL number-crunching. The next chapter applies these functions to process images, which OpenCL represents with image objects.

Image processing

This chapter covers

- Understanding the data types used in OpenCL image processing
- Invoking functions that read, write, and access image data
- Interpolating between pixel colors using samplers

Memory objects package data sent between a host and a device, and as discussed in chapter 3, they come in two types: buffer objects and image objects. Buffer objects transfer general-purpose data, and so far, all of the example code in this book has relied exclusively on buffer objects.

Now we're going to switch gears and focus on image objects. In theory, you could store an image's data in a buffer object and access its pixels as regular buffer data. But there are four important reasons to use image objects instead:

- On GPUs, image data is stored in special global memory called *texture memory*. Unlike regular global memory, texture memory is cached for rapid access.
- The functions used to read and write image data can be invoked without regard to how the pixel data is formatted, so long as the format is supported by OpenCL.

- Special data structures called *samplers* make it possible to configure how color information is read from an image.
- OpenCL provides functions that return image-specific information, such as an image's dimensions, pixel format, and bit depth.

This chapter will discuss these characteristics, and a large part of the discussion will be centered on image-related functions. These functions will be presented in detail and then combined in an example application that scales image data. But before you can call these functions, you need a solid grasp of the data structures used in OpenCL image processing.

> **NOTE** Some OpenCL-compliant devices don't support image processing. To check for image support from the host, call `clGetDeviceInfo` with the `CL_DEVICE_IMAGE_SUPPORT` option. If the result is `CL_FALSE`, the device doesn't support images. On the kernel, the `__IMAGE_SUPPORT__` macro will be set to 1 if images are supported. If not, the macro will be undefined.

6.1 Image objects and samplers

When it comes to processing images in OpenCL, the two primary data structures are image objects and samplers. Image objects serve as the storage mechanism that host applications use to transfer pixel data to and from a device. When the device receives the image data, samplers tell it how to read color values.

To keep things interesting, OpenCL gives different names to these structures depending on whether they're on the host or the device. On the host, image objects are represented by `cl_mem` structures, and samplers are represented by `cl_sampler` structures. On the device, image objects are `image2d_t` or `image3d_t` structures, and samplers are `sampler_t` structures. This section discusses each of these data types and how they're processed on the host and device.

6.1.1 Image objects on the host: cl_mem

All memory objects are represented by the `cl_mem` data type, and there are no separate types to distinguish buffer objects from image objects. Instead, to create a buffer object, you can call `clCreateBuffer` or `clCreateSubBuffer`. To create an image object, you can call `clCreateImage2d` or `clCreateImage3d`. Chapter 3 discussed the parameters of these two functions, but to review, their signatures are as follows:

```
clCreateImage2D (cl_context context, cl_mem_flags opts,
    const cl_image_format *format, size_t width, size_t height,
    size_t row_pitch, void *data, cl_int *error)

clCreateImage3D (cl_context context, cl_mem_flags opts,
    const cl_image_format *format, size_t width, size_t height,
    size_t depth, size_t row_pitch, size_t slice_pitch,
    void *data, cl_int *error)
```

NOTE Chapter 3 explains the parameters of these functions in detail. Table 3.1 lists the different values available for the `cl_mem_flags` parameter and table 3.2 lists the values available for the `cl_channel_type` parameter. Figure 3.2 depicts how the geometric parameters (`width`, `height`, and `depth`) relate to the image's shape.

As an example, the following code creates a `cl_image_format` structure and uses it to create a two-dimensional image object. Each pixel in the image contains 32 bits: eight bits for the red, blue, green, and alpha channels each:

```
cl_image_format format;
format.image_channel_order = CL_RGBA;
format.image_channel_data_type = CL_UNSIGNED_INT8;

image = clCreateImage2D(context, CL_MEM_READ_ONLY | CL_MEM_USE_HOST_PTR,
        &format, width, height, 0, (void*)data, &err);
```

Once an image object is created, it can be sent to a device as an argument of the kernel function. This works just as it does for buffer objects. If you call `clSetKernelArg` with the `cl_mem` object, the kernel function will be able to access the image as a regular argument. For example, the following code makes the preceding image object an argument of the `image_knl` kernel:

```
clSetKernelArg(image_knl, 0, sizeof(cl_mem), &image);
```

When the image object is no longer needed, its memory can be deallocated with the `clReleaseMemObject` function. In this example, the image memory can be freed by calling `clReleaseMemObject(image)`.

6.1.2 Samplers on the host: cl_sampler

Before a kernel can read image data, it needs certain pieces of information, such as how the coordinates are formatted and how to interpret coordinates that go beyond the image's size. It also needs to know how to interpolate colors between pixel values. All of this information is stored in a data structure called a *sampler.*

Samplers can be created by the host application or within the kernel. Host applications create `cl_sampler` objects by calling `clCreateSampler`, whose signature is as follows:

```
cl_sampler clCreateSampler(cl_context context, cl_bool normalized_coords,
    cl_addressing_mode addressing_mode, cl_filter_mode filter_mode,
    cl_int *errcode_ret)
```

The first and last parameters are straightforward, but the parameters in between are completely new:

- `normalized_coords`—Identifies whether coordinates are normalized (given from 0.0–1.0)
- `addressing_mode`—Identifies how the kernel should process coordinates beyond the maximum value
- `filter_mode`—Identifies how the kernel interpolates color values between pixels

These parameters are important to understand. If you configure a sampler with the wrong properties, the kernel will read the wrong colors from the image.

NORMALIZED COORDINATES AND NORMALIZED COLORS

In general, kernels process images by reading color values from an image object, operating on the color values, and writing the color values to a second image object. A kernel reads a color value at a given point by defining coordinates, and it can provide these coordinates in one of three ways:

- Integer—Coordinates are given in a vector of integers from 0 to MAX_DIM in each dimension. If an image has dimensions 121 by 81, the color value at the center can be accessed with coordinates (60, 40).
- Floating-point—Coordinates are given in a vector of floats from 0.0 to MAX_DIM in each dimension. If an image has dimensions 121 by 81, the color value at the center can be accessed with coordinates (60.0, 40.0).
- Normalized floating-point—Coordinates are given in a vector of floats from 0.0 to 1.0 in each dimension. If an image has dimensions 121 by 81, the color value at the center can be accessed with coordinates (0.5, 0.5).

Normalized coordinates aren't a concern when coordinates are given as integers, but they become useful when you want to process an image with unknown dimensions. This situation arises frequently when you work with OpenGL textures, which are discussed in chapter 16. To specify that coordinates should be read in normalized form, set the second parameter of clCreateSampler to CL_TRUE. Otherwise, set this parameter to CL_FALSE.

It's crucial to know the difference between normalized coordinates and normalized colors. Color normalization removes the color's intensity level by dividing each component by the sum of the components. Intensity is the technical term for a color's *brightness*—color normalization makes colors equally vivid. If a pixel's components are given by (R, G, B), the normalized components are computed as follows:

$$R' = \frac{R}{R + G + B}$$

$$G' = \frac{G}{R + G + B}$$

$$B' = \frac{B}{R + G + B}$$

After these floating-point values are computed, the results are scaled to occupy the pixel's full integer range. For example, if a pixel contains 8-bit RGB components, each normalized result is scaled to an integer value between 0 and 255.

ADDRESSING MODE

The third parameter of clCreateSampler has type cl_addressing_mode. This tells the kernel how to read color values at coordinates beyond the image's size. For example, if an image's size is 60 by 80, its pixel coordinates run from (0, 0) to (59, 79). If the kernel asks for color values at (150, 200) or (–5, –10), the addressing mode will determine what color should be returned. If the addressing mode holds these color values to those on the image's border or a default border color, we say that it *clamps* the output color.

The five possible values for cl_addressing_mode are as follows:

- CL_ADDRESS_NONE—Color values beyond the image's maximum dimensions are undefined.
- CL_ADDRESS_CLAMP—Colors beyond the maximum dimensions are set to a specific border color, which is black by default
- CL_ADDRESS_CLAMP_TO_EDGE—Colors beyond the maximum dimensions are set equal to the pixels at the edge of the image
- CL_ADDRESS_REPEAT—In-range coordinates are repeated, so if one of the maximum dimensions is N, an out-of-range coordinate X is set equal to $X \bmod N$ (only available with normalized coordinates)
- CL_ADDRESS_MIRRORED_REPEAT—Out-of-range coordinates are set equal to the reflections of their corresponding in-range values (only available with normalized coordinates)

The images in figure 6.1 demonstrate what happens when a kernel reads pixels at coordinates beyond the image's range. In each case, the coordinates run from below the minimum and above the maximum.

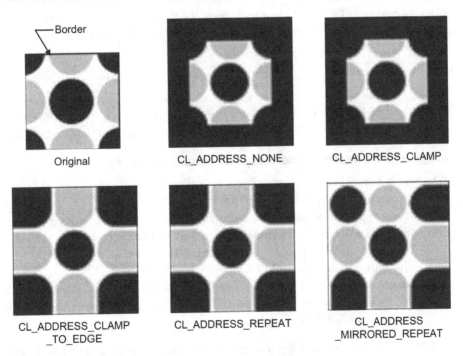

Figure 6.1 Output images with different addressing modes

INTERPOLATION AND FILTER MODE

If you specify coordinates with integers, you'll always get the color value that corresponds to the given pixel. But if coordinates are given as floating-point values, the result will be an *interpolated* value. Interpolation is the process of computing an unknown data point between known data points, and it's crucial when images need to be enlarged or shrunk. For example, if the user zooms in on an image, the renderer will need to display pixels between those of the original image.

OpenCL supports two methods of image interpolation: nearest-neighbor interpolation and bilinear interpolation. The purpose of the `filter_mode` parameter of `clCreateSampler` is to specify which interpolation method should be used. If `filter_mode` is set to `CL_FILTER_NEAREST`, the sampler will compute in-between color values using nearest-neighbor interpolation. If the parameter is set to `CL_FILTER_LINEAR`, the sampler will use bilinear interpolation for 2D images and trilinear interpolation for 3D images. Section 6.3 discusses the nearest-neighbor interpolation and bilinear interpolation methods.

The following code creates a `cl_sampler` whose coordinates are given in normalized form. It clamps out-of-range coordinates to those at the image's border and computes in-between pixels using bilinear interpolation:

```
cl_sampler clCreateSampler(ctx, CL_TRUE, CL_ADDRESS_CLAMP_TO_EDGE,
    CL_FILTER_LINEAR);
```

After the host creates a sampler, the sampler can be made a kernel argument using `clSetKernelArg`. This works just as it does for memory objects, except the last argument is a pointer to a `cl_sampler` instead of a `cl_mem`. The following code shows how this works:

```
clSetKernelArg(kernel, 0, sizeof(cl_sampler), &ex_sampler);
```

The `clReleaseSampler` function, like all `clReleaseXX` functions, reduces the reference count of a sampler object. When the reference count goes to 0, the structure is deallocated. The function `clRetainSampler` increases the count of a `cl_sampler`.

6.1.3   *Image objects on the device: image2d_t and image3d_t*

When a host transfers an image object to a device, the device's kernel function will access the image object as one of its parameters. The parameter's data type depends on the image's dimensionality. A two-dimensional image object will be received as an `image2d_t` and a three-dimensional image object will be received as an `image3d_t`.

Buffer object parameters can take `__global` or `__kernel` modifiers that designate where the buffer's object should be stored on the device. But because many devices store images in dedicated memory, `image2d_t` and `image3d_t` parameters are preceded by `__read_only` or `__write_only`. That is, an image object can read from or written to, but not both.

NOTE The default modifier for image objects is `__read_only`. The leading underscores can be omitted.

An example will help clarify how kernels access images. Suppose you want a kernel to read from a three-dimensional image called my_mpeg and write to a two-dimensional image called my_jpg. After creating the two cl_mem structures with clCreateImage3D and clCreateImage2D, your host application might use the following code to make them into kernel arguments:

```
clSetKernelArg(kernel, 0, sizeof(cl_mem), &my_mpeg);
clSetKernelArg(kernel, 1, sizeof(cl_mem), &my_jpg);
```

Let's say the name of the function is image_proc and its only arguments are the image objects and the sampler. The kernel declaration could be given as follows:

```
__kernel void image_proc(read_only image3d_t empg,
                         write_only image2d_t ejpg)
```

Note that these arguments aren't pointers. Unlike data in a buffer object, image data isn't meant to be accessed directly using memory operations. Instead, OpenCL provides a range of functions that read and write image data, and we'll discuss these shortly.

6.1.4 *Samplers on the device: sampler_t*

As discussed earlier, host applications can transfer cl_sampler structures to the kernel by calling setKernelArg. The kernel receives these arguments as sampler_t structures, and unlike image objects, you can place them in global or constant memory using the __global or __constant modifier.

For example, if the host transfers a sampler argument to a kernel called image_proc as its only parameter, the kernel declaration can be coded as follows:

```
__kernel void image_proc(__global sampler_t smplr)
```

Thankfully, OpenCL provides an easier way to work with samplers. With a single statement in the kernel, you can create a sampler_t structure and set its properties. This makes it unnecessary to call clSetKernelArg. This statement takes the following form:

```
const sampler_t sampler_name = sampler_properties
```

The sampler_properties expression configures the properties of the sampler, which tell the kernel how to read data from an image object. The names of these properties are similar to the parameters of clCreateSampler. On the kernel, sampler properties are specified with the following values:

- CLK_NORMALIZED_COORDS_TRUE or CLK_NORMALIZED_COORDS_FALSE—Specifies whether image coordinates are normalized (0.0–1.0). By default, coordinates are assumed to be normalized.
- CLK_ADDRESS_CLAMP, CLK_ADDRESS_CLAMP_TO_EDGE, CLK_ADDRESS_REPEAT, CLK_ADDRESS_MIRRORED_REPEAT, or CLK_ADDRESS_NONE—Defines what color values are returned when coordinates exceed the image boundaries.
- CLK_FILTER_NEAREST or CLK_FILTER_LINEAR—Identifies how color values are interpolated between pixels.

As an example, the `sampler_t` defined in the following statement tells the kernel that coordinates are normalized, coordinates outside the boundaries should be clamped to the boundary values, and the color at a point should be set to that of the nearest pixel:

```
__constant sampler_t sampler = CLK_NORMALIZED_COORDS_TRUE |
                               CLK_ADDRESS_CLAMP_TO_EDGE |
                               CLK_FILTER_NEAREST;
```

Once you've created a sampler, you can use it in one of OpenCL's many functions for reading image data. The next section discusses these and other image-related functions.

6.2   Image processing functions

Once you understand the basics of image objects and samplers, you're ready to invoke the functions that access them in code. OpenCL provides a number of image processing functions that can be run inside kernels, and they fall into three categories:

- *Read functions*—Return color values at a given coordinate
- *Write functions*—Set color values at a given coordinate
- *Information functions*—Provide data about the image object, such as its dimensions and pixel properties

This section discusses the functions in each of these categories. Afterward, we'll examine an example application that reads pixels from one image, modifies their values, and writes the modified values to a second image.

6.2.1   Image read functions

The functions in table 6.1 read vectors from image objects, and they all have essentially the same parameters. The differences between them involve whether the returned vector contains floating-point values or integers, and whether the image object is two-dimensional or three-dimensional.

Table 6.1   Kernel functions for reading image data

Function	Purpose
`float4 read_imagef(image2d_t img, sampler_t sampler, int2/float2 coord)`	Reads a `float4` vector from a 2D image at the location given by `coord`
`int4 read_imagei(image2d_t img, sampler_t sampler, int2/float2 coord)`	Reads an `int4` vector from a 2D image at the location given by `coord`
`uint4 read_imageui(image2d_t img, sampler_t sampler, int2/float2 coord)`	Reads a `uint4` vector from a 2D image at the location given by `coord`
`float4 read_imagef(image3d_t img, sampler_t sampler, int4/float4 coord)`	Reads a `float4` vector from a 3D image at the location given by `coord`

Table 6.1   Kernel functions for reading image data *(continued)*

Function	Purpose
`int4 read_imagei(image3d_t img,` `    sampler_t sampler, int4/float4 coord)`	Reads an `int4` vector from a 3D image at the location given by `coord`
`uint4 read_imageui(image3d_t img,` `    sampler_t sampler, int4/float4 coord)`	Reads a `uint4` vector from a 3D image at the location given by `coord`

Each of these functions accepts an image object, a sampler, and a vector containing coordinates. Each returns a vector containing pixel data, and the vector's data type depends on the function name: `read_imagef` returns a `float4`, `read_imagei` returns an `int4`, and `read_imageui` returns a `uint4`. If the image object is an `image2d_t`, the coordinates must be given in an `int2` or `float2`. If the image object is an `image3d_t`, the coordinates must be given in an `int4` or `float4`.

For example, suppose you want to read the color from a two-dimensional image object called `image` at coordinates (3, 4). If you want the color value as a `float4` vector, you'd make the following function call:

```
float4 color = read_imagef(image, sampler, (int2)(3, 4));
```

The range of values returned by `read_imagef` is determined by the image format. If the pixels are given in an unsigned normalized format (`CL_UNORM_INT8`, `CL_UNORM_INT16`, `CL_UNORM_INT101010`, `CL_UNORM_SHORT565`, or `CL_UNORM_SHORT555`), the function will return values between 0.0 and 1.0. If pixels are given in a signed normalized format (`CL_SNORM_INT8` or `CL_SNORM_INT16`), `read_imagef` will return values between –0.5 and 0.5. If pixels are given in `CL_HALF_FLOAT` or `CL_FLOAT`, the function will return regular floating-point values.

After you've read a vector from an image object, it's important to know how the color components are contained within the vector. For example, suppose the image has the `CL_R` channel order (single color: red) and you read a `uint4` vector. Which of the vector's components is the red channel? What about the channels in a grayscale image? Table 6.2 answers these questions for each channel order supported by OpenCL. R, G, B, and A correspond to red, green, blue, and alpha channels, and x refers to padding.

Table 6.2   Color vector returned by read_image

Channel order	Vector storage (integer)
`CL_R, CL_Rx`	`(R, 0, 0, 1)`
`CL_A`	`(0, 0, 0, A)`
`CL_RG, CL_RGx`	`(R, G, 0, 1)`
`CL_RA`	`(R, 0, 0, A)`

Table 6.2   Color vector returned by read_image *(continued)*

Channel order	Vector storage (integer)
CL_RGB, CL_RGBx	(R, G, B, 1)
CL_RGBA, CL_BGRA, CL_ARGB	(R, G, B, A)
CL_INTENSITY	(I, I, I, I)
CL_LUMINANCE	(L, L, L, 1)

The numbers in this table are all integers, but if the vector is returned by read_imagef, its components will be floating-point. For example, if an image object's pixels have the CL_RG format, the vector returned by read_imagef will contain [R, G, 0.0, 1.0], where R and G are the red and green components of the pixel.

6.2.2   *Image write functions*

In addition to reading pixel data, OpenCL functions also make it possible to write pixel data to an image object. Table 6.3 lists each of them, and unlike the functions in the preceding table, these don't require sampler objects.

Table 6.3   Kernel functions for writing data to images

Function	Purpose
void write_imagef(image2d_t img, int2 coord, float4 color)	Writes a float4 color to a 2D image at the location given by coord
void write_imagei(image2d_t img, int2 coord, int4 color)	Writes an int4 color to a 2D image at the location given by coord
void write_imageui(image2d_t img, int2 coord, uint4 color)	Writes an uint4 color to a 2D image at the location given by coord
void write_imagef(image3d_t img, int4 coord, float4 color)	Writes a float4 color to a 3D image at the location given by coord
void write_imagei(image3d_t img, int4 coord, int4 color)	Writes an int4 color to a 3D image at the location given by coord
void write_imageui(image3d_t img, int4 coord, uint4 color)	Writes a uint4 color to a 3D image at the location given by coord

As shown, the color value can be given as a vector containing floats, ints, or uints. In contrast, the coordinates must always be given as signed integers.

Writes to three-dimensional image objects are *not* supported by default. This capability is provided through the cl_khr_3d_image_writes extension. Therefore, if you intend to modify data in an image3d_t, you need to check for this extension and add the following line to your kernel:

```
#pragma OPENCL EXTENSION cl_khr_3d_image_writes: enable
```

To specify a color to be written, you need to use the vector formats listed in the second column of table 6.2. For example, if the RGB components of a pixel are [132, 15, 44], you can write the pixel data to a CL_RGB image called img with the following code:

```
write_imageui(img, coord, (uint4)(132, 15, 44, 0));
```

If you don't know the channel order of an image's pixels, you can't write data to its pixels. Instead, you need OpenCL's functions for obtaining image information, which form the topic of the next discussion.

6.2.3 Image information functions

The functions in table 6.4 return information about the structure and content of an image. More specifically, they make it possible to determine an image's dimensions and the properties of its pixels.

Table 6.4 Kernel functions for obtaining image information

Function	Purpose
int get_image_width(image2d_t/image3d_t image)	Returns the width of the image
int get_image_height(image2d_t/image3d_t image)	Returns the height of the image
int get_image_depth(image3d_t image)	Returns the depth of the 3D image
int2 get_image_dim(image2d_t image)	Returns the width and height of a 2D image as an int2 vector
int4 get_image_dim(image3d_t image)	Returns the width, height, and depth of a 3D image as an int2 vector
int get_image_channel_data_type(image2d_t/image3d_t image)	Returns the channel data type of the image (CLK_UNORM_INT8, CLK_SIGNED_INT32, and so on)
int get_image_channel_order(image2d_t/image3d_t image)	Returns the channel of the image (CLK_A, CLK_RGB, CLK_INTENSITY, and so on)

These functions are easy to use and understand. The only difficulty involves remembering the difference between channel data type and channel order—channel data type tells you how the bits in each channel are formatted, and channel order tells you what channels are present and the order in which they're stored. Both of these values are provided as ints, and the cl.h header file shows the constants represented by these ints.

6.2.4 A simple example

Now that we've looked at the relevant data types and functions, it's time to see how they're used in practice. The example application in this discussion creates one work-item for each pixel of the 4-by-4 image shown on the left side of figure 6.2. Each

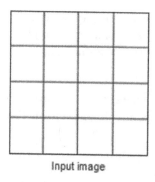

Input image

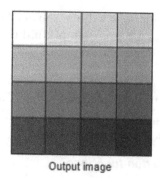

Output image

Figure 6.2 Selective image darkening (grid lines added for clarity)

work-item reads the color value of its corresponding pixel, subtracts a number, and writes the new value to a second image. The right-hand side of figure 6.2 shows what the second image looks like.

The following code implements this darkening process. Notice that the kernel doesn't accept a sampler as one of its function arguments. Instead, it creates a sampler_t structure called sampler by declaring it before the function.

Listing 6.1   Simple image processing: simple_image.cl

```
__constant sampler_t sampler = CLK_NORMALIZED_COORDS_FALSE |
    CLK_ADDRESS_CLAMP | CLK_FILTER_NEAREST;

__kernel void simple_image(read_only image2d_t src_image,
                           write_only image2d_t dst_image) {

  uint offset = get_global_id(1) * 0x4000 + get_global_id(0) * 0x1000;

  int2 coord = (int2)(get_global_id(0),
                      get_global_id(1));                    Read input
  uint4 pixel = read_imageui(src_image,                     pixel
                   sampler, coord);

  pixel.x -= offset;                                        Modify/write
  write_imageui(dst_image, coord, pixel);                   output pixel
}
```

Each work-item reads a color value as a uint4 vector and subtracts a value from the vector's first component. Because the image is grayscale, this is the only component that needs to be changed. The value subtracted from the pixel increases with the work-item's ID, and this is why the pixels get darker from the upper left to the lower right.

By default, the host application reads input image data from blank.png and writes the output data to output.png. To read PNG (Portable Network Graphics) images, the code relies on the open-source PNG library, called libpng. The routines in this library make it possible to read, analyze, and modify PNG images. GNU users can obtain libpng from the home site at http://libpng.sourceforge.net/index.html. Windows users can obtain the library from http://gnuwin32.sourceforge.net/packages/libpng.htm.

This kernel changes the image's brightness by subtracting a constant. Similarly, an image's contrast can be altered by multiplying its color values by a constant. The next section explores another important operation: how to enlarge and reduce images using interpolation.

6.3 Image scaling and interpolation

In addition to adjusting brightness and contrast, one of the most common image processing routines is scaling: reducing or enlarging the size of an image. Image enlargement is the greater problem because it involves adding pixels instead of removing them. If an $N * N$ image is enlarged k times, the result is a $kN * kN$ image. The central question is this: how can you obtain the color values of the extra $(k^2-1)N^2$ pixels in the enlarged image?

One method is to repeat the pixels from the original image. This is easy to understand, and this method is called *nearest-neighbor interpolation*. But you can also draw lines connecting the centers of pixels and use those lines to approximate points in between. This method, called *bilinear interpolation*, requires more work but produces better-looking results.

This section explores both of these methods, and thankfully, we don't need to write much code. If it's properly configured, a sampler can tell the kernel to perform nearest-neighbor interpolation (CLK_FILTER_NEAREST) or bilinear interpolation (CLK_FILTER_LINEAR) automatically.

> **NOTE** Pixel interpolation is performed only if an image's coordinates are given as floating-point values. If coordinates are given as integers, the result will always be a pixel's exact color.

6.3.1 Nearest-neighbor interpolation

If a sampler's filtering property is set to CLK_FILTER_NEAREST, it will interpolate between points using nearest-neighbor interpolation. This means that if a point is closer to pixel A than any other pixel, the sampled color at that point will be set equal to the color of pixel A.

If this method is used to enlarge an image, the resulting image will contain only the colors in the original. If an image is enlarged k-fold, each of its colors will be repeated k times. This is shown in figure 6.3, which depicts four adjacent pixels repeated three times.

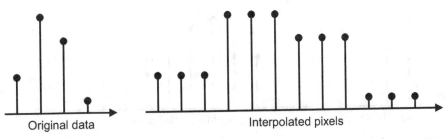

Original data   Interpolated pixels

Figure 6.3   Nearest-neighbor data expansion

Figure 6.4   Image enlargement using nearest-neighbor interpolation

Nearest-neighbor interpolation executes quickly because it doesn't require any mathematical computation. But when used for enlargement, the result tends to look grainy and pixelated. This is shown in figure 6.4.

The problem with the enlarged image is the abrupt changes between pixel values. Even in grayscale, it's clear that the car's colors change discontinuously from one point to the next.

6.3.2   *Bilinear interpolation*

We can improve upon nearest-neighbor interpolation by employing bilinear interpolation, which can be configured for samplers by setting CLK_FILTER_LINEAR. Using this method, if a point lies between pixels in a rectangular image, its sampled color will be set equal to a linear combination of the pixels' colors.

To understand how this sampled color is computed, it helps to start with the one-dimensional case. Suppose point P lies on a line between two adjacent pixels, A and B. To identify the location of P relative to A and B, we use a parameter called t. The distance from P to the center of A is given by t, and the distance from P to the center of B is given by $1 - t$. The linear interpolation sets the color at P with the following equation:

$$Color(P) = t \times Color(A) + (1 - t) \times Color(B)$$

It should be clear that if $t = 1$, the color at P equals the color at A. Similarly, if $t = 0$, the color at P equals the color at B. If $t = 0.5$, the resulting color will be an average of the color of A and the color of B. The resulting color value from A to B follows a straight line, and figure 6.5 depicts the lines used to interpolate values between four pixels. Note the difference between this data expansion and that shown in figure 6.3.

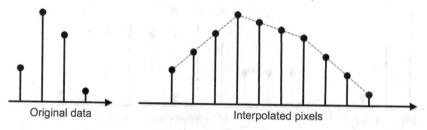

Original data   Interpolated pixels

Figure 6.5   Data expansion using linear interpolation

In two dimensions, this process is called bilinear interpolation. Here, we assume that point P lies between four adjacent pixels: A, B, C, and D. With this arrangement, each point needs two interpolation parameters, t^1 and t^2. Figure 6.6 shows the relationship between the points, pixels, and interpolation parameters.

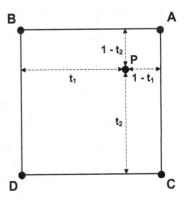

Figure 6.6 Pixels and points in bilinear interpolation

You can compute the color at P by extending the preceding equation to two dimensions. The new equation is as follows:

$$
\begin{aligned}
Color(P) = {}& t_1 \times t_2 \times Color(A) \\
& + (1 - t_1) \times t_2 \times Color(B) \\
& + t_1 \times (1 - t_2) \times Color(C) \\
& + (1 - t_1) \times (1 - t_2) \times Color(D)
\end{aligned}
$$

You can see that if $t_1 = 1$ and $t_2 = 1$, the color at P equals the color at A. If $t_1 = 0$ and t_2 equals 0, the color at P equals the color at D. If t_1 and t_2 both equal 0.5, the color at P equals the average of the colors A, B, C, and D.

Figure 6.7 shows what happens to the sports car when the image is enlarged using bilinear transformation. Because of the lines drawn between pixels, the enlarged image looks less pixelated than that shown in figure 6.4.

This is a significant improvement over nearest-neighbor interpolation, and if you're using a sampler to interpolate between floating-point values, the `CLK_FILTER_LINEAR` option will give you better results than `CLK_FILTER_NEAREST`. But there are three points to keep in mind when setting this option:

- The `CLK_FILTER_LINEAR` option is only available if coordinates are given as floating-point values.
- This option is only available for `read_imagef`. If `read_imageui` or `read_imagei` are called with a sampler set to `CLK_FILTER_LINEAR`, the results will be undefined.
- Some OpenCL-compliant devices don't support bilinear interpolation. In this case, interpolation may be emulated in hardware.

Figure 6.7 Image enlargement using bilinear interpolation

6.3.3   *Image enlargement in OpenCL*

If an image with dimensions w by h is enlarged k times, the resulting image will contain k^2wh pixels. The sampler's interpolation setting defines whether the color values of the additional pixels are obtained using nearest-neighbor interpolation or bilinear interpolation.

The code in the following listing creates a sampler with the CLK_FILTER_NEAREST setting, so it will choose color values using nearest-neighbor interpolation.

Listing 6.2   Image interpolation: interp_image.cl

```
constant sampler_t sampler = CLK_NORMALIZED_COORDS_FALSE
      | CLK_ADDRESS_CLAMP | CLK_FILTER_NEAREST;

__kernel void interp(read_only image2d_t src_image,
                   write_only image2d_t dst_image) {
   float4 pixel;

   float2 input_coord = (float2)
        (get_global_id(0) + (1.0f/(SCALE*2)),         Set initial
         get_global_id(1) + (1.0f/(SCALE*2)));        coordinates
   int2 output_coord =
      (int2)(SCALE*get_global_id(0),
      SCALE*get_global_id(1));

   for(int i=0; i<SCALE; i++) {
      for(int j=0; j<SCALE; j++) {
         pixel = read_imagef(src_image, sampler,
            (float2)(input_coord +                    Read/write
            (float2)(1.0f*i/SCALE, 1.0f*j/SCALE)));    pixels
         write_imagef(dst_image, output_coord +
            (int2)(i, j), pixel);
      }
   }
}
```

If SCALE is set to k, each work-item will read k^2 values from an input image and write k^2 values to the output image. These input coordinates are given as floating-point values, and their locations must be spread evenly across the image. Figure 6.8 demonstrates how a work-item reads 25 values within a pixel when the scaling factor is set to 5.

If nearest-neighbor interpolation is used, all 25 read operations will return the same result: the color value of the pixel. But if bilinear interpolation is used, the read operations will return a value somewhere between the pixel's color value and that of the neighboring pixel.

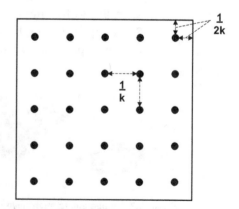

Figure 6.8   Coordinate placement within a pixel

6.4   *Summary*

High-speed image processing is one of OpenCL's most important strengths, and the OpenCL standard defines a number of image-related data types and functions. If a kernel processes images, it receives the image data as an image object, which can be an `image2d_t` or an `image3d_t`. To read data from the image object, the kernel needs a `sampler_t` structure. This controls how the kernel evaluates coordinates and interpolates data.

OpenCL's image processing functions fall into three categories: those that read data from an image object, those that write data to an image object, and those that access information related to the image, such as its dimensions and pixel properties. The read functions require a sampler, and the coordinates can be given as integer or floating-point values. The write functions, however, require integer coordinates. In addition, three-dimensional images can't be written to unless the device supports the `cl_khr_3d_image_writes` extension.

Samplers play an important role in image processing by configuring how color data is interpolated between pixels. OpenCL provides two interpolation methods: nearest-neighbor interpolation is set with `CLK_FILTER_NEAREST` and bilinear interpolation is set with `CLK_FILTER_LINEAR`. When used to scale images, nearest-neighbor interpolation repeats pixels in the original image. This method executes quickly, but bilinear interpolation generally produces better results. Bilinear interpolation computes colors between pixels using a line that connects the pixels' centers. This interpolation method is only available if coordinates and color values are given in floating-point form.

In the next chapter, we'll examine some of OpenCL's more advanced capabilities. First, we'll look at OpenCL events and how they can be used to profile kernel execution. Then we'll explore how OpenCL makes it possible to synchronize kernel execution among work-items.

Events, profiling, and synchronization

7

This chapter covers
- Configuring events and event-handling
- Using profiling to measure processing time
- Synchronizing work-item execution

Preceding chapters have dealt with the *what* and *how* of OpenCL operations; this chapter deals with *when*. We're not going to look at new types of operations, but instead you'll learn how to monitor operations we've already encountered.

The concept of an event is central to this discussion. In OpenCL, an event is a data structure that corresponds to an occurrence. One event might monitor the completion of a data transfer operation and another might monitor the execution of a kernel. You can use events in three main ways:

- *Host notification*—An event can notify the host that a command has completed its execution on a device
- *Command synchronization*—An event can force commands to delay their execution until another event's occurrence has taken place
- *Profiling*—An event can monitor how much time a command takes to execute

The third use is particularly interesting. Profiling is a vital tool in high-performance application development because it allows you to evaluate the performance of computing hardware and coding methods. With profiling, you can compare devices, kernels, and data partitioning strategies. This chapter will not only explain profiling; it will also show how profiling can be used to test different aspects of OpenCL's operation.

The last part of this chapter examines work-item synchronization. Normally, when work-items are generated for a kernel, they execute in a disordered, nondeterministic fashion. This is fine when work-items access different memory regions, but it causes problems when work-items need to process the same data. OpenCL provides capabilities for ordering the processing of work-items, and we'll look at these capabilities in detail.

But to start, this chapter will discuss the topic of OpenCL host notification events. These allow host applications to monitor commands executing on a device.

7.1 Host notification events

Every OpenCL event corresponds to an occurrence, and the majority of these occurrences involve commands and command queues. So before we continue, let's review these important topics. When a host wants to send a task to a device, it creates a command queue and dispatches a command to the queue. This command may involve executing a kernel, transferring data between the host and device, or mapping device memory to host memory. Chapters 2 and 3 discuss commands and command queues in detail.

After the host enqueues a command, it has no control over how the command will be processed, but it can receive notification when the command completes its execution. This notification is made possible by *events*, which are represented in code by `cl_event` data structures. The goal of this section is to explain how `cl_events` can be configured to execute a host function when a command completes.

An example will show how host notification works. Suppose you want to transfer a great deal of data from a device to the host using `clEnqueueReadBuffer`. This may take some time, so you make the function nonblocking by setting its third argument to `CL_FALSE`. Because `clEnqueueReadBuffer` returns immediately, the host can perform other tasks while the data transfer continues.

When the data transfer is complete, you may want the host application to respond by processing the data. To make this possible in code, you need to declare a `cl_event` and configure two associations. First, you need to associate the event with the data transfer command. Then you need to associate the event with a function to be called on the host when the transfer command finishes. This type of function is called a *callback function*.

7.1.1 Associating an event with a command

Chapters 2 and 3 discussed the many different functions that dispatch commands to a command queue. Their names start with `clEnqueue` and they all accept a pointer to a cl_event as their final argument. For example, clEnqueueTask enqueues a command that tells the device to execute a kernel. Its signature is as follows:

```
cl_int clEnqueueTask (cl_command_queue queue, cl_kernel kernel,
    cl_uint num_events, const cl_event *wait_list, cl_event *event)
```

In all of our example code so far, we've set the last argument to NULL. But if this argument points to a valid cl_event, functions like clEnqueueTask will associate the cl_event with the enqueued command. For example, the following code associates ev with the function's kernel-execution command:

```
cl_event ev;
clEnqueueTask(queue, kernel, 0, NULL, &ev);
```

Note that you don't have to call a separate function to create the cl_event. Once you declare the structure, you can use it in clEnqueueTask or any command-enqueuing function.

As clEnqueueTask enqueues the kernel-execution command, it initializes ev and associates it with the new command. If ev has a callback function, the function will be invoked when ev's command completes its execution. We'll look at callback functions next.

7.1.2   *Associating an event with a callback function*

When you associate a callback function with an event, the function will execute when the command associated with the event completes its operation. The clSetEventCallback function creates this association. Its signature is as follows:

```
cl_int clSetEventCallback(cl_event event, cl_int callback_type,
    void (CL_CALLBACK  *func_name) (cl_event event, cl_int status,
    void *data), void *data)
```

The second argument, callback_type, identifies the type of command status you're interested in monitoring. At the time of this writing, the only accepted value is CL_COMPLETE. The third argument is a pointer to a callback function, and the fourth points to data that will be sent to the callback function when it's invoked. For example, the following code associates the callback function process with the event ev:

```
clSetEventCallback(ev, CL_COMPLETE, &process, NULL);
```

Now let's look at coding the callback function. All event-related callback functions must return void, and they must all accept the same three argument types. The required callback signature is as follows:

```
void CL_CALLBACK func_name(cl_event event, cl_int status, void *data)
```

The first argument provides the cl_event data structure that triggered the callback, and the second presents the event's status. The last argument points to the data that was defined as the last argument of clSetEventCallback. CL_CALLBACK is a macro that evaluates to _stdcall on Windows systems. On other operating systems, this macro is blank.

The following listing presents code for a simple callback function called process, which interprets the incoming data as text and prints the text. Inside the main function, the code declares a cl_event and associates it with process:

Listing 7.1 Basic callback configuration

```
void CL_CALLBACK process(cl_event event, cl_int status, void *data) {
   printf("%s\n", (char*)data);
}

int main() {
   ...
   cl_event ev;
   char[] msg = "Hello world!";
   ...
   cl_int clSetEventCallback(ev, CL_COMPLETE, &process, (void*)msg);
   ...
}
```

This code configures ev so that process will be called when ev's corresponding command completes. Next, we'll look at a full example that demonstrates how host notification works.

7.1.3 A host notification example

The following code creates and configures two callback events, kernel_event and read_event. The first is associated with a kernel-execution command and the second is associated with a command that reads data from the device. These events are also associated with callback functions: kernel_complete and read_complete.

NOTE The clSetEventCallback function is new in OpenCL 1.1 and won't compile on systems that don't support this standard.

Listing 7.2 Host notification: callback.c

```
...
void CL_CALLBACK kernel_complete(cl_event e, cl_int status, void* data) {
   printf("%s", (char*)data);
}
void CL_CALLBACK read_complete(cl_event e, cl_int status, void* data) {

   int i;
   cl_bool check;
   float *buffer_data;

   buffer_data = (float*)data;
   check = CL_TRUE;
   for(i=0; i<4096; i++) {
      if(buffer_data[i] != 5.0) {
         check = CL_FALSE;
         break;
      }
   }
```

```
        if(check)
            printf("The data has been initialized successfully.\n");
        else
            printf("The data has not been initialized successfully.\n");
    }

    int main() {

        char *kernel_msg;
        float data[4096];
        cl_mem data_buffer;
        cl_event kernel_event, read_event;

        ...

        err = clEnqueueTask(queue, kernel, 0,              Associate kernel_event
                NULL, &kernel_event);                      with command
        if(err < 0) {
            perror("Couldn't enqueue the kernel");
            exit(1);
        }

        err = clEnqueueReadBuffer(queue, data_buffer,      Associate read_event
                CL_FALSE, 0, sizeof(data), &data,          with command
                0, NULL, &read_event);
        if(err < 0) {
            perror("Couldn't read the buffer");
            exit(1);
        }

        kernel_msg = "The kernel finished successfully.\n\0";
        err = clSetEventCallback(kernel_event, CL_COMPLETE,  Set kernel_event
                &kernel_complete, kernel_msg);               callback function
        if(err < 0) {
            perror("Couldn't set callback for event");
            exit(1);
        }
        clSetEventCallback(read_event, CL_COMPLETE,          Set read_event
                &read_complete, data);                       callback function
        ...
        clReleaseEvent(read_event);
        clReleaseEvent(kernel_event);
        ...
    }
```

It's important to note that `clSetEventCallback` must be called *after* the command-enqueuing functions. If you reverse the order, you'll receive a segmentation fault.

It's also important to note that the `clEnqueueTask` and `clEnqueueReadBuffer` functions are both nonblocking, which means they don't wait for their commands to finish executing. You can test this by adding a `printf` statement before the end of the main function. This will be called before either callback function because the two commands are still executing on the device.

We've examined how events can notify a host of a command's execution, but this isn't their only purpose. Events can also be used to establish order among executing commands. We'll look at this in the next section.

7.2   Command synchronization events

By default, command queues process commands in the order in which they're enqueued. But if commands are dispatched to different command queues in a context, there is no way of telling what order they'll be executed in. With events, however, you can establish your own order for the commands' execution. That is, you can force one or more commands to wait until a set of events have completed. These sets of delaying events are called *wait lists*.

I've said that events correspond to occurrences, but now I need to be more specific. If an event is associated with a command's execution, it's a *command event*. If an event is associated with an occurrence within a host application, it's a *user event*. This section discusses both types of events and then examines three other functions that synchronize commands.

7.2.1   Wait lists and command events

As discussed earlier, if you set the last argument of an enqueuing function, such as clEnqueueTask, to point to a cl_event, that event will be associated with the enqueued command. We'll call this type of event a command event. You've seen how this cl_event can be associated with a callback function, but you can also add it to the *wait list* of another command.

Every OpenCL command has a wait list made up of cl_event structures. If a command's wait list is NULL, it can start executing as soon as it reaches the end of the command queue. If the command's wait list isn't NULL, then for every cl_event in the list, the command must halt until the event's corresponding occurrence has completed.

To configure a command's wait list, you need to set the third-to-last and second-to-last arguments in the function that enqueues the command. If you look back at the signature of clEnqueueTask, you'll see that these arguments are as follows:

- cl_uint num_events—Number of cl_event structures in the command's wait list
- const cl_event *wait_list—Pointer to the cl_events in the wait list

An example will clarify how wait lists are configured. Suppose you want the execution of kernel_c in queue_c to start after kernel_a in queue_a and kernel_b in queue_b have finished executing. The following code shows how this can be accomplished:

```
cl_event kernel_event[2];
clEnqueueTask(queue_a, kernel_a, 0, NULL, &kernel_event[0]);
clEnqueueTask(queue_b, kernel_b, 0, NULL, &kernel_event[1]);
clEnqueueTask(queue_c, kernel_c, 2, kernel_event, NULL);
```

In this case, the wait list of the last command consists of two cl_events. The first cl_event corresponds to the execution of kernel_a and the second corresponds to the execution of kernel_b. Because these events are in the wait list, kernel_c's execution will wait until the other kernels' executions have completed. Figure 7.1 depicts this graphically.

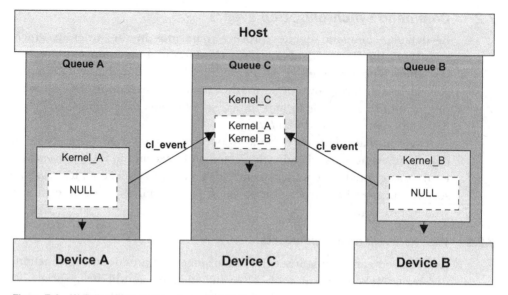

Figure 7.1 Wait lists and command synchronization

In this figure, the dotted lines surround the commands' wait lists. Because the wait lists of the commands in queue A and queue B are NULL, the commands can execute without delay. But the command in queue C must wait until the other two commands have finished.

7.2.2 *Wait lists and user events*

The preceding discussion explained how to stall commands with command events. If the preceding discussion was clear, you'll have no trouble understanding how to stall commands with *user events*. Once again, the goal is to halt a command's execution by placing cl_event structures in its wait list.

There's a large difference between command events and user events. Command events correspond to commands executing on the device, but a user event is generated by the host application. With a user event, you can stall a command's execution from the *host*, not the device. (I think *host event* would be a better term, but no one listens to me.)

As its name implies, the clCreateUserEvent function creates user events. This is a simple function and its signature is as follows:

```
cl_event clCreateUserEvent(cl_context context, cl_int *err)
```

The cl_event returned by this function can be placed in a command's wait list. You don't have to identify a command queue, so you can use the same user event with multiple devices.

If you add a user event to a command's wait list, the execution of the command will halt until the host application updates the event's status. This is accomplished by calling clSetUserEventStatus, whose signature is as follows:

```
cl_int clSetUserEventStatus(cl_event event, cl_int status)
```

At the time of this writing, the status parameter can only be set to CL_COMPLETE (which evaluates to 0) or a negative value. If status is set to CL_COMPLETE, any commands waiting on the user event will be allowed to execute. If status is set to a negative number, any commands waiting on the user event will be terminated.

As an example, the following code creates a user event e and configures it to stall the execution of a kernel. Then, at a later point in the code, the host application allows the kernel to execute by calling clSetUserEventStatus with CL_SUCCESS:

```
cl_event e;
...
e = clCreateUserEvent(context, &err);
...
clEnqueueTask(queue, kernel, 1, &e, NULL);
...
clSetUserEventStatus(e, CL_SUCCESS);
...
clReleaseEvent(e);
```

Listing 7.3 demonstrates how user events, command events, and callback functions can work together. The host application sends two commands to the device: one that executes a kernel and one that reads the kernel's output data. The read command stalls until the kernel-execution command is finished, and the kernel-execution command stalls until a user event has completed. Once the user presses a key, the user event completes and both commands execute. When the read command finishes, it invokes the callback function read_complete.

NOTE Like the clSetEventCallback function discussed earlier, user events are new in OpenCL 1.1. This code will compile only on devices that support the 1.1 standard.

Listing 7.3 Stalling commands with user events: user_event.c

```
void CL_CALLBACK read_complete(cl_event e,
      cl_int status, void* data) {

   float *float_data = (float*)data;
   printf("New data: %4.2f, %4.2f, %4.2f, %4.2f\n",
      float_data[0], float_data[1], float_data[2], float_data[3]);
}

int main() {
   ...
   cl_event user_event, kernel_event, read_event;
   ...
   user_event = clCreateUserEvent(context, &err);       Create
   if(err < 0) {                                         user event
      perror("Couldn't enqueue the kernel");
      exit(1);
   }
   err = clEnqueueTask(queue, kernel, 1, &user_event,    Enqueue kernel
         &kernel_event);                                 command
   if(err < 0) {
```

```
      perror("Couldn't enqueue the kernel");
      exit(1);
   }

   err = clEnqueueReadBuffer(queue, data_buffer,            ❶ Enqueue read
         CL_FALSE, 0, sizeof(data), data, 1,                   command
      &kernel_event, &read_event);
   if(err < 0) {
      perror("Couldn't read the buffer");
      exit(1);
   }

   err = clSetEventCallback(read_event, CL_COMPLETE,        Set callback
         &read_complete, data);                             function
   if(err < 0) {
      perror("Couldn't set callback for event");
      exit(1);
   }

   sleep(1);
   printf("Old data: %4.2f, %4.2f, %4.2f, %4.2f\n",
      data[0], data[1], data[2], data[3]);
   printf("Press ENTER to continue.\n");
   getchar();
                                                            Complete
   clSetUserEventStatus(user_event, CL_SUCCESS);            user event

   clReleaseEvent(read_event);
   clReleaseEvent(kernel_event);                            Deallocate
   clReleaseEvent(user_event);                              resources
   ...
}
```

The clEnqueueReadBuffer function ❶ is set to be nonblocking, and this is important. If the blocking parameter were changed to CL_TRUE, the function wouldn't complete until the read operation is finished, but the read command stalls on the kernel-execution command, which won't execute until the user event completes. If clEnqueueReadBuffer is waiting, the code following this function wouldn't run and the entire application would hang.

7.2.3 *Additional command synchronization functions*

The preceding discussion explained how to force commands to stall until an individual command completes its execution. But you can also stall commands until a group of commands have completed their execution. The functions discussed in this section make this synchronization possible by dispatching three new types of commands: marker commands, wait commands, and barrier commands.

MARKER COMMANDS

We've already discussed how to associate an event with a command's execution. The clEnqueueMarker function, however, enqueues a command called a *marker command* and associates an event with the execution of every command preceding it. Its signature is as follows:

```
cl_int clEnqueueMarker(cl_command_queue command_queue, cl_event *event)
```

Host

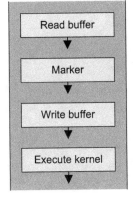

**Command
queue**

Device

Figure 7.2 The marker command

This function associates event with the marker command, and event can be placed in a wait list or be used to notify the host. For example, figure 7.2 shows a command queue in which the third command enqueued by the host is a marker command. The cl_event associated with the marker will complete when the first two commands have completed.

The following code configures the marker command to invoke a callback function called process:

```
void CL_CALLBACK process(cl_event event, cl_int status, void *data) {
    ...
}

int main() {
    ...
    cl_event ev;
    ...
    cl_int clSetEventCallback(ev, CL_COMPLETE, &process, NULL);
    ...
    cl_int clEnqueueMarker(cl_command_queue queue, ev);
}
```

WAIT COMMANDS

The command generated by clEnqueueWaitForEvents, called a *wait command*, tells the command queue not to execute any following commands until the events in its wait list have reached a completed state. The signature of this function is as follows:

```
cl_int clEnqueueWaitForEvents(cl_command_queue queue, cl_uint num_events,
    const cl_event *wait_list)
```

The last two arguments create a wait list similar to those of other command-enqueuing functions we've encountered. But instead of stalling a single command, the events in this wait list stall every following command in the queue. This is shown in figure 7.3.

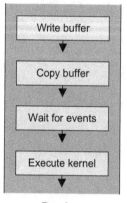

Figure 7.3   The wait command

In this figure, the wait command tells the queue not to process the copy or write commands until the events in its wait list have completed. The following code shows how `clEnqueueWaitForEvents` can be configured to respond to a user-created event:

```
cl_event e;
...
e = clCreateUserEvent(context, &err);
...
clEnqueueWaitForEvents(queue, 1, &e);
...
clSetUserEventStatus(e, CL_SUCCESS);
```

Here, the command dispatched by `clEnqueueWaitForEvents` prevents all following commands on the queue from executing. But when `clSetUserEventStatus` is called, the user event will complete, and succeeding commands will be able to execute.

BARRIER COMMANDS

The `clEnqueueBarrier` function doesn't accept or configure events, but its purpose is so similar to that of `clEnqueueWaitForEvents` that it's worth discussing here. Both functions prevent later commands on the queue from executing, but `clEnqueueBarrier` doesn't use a wait list. Instead, it enqueues a command called a *barrier command*. This forces following commands to stall until preceding commands have completed their execution. The signature couldn't be simpler:

```
cl_int clEnqueueBarrier(cl_command_queue queue)
```

Barriers are necessary when you have one set of commands that need to be executed before a second set of commands. With a barrier command, you don't have to deal with events and callback functions. The barrier will automatically prevent any following commands from executing until every preceding command has executed.

7.2.4   Obtaining data associated with events

The callback functions presented in this section have accessed the function's `data` parameter but not its `event` parameter. But by calling `clGetEventInfo`, you can access a great deal of information about an event, such as its context, command queue, and the type of its associated command. The signature for this function is as follows:

```
cl_int clGetEventInfo(cl_event event, cl_event_info param_name,
  size_t param_value_size, void *param_value, size_t *param_size)
```

This works like the clGet*XX*Info functions discussed in chapters 2 and 3. The only difference is the cl_event_info argument, which identifies the type of information you'd like to access. Table 7.1 lists the possible values this argument can take.

Table 7.1 Event information parameters (`cl_event_info`)

Parameter name	Parameter value	Purpose
CL_EVENT_CONTEXT	cl_context	Returns the context used to create the event
CL_EVENT_COMMAND QUEUE	cl_command_queue	Returns the command queue used to create the event
CL_EVENT_COMMAND EXECUTION_STATUS	cl_int	Returns the status of the corresponding command (CL_QUEUED, CL_SUBMITTED, CL_RUNNING, CL_COMPLETE, or a negative error value)
CL_EVENT_COMMAND TYPE	cl_command_type	Identifies the nature of the occurrence corresponding to the cl_event (see table 7.2)
CL_EVENT_REFERENCE_ COUNT	cl_uint	Returns the number of times the event has been referenced

Most of these entries are simple, but CL_EVENT_COMMAND_EXECUTION_STATUS and CL_EVENT_COMMAND_TYPE merit explanation. So far, the only command status we've dealt with is CL_COMPLETE, which is the status of a command after its execution has finished. But the full lifecycle of a command consists of four stages:

1 *Queued*—The command is placed in the command queue (identified by CL_QUEUED).

2 *Submitted*—The command is submitted to the device (identified by CL_SUBMITTED).

3 *Running*—The command is being executed on the device (identified by CL_RUNNING).

4 *Complete*—The command's execution has finished (identified by CL_COMPLETE).

Future versions of OpenCL may support full access to a command's status, but at the time of this writing, clSetEventCallback and clSetUserEventStatus only work properly for the CL_COMPLETE stage.

If the information parameter is set to CL_EVENT_COMMAND_TYPE, the returned value will identify the nature of the command associated with the event. The data type of the result is an enumerated type called cl_command_type. Table 7.2 lists the different values this type may take.

Table 7.2 Command types (`cl_command_type`)

Type	Type
CL_COMMAND_NDRANGE_KERNEL	CL_COMMAND_MAP_IMAGE
CL_COMMAND_TASK	CL_COMMAND_UNMAP_MEM_OBJECT
CL_COMMAND_NATIVE_KERNEL	CL_COMMAND_READ_BUFFER_RECT
CL_COMMAND_READ_BUFFER	CL_COMMAND_WRITE_BUFFER_RECT
CL_COMMAND_WRITE_BUFFER	CL_COMMAND_COPY_BUFFER_RECT
CL_COMMAND_COPY_BUFFER	CL_COMMAND_MARKER
CL_COMMAND_READ_IMAGE	CL_COMMAND_ACQUIRE_GL_OBJECTS
CL_COMMAND_WRITE_IMAGE	CL_COMMAND_RELEASE_GL_OBJECTS
CL_COMMAND_COPY_IMAGE	CL_COMMAND_GL_FENCE_SYNC_OBJECT_KHR
CL_COMMAND_COPY_BUFFER_TO_IMAGE	CL_COMMAND_ACQUIRE_D3D10_OBJECTS_KHR
CL_COMMAND_COPY_IMAGE_TO_BUFFER	CL_COMMAND_RELEASE_D3D10_OBJECTS_KHR
CL_COMMAND_MAP_BUFFER	CL_COMMAND_USER

Most of these names should be easily recognizable, because they correspond to functions that enqueue commands. For example, the `CL_COMMAND_READ_BUFFER` type corresponds to a command enqueued by `clEnqueueReadBuffer`. But the last entry, `CL_COMMAND_USER`, doesn't correspond to a function that enqueues a command. It identifies a `cl_event` as a user event created by `clCreateUserEvent`.

Two examples will help clarify how `clGetEventInfo` is used in code. The following callback function calls `clGetEventInfo` to obtain the command queue associated with the event. If the event is a user event, `cq` will be set to NULL:

```
void CL_CALLBACK get_queue(cl_event e, cl_int status, void* data) {
   cl_command_queue cq;

   cl_int clGetEventInfo(e, CL_EVENT_COMMAND_QUEUE, sizeof(cq),
      &cq, NULL);
   ...
}
```

The callback function in the following listing determines whether the `cl_event` is associated with a command that reads, writes, or copies a buffer.

Listing 7.4 Determining the command type associated with an event

```
void CL_CALLBACK get_type(cl_event e, cl_int status, void* data) {
   cl_command_type type;

   cl_int clGetEventInfo(e, CL_EVENT_COMMAND_TYPE,
      sizeof(type), &type, NULL);

   switch(type) {
```

```
      case CL_COMMAND_READ_BUFFER:
         ...
      break;

      case CL_COMMAND_WRITE_BUFFER:
         ...
      break;

      case CL_COMMAND_COPY_BUFFER:
         ...
      break;
   }
}
```

At this point, you should have a solid understanding of events, including how to configure them in code and obtain information about them. The next section presents profiling, which uses events to determine how long a command takes to execute.

7.3 Profiling events

Chapter 1 explained a great deal about OpenCL's vector processing and parallel programming, and how they provide improved performance over traditional C/C++. But without actual timing data, it's all talk. You can spend hundreds of dollars on a top-of-the-line graphics card, but until you test its performance, you can't be certain you got your money's worth.

This section puts aside the promises and gets to the numbers. We're going to discuss how profiling events work in OpenCL and how to use them to measure timing. Specifically, we'll start by examining profiling events and how they're configured in code. Then we'll use these events to time data transfer operations and kernel execution.

7.3.1 Configuring command profiling

To obtain timing information about a command, you need to follow three steps:

1 Set the CL_QUEUE_PROFILING_ENABLE flag when you create a command queue with clCreateCommandQueue.
2 Associate a cl_event with the command you want to profile. As discussed earlier, this is done by making the event's pointer the last argument of the function that enqueues the command.
3 After the command completes its execution, call clGetEventProfilingInfo to access the cl_event and obtain information about the command's timing.

Easy, isn't it? The first step enables profiling for the command queue, which means that OpenCL will record when commands in the queue change state. The second step identifies the cl_event that will store the timing data for a specific command, and the last step obtains the data from the cl_event. The signature of the clGetEventProfiling-Info function is as follows:

```
cl_int clGetEventProfilingInfo(cl_event event, cl_profiling_info param,
   size_t param_value_size, void *param_value, size_t *param_value_size_ret)
```

This works exactly like the `clGetEventInfo` function we examined earlier. The only difference is that the second parameter must be a `cl_profiling_info` value instead of a `cl_event_info` value. Table 7.3 lists the values of the `cl_profiling_info` enumerated type.

Table 7.3   Profiling information parameters (`cl_profiling_info`)

Parameter name	Value	Purpose
CL_PROFILING_COMMAND_QUEUED	cl_ulong	Returns the time in nanoseconds for when the command was enqueued
CL_PROFILING_COMMAND_SUBMIT	cl_ulong	Returns the time in nanoseconds for when the command was submitted to the device
CL_PROFILING_COMMAND_START	cl_ulong	Returns the time in nanoseconds for when the command's execution started
CL_PROFILING_COMMAND_END	cl_ulong	Returns the time in nanoseconds for when the command's execution ended

In each case, the data provided by `clGetEventProfilingInfo` is a 64-bit value that identifies the time in nanoseconds (billionths of a second) when a command changed state. To determine how long a command remained in a queue, call `clGetEvent-ProfilingInfo` once with the `CL_PROFILING_COMMAND_SUBMIT` flag set and again with the `CL_PROFILING_COMMAND_QUEUED` flag, and then subtract the queued time from the submitted time. Similarly, to find out how long the command took to execute, call `clGetEventProfilingInfo` once with `CL_PROFILING_COMMAND_START` and once with `CL_PROFILING_COMMAND_END`, and subtract the start time from the end time.

The profiling times are given in billionths of a second, called *nanoseconds* or ns. But not every device can resolve time down to individual nanoseconds. To determine the resolution of a device, call `clGetDeviceInfo` with `CL_DEVICE_PROFILING_TIMER_RESOLUTION` set as the second argument. This is shown in the following code:

```
size_t time_res;

clGetDeviceInfo(device, CL_DEVICE_PROFILING_TIMER_RESOLUTION,
   sizeof(time_res), &time_res, NULL);
```

This produces a `size_t` value that tells you how many nanoseconds elapse between each change in the timer's value. The timing resolution on my MacBook (Nvidia 9400M) is 1000 ns. On my AMD 5850, the resolution is 1 ns.

A basic example will demonstrate how command profiling works. The following code creates a command queue with profiling enabled, enqueues a command to read a buffer object, and accesses the command's timing data with `clGetEventProfilingInfo`.

Listing 7.5   Basic profiling

```
cl_event timing_event;
cl_ulong time_start, time_end, read_time;
```

```
queue = clCreateCommandQueue(context, device,
    CL_QUEUE_PROFILING_ENABLE, NULL);

clEnqueueReadBuffer(queue, data_buffer, TRUE, 0,
    sizeof(data), data, 0, NULL, &timing_event);

clGetEventProfilingInfo(timing_event, CL_PROFILING_COMMAND_START,
    sizeof(time_start), &time_start, NULL);

clGetEventProfilingInfo(timing_event, CL_PROFILING_COMMAND_END,
    sizeof(time_end), &time_end, NULL);

read_time = time_end - time_start;
```

Now that you understand how profiling works, let's put it to use. First, we'll determine whether it's faster to transfer data using read/write operations or memory maps. Second, we'll investigate how the timing of kernel execution changes as you add more work-items.

7.3.2 *Profiling data transfer*

As explained in chapter 3, there are two ways to transfer data between a host and a device. You can call functions that enqueue read/write commands such as clEnqueueReadBuffer or clEnqueueWriteImage. Alternatively, you can map a memory object to host memory with a function like clEnqueueMapBuffer. Then, once you've processed the mapped data, you can unmap the memory region with clEnqueueUnmapMemObject. For file access, memory mapping usually provides improved performance. But what about OpenCL data transfer? We can find out using event profiling.

The code in the following listing contains an iteration loop that tests the average time taken by the commands enqueued by clEnqueueReadBuffer versus clEnqueue-MapBuffer. The PROFILE_READ macro determines which method will be used to transfer data. To save space, the error handling code has been removed.

> **Listing 7.6 Profiling data transfer: profile_read.c**

```
...
total_time = 0.0f;
for(i=0; i<NUM_ITERATIONS; i++) {
    clEnqueueTask(queue, kernel, 0, NULL, NULL);

#ifdef PROFILE_READ

    clEnqueueReadBuffer(queue, data_buffer,          Read data
        CL_TRUE, 0, sizeof(data), data, 0,           from buffer
        NULL, &prof_event);

#else

    mapped_memory = clEnqueueMapBuffer(queue,        Create
        data_buffer, CL_TRUE, CL_MAP_READ, 0,        memory map
        sizeof(data), 0, NULL, &prof_event, &err);

#endif
```

```
clGetEventProfilingInfo(prof_event,
    CL_PROFILING_COMMAND_START,
    sizeof(time_start), &time_start, NULL);
clGetEventProfilingInfo(prof_event,
    CL_PROFILING_COMMAND_END,
    sizeof(time_end), &time_end, NULL);
total_time += time_end - time_start;
```

Measure read time

```
#ifndef PROFILE_READ

    /* Unmap the buffer */
    err = clEnqueueUnmapMemObject(queue, data_buffer, mapped_memory,
        0, NULL, NULL);
    if(err < 0) {
        perror("Couldn't unmap the buffer");
        exit(1);
    }

#endif
}
#ifdef PROFILE_READ
    printf("Average read time: %lu\n", total_time/NUM_ITERATIONS);
#else
    printf("Average map time: %lu\n", total_time/NUM_ITERATIONS);
#endif
```

Figure 7.4 presents the results of the data transfer experiments I conducted by running the code in listing 7.6 on my AMD 5850 graphics card. Two thousand iterations were performed for each data point.

For every data size tested, memory maps transfer data faster than read commands. The performance improvement increases with the amount of data transferred.

It's important to note that, for the map times, only the clEnqueueMapBuffer function was profiled. The clEnqueueUnmapMemObject function was not timed. It's also worth noting that the time taken for the data transfer is generally much less than the total time taken for the command to complete its execution.

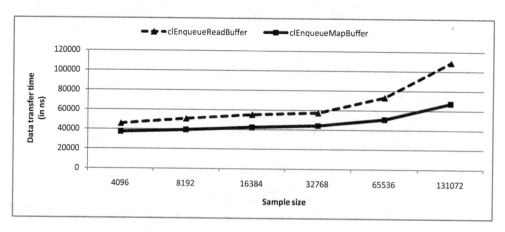

Figure 7.4 Comparison of data transfer speeds

7.3.3 *Profiling data partitioning*

In most of the example code so far, we've used clEnqueueTask to enqueue kernel-execution commands. This is a simple function, but it doesn't let us access one of OpenCL's most important capabilities: data partitioning.

As explained in chapter 3, data partitioning allows you to divide the execution of a kernel into multiple work-items. In theory, the time needed to execute a kernel should drop as more work-items are generated. But how true is this in practice? To find out, we need to profile the clEnqueueNDRangeKernel function. Like clEnqueueTask, this enqueues a kernel-execution command, but it accepts additional arguments that specify how the kernel's execution should be partitioned. This is a complex function, so let's look at its signature:

```
clEnqueueNDRangeKernel(cl_command_queue queue, cl_kernel kernel,
    cl_uint work_dims, const size_t *global_work_offset,
    const size_t *global_work_size, const size_t *local_work_size,
    cl_uint num_events, const cl_event *wait_list, cl_event *event)
```

The third argument, work_dims, identifies the dimensionality of the data. The fifth argument, global_work_size, identifies how many work-items should be generated for each dimension. The last argument, event, accepts a cl_event that will be used to monitor the kernel-execution command.

The following listing shows the iteration loop I used to profile the kernel-execution commands enqueued by clEnqeueueNDRangeKernel.

Listing 7.7 Profiling data partitioning: profile_items.c

```
...
total_time = 0.0f;
for(i=0; i<NUM_ITERATIONS; i++) {

   clEnqueueNDRangeKernel(queue, kernel, 1, NULL,
         &num_items, NULL, 0, NULL, &prof_event);
   if(err < 0) {
      perror("Couldn't enqueue the kernel");
      exit(1);
   }
   clFinish(queue);                                    Wait for
                                                       completion

   clGetEventProfilingInfo(prof_event,
         CL_PROFILING_COMMAND_START,                   Measure
         sizeof(time_start), &time_start, NULL);       start time
   clGetEventProfilingInfo(prof_event,
         CL_PROFILING_COMMAND_END,              Measure
         sizeof(time_end), &time_end, NULL);    end time
   total_time += time_end - time_start;
}
printf("Average time = %lu\n", total_time/NUM_ITERATIONS);
...
```

This is similar to the code in listing 7.6, but an important difference is the use of the clFinish function. In listing 7.6, clEnqueueReadBuffer and clEnqueueMapBuffer

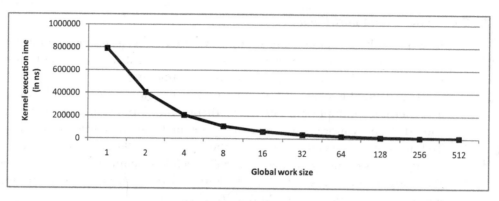

Figure 7.5   Kernel execution with varying global work sizes

were set to block, but `clEnqueueNDRangeKernel` is nonblocking. Therefore, the function returns before the kernel completes its execution. This is a problem because the following lines of code measure the start and end of the kernel's execution. We could measure the timing in a callback function, but with `clFinish`, we can be sure that the application will wait until the kernel's execution completes.

Figure 7.5 presents the results of the data partitioning experiments I conducted by running the code in listing 7.7 on my AMD 5850 graphics card. Each data set consisted of 4,096 integers, and 2,000 iterations were performed for each data point.

This graph clearly shows the importance of partitioning kernels into work-items. Initially, as the experiment proceeds from one work-item to two and four work-items, the execution time drops in half as the number of work-items doubles. The performance improvement continues for larger work sizes, but not as dramatically.

The host application sends two arguments to the kernel. The first is a buffer object that contains integers to be processed. The second argument identifies the number of integers contained in the buffer object. Each work-item uses this second value (called `num_ints`) and the global work size to determine how many vectors it should process. This is given in the following line of code, taken from profile_items.cl:

```
int num_vectors = num_ints/(4 * get_global_size(0));
```

This code ensures that each work-item will access different data than every other work-item. But what if you want the work-items to work together and access common data? In this case, you'll need synchronization, which we'll discuss in the next section.

7.4   *Work-item synchronization*

For the purposes of this book, we'll define *synchronization* as the process of ensuring that computing tasks are performed in order. OpenCL provides two kinds of synchronization: command synchronization and work-item synchronization. We've already examined *command synchronization* earlier in this chapter. This establishes order among commands using events or functions like `clEnqueueBarrier`.

So far, work-item synchronization hasn't been necessary. Our work-items have all accessed different regions of memory, so it hasn't mattered when they start or finish processing their data. But ordering work-items becomes vital when multiple work-items need to access the same data. For example, if you're performing a large dot product of two vectors, each work-item must be able to access and modify the final sum.

Commands can only be synchronized if their command queues belong to the same context. Similarly, work-items can only be synchronized if they're in the same work-group. Chapter 3 explained how to configure work-groups using `clEnqueueNDRangeKernel`. Chapter 4 discussed the kernel functions that access work-group configuration data.

To take the fullest advantage of work-group partitioning, you need to know more than just the functions. You need to understand how work-groups relate to device resources. Chapter 4 discussed the OpenCL device model, but let's quickly review three of the main address spaces:

- Memory specific to a processing element is called *private memory*.
- Memory specific to a compute unit is called *local memory*.
- Memory accessible throughout a device is called *global memory*.

The memory access between a processing element and its private memory is the fastest memory access on the device. Local memory access is slower, and global memory access is slower still. Therefore, for high-performance data processing, you need to use private and local memory as much as possible.

But a problem arises. When multiple work-items process the same data in local memory, their disordered execution can cause errors. To prevent these errors, we need to synchronize work-item execution, and OpenCL provides two methods of doing this. The first method involves fences and barriers, and the second involves atomic operations.

7.4.1 Barriers and fences

Earlier in this chapter, we looked at the `clEnqueueBarrier` function, which helps make command synchronization possible. A barrier command prevents all following commands from executing until every preceding command has completed its execution.

To synchronize work-items in a work-group, OpenCL provides a similar capability with the `barrier` function. This forces a work-item to wait until every other work-item in the group reaches the barrier. Its signature is given as follows:

```
void barrier(cl_mem_fence_flags flags)
```

By creating a barrier, you can make sure that every work-item has reached the same point in its processing. This is a crucial concern when the work-items need to finish computing an intermediate result that will be used in future computation.

For example, suppose you want a work-group to compute the momentum of a large, complex object. The first task involves determining the object's volume. The second task computes the momentum by multiplying this volume by the object's density and velocity. You might start with kernel code like the following:

```
compute_volume();
compute_momentum();
```

But there's a problem. If a work-item starts processing `compute_momentum` before the other work items have finished computing the volume, it will arrive at an inaccurate result because it's using an incomplete value for the volume. We can fix this problem by inserting a barrier between the two tasks:

```
compute_volume();
barrier(CLK_LOCAL_MEM_FENCE);
compute_momentum();
```

The `CLK_LOCAL_MEM_FENCE` flag specifies that the barrier will affect memory operations related to the work-group's local memory. In the example, each work-item must finish accessing local memory before the function following the barrier can start. Similarly, if the flag is set to `CLK_GLOBAL_MEM_FENCE`, the barrier will synchronize work-items' access to global memory.

> **NOTE** The barrier function only synchronizes work-items within a single work-group. At the time of this writing, there is no way to synchronize work-items in different work-groups except by launching a new kernel.

Fences are similar to barriers, but they make it possible to synchronize specific memory operations. That is, some fences affect read operations and others synchronize write operations. OpenCL provides three fence functions that synchronize kernel memory access, and table 7.4 lists all of them.

Table 7.4   Kernel fence functions

Parameter name	Purpose
void read_mem_fence (cl_mem_fence_flags flags)	Stalls further reads from memory until every preceding memory read has completed
void write_mem_fence (cl_mem_fence_flags flags)	Stalls further writes to memory until every preceding write operation has completed
void mem_fence (cl_mem_fence_flags flags)	Stalls further read/write operations until every preceding read/write operation has completed

The `flags` argument of these functions can take the same two values as the `flags` argument of `barrier`: `CLK_LOCAL_MEM_FENCE` to synchronize local memory access or `CLK_GLOBAL_MEM_FENCE` to synchronize global memory access.

7.4.2   *Atomic operations*

Consider the following line of code:

```
x -= 4;
```

This operation performs three suboperations: it reads the value of x, subtracts 4, and stores the updated value. If work-items access different regions of memory, these suboperations will always be performed in order. But problems can arise if multiple work-items access x at the same time.

This can be clarified with an example. Suppose work-item *A* and work-item *B* both process x -= 4, where x is set to 20. The following suboperations may result:

1. Work-item *A* reads the value of x as 20.
2. Work-item *B* reads the value of x as 20.
3. Work-item *A* computes $20 - 4 = 16$.
4. Work-item *A* stores 16 to memory.
5. Work-item *B* computes $20 - 4 = 16$.
6. Work-item *B* stores 16 to memory.

The resulting value of x is 16, which is the wrong answer. But if one work-item is forced to wait until the other finishes, the result will be 12, the correct answer.

The problem is that the operation defined by the -= operator isn't *atomic*. An atomic operation can't be interrupted. If we could find a way to perform -= atomically, work-item *B* won't start until after work-item *A* finishes, and successive work-items won't start until after work-item *B* finishes.

OpenCL makes this possible, not only for subtraction assignments, but also for a number of other a basic mathematic and logical operations. Table 7.5 lists the functions that perform 32-bit atomic operations.

Table 7.5 Atomic operations (32-bit)

Parameter name	Purpose
u/int atomic inc (volatile __(g|l) u/int *x)	Increments the value stored at x (*x += 1)
u/int atomic dec (volatile __(g|l) u/int *x)	Decrements the value stored at x (*x -= 1)
u/int atomic add (volatile __(g|l) u/int *x, u/int val)	Adds a 32-bit val to the value stored at x (*x += val)
u/int atomic sub (volatile __(g|l) u/int *x, u/int val)	Subtracts a 32-bit val from the value stored at x (*x -= val)
u/int atomic and (volatile __(g|l) u/int *x, u/int val)	Sets x equal to the conjunction of a 32- bit val and the value stored at x (*x &= val)
u/int atomic or (volatile __(g|l) u/int *x, u/int val)	Sets x equal to the disjunction of a 32- bit val and the value stored at x (*x |= val)
u/int atomic xor (volatile __(g|l) u/int *x, u/int val)	Sets x equal to the exclusive disjunction of a 32-bit val and the value stored at x (*x ^= val)

Table 7.5   Atomic operations (32-bit) *(continued)*

Parameter name	Purpose
u/int atomic max (volatile __(g|l) u/int *x, u/int val)	Sets x equal to the maximum of a 32-bit val and the value stored at x (x = max(*x, val))
u/int atomic min (volatile __(g|l) u/int *x, u/int val)	Sets x equal to the maximum of a 32-bit val and the value stored at x (x = max(*x, val))
u/int atomic xchg (volatile __(g|l) u/int *x, u/int val)	Swaps x with the 32-bit val (*x = val)
float atomic xchg (volatile __(g|l) float *x, float val)	Swaps x with the 32-bit floating-point val (*x = val)

u/int atomic cmpxchg
    (volatile __(g|l) u/int *x, u/int cmp,
    u/int val)
	Compares the value stored at x to cmp, and sets the value to val if they're equal ((*x == cmp) ? val : *x)

Each of these functions updates scalar values in global or local memory, and each returns the original value of *x. With the exception of atomic_xchg, these operations involve ints or unsigned ints. Integer types can't be combined. That is, if you compute the difference of *x and val atomically, they must both be ints or both unsigned ints.

NOTE   The availability of these atomic functions depends on the extensions supported by the target device. Section 6.11.10 of the OpenCL standard lists the extensions related to atomic functions.

The next listing demonstrates how atomic operations are used. It declares two variables in the local memory space and increments both. The first variable is incremented using the ++ operator whereas the second uses atomic_inc.

Listing 7.8   Testing atomic operations: atomic.cl

```
__kernel void atomic(__global int* x) {

    __local int a, b;

    a = 0;
    b = 0;

    a++;                  ←⎤ Regular
    atomic_inc(&b);       ←⎤ increment
                            ⎤ Atomic
    x[0] = a;               ⎦ increment
    x[1] = b;
}
```

On my system, the results are as follows:

```
Increment: 1
Atomic increment: 4
```

The variables a and b are stored in local memory, so each is allocated once for each compute unit. The host application generates four work-items to execute the kernel, so a and b are both incremented four times. When a is incremented, the four work-items read and modify its value without synchronization. Therefore, the operations are performed in parallel and the result is 1. But when b is incremented, the atomic operation forces the work-items to read and modify its value in sequence. This is why the incremented result for b is 4.

7.4.3 *Atomic commands and mutexes*

One of the most important uses of atomic commands is to enable the operation of *mutexes*, also called semaphores. A mutex (mutual exclusion) ensures that only one work-item can access data at a time. In software, mutexes are commonly implemented as variables that can take one of two values: a locked value and an unlocked value.

Before accessing protected data, each work-item must check the mutex's value. If the mutex is set to its locked value, it means the data is already being processed. But if a work-item finds the mutex in its unlocked value, then it will set the mutex to its locked value, process the data, and then set the mutex to its unlocked state.

A mutex is like a lock on a dressing room. When the dressing room is unlocked, anyone can come in. But when a person enters the room, they lock the door, thereby preventing others from entering. When the person is finished, they unlock the door and leave.

The check-unlock procedure must be performed atomically, or two work-items might find the mutex unlocked at the same time. To implement this procedure, the atomic_cmpxchg function is ideal. It performs the C ternary operator (((*x == cmp) ? val : *x) atomically. That is, it checks whether *x equals cmp, and if so, it changes *x to val. If not, *x remains unchanged. atomic_cmpxchg returns the original value of *x.

Let's choose 0 as the unlocked value of our mutex and 1 as the locked value. Then we can use atomic_cmpxchg to check-unlock a local variable called mutex with the following code:

```
if (atomic_cmpxchg(&mutex, 0, 1) == 0) {
   process_critical_data();
   atomic_xchg(&mutex, 0);
}
```

Here, the work-item atomically checks the value of mutex, and if it equals 0 (unlocked), the work-item sets its value to 1 (locked). Then the work-item processes critical data and unlocks mutex by setting its value to 0.

Similarly, you can implement a spinlock by calling atomic_cmpxchg in a while loop. A spinlock prevents a work-item from continuing execution until it has unlocked the mutex. This is shown in the following line of code:

```
while(atomic_cmpxchg(&mutex, 0, 1) == 1);
```

The following listing shows how mutexes can be used to synchronize work-items. The LOCK macro invokes atom_cmpxchg and the UNLOCK macro invokes atom_xchg.

Listing 7.9 Mutex-based synchronization: mutex.cl

```
#pragma OPENCL EXTENSION cl_khr_global_int32_base_atomics : enable

#define LOCK(a)   atom_cmpxchg(a, 0, 1)
#define UNLOCK(a) atom_xchg(a, 0)

__kernel void mutex(__global int *mutex, __global int *sum) {

   while(LOCK(mutex));
   *sum += 1;                                              Increment
   UNLOCK(mutex);                                          sum

   int waiting = 1;
   while(waiting) {
      while(LOCK(mutex));
      if(*sum == get_global_size(0)) {                     Wait for
         waiting = 0;                                      completion
      }
      UNLOCK(mutex);
   }
}
```

When the kernel executes, each work-item reaches the spinlock and waits until `mutex` equals 0. When it's unlocked, the work-item locks `mutex`, increments `sum`, and unlocks `mutex`. Afterward, the work-item waits until `sum` equals the total number of work-items. At this point, all of the work-items executing the kernel are synchronized.

The host application sets the local size to 1, which means each work-item executing the kernel belongs to a different work-group. This may seem surprising because I mentioned earlier that work-items in different work-groups can only be synchronized by restarting the kernel. As it turns out, there's a catch.

The catch is that the number of work-items executing this kernel can't exceed the number of compute units on the device. For example, if a device contains 16 compute units, then the 16 work-items (each in a different work-group) can execute concurrently and they can be synchronized with the mutex. But if you attempt to execute this kernel with 17 work-groups, the device will stall because the first 16 work-groups will wait for the seventeenth to access the mutex. But the seventeenth can't start until one of the 16 compute units is available.

If you execute this kernel with work-items in the same work-group, the kernel will hang. This is because work-items in the same work-group combine their individual reads and writes to global memory into a single memory operation for the entire group. The work-items can't access global memory separately, so they can't lock and unlock the `mutex` at different times.

7.4.4 *Asynchronous data transfer*

The code in listing 7.8 declares two variables in local memory and transfers their values to global memory. This is fine for individual scalars and vectors, but it can be time-consuming to transfer a great deal of data between local and global memory in this manner. For large data sizes, it's more efficient for a kernel to start the data transfer and perform other activities while the transfer completes. This is called *asynchronous data transfer.*

OpenCL enables asynchronous data transfer with a series of functions that copy data between local and global memory. Table 7.6 lists each of them along with the operation they perform.

Table 7.6   Asynchronous data transfer

Function name	Purpose

`event_t async_work_group_copy`
`    (__local all *dst,`
`    const __global all *src,`
`    size_t num, event_t event)`
 	
`event_t async_work_group_copy`
`    (__global all *dst,`
`    const __local all *src,`
`    size_t num, event_t event)`
	Copies data between local and global memory. Returns an `event_t` that represents the status of the data transfer.

`event_t async_work_group_strided_copy`
`    (__local all *dst,`
`    const __global all *src,`
`    size_t num, size_t src_stride,`
`    event_t event)`
 	
`event_t async_work_group_strided_copy`
`    (__global gentype *dst,`
`    const __local gentype *src,`
`    size_t num, size_t dst_stride,`
`    event_t event)`
	Transfers strided data between local memory and global memory. Returns an `event_t` that represents the status of the data transfer.

`void wait_group_events(int num_events,` `    event_t *wait_list)`	Accepts one or more `event_t` structures, and waits for the corresponding data transfers to complete.
`void prefetch(const __global all *mem,` `    size_t num)`	Reads data into the global cache.

The `async_work_group_copy` and `async_work_group_strided_copy` functions have two variations. The first variation transfers data from local memory to global memory, and the second transfers data from global memory to local memory. In both cases, the num argument identifies how many elements of the given type will be transferred.

Unlike `async_work_group_copy`, `async_work_group_strided_copy` accepts an additional parameter that identifies how many elements lie between those to be transferred. This parameter is referred to as the *stride*, and it becomes helpful when you need to copy sequential data from global memory to or from multiple compute units. The first variation of `async_work_group_strided_copy` accepts a `src_stride` argument that identifies the stride of the data to be copied from global memory. The second variation accepts a `dst_stride` argument that identifies the stride of the data to be copied to global memory.

Both copy functions return an `event_t` structure that acts like the `cl_event` structure used in host applications. This `event_t` represents the status of the transfer, and it can be associated with other data transfers by making it the last argument of the corresponding copy functions. There's no way to associate the `event_t` with a callback function, but you can wait for one or more `event_t` structures by calling `wait_group_events`. The following code shows how this works:

```
event_t e = async_work_group_copy(glob_data, loc_data, 10, (event_t) 0);
async_work_group_copy(loc_data, glob_data, 10, e);
...
wait_group_events(1, &e);
```

In this code, the first function call transfers data from local memory to global memory and the second call transfers data from global memory to local memory. The `wait_group_events` function waits for both transfers to complete.

The last function in table 7.6, `prefetch`, reads data into the global cache. Like the two copy functions, it can transfer data of any type except vectors containing three components. But it doesn't return an `event_t`, so there is no way to be certain when the operation has completed.

7.5   Summary

This chapter has discussed three advanced topics of OpenCL programming, and all of them relate to timing and control. With events, you can keep track of when operations are finished and respond to their completion. With profiling, you can determine the amount of time taken by devices to perform various tasks. With work-item synchronization, you can establish an order in the execution of work-items, which normally execute in a nondeterministic fashion.

An OpenCL event, represented by a `cl_event` data structure, corresponds to the completion of a task. On the device, an event's task may involve the execution of a kernel or the transfer of data to or from the host. But as you've seen, events can also be generated on the host. In this case, you simply need to invoke `clSetUserEventStatus` to set an event's status as completed.

Events become particularly important when you need to measure how long a command took to execute. In this case, the function to know is `clGetEventProfilingInfo`. This analyzes a `cl_event` corresponding to a command and returns how much time was taken between status changes of the event.

Work-item synchronization is only necessary when an algorithm demands access to shared data. In this case, you need to ensure that work-items access data in an organized fashion and complete their memory access by specific checkpoints. You can set these checkpoints using barriers and fences. To keep multiple work-items from accessing data at once, you need atomic operations. These operations are uninterruptible, which means that work-items will always perform the operation without interruption.

In the next chapter, we'll break completely from OpenCL host programming in C. We'll look at programming in C++, and see the advantages that object-oriented programming provide when used in high-performance computing.

Development with C++   8

This chapter covers

- Creating kernels with the C++ Wrapper API
- Enqueuing commands with the CommandQueue class
- Processing events with the Event and UserEvent classes

When I need to crunch numbers at high speed, I prefer to write code in C. This is because my favorite compilers are optimized for high-speed processing, the executables tend to be small, and there's usually plenty of code available on the internet from which I can draw inspiration.

But when my application needs to do more than just crunch numbers, such as animate an assemblage of moving parts, I prefer an object-oriented (OO) language like C++. This gives me the benefits associated with OO programming, such as polymorphism, inheritance, and encapsulation. It also provides a wealth of capabilities through the C++ Standard Template Library (STL) and the Boost libraries.

The OpenCL Working Group provides a C++ Wrapper API that makes it possible to code full-featured OpenCL host applications in C++. This API provides many advantages over the regular C API, and three of the most important advantages are as follows:

- *No need to dynamically allocate arrays*—The C++ wrapper relies on Vectors instead of arrays, so there's no need to dynamically allocate memory to store multiple platforms, multiple devices, or data from a call to get*XX*Info.
- *Simpler function calls*—Partly because of the preceding point, C++ functions usually require fewer arguments than their C counterparts.
- *No reference counts or deallocation functions*—The C API requires that data structures be deallocated with functions like free and clReleaseCommandQueue. But with C++, object deallocation is handled by default.

Given the size of the C++ API, this chapter can't discuss every class and function in detail. But it will present a large portion of them. After discussing how kernels are created in C++, we'll look at how to set kernel arguments. We'll also look at how to code command queues in C++ that send tasks to devices. The last part of this chapter explores C++ event processing.

> **NOTE**   For more information on C++, I heartily recommend *C++/CLI in Action* by Nishant Sivakumar and *C++ Concurrency in Action* by Anthony Williams. Both books provide thorough discussions of their subject material and contain helpful examples that demonstrate how the theory is implemented in code.

But before discussing host application development, it's important to examine three important topics. The next section presents two classes defined in the cl.hpp header that replace classes in the STL: cl::vector and cl::string. It also shows how the C++ API manages exception handling.

8.1   Preliminary concerns

Regular C code relies on arrays for data collection, but C++ uses strings to hold characters and vectors to hold everything else. The STL provides string and vector classes, but the C++ Wrapper API provides alternatives. This section will explain how to access these alternative classes and use them in code.

Whereas C uses integer codes to test for errors, C++ makes use of exception handling. OpenCL disables exceptions by default, but this section will discuss how to enable them in your code.

8.1.1   Vectors and strings

If you look through the function signatures in the C++ API, you'll see many references to VECTOR_CLASS and STRING_CLASS. These macros identify which classes will be employed to represent vectors and strings. You can choose between std::vector/std::string and cl::vector/cl::string or create your own custom classes.

By default, the C++ Wrapper API relies on the std::vector and std::string classes. But to support platforms for which the STL is unavailable, the creators of the C++ Wrapper coded their own replacements. If you look through the cl.hpp header file, you'll find two new classes: cl::vector and cl::string.

OPENCL VECTORS

The cl::vector class is similar to std::vector, but many functions are missing. With a cl::vector, you can't call resize, reserve, insert, erase, or swap. But in many host applications, you won't miss these functions because vectors are commonly initialized when they're first used. To use cl::vectors instead of std::vectors, insert the following definition in your host application:

```
#define __NO_STD_VECTOR
```

By default, the maximum capacity of a cl::vector is 10, but this can be increased by redefining the __MAX_DEFAULT_VECTOR_SIZE macro. For example, if you have 20 OpenCL devices connected, you could use the following definition:

```
#define __MAX_DEFAULT_VECTOR_SIZE 20
```

If you'd rather not rely on std::vector or cl::vector, you can use your own custom class. This class must implement the std::vector interface, and the VECTOR_CLASS macro must be set to the class's name. In addition, the __USE_DEV_VECTOR macro must be defined.

For example, if MyVector is a template-based container class that follows the std::vector interface, you can make sure the API uses this with the following definitions:

```
#define __USE_DEV_VECTOR
#define VECTOR_CLASS MyVector
```

OPENCL STRINGS

The cl::string class has much in common with the std::string class, but besides the constructors and destructors, the only member functions are size, length, and c_str. Therefore, if you need to manipulate strings in your host application, you may be better off with the default, std::string. But if you prefer the cl::string class, you'll need to define the __NO_STD_STRING macro. That is, insert the following line into your code:

```
#define __NO_STD_STRING
```

You can also identify a custom class to serve as the string replacement. This class must implement the std::string interface, and the STRING_CLASS macro must be set equal to the class's name. In addition, the __USE_DEV_STRING macro must be defined. If you'd like the host application to store characters with NewString, you'll need to add the following definitions:

```
#define __USE_DEV_STRING
#define STRING_CLASS NewString
```

8.1.2 Exceptions

In C and C++, many OpenCL functions return or set a cl_int that identifies the function's completion status. If the error code equals 0, the function completed successfully. A negative code indicates an error.

These codes are fine for C programs, but C++ provides *exception handling*, which allows you to separate error handling routines from the main code. OpenCL disables exceptions by default, but you can enable them with the following macro definition:

```
#define __CL_ENABLE_EXCEPTIONS
```

Once you've set this definition, you can add `try` and `catch` blocks to your program. Inside the `catch` block, you can obtain error information by calling two functions of the `cl::Error` class:

- what—Identifies the C function that caused the error
- err—Returns the error code of the C function

The following example shows how exception handling can be enabled and coded in a host application:

```
#define __CL_ENABLE_EXCEPTIONS
...
try {
    process_data...
}
catch(Error e) {
    std::cout << e.what() << ": Error code " << e.err() << std::endl;
}
```

If an error occurs within the `try` block, the `catch` block will print the C function that produced the error and the function's error code. Note that `__CL_ENABLE_EXTENSIONS` must be defined for the exception handling to work properly.

The `cl::vector`, `cl::string`, and `cl::Error` classes are all disabled by default. But because they're defined in the cl.hpp header, you can be sure they will behave the same way on different operating systems and processors. This isn't necessarily true when it comes to classes in the STL.

In the next section, we'll start looking at more interesting classes of the C++ Wrapper API. These are the classes that make it possible for the host application to create kernel functions.

8.2   *Creating kernels*

In a C host application, the main OpenCL data structures are `cl_platform`, `cl_device`, `cl_context`, `cl_program`, and `cl_kernel`. Conveniently, the C++ wrapper provides classes with similar names: `Platform`, `Device`, `Context`, `Program`, and `Kernel`. This section presents each of these classes and many of their associated member functions.

8.2.1   *Platforms, devices, and contexts*

In much of our example C code, the first step has been to access `cl_platforms` by calling `clGetPlatformIDs`. With these data structures, you can obtain information about the installed platforms with `clGetPlatformInfo` or discover connected devices with clGetDeviceIDs. Each device is represented by a `cl_device_id` structure, which can be used to create a context, represented by a `cl_context`.

With the C++ Wrapper API, you can accomplish the same results with the `Platform`, `Device`, and `Context` classes. We'll look at the `Platform` class first.

THE PLATFORM CLASS

A `Platform` object represents an installed platform on the development system, such as Nvidia's platform or AMD's platform. To obtain `Platform` objects, you need to call the static function `Platform::get`. This returns a vector containing a `Platform` object for each installed platform on the system, and its signature is as follows:

```
static cl_int Platform::get(VECTOR_CLASS<Platform>* platforms)
```

This simple function only takes one argument, as compared to the three arguments required by `clGetPlatformIDs`. The reason for this is that C++ vectors are dynamically allocated, so you don't have to allocate memory in advance.

The `getInfo` member function is even simpler. Whereas `clGetPlatformInfo` takes five arguments, the C++ function `Platform::getInfo` takes only two. Its signature is as follows:

```
cl_int Platform::getInfo(cl_platform_info name, STRING_CLASS* param)
```

The first argument takes any of the `cl_platform_info` values listed in table 2.2. The following code shows how `getInfo` is used. It accesses the extensions supported by a `Platform` called `platform` and places the data in a string called `ext_data`:

```
err = platform.getInfo(CL_PLATFORM_EXTENSIONS, ext_data);
```

This is much simpler to use than `clGetPlatformInfo`, but there's a way to access platform data that's even simpler. By making the `cl_platform_info` value a template parameter of `getInfo`, you can access the same data in the following manner:

```
ext_data = platform.getInfo<CL_PLATFORM_EXTENSIONS>();
```

It doesn't get much simpler than this. And the wonderful thing is that every `clGetXXInfo` function discussed in previous chapters has a `getInfo` equivalent that can be invoked in the same way.

> **NOTE** The `getInfo` functions of other OpenCL classes (`Device::getInfo`, `Program::getInfo`, `Kernel::getInfo`, and so on) work in the same manner as `Platform::getInfo`, so we won't discuss these functions further.

The most important capability of a `Platform` object is that it allows you to access `Device` objects associated with the installed platform. For example, if a `Platform` represents an AMD installation, you can use it to access every connected CPU or GPU associated with AMD. The function that makes this possible is `getDevices`, and its signature is as follows:

```
cl_int Platform::getDevices(cl_device_type type,
    VECTOR_CLASS<Device>* devices)
```

This function initializes a vector containing every Device object of the given type associated with the platform. We'll look at Devices and Contexts next.

THE DEVICE AND CONTEXT CLASSES

We've seen how to access Device objects through Platform::getDevices, but you can also create Device objects from cl_device_id structures. The Device constructor accepts a pointer to a cl_device_id, and it can be used as follows:

```
Device d(&dev_id);
```

Once you've decided which Device objects you want to execute your kernels, you can use them to create a Context. There are two ways to do this. The first method involves creating a Context from a vector of Device objects. The signature for this constructor is as follows:

```
Context(VECTOR_CLASS<Device>& devices, cl_context_properties* props = NULL,
    void (CL_CALLBACK* pfn_notify)(const char* errorinfo,
        const void* info_size, ::size_t cb, void * user_data) = NULL,
    void* user_data = NULL, cl_int* err = NULL)
```

The arguments of this function are almost exactly like those of the clCreateContext function we looked at in chapter 2. The only differences are that the constructor requires a vector of Device objects instead of an array of cl_device_id structures, and you don't have to identify how many elements are in the vector. Because of the constructor's default values, the only required parameter is the Device vector.

The second constructor defined by the Context class creates a Context containing all connected devices of a given type. Here is the signature for this constructor:

```
Context(cl_device_type type, cl_context_properties* props = NULL,
    void (CL_CALLBACK* pfn_notify)(const char* errorinfo,
        const void* info_size, ::size_t cb, void* user_data) = NULL,
    void * user_data = NULL, cl_int * err = NULL)
```

This constructor corresponds to the C function clCreateContextFromType. The only required parameter is the type of device you're interested in, and table 2.3 lists the five different device types available.

The code in the following listing shows how Platform, Device, and Context objects are used in practice. It accesses the first installed platform and places its devices in a std::vector. Then it creates a Context containing the devices and prints the name of each.

Listing 8.1   Testing a context in C++: full_context.cpp

```
#define __CL_ENABLE_EXCEPTIONS
#define __NO_STD_STRING

#include <iostream>

#ifdef MAC
#include <OpenCL/cl.hpp>
#else
#include <CL/cl.hpp>
```

```
#endif

using namespace std;

int main(void) {
    vector<cl::Platform> platforms;
    vector<cl::Device> platformDevices, allDevices, ctxDevices;
    cl::string device_name;
    cl_uint i;

    try {
        cl::Platform::get(&platforms);                     // Access platform
        platforms[0].getDevices(CL_DEVICE_TYPE_ALL,        // devices
            &platformDevices);

        cl::Context context(platformDevices);
        ctxDevices =
            context.getInfo<CL_CONTEXT_DEVICES>();
        for(i=0; i<ctxDevices.size(); i++) {
            device_name =
                ctxDevices[i].
                getInfo<CL_DEVICE_NAME>();                 // Create context and
            cout << "Device: "                             // display devices
                << device_name.c_str()
                << endl;
        }
    }
    catch(cl::Error e) {
        cout << e.what() << ": Error code "                // Handle
            << e.err() << endl;                            // errors
    }
    return 0;
}
```

If this had been coded in C, the listing would probably be at least twice as long. But thanks to C++'s vectors and exception handling, we can perform the same operations in a cleaner, more organized manner.

The __NO_STD_STRING definition at the start of the listing means we'll be dealing with cl::strings instead of std::strings. This makes no difference for the most part. But when the code displays the device names, it has to call c_str to convert the cl::string into a form that can be directed to the output stream. If device_name had been a std::string, you could have displayed the result with cout << device_name, but because it's a cl::string, the code uses cout << device_name.c_str().

The vectors used in this code are std::vector objects, not cl::vector objects. This is because the insert function is needed. cl::vectors are fine for most applications, but if you need to resize or concatenate vectors, you may be better off with the std::vector class.

8.2.2 Programs and kernels

Once you've created a Context object, the next step is to create a Program object to contain the code that will be executed on the context's devices. After you've created a Program, you'll need to compile the code for the target devices and then create Kernel objects from the compiled functions.

CREATING A PROGRAM OBJECT

The Program class provides two constructors: one that creates a Program from source code (text) and one that creates a Program from binary code. Their signatures are as follows:

```
Program(const Context& context, const Sources& sources, cl_int* err = NULL)

Program(const Context& context, const VECTOR_CLASS<Device>& devices,
    const Binaries& binaries, VECTOR_CLASS<cl_int>* binaryStatus = NULL,
    cl_int* err = NULL)
```

The first constructor depends on a Sources data type and the second depends on a Binaries data type. These types are defined in cl.hpp as follows:

```
typedef VECTOR_CLASS<std::pair<const char*, ::size_t> > Sources;

typedef VECTOR_CLASS<std::pair<const void*, ::size_t> > Binaries;
```

Both of these types are vectors that contain pair objects. In a Sources object, each pair contains a char* and the size of the corresponding text in bytes. To create a Program from a text file, you'll need to convert the file into a Sources object. To do this, you can use a three-step process:

1 Create an input file stream (ifstream) using the filename.
2 Form an iterator (istreambuf_iterator) to create a string from the file stream.
3 Create a pair containing the string characters and the size of the string (plus one).

For example, to create a Program from a file called kernel.cl, you could use code similar to the following:

```
std::ifstream programFile("kernel.cl");

std::string programString(std::istreambuf_iterator<char>(programFile),
    (std::istreambuf_iterator<char>()));

cl::Program::Sources source(1,
    std::make_pair(programString.c_str(), programString.length()+1));

cl::Program program(context, source);
```

As shown, the length of the source text must be set to the length of the string plus one. This additional character must be included because the c_str function automatically appends a null-termination character to the end of the char array.

BUILDING A PROGRAM OBJECT

As discussed in chapter 2, each OpenCL framework provides a runtime compiler that builds device-specific binaries. In C, this compiler is invoked using clBuildProgram. In C++, programs are compiled using the build function of the Program class. The signature for this function is as follows:

```
cl_int Program::build(
    const VECTOR_CLASS<Device> devices, const char* options = NULL,
    (CL_CALLBACK* pfn_notify) (cl_program, void* user_data) = NULL,
    void* data = NULL)
```

The first argument is a vector containing the Device objects that will be targeted by the compiler. The second argument identifies options to constrain the build process, such as what types of errors should be reported and which mathematical operations should be allowed. Chapter 2 discusses these options in detail and table 2.7 lists each of them.

For example, the following code builds a Program that targets the devices in a vector called targets. It also tells the compiler to allow atomic multiply-and-add (MAD) operations. The last two arguments are set to their default values, which equal NULL:

```
program.build(targets, "-cl-mad-enable");
```

If an error occurs during the build, it's important to obtain as much information as possible. Chapter 2 explained the clGetProgramBuildInfo function and the different types of information available. In C++, the getBuildInfo function accomplishes the same result. This works like the getInfo function we examined earlier. To access the build log, you could use the following code:

```
cl::string log = program.getBuildInfo<CL_PROGRAM_BUILD_LOG>();
```

If the build completes without error, the log will be empty. You can also call getBuildInfo with the CL_PROGRAM_BUILD_OPTIONS flag to obtain the build options.

CREATING KERNELS

OpenCL provides two ways to create kernels from a program. You can create a kernel for every kernel function inside a program, or you can create a single kernel for a specific function. In C, these two options are accomplished with clCreateKernelsInProgram and clCreateKernel, respectively.

In C++, you can create a kernel for every kernel function in a Program with createKernels. The signature of this simple function is as follows:

```
cl_int Program::createKernels(const VECTOR_CLASS<Kernel>* kernels)
```

The following code demonstrates the use of this function. It declares a cl::vector of Kernel objects to be initialized by the createKernels function:

```
cl::vector<cl::Kernel> kernels;
cl_int Program::createKernels(kernels);
```

To create a single kernel, you need to call the constructor of the Kernel class. This is its signature:

```
Kernel::Kernel(const Program& program, const char* name,
    cl_int* err = NULL)
```

As an example, let's say there's a kernel function called kernel_func within a program called prog. To create a kernel for kernel_func, you'd use the following code:

```
cl::Kernel kernel(prog, kernel_func);
```

The following code demonstrates both methods of creating kernels. After forming a Program from the kernels.cl file, it creates three individual Kernel objects using the Kernel constructor. Then it initializes a vector of Kernel objects by calling createKernels.

Listing 8.2   Creating kernels in C++: create_kernels.cpp

```
...
cl::Platform::get(&platforms);
platforms[0].getDevices(CL_DEVICE_TYPE_GPU, &devices);    Place GPU
cl::Context context(devices);                             devices in vector

std::ifstream programFile("kernels.cl");
std::string programString(
       std::istreambuf_iterator<char>(programFile),
       (std::istreambuf_iterator<char>()));
cl::Program::Sources source(1,                            Create and
       std::make_pair(programString.c_str(),              build program
       programString.length()+1));
cl::Program program(context, source);
program.build(devices);

cl::Kernel addKernel(program, "add");                     Create individual
cl::Kernel subKernel(program, "subtract");                kernels
cl::Kernel multKernel(program, "multiply");
                                                          Create all kernels
program.createKernels(&allKernels);                       in program
for(unsigned int i=0; i<allKernels.size(); i++) {
   kernelName = allKernels[i].getInfo<CL_KERNEL_FUNCTION_NAME>();
   std::cout << "Kernel: " << kernelName << std::endl;
}
...
```

This listing is straightforward to understand, and the code used to build a Program closely resembles the example code presented earlier. You can rely on cl::vectors in this code because there's no need to add or remove elements. But this code can't use cl::strings because a cl::string can't be formed from an input file stream buffer iterator (istreambuf_iterator).

This section has discussed how to create Kernel objects using the C++ API, but there's still a lot of work to be done before you can deploy these kernels to a device. For one thing, you need to create the kernels' arguments. This is the topic of the next section.

8.3   *Kernel arguments and memory objects*

Every kernel function returns void, so if it's going to process input data and produce output data, it has to rely on its arguments. One of the responsibilities of the host application is to configure these arguments before the kernel is sent to the device. If an argument provides input, the host needs to set the size and content of the input data. If an argument stores output, the host only needs to set the size.

In both cases, the host application relies on the setArg function of the Kernel class. The signature of this function is as follows:

```
template <typename T>
cl_int Kernel::setArg(cl_uint index, T value)
```

In this signature, index identifies the order of the argument in the function's parameter list. T identifies the data that will be sent to the kernel. The exact data type of T is determined at compile time, but it can be any of the following:

- cl::Sampler—T is a sampler that will be used to process an image object.
- cl::Memory—T is a memory object (buffer object or image object) that will be passed to the kernel by reference.
- General data—T contains data that will be passed to the kernel by value.
- cl::LocalSpaceArg—The argument will be stored in the device's local space.

The first option, cl::Sampler, corresponds to the samplers discussed in chapter 6. The rest of this section will discuss the last three options. We'll start by discussing memory objects and then look at creating arguments from general data or cl::LocalSpaceArg objects.

8.3.1 Memory objects

A memory object is an instantiation of the cl::Memory class. This contains data that will be passed to the kernel by reference. The two types of memory objects are buffer objects, which store one-dimensional data, and image objects, which store multidimensional data.

Figure 8.1 presents the cl::Memory class hierarchy. The functions in each class are presented without their arguments.

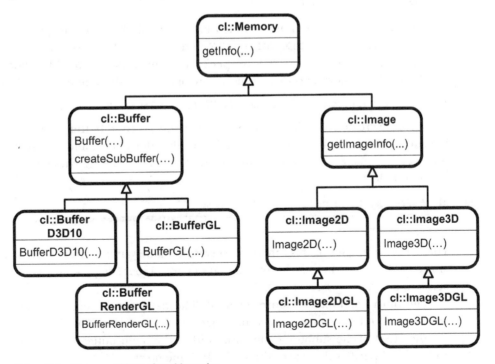

Figure 8.1 Memory object class hierarchy

The cl.hpp header contains definitions for the classes ending in GL and D3D10, but they aren't mentioned in the C++ Wrapper API documentation. For this reason, we'll limit our discussion to buffer objects (cl::Buffer) and image objects (cl::Image, cl::Image2D, and cl::Image3D).

BUFFER OBJECTS

If you need to transfer a memory object to a kernel that doesn't involve images or graphics, you should make the memory object a buffer object. This is represented by the cl::Buffer class, whose constructor is as follows:

```
Buffer::Buffer(const Context& context, cl_mem_flags flags,
    ::size_t size, void* host_ptr = NULL, cl_int* err = NULL)
```

The host_ptr parameter identifies data on the host that will be used to form a buffer. The size parameter identifies the size of the data to be contained inside the buffer. The flags parameter identifies the read/write capability of the buffer relative to the device and the nature of the buffer memory's allocation on the host. Chapter 3 explains these parameters in detail, and table 3.1 lists the different flags and their purposes.

If a kernel argument is intended to provide input, the host should set its readability to CL_MEM_READ_ONLY or CL_MEM_READ_WRITE. In this case, host_ptr must not be NULL. This is shown in the following code, which creates a cl::Buffer containing 128 bytes starting at the memory region referenced by host_mem:

```
cl::Buffer buff(context, CL_MEM_READ_ONLY | CL_MEM_COPY_HOST_PTR,
    128, host_mem, &err);
```

If a kernel argument is intended to hold output exclusively, the memory object's readability should be set to CL_MEM_WRITE_ONLY. In this case, host_ptr should be set to NULL but the size parameter still needs to specify how much space should be allocated on the device. The following code creates a write-only buffer that will hold 256 bytes:

```
cl::Buffer buff(context, CL_MEM_WRITE_ONLY, 256, NULL, &err);
```

Once you've created a buffer object, you can create a second buffer object whose data is a subset of that of the first. This is called a subbuffer object, and it's created using the createSubBuffer function of the cl::Buffer class. The signature for this function is as follows:

```
cl::Buffer Buffer::createSubBuffer(cl_mem_flags flags,
    cl_buffer_create_type buffer_type, const void* buffer_create_info,
    cl_int* err = NULL)
```

The flags parameter in this function accepts the same values as the flags parameter of the Buffer constructor. The second parameter, cl_buffer_create_type, can only be set to CL_BUFFER_CREATE_TYPE_REGION.

The third parameter is more involved. The data type is const void*, but the pointer must reference memory containing two size_t values. The first size_t specifies the offset of the subbuffer's memory within the main buffer's memory. The second size_t specifies the size of the subbuffer's memory.

For example, if a main buffer contains 200 `float`s and you want to create a subbuffer containing `float`s 70–89, you could use the following function:

```
size_t config[2] = {70*sizeof(float), 20*sizeof(float)};
subBuffer = mainBuffer.createSubBuffer(CL_MEM_READ_ONLY |
    CL_MEM_COPY_HOST_PTR, CL_BUFFER_CREATE_TYPE_REGION, (void*)config);
```

The code in the following listing creates two buffers, `mainBuffer` and `subBuffer`, and makes them arguments of a `Kernel`. Then it displays the sizes and locations of their memory regions on the host.

NOTE This code relies on subbuffers, which were introduced in OpenCL 1.1. This code will execute only on devices that support 1.1 capabilities.

Listing 8.3 Creating a subbuffer in C++: sub_buffer.cpp

```
...
cl::Buffer mainBuffer(context,
    CL_MEM_READ_ONLY | CL_MEM_COPY_HOST_PTR,                    Make mainBuffer
    sizeof(data), data);                                       kernel argument
kernel.setArg(0, mainBuffer);

size_t config[2] = {70*sizeof(float), 20*sizeof(float)};
subBuffer = mainBuffer.createSubBuffer(                        Make subBuffer
    CL_MEM_READ_ONLY | CL_MEM_COPY_HOST_PTR,                   kernel argument
    CL_BUFFER_CREATE_TYPE_REGION, (void*)config);
kernel.setArg(1, subBuffer);

std::cout << "Main buffer size: "
    << mainBuffer.getInfo<CL_MEM_SIZE>()
    << std::endl;
std::cout << "Main buffer memory location: "
    << mainBuffer.getInfo<CL_MEM_HOST_PTR>()                   Create individual
    << std::endl;                                              kernels
std::cout << "Sub-buffer size: "
    << subBuffer.getInfo<CL_MEM_SIZE>() << std::endl;
std::cout << "Sub-buffer memory location: "
    << subBuffer.getInfo<CL_MEM_HOST_PTR>()
    << std::endl;
...
```

On my system, this is the output of the sub_buffer executable:

```
Main buffer size: 800
Main buffer memory location: 0x2596000
Sub-buffer size: 80
Sub-buffer memory location: 0x2596118
```

This output shows that the size of the subbuffer's data is 80 bytes, which equals 20 * `sizeof(float)`. The memory location of the subbuffer's data has an offset of 0x118 from the start of the main buffer's data. This equals 280, or 70 * `sizeof(float)`.

IMAGE OBJECTS

As discussed in chapter 6, OpenCL provides many capabilities for processing images inside kernels. But before a kernel can process an image, the host needs to transfer it to the device as an image object. In C++, if the host needs to send pixel data or texture data to a device, it should package the data inside a `cl::Image` object.

The `cl::Image` class doesn't provide a public constructor, so host applications must create instances of its subclasses. As shown in figure 8.1, its subclasses are distinguished by the dimensionality of the image data. If the image data is two-dimensional, the host should create a `cl::Image2D` object. If the image data is three-dimensional (such as in a succession of images), the host should create a `cl::Image3D` object. The constructors of the `cl::Image2D` object and `cl::Image3D` object are as follows:

```
cl::Image2D::Image2D(Context& context, cl_mem_flags flags,
    ImageFormat format, ::size_t width, ::size_t height,
    ::size_t row_pitch = 0, void* host_ptr = NULL, cl_int* err = NULL)
```

```
cl::Image3D::Image3D(const Context& context, cl_mem_flags flags,
    ImageFormat format, ::size_t width, ::size_t height, ::size_t depth,
    ::size_t row_pitch = 0, ::size_t slice_pitch = 0,
    void* host_ptr = NULL, cl_int* err = NULL)
```

The `flags` parameter takes the same values as the `flags` parameter of the `Buffer` constructor, but the next four arguments are entirely different. The `format` argument specifies the nature of the image data by providing an `ImageFormat` object, which wraps around the `cl_image_format` data structure discussed in chapter 3. An `ImageFormat` object can be formed with the following function:

```
ImageFormat(cl_channel_order order, cl_channel_type type)
```

Here, the `cl_channel_order` defines what channels are present and the order in which they're stored. This is an enumerated type, and most of its values involve red, green, blue, and alpha channels: `CL_RGB`, `CL_RGBA`, `CL_ARGB`, `CL_BGRA`, `CL_RG`, `CL_RA`, `CL_R`, and `CL_A`. Other values add bit padding, represented by x: `CL_RGBx`, `CL_RGx`, and `CL_Rx`. `CL_INTENSITY` measures alpha (opacity) independent of color, and `CL_LUMINANCE` is used for grayscale images.

The `cl_channel_type` identifies the numerical data types and data sizes used to specify the image's channel data. For example, if each channel is represented by a 16-bit unsigned short, you'd set the type to `CL_UNSIGNED_INT16`. Table 3.2 lists all the possible values of `cl_channel_type`.

For example, to create an `ImageFormat` that represents the RGBA format, you'd make the following declaration:

```
cl::ImageFormat format(CL_RGBA, CL_UNSIGNED_INT8);
```

Returning to the two image constructors, the arguments following `format` identify the geometry of the image data. For two-dimensional images, this consists of the width, height, and row pitch. For three-dimensional images, this consists of the width, height, depth, row pitch, and slice pitch. Figure 8.2 depicts the geometry of a three-dimensional image.

In both constructors, the `row_pitch` argument identifies how many bytes are in each row. If `row_pitch` is set to 0, OpenCL will assume its value equals width * (pixel

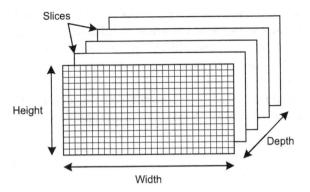

Figure 8.2 Geometry of a three-dimensional image object

size). The `cl::Image3D` object constructor accepts a `slice_pitch` argument that identifies the number of bytes in each two-dimensional image, or slice. If `slice_pitch` is set to 0, its value will be set to `row_pitch * height`.

The following code creates a three-dimensional image object from four slices of 800 * 600 pixels each. The pixels are provided in the RGBA format:

```
#define NUM_ROWS 600
#define NUM_COLS 800
#define NUM_SLICES 4

unsigned char rgb_data[NUM_SLICES][NUM_ROWS][NUM_COLS];
cl::ImageFormat format(CL_RGBA, CL_UNSIGNED_INT8);

cl::Image3D image(context, CL_MEM_READ_ONLY | CL_MEM_COPY_HOST_PTR,
    format, NUM_COLS, NUM_ROWS, NUM_SLICES, 0, 0, (void*)rgb_data);
```

Once you've created an image object, you can obtain information about it in two ways. First, the `getInfo` function of the `cl::Memory` class provides general information about the memory object, such as the size and address of its data.

Second, the `getImageInfo` function of the `cl::Image` class provides information specific to images, such as its pixel format and geometry. Table 3.3 lists the different kinds of information available.

As an example, the following code accesses information about the `cl::Image3D` object created earlier. It calls `getInfo` to determine the number of bytes in the data and then calls `getImageInfo` to determine how many bytes are in a slice:

```
size_t image_size = image.getInfo<CL_MEM_SIZE>();
size_t slice_size = image.getImageInfo<CL_IMAGE_SLICE_PITCH>();
```

8.3.2 General data arguments

If a kernel has memory objects as arguments, the memory object data will be stored in the device's global or constant memory after the kernel is transferred to the device. Therefore, in the kernel function's parameter list, each parameter corresponding to a memory object must be preceded by `__global` or `__constant`. The parameter must be a pointer because kernels access memory object data by reference.

If you set the last parameter of setArg to a general data object, the data will be passed by value. In this case, the corresponding argument in the kernel function must *not* be a pointer and it must *not* have any address space designation. Without an address space designation, the object will be stored in the private memory of each work-item executing the kernel.

An example will help make this clear. The following code creates a buffer object and an integer, and then calls setArg twice to make them arguments of kernel:

```
cl::Buffer buff(...);
int x = 10;

kernel.setArg(0, buff);
kernel.setArg(1, x);
```

Because buff and x are the kernel's arguments, the kernel function's parameter list must look something like this:

```
__kernel void foo(__global float* data, int num) {
...
}
```

The first argument must be a pointer, and its address space can be set to __global or __constant. The second argument, however, must not be a pointer, and its data will be stored in the private address space.

8.3.3   *Local space arguments*

In some kernel functions, you may want arguments to be stored in the local address space instead of the global, constant, or private spaces. This poses a problem, though, because the host can't directly read or write to local memory.

But if setArg is called with a cl::LocalSpaceArg object, the device will allocate memory for the argument in local space. This argument won't have any initial value—it must be initialized by work-items as they execute.

In other words, the entire purpose of cl::LocalSpaceArg is to identify how many bytes should be allocated for an uninitialized argument in local memory. This is shown by the structure's definition, which is as follows:

```
struct LocalSpaceArg {
    ::size_t size_;
};
```

You can create a LocalSpaceArg structure by calling the __local method, which accepts a size_t parameter. For example, the following code creates a LocalSpaceArg containing 64 bytes, and then makes it the first argument of kernel:

```
cl::LocalSpaceArg arg = cl::__local(64);
kernel.setArg(0, arg);
```

If arg is the only argument of the kernel, the kernel function argument must be a pointer preceded by the __local designation. This is shown in the following code:

```
__kernel void foo(__local float* data) {
...
}
```

Now that you understand how to add arguments to kernels in C++, you're ready to create and dispatch kernel-execution commands. But first, you need to create and configure a CommandQueue. The next section discusses the CommandQueue class and its associated functions. In both cases, the host application relies on the setArg function

8.4 Command queues

In C++, all the functions needed to enqueue commands—from kernel-execution commands to data transfer commands—are contained within the CommandQueue class. This section will explore these commands in detail, but first we need to look at how new CommandQueue objects are created.

8.4.1 Creating CommandQueue objects

A command queue makes it possible for the host to direct processing tasks to a device. Therefore, unlike Context and Program objects, a CommandQueue must be created with one specific Device object. This is shown by its constructor:

```
CommandQueue::CommandQueue(const Context& context, const Device& device,
    cl_command_queue_properties properties = 0, cl_int* err = NULL)
```

By default, the CommandQueue sends commands to the device in the order in which the host enqueued them. But if the properties parameter is set equal to CL_QUEUE_OUT_OF_ORDER_EXEC_MODE_ENABLE, the device will process commands in an out-of-order fashion. If properties is set to CL_QUEUE_PROFILING_ENABLE, the command queue will monitor the timing of each command in the queue. This timing information can be retrieved using profiling events, which will be discussed in the next section.

The following line of code constructs a CommandQueue capable of sending commands from the host to a Device object called device. This queue is configured to monitor the timing of enqueued commands:

```
cl::CommandQueue queue(context, device, CL_QUEUE_PROFILING_ENABLE);
```

8.4.2 Enqueuing kernel-execution commands

The CommandQueue class provides two functions that tell a device to execute kernel code. The simpler of the two is enqueueTask. This enqueues a command that executes a kernel using one work-item and no work-groups. Its signature is as follows:

```
cl_int CommandQueue::enqueueTask(const Kernel& kernel,
    const VECTOR_CLASS<Event> *wait_list = NULL, Event *event = NULL)
```

The only required parameter is the Kernel object, and the other parameters will be discussed in the next section. For example, to enqueue a command to execute kernel without event-processing, you'd make the following function call:

```
queue.enqueueTask(kernel);
```

This function is simple to code, but because it only configures a single work-item to execute the kernel, the kernel code won't be processed efficiently. To enqueue a command that will execute a kernel using multiple work-items and work-groups, you need to invoke enqueueNDRangeKernel. This function's signature is as follows:

```
cl_int cl::CommandQueue::enqueueNDRangeKernel(const Kernel& kernel,
    const NDRange& offset, const NDRange& global_size,
    const NDRange& local_size, const VECTOR_CLASS<Event>* events = NULL,
    Event* event = NULL)
```

The three new arguments—offset, global_size, and local_size—must all be provided as NDRange objects. An NDRange is a container of size_t values, and if the kernel data has *N* dimensions, each NDRange must hold *N* size_t values.

Chapters 3 and 4 discuss work-items in detail, but we'll briefly review the topic here. A work-item is a parallel implementation of an executing kernel. In general, the more work-items you have, the faster the kernel will be processed. The global_size argument identifies how many work-items should be generated for each dimension of data.

Each work-item has a unique identifier called a global ID. The offset argument identifies the first global ID that will be assigned to a work-item. Successive global IDs will be incremented from this offset value.

As discussed in chapters 4 and 7, OpenCL makes it possible to synchronize the processing of work-items so long as they're placed into groups with shared memory. These groups are called work-groups, and the local_size parameter identifies how many work-items should be placed in a work-group per dimension.

A good way to depict work-items and work-groups is through an index space. Figure 8.3 presents an index space in which each grayed box represents a work-item. There are 12 * 4 work-items split into eight work-groups composed of 3 * 2 work-items each. The offset coordinates are (3, 3), so the first work-item will have a global ID of (3, 3).

The following code invokes enqueueNDRangeKernel to execute a kernel using the partitioning scheme depicted in the figure:

```
cl::NDRange offset(3, 3);
cl::NDRange global_size(12, 4);
cl::NDRange local_size(3, 2);

queue.enqueueNDRangeKernel(kernel, offset, global_size, local_size);
```

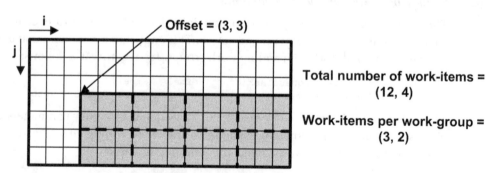

Figure 8.3   Index space for an example kernel partition

Because the kernel data has two dimensions, each NDRange constructor must have two elements. The NDRange class provides four constructors that accept 0, 1, 2, and 3 size_t elements respectively.

8.4.3 *Read/write commands*

Chapter 3 discussed the C functions that enqueue commands that transfer data. The simplest of these are the read/write commands. A read command transfers a memory object from the device to the host, and a write command transfers a memory object from the host to a device.

Table 8.1 lists the functions of the CommandQueue class that enqueue read and write commands. Depending on the function, some commands transfer buffer objects and others transfer image objects.

Table 8.1 C++ functions that read/write memory objects

Function	Purpose

`cl_int CommandQueue::enqueueReadBuffer(`
`    const Buffer& buffer, cl_bool blocking,`
`    ::size_t offset, ::size_t size, const void* ptr,`
`    const VECTOR_CLASS<Event>* wait_list = NULL,`
`    Event* event = NULL)`
	Transfers data from a buffer object to the host

`cl_int CommandQueue::enqueueWriteBuffer(`
`    const Buffer& buffer, cl_bool blocking,`
`    ::size_t offset, ::size_t size, const void *ptr,`
`    const VECTOR_CLASS<Event>* wait_list = NULL,`
`    Event* event = NULL)`
	Writes data from the host to a buffer object

`cl_int CommandQueue::enqueueReadImage(`
`    const Image& image, cl_bool blocking,`
`    const size_t<3>& origin,`
`    const size_t<3>& region,`
`    ::size_t row_pitch, ::size_t slice_pitch,`
`    void *ptr,`
`    const VECTOR_CLASS<Event>* wait_list = NULL,`
`    Event* event = NULL)`
	Transfers data from an image object to the host

`cl_int CommandQueue::enqueueWriteImage(`
`    const Image& image, cl_bool blocking,`
`    const size_t<3>& origin,`
`    const size_t<3>& region,`
`    ::size_t row_pitch, ::size_t slice_pitch,`
`    const void *ptr,`
`    const VECTOR_CLASS<Event>* wait_list = NULL,`
`    Event* event = NULL)`
	Transfers data from the host to an image object

Table 8.1   C++ functions that read/write memory objects *(continued)*

Function	Purpose

`cl_int CommandQueue::enqueueReadBufferRect(`
`   const Buffer& buffer, cl_bool blocking,`
`   const size_t<3>& buffer_offset,`
`   const size_t<3>& host_offset,`
`   const size_t<3>& region,`
`   ::size_t buffer_row_pitch,`
`   ::size_t buffer_slice_pitch,`
`   ::size_t host_row_pitch,`
`   ::size_t host_slice_pitch, void *ptr,`
`   const VECTOR_CLASS<Event>* wait_list = NULL,`
`   Event* event = NULL)`
	Transfers a rectangular portion of data from a buffer object to the host

`cl_int CommandQueue::enqueueWriteBufferRect(`
`   const Buffer& buffer, cl_bool blocking,`
`   const size_t<3>& buffer_offset,`
`   const size_t<3>& host_offset,`
`   const size_t<3>& region,`
`   ::size_t buffer_row_pitch,`
`   ::size_t buffer_slice_pitch,`
`   ::size_t host_row_pitch,`
`   ::size_t host_slice_pitch, void *ptr,`
`   const VECTOR_CLASS<Event>* wait_list = NULL,`
`   Event* event = NULL)`
	Transfers a rectangular portion of data from the host to a buffer object

In each case, the data is transferred between the `cl::Buffer`/`cl::Image` parameter and the `void* ptr` parameter. In a read operation, data is transferred from the `cl::Buffer`/`cl::Image` on the device to the `ptr` memory on the host. In a write operation, this is reversed.

These functions closely resemble their C counterparts, which chapter 3 examined at length. The only differences are that the functions in table 8.1 use C++ data types, and they don't require a parameter that specifies the number of events in the wait list.

Because of the strong similarity between the C functions and C++ functions, this chapter won't delve into the individual data transfer functions. Instead, we'll rewrite chapter 3's buffer_test.c example in C++. Figure 8.4 depicts the transfer operation graphically and listing 8.4 presents its implementation in C++.

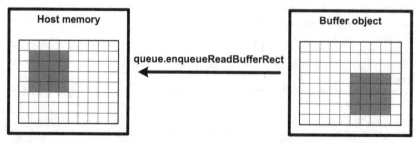

Figure 8.4   Transferring a rectangular buffer section to the host in C++

Listing 8.4 Reading rectangular data from a buffer in C++: buffer_test.cpp

```
...
cl::Buffer matrixBuffer(context,
      CL_MEM_READ_WRITE | CL_MEM_COPY_HOST_PTR,
      sizeof(zeroMatrix), zeroMatrix);
kernel.setArg(0, matrixBuffer);

cl::CommandQueue queue(context, devices[0]);
queue.enqueueTask(kernel);
queue.enqueueWriteBuffer(matrixBuffer, CL_TRUE, 0,           Write to
      sizeof(fullMatrix), fullMatrix);                        buffer

bufferOrigin.push_back(5*sizeof(float));
bufferOrigin.push_back(3);
bufferOrigin.push_back(0);
hostOrigin.push_back(1*sizeof(float));
hostOrigin.push_back(1);
hostOrigin.push_back(0);
region.push_back(4*sizeof(float));
region.push_back(4);
region.push_back(1);
queue.enqueueReadBufferRect(matrixBuffer, CL_TRUE,
      bufferOrigin, hostOrigin, region,                       Read rectangle
      10*sizeof(float), 0,                                    from buffer
      10*sizeof(float), 0, zeroMatrix);
...
```

Most of the code in this listing is devoted to initializing the cl::size_t<3> arguments of the enqueueReadBufferRect function: bufferOrigin, hostOrigin, and region. There is no constructor for this type, so you must call the push_back function or set the elements of the vector directly.

8.4.4 *Memory mapping and copy commands*

Besides read/write operations, OpenCL provides two additional methods of transferring data. First, you can map a region of host memory to a memory object on the device and transfer data using traditional memory I/O routines. The memory map is created with the enqueueMapBuffer and enqueueMapImage functions of the CommandQueue class, and it's destroyed with enqueueUnmapMemObject. Second, you can copy data between memory objects. This makes it convenient to transfer data between connected devices or between an image object and a buffer object.

Table 8.2 lists the CommandQueue functions that make memory-mapping and data copying possible. Each function signature is followed by a description of the command it enqueues.

These C++ functions look and behave like corresponding C functions in tables 3.6 and 3.7. To demonstrate how they work, the code in listing 8.5 performs six steps:

1 Send two buffer objects, buffer A and buffer B, to the device as kernel arguments.
2 Copy the content of buffer A to buffer B with enqueueCopyBuffer.
3 Map buffer B to host memory with enqueueMapBuffer.
4 Copy mapped memory on the host to an array with memcpy.
5 Unmap the memory map with enqueueUnmapMemObject.
6 Verify that the array contains the original content of buffer A.

Table 8.2   C++ Functions that map/unmap memory and copy memory objects

Function	Purpose
| ```cpp
void* CommandQueue::enqueueMapBuffer(
    const Buffer& buffer, cl_bool blocking,
    cl_map_flags map_flags,
    ::size_t offset, ::size_t size,
    const VECTOR_CLASS<Event>* wait_list = NULL,
    Event* event = NULL, cl_int* err = NULL)
``` | Maps a region of a buffer object to host memory |
| ```cpp
void* CommandQueue::enqueueMapImage(
    const Image& image, cl_bool blocking,
    cl_map_flags map_flags,
    ::size_t<3>& origin, ::size_t<3>& region,
    ::size_t* row_pitch, ::size_t* slice_pitch,
    const VECTOR_CLASS<Event>* wait_list = NULL,
    Event* event = NULL, cl_int* err = NULL)
``` | Maps a rectangular region of an image object to host memory |
| ```cpp
cl_int CommandQueue::enqueueUnmapMemObject(
    const Memory& mem_object, void* mapped_ptr,
    const VECTOR_CLASS<Event>* wait_list = NULL,
    Event* event = NULL)
``` | Unmaps an existing memory object from host memory |
| ```cpp
cl_int CommandQueue::enqueueCopyBuffer(
    const Buffer& src, const Buffer& dst,
    ::size_t src_offset, ::size_t dst_offset,
    ::size_t size,
    const VECTOR_CLASS<Event>* wait_list = NULL,
    Event* event = NULL)
``` | Copies data from a source buffer object to a destination buffer object |
| ```cpp
cl_int CommandQueue::enqueueCopyImage(
    const Image& src, const Image& dst,
    const size_t<3>& src_origin,
    const size_t<3>& dst_origin,
    const size_t<3>& region,
    const VECTOR_CLASS<Event>* wait_list = NULL,
    Event* event = NULL)
``` | Copies data from a source image object to a destination image object |
| ```cpp
cl_int CommandQueue::enqueueCopyBufferToImage(
    const Buffer& src, const Image& dst,
    const ::size_t src_offset,
    const size_t<3>& dst_origin,
    const size_t<3>& region,
    const VECTOR_CLASS<Event>* wait_list = NULL,
    Event* event = NULL)
``` | Copies data from a source buffer object to a destination image object |
| ```cpp
cl_int CommandQueue::enqueueCopyImageToBuffer(
    const Image& src, const Buffer& dst,
    const size_t<3>& src_origin,
    const size_t<3>& region,
    const ::size_t dst_offset,
    const VECTOR_CLASS<Event>* wait_list = NULL,
    Event* event = NULL)
``` | Copies data from a source image object to a destination buffer object |
```

Listing 8.5   Copying and mapping buffer objects in C++: map_copy.cpp

```
...
cl::Buffer bufferA(context,                                    Create buffer
      CL_MEM_READ_WRITE | CL_MEM_COPY_HOST_PTR,                objects
      sizeof(dataA), dataA);
cl::Buffer bufferB(context,
      CL_MEM_READ_WRITE | CL_MEM_COPY_HOST_PTR,
      sizeof(dataB), dataB);

kernel.setArg(0, bufferA);
kernel.setArg(1, bufferB);

cl::CommandQueue queue(context, devices[0]);
queue.enqueueTask(kernel);

queue.enqueueCopyBuffer(bufferA, bufferB,                      Copy buffer
                  0, 0, sizeof(dataA));                        data

mappedMemory = queue.enqueueMapBuffer(bufferB, CL_TRUE,        Map second
      CL_MAP_READ, 0, sizeof(dataB));                          buffer to host

memcpy(results, mappedMemory, sizeof(dataB));                 Unmap
queue.enqueueUnmapMemObject(bufferB, mappedMemory);           memory
...
```

As you use the map/unmap functions from table 8.2, remember that the enqueueMapBuffer and enqueueMapImage functions both return void pointers to identify the mapped memory regions on the host. These are the only functions in the table that don't return an error code.

There are three functions of the CommandQueue class that haven't been mentioned in this section. That's because they're commonly associated with event processing, which is the topic of the next section.

8.5   *Event processing*

Events make it possible to respond to occurrences on the host and the device. The C++ Wrapper API provides the Event class to represent these occurrences, and Event objects can be created easily because the class's constructor takes no arguments.

Events can be used in three main ways: host notification, command synchronization, and profiling. Chapter 7 explained the theory behind these methods in detail. In this section, we'll focus instead on the C++ classes and functions that make event processing possible.

8.5.1   *Host notification*

Events can be configured to call a host function (called a *callback function*) when a command on the device completes its execution. The configuration process requires that the Event be associated with both an enqueued command and a callback function.

Associating an Event with a command is simple. If you look back on tables 8.1 and 8.2, you'll see that the last argument of almost every function is a pointer to an Event object. When you make an Event the last argument of one of these functions, the Event will be associated with the command enqueued by the function. For example, the following code creates an Event called e and associates it with a command that memory-maps a buffer object to host memory:

```
Event e();
q.enqueueMapBuffer(buff, CL_TRUE, CL_MAP_READ, 0, sizeof(data), NULL, &e);
```

Associating an Event with a callback function is slightly more complicated. The function that creates this association is Event::setCallback, and its signature is as follows:

```
cl_int Event::setCallback(cl_int type, void (CL_CALLBACK* pfn_notify)
    (cl_event event, cl_int command_exec_status, void* user_data),
    void* user_data = NULL)
```

This function signature is close to that of clSetEventCallback, which was discussed in chapter 7. The first parameter must be set to CL_COMPLETE, because at the time of this writing, a command Event can be associated only with a command's completion. The second parameter is a pointer to the callback function, and the third parameter identifies data that will be sent to the callback function. As an example, the following code associates the Event e with a callback function called computeData:

```
e.setCallback(CL_COMPLETE, &computeData, NULL);
```

In both C and C++, callback functions must accept the same data types in the same order. The required signature for a callback function is as follows:

```
void CL_CALLBACK func_name(cl_event event, cl_int status, void *data)
```

Notice that the first parameter is a cl_event structure, not an Event object. Therefore, if you want to examine an event's properties in a callback function, you need to invoke the clGetEventInfo function discussed in chapter 7, not cl::Event::getInfo.

The following code demonstrates how callback functions are coded in C++. This application executes a kernel, reads a buffer object, and then uses a callback to test the accuracy of the output data.

Listing 8.6   Events and callback functions in C++: callback.cpp

```
void CL_CALLBACK checkData(cl_event event,
    cl_int status, void* data) {

  int i;
  cl_bool check;
  int *buffer_data;

  buffer_data = (int*)data;                              Define callback
  check = CL_TRUE;                                        function
  for(i=0; i<100; i++) {
    if(buffer_data[i] != 2*i) {
      check = CL_FALSE;
      break;
    }
  }
}
```

```
    if(check)
        std::cout << "The data is accurate."
                    << std::endl;
    else
        std::cout << "The data is not accurate."
                    << std::endl;
}
int main(void) {
    ...
    cl::Event callbackEvent;
    int i, data[100];
    ...
    queue.enqueueReadBuffer(buffer,
            CL_FALSE, 0, sizeof(data),
            data, NULL, &callbackEvent);

    callbackEvent.setCallback(CL_COMPLETE,
            &checkData, (void*)data);
    ...
}
```

Define callback function

Read kernel output

Set callback function

This code demonstrates how to direct data from a memory object to a callback function and verify the data inside the callback function. This process becomes particularly useful when you enqueue time-consuming commands involving kernel execution or data transfer.

8.5.2 Command synchronization

In tables 8.1 and 8.2, most of the command-enqueuing functions accept a vector of Event objects as their second-to-last parameter. These Events form the *wait list* of the enqueued command. Before a command can execute, the occurrence corresponding to each Event in its wait list must complete.

If an Event corresponds to a command's completion on the device, we'll refer to it as a command event. If it corresponds to an occurrence on the host, we'll refer to it as a user event. We'll look at how both types of events are used to synchronize commands.

COMMAND EVENTS

Command events are helpful when you need to synchronize commands in different command queues. For example, the following code associates the Event e1 with a kernel-execution command in CommandQueue q1. Then it places e1 in the wait list of a write command in CommandQueue q2:

```
q1.enqueueTask(kernel, NULL, &e1);
cl::vector<cl::Event> waitList;
waitList.push_back(e1);
q2.enqueueWriteBuffer(buff, CL_TRUE, 0, sizeof(data), data, &waitList);
```

Because e1 is in the wait list of the write command, the write operation won't start until the kernel-execution command in q1 has completed its execution. Note that a wait list must be provided as a vector containing cl::Event objects, not just as a pointer to a cl::Event array.

USER EVENTS

In addition to command events, user events can also be placed in a command's wait list. This will force the command's execution to wait until the host application sets the user event's status to CL_COMPLETE. The C++ Wrapper API provides a separate class for user events called UserEvent, and its constructor is as follows:

```
UserEvent::UserEvent(Context& context, cl_int* err = NULL)
```

After a UserEvent is created, it can be placed in a command's wait list. Then, to allow the command to execute, the host application must call the event's setStatus function. The signature of setStatus is as follows:

```
cl_int UserEvent::setStatus(cl_int status)
```

If this function is called with the status argument set to CL_COMPLETE, any commands waiting on the event will stop waiting and start executing. If status is set to a negative value, this will be interpreted as an error condition, and any commands waiting on the event will terminate.

The code in the following listing shows how user events are coded in C++. The host application forces a kernel-execution command to wait until the user presses a key. When the kernel finishes executing, its associated event invokes a callback function that displays an output message.

Listing 8.7   User event processing in C++: user_event.cpp

```
void CL_CALLBACK printMessage(cl_event event,
     cl_int status, void* data) {
   std::cout << "The kernel has executed." << std::endl;     Define callback
}                                                             function

int main(void) {
   ...
   cl::Event callbackEvent;
   ...
   cl::UserEvent userEvent(context);
   cl::vector<cl::Event> waitList;                           Configure
   waitList.push_back((cl::Event)userEvent);                 wait list
   cl::CommandQueue queue(context, devices[0]);
   queue.enqueueTask(kernel, &waitList, &callbackEvent);

   callbackEvent.setCallback(CL_COMPLETE, &printMessage);
   std::cout << "Press ENTER to execute kernel." << std::endl;
   getchar();                                                Set event
   userEvent.setStatus(CL_COMPLETE);                         completion
   ...
}
```

The userEvent in the wait list forces the kernel-execution command to stall until the user presses the Enter key. But once the setStatus function is called, the kernel can execute normally.

8.5.3 *Profiling events*

Profiling makes it possible to precisely gauge the timing of high-performance applications. The goal is to obtain the times associated with a command's changes in status, and subtract these times to determine how long the command spent in one of the stages. To configure profiling in C++, you need to take three steps:

1 Set the `CL_QUEUE_PROFILING_ENABLE` flag when you create the command queue.
2 Associate an `Event` object with the command to be profiled.
3 After the command executes, call `getProfilingInfo` to obtain information about its timing.

The `getProfilingInfo` function works like the `getInfo` functions in other classes. This function accepts one of four template values that identify the stages of a command's processing: `CL_PROFILING_COMMAND_QUEUED`, `CL_PROFILING_COMMAND_SUBMIT`, `CL_PROFILING_COMMAND_START`, and `CL_PROFILING_COMMAND_END`. These stages are discussed further in chapter 7 and listed in table 7.3.

As an example, the following code shows how `getProfilingInfo` can be used to obtain the time when a command began its execution on the device:

```
cl_ulong start = event.getProfilingInfo<CL_PROFILING_COMMAND_START>();
```

The following code demonstrates how simple it is to profile command execution with C++. It associates an `Event` `profileEvent` with a kernel-execution command, and calls `getProfilingInfo` twice to obtain the starting and ending times for the execution.

Listing 8.8 Profiling kernels in C++: profile.cpp

```
...
cl::CommandQueue queue(context, devices[0], CL_QUEUE_PROFILING_ENABLE);
queue.enqueueTask(kernel, NULL, &profileEvent);
queue.finish();

start = profileEvent.getProfilingInfo<CL_PROFILING_COMMAND_START>();
end = profileEvent.getProfilingInfo<CL_PROFILING_COMMAND_END>();
std::cout << "Elapsed time: " << (end-start) << " ns." << std::endl;
...
```

The time values returned by `getProfilingInfo` are given in billionths of a second, called nanoseconds or ns. But not all compliant devices can resolve time down to individual nanoseconds. To see how precisely a device can measure time, call the `getInfo` function of a `Device` object with the `CL_DEVICE_PROFILING_TIMER_RESOLUTION` template value.

8.5.4 *Additional event functions*

The C++ Wrapper API provides event-related routines that aren't directly related to host notification, command synchronization, or profiling. Here, we'll look at the wait functions of the `Event` class and the additional synchronization functions of the `CommandQueue` class.

WAIT FUNCTIONS

Each `Event` object corresponds to an occurrence, and we've discussed how to stall a command's execution until the occurrence finishes. But you can also stall the host application using the two wait functions of the `Event` class.

The first function is called `wait`, and it doesn't require any arguments. It forces the host application to halt until the `Event`'s occurrence completes. For example, if event is associated with an occurrence that hasn't completed yet, the following code will force the host application to stall:

```
event.wait();
```

Similarly, the static function `waitForEvents` forces the host application to halt until a group of event occurrences have completed. Its signature is as follows:

```
static cl_int cl::Event::waitForEvents(const VECTOR_CLASS<Event>& events)
```

You can think of `waitForEvents` as a wait list for the host application. Once every event occurrence has completed, the host application can continue executing.

ADDITIONAL QUEUE COMMANDS

We've looked at functions that enqueue kernel-execution commands, data transfer commands, and memory-map commands. But the `CommandQueue` class provides three additional functions that enqueue commands that relate to synchronization:

- `enqueueMarker(Event *e = NULL)`—Enqueues a marker command and associates an `Event` with the execution of every command preceding it. This `Event` can be used to synchronize other commands or notify the host.
- `enqueueWaitForEvents(const VECTOR_CLASS<Event>& waitList))`—Enqueues a wait command that forces following commands to halt until the occurrences corresponding to each `Event` in the wait list have completed.
- `enqueueBarrier()`—Enqueues a barrier command that forces all following commands to halt until all preceding commands have completed their execution.

Unlike other command synchronization methods, these functions only affect commands within a single command queue. They become particularly important when a queue is configured to process commands out of order.

The wait command enqueued by `enqueueWaitForEvents` and the barrier command enqueued by `enqueueBarrier` both stall succeeding commands in the queue. The wait command stalls the queue until the occurrences corresponding to the `Events` in its wait list have completed. The barrier command stalls the queue until every preceding command has finished executing.

8.6   *Summary*

With the C++ Wrapper API, you can build applications that combine the high performance of OpenCL and the high-level object-oriented features of C++. C++ programming is usually considered to be more complicated than C programming, but if you compare the code listings in this chapter with those of previous chapters, I'm sure you'll agree that you can obtain the same results with much less code by using C++.

This chapter has discussed the C++ API for OpenCL, and we started with the process of creating kernels. Instead of data structures like `cl_platform_id` and `cl_context`, we rely on objects instantiated from classes such as `cl::Platform` and `cl::Context`. Not only does this provide greater organization, but it also makes the code simpler. For example, if you want information about an object, you can simply call `getInfo` with a template instead of calling functions like `clGetPlatformInfo` and `clGetDeviceInfo` with their many parameters.

After explaining how to create kernels, this chapter discussed kernel arguments and the command queue. The C++ functions are quite similar to the C functions, but there are two points to keep in mind. First, *every* command-enqueuing function, from `enqueueTask` to `enqueueReadBufferRect`, is a member function of the `CommandQueue` class. Second, the C++ API provides its own `size_t` class that accepts a template with a numerical value.

The last topic explored in this chapter involves event processing. Again, the C++ code resembles C code, but whereas C code relies on the `cl_event` structure, the C++ API provides two classes representing events. The `Event` class corresponds to general occurrences, and the `UserEvent` class corresponds to occurrences on the host. Both types of objects can be placed in wait lists to synchronize the execution of commands.

Although C++ provides many advantages over C, neither C executables nor C++ executables are cross-platform. When you build a C/C++ application for one operating system, it won't run on other systems without some sort of conversion. In the next chapter, we'll look at Java APIs for OpenCL, which will enable you to build classes that can be run immediately on multiple operating systems.

Development
with Java and Python

This chapter covers

- Building Java-based OpenCL classes with Aparapi
- Using the JavaCL toolset to build host applications in Java
- Creating Python-based host applications with the PyOpenCL toolset

In chapter 1, I explained that OpenCL makes it possible to "write once, run on anything," and I contrasted that with Java's motto, "Write once, run anywhere." In this chapter, we're going to combine the two and obtain the best of both worlds. That is, we're going to explore how to build high-performance applications using Java and OpenCL. Then we're going to investigate host application development with Python.

> **TIP** If you're unfamiliar with Java, I strongly recommend reading *Head First Java* by Kathy Sierra and Bert Bates (O'Reilly, 2005). If you'd like to know more about Python, you can't do much better than *The Quick Python Book, Second Edition* by Vern Ceder (Manning, 2010).

This chapter presents three freely available toolsets that allow you to access OpenCL's capabilities using object-oriented development:

- Aparapi—Released by AMD and translates Java and deploys kernel code
- JavaCL—Released by Olivier Chafik and binds Java classes to the structures in an OpenCL host application
- PyOpenCL—Released by Andreas Klöckner and makes it possible to code host applications in Python

This chapter will look at these toolsets and discuss their capabilities and coding practices. This presentation won't be exhaustive, and we won't examine every function of every class in the three APIs. But it will provide plenty of example code to show how their classes are used in practice.

NOTE In addition to Aparapi and JavaCL, Michael Bien of the JogAmp project has released JOCL, which provides a Java-OpenCL binding similar to JavaCL. The main page for JOCL is http://jogamp.org/jocl/www.

AMD's Aparapi toolset is the newest of the three OpenCL-based offerings. We'll examine it first.

9.1 *Aparapi*

In September 2010, AMD released the alpha version of its Aparapi (pronounced AP-ar-AP-ee) tool on its website, http://developer.amd.com. This remarkable package makes it easy to write and dispatch kernels from Java classes, but there are a few points to be aware of in advance:

- An Aparapi kernel can execute on the host's Java Virtual Machine (JVM) or on a single graphics card, but only if the graphics card was released by AMD/ATI.
- The Aparapi tools only support 32-bit Windows (Windows 7, Vista, or XP) and 32-bit/64-bit Linux (openSUSE, Ubuntu, and Red Hat Enterprise Linux) systems.
- According to the End User License Agreement, Aparapi is available only for testing, debugging, and evaluation. You can't modify or distribute any part for any reason.

To understand Aparapi, it helps to contrast it with the C++ Wrapper API we looked at in chapter 8. The C++ API is a *binding*, which means it provides an interface from the routines of one language (C++) to those of another (C). It's a thorough binding because it allows you to build C++ host applications with the same breadth of functionality as C host applications.

In contrast, Aparapi isn't a thorough binding. At the time of this writing, you can't access platforms, devices, contexts, or command queues. But Aparapi's great strength is that you can code *kernels* in a high-level language, which is more than you can accomplish in C++.

This section will explain Aparapi's `Kernel` class and show you how to write Java code that defines and executes kernels. But first, you need to understand how to obtain Aparapi and install it on your development system.

9.1.1   *Aparapi installation*

AMD's Aparapi page is http://developer.amd.com/zones/java/aparapi/Pages/default.aspx. If you scroll to the bottom of the page, you'll see links for Aparapi files directed toward 32-bit Windows and 32-bit/64-bit Linux. To obtain Aparapi, click the link that corresponds to your system, accept the license agreement, and save the zip file to your development computer.

> **NOTE**   Before you install Aparapi, you must have the AMD OpenCL framework installed. Appendix A explains how to obtain this and install it on your system.

When you decompress the archive, you'll find a number of files inside. The two most important files are these:

- *aparapi.jar*—This Java Archive (JAR) contains the class files that Aparapi requires to function
- *aparapi.dll (Windows) or libaparapi.so (Linux)*—This dynamic library serves as an interface between the classes in the JAR file and the installed OpenCL library.

The dynamic library must be placed in a directory where the loader will automatically find it. For example, a Linux user can place the libaparapi.so file in /usr/local. A Windows user can place the aparapi.dll file in C:\Windows\System32.

To build an Aparapi-based class, the compiler must know the name and location of aparapi.jar. If you're running javac from the command line, you can set this location using the -cp flag, which defines the compiler's classpath.

9.1.2   *The Kernel class*

The Aparapi documentation is located in the docs folder in the decompressed archive. If you look through the index.html file, you'll find a top-level link for a single class: Kernel. This is Aparapi's central class, and in essence, the entire purpose of an Aparapi application is to configure code for a Kernel object and execute it.

Working with Kernel objects is so simple that the best way to understand it is to look at an example. The following listing presents a basic Kernel object that executes four rounding functions.

Listing 9.1   Kernel rounding with Aparapi: AparapiRound.java

```
import com.amd.aparapi.Kernel;

public class AparapiRound {

    public static void main(String[] args) {

        final float[] input =
            new float[]{-6.5f, -3.5f, 3.5f, 6.5f};
        final float[] rintOutput =
            new float[input.length];                    Construct input/
        final float[] roundOutput =                     output arrays
            new float[input.length];
        final float[] ceilOutput =
```

```
        new float[input.length];
   final float[] floorOutput =
        new float[input.length];

Kernel kernel = new Kernel(){
     public void run() {
        for(int i=0; i<4; i++) {
            rintOutput[i]  = rint(input[i]);
            roundOutput[i] = round(input[i]);
            ceilOutput[i]  = ceil(input[i]);
            floorOutput[i] = floor(input[i]);
        }
     }
};

kernel.execute(1);
...

   }
}
```

**Construct input/
output arrays**

**Perform rounding
operations**

**Execute
kernel**

It may not look like it, but the code in this listing represents both a host application *and* a kernel. This kernel accepts an array of floats and executes the rint, round, ceil, and floor functions. You may recall these functions from chapter 5, which discussed them as part of the overall presentation of kernel functions.

It's no coincidence that the Java methods inside the Kernel object have the same names as the C-based kernel functions. The Kernel class contains a long list of methods that exactly correspond to those used by OpenCL kernels. If you provide code for the Kernel's abstract run method, this code will be translated into an OpenCL kernel when the execute method is invoked. The execute method will also compile the kernel and dispatch it to the target for execution.

Aparapi doesn't allow you to access connected devices in code, so you can't select a specific target for the translated kernel. Instead, the Kernel class provides the setExecutionMode method. This accepts one of four values:

- Kernel.EXECUTION_MODE.GPU—Execute on the first accessible GPU
- Kernel.EXECUTION_MODE.CPU—Execute on the first accessible CPU
- Kernel.EXECUTION_MODE.JTP—Execute on the JVM using a Java thread pool
- Kernel.EXECUTION_MODE.SEQ—Execute using a single loop

By default, the execute method searches for three things: the Aparapi dynamic library, the AMD OpenCL framework, and a compliant GPU. If it finds all three, then it sends the kernel to the GPU for execution. But if any of these is missing, Aparapi executes the kernel on the host's JVM using a Java thread pool. AMD recommends that you leave this default behavior unchanged, but you can customize this with setExecutionMode. For example, if you want to execute the Kernel object kernel on an OpenCL-compliant CPU, you can insert the following code:

```
kernel.setExecutionMode(Kernel.EXECUTION_MODE.CPU);
```

At this point, all of the code in listing 9.1 should make sense—except for one minor point. Why is the execute method called with an argument of 1? The answer has to do with how Aparapi processes work-items. We'll look at this next.

9.1.3 *Work-items and work-groups*

As explained in chapters 3 and 4, a work-item is a parallel execution of a kernel. In general, the more work-items you have, the faster the kernel will execute. Work-item configuration is an important aspect of OpenCL, and Aparapi provides two ways to set the number of work-items generated for a kernel.

The first way is to invoke the execute method. The argument of execute is an integer that identifies how many work-items will be generated. For example, in listing 9.1, the argument of execute is 1, which means the kernel will be executed by a single work-item.

The second way to configure the number of work-items is through the setSizes method. The signature of this method is as follows:

```
protected void setSizes(int globalSize, int localSize)
```

The first argument identifies how many total work-items will be generated to execute the kernel. The second argument identifies how many work-items are contained within a work-group. As discussed in chapters 3 and 4, a work-group is a collection of work-items that can access the same block of local memory.

For example, suppose you want to execute a kernel with 32 work-items split into 8 work-groups of 4 work-items each. In that case, you'd invoke setSizes in the following manner:

```
Kernel kernel = new Kernel() {

    public void setSizes(int gSize, int lSize) {
        super.setSizes(32, 4);
    }

    public void run() {...}
};
```

Once you've set how many work-items and work-groups you want to use, you can access this information from inside the kernel with the following six methods:

- getGlobalId()—Returns the unique identifier of the work-item
- getGlobalSize()—Returns the total number of work-items
- getGroupId()—Returns the unique identifier of the work-group
- getLocalId()—Returns the identifier of the work-item within the work-group
- getLocalSize()—Returns the number of work-items in the item's work-group
- getNumGroups()—Returns the number of work-groups

It's important to distinguish between getGlobalId(), getLocalId(), and getGroupId(). The first method returns the work-item's unique ID among all other work-items generated for the kernel. getLocalId returns the work-item's ID within the work-group; work-items in other work-groups may have the same local ID. Lastly, getGroupId returns the identifier for the work-group containing the work-item.

The following code demonstrates how these methods are used. It configures the Kernel to be executed by 32 work-items split into 8 work-groups. Each work-item produces a float that identifies its global ID, global size, local ID, and local size.

Listing 9.2 Work-item information: AparapiItems.java

```
import com.amd.aparapi.Kernel;

public class AparapiItems {

    public static void main(String[] args) {
        final int numItems = 8;
        final int numGroups = 4;
        final float[] itemInfo = new float[numItems];

        Kernel kernel = new Kernel() {
            public void setSizes(int gSize, int lSize) {        Set work-items
                super.setSizes(numItems, numGroups);            and work-groups
            }

            public void run() {
                itemInfo[getGlobalId()] =                       Combine global
                    getGlobalId() * 10.0f +                     and local info
                    getGlobalSize() + getLocalId()*0.1f +
                    getLocalSize() * 0.01f;
            }
        };

        kernel.execute(numItems);                              Execute
                                                               kernel
        for(int i=0; i<numItems; i++)
            System.out.println(itemInfo[i]);
    }
}
```

Aparapi functions like getGlobalId and getLocalSize are similar to the C functions get_global_id and get_local_size, but there's one important difference. In Aparapi, there's no way to set the dimensionality of the data: the index space must be one-dimensional. If you're processing images or successions of images, this is an important drawback.

Another drawback is Aparapi's lack of vector support. With Aparapi, there's no way to process float4s, int8s, or char16s. Kernels are limited to processing scalar values.

Because of these drawbacks and the severely limiting license, I can't recommend using Aparapi for professional OpenCL development. But if you want to test kernel functions with one-dimensional work-items and work-groups, Aparapi is the simplest method available. In the next section, we'll look at JavaCL, which provides all the flexibility and complexity of regular host application development.

9.2   *JavaCL*

At the start of chapter 8, I described all the advantages of coding host applications using the C++ Wrapper API: object-oriented programming, no need to call malloc, and the simplicity of the function calls. JavaCL provides these advantages as well, but in most cases, the JavaCL methods are even simpler to work with than the C++ functions.

JavaCL is a Java binding for OpenCL released by Olivier Chafik as part of the NativeLibs4Java toolset. JavaCL enables developers to build full-featured OpenCL host applications, and the only drawback I've encountered is that it currently doesn't support OpenCL 1.1. This is probably because Mac OS doesn't support OpenCL 1.1 yet.

> **NOTE**   The toolset provides two JavaCL implementations: one that relies on the Java Native Access (JNA) and one that relies on BridJ. The discussion in this section focuses on the former.

This section will discuss how to use JavaCL to build applications. But first, let's look at how to obtain and install the package.

9.2.1   JavaCL installation

Installing JavaCL is as simple as it gets. Unlike Aparapi, which consists of a dynamic library and a JAR, JavaCL contains only a JAR. The JAR's name is javacl-jna-*x-y-z*-shaded.jar. The "jna" term means that the JAR communicates with the OpenCL library through JNA. The "shaded" term means that there are no additional dependencies. To obtain the JAR, open a browser to http://code.google.com/p/javacl/downloads/list, click the link with the JAR's name, and download the file to your computer.

Chafik has released JavaCL under the GNU Lesser General Public License (LGPL). This means you can incorporate the JAR in your own Java application and release the application under any license, so long as your application isn't a *derivative work*. The legal definitions of what constitutes a derivative work aren't helpful, but in a *Linux Journal* article (www.linuxjournal.com/article/6366), Lawrence Rosen, general counsel for the Open Source Initiative, states that "The meaning of derivative work will not be broadened to include software created by linking to library programs that were designed and intended to be used as library programs."

Once you've downloaded the JavaCL JAR, you can access its classes by adding it to your Java classpath. We'll look at these classes next.

9.2.2   Overview of JavaCL development

Table 9.1 lists 11 of the most important classes of JavaCL, their corresponding C data structures, and a handful of their methods. The table lists the classes in the order in which they're commonly encountered in code.

Table 9.1   Important classes of the JavaCL API

JavaCL class	C data structure	Important methods
JavaCL	–	listPlatforms, getBestDevice, createContext, createBestContext
CLPlatform	cl_platform	getName, getProfile, listAllDevices, listCPUDevices, listGPUDevices, getBestDevice, createContext

Table 9.1 Important classes of the JavaCL API *(continued)*

JavaCL class	C data structure	Important methods
CLDevice	cl_device	getName, getExtensions, createQueue, createProfilingQueue, getMaxComputeUnits
CLContext	cl_context	createProgram, createBuffer, createImage2D, createImage3D, createDefaultQueue, createProfilingQueue
CLProgram	cl_program	addSource, build, createKernel, createKernels, defineMacro
CLKernel	cl_kernel	enqueueTask, enqueueNDRange, setArg, getFunctionName, getProgram
CLQueue	cl_command_queue	finish, flush, enqueueMarker, enqueueBarrier, enqueueWaitForEvents
CLMem	cl_mem	getByteCount, getContext
CLBuffer	cl_mem (buffer object)	read, write, map, unmap, copyTo
CLImage2D/ CLImage3D	cl_mem (image object)	read, write, map, unmap, copyTo, getFormat

The classes in table 9.1 closely resemble the C++ classes we looked at in chapter 8, but there are four significant differences:

- JavaCL classes start with CL and are part of the com.nativelibs4java.opencl package instead of the CL namespace.
- In C++, the enqueueTask and enqueueNDRangeKernel functions are contained in the CommandQueue class. In JavaCL, enqueueTask and enqueueNDRange are provided by the CLKernel class.
- JavaCL contains simple data in arrays and Strings. You don't have to be concerned about whether to use cl::vector/cl::string or std::vector/std::string.
- C++ supports default arguments, so you can frequently leave off parameters of a function. Java doesn't support this, but JavaCL provides many overloaded methods that accomplish the same result with different numbers of arguments.

Only one of the classes in table 9.1 has a constructor: JavaCL. JavaCL has no equivalent in C or C++, but it's usually the first class you need to access when creating kernels in code. We'll discuss this next.

9.2.3 Creating kernels with JavaCL

Chapter 2 explained the six OpenCL data structures that work in conjunction to form kernels, and each has a corresponding class in table 9.1. In discussing these classes, we'll look at the CLPlatform and CLDevice classes first and then proceed to the CLContext and CLQueue classes. Then we'll discuss how to compile and dispatch kernel code with the CLProgram and CLKernel classes.

PLATFORMS AND DEVICES

In coding a JavaCL application, the first class you need to know is `JavaCL`. The static methods of this class construct and return other OpenCL-related objects. For example, its `listPlatforms` method returns an array of `CLPlatform` objects and serves the same purpose as the C function `clGetPlatformIds`.

Once you've obtained one or more `CLPlatform`s, you can access their devices with `listAllDevices`, `listCPUDevices`, or `listGPUDevices`. These methods accept a boolean parameter that identifies whether the method should return only available devices. This is shown in the following code:

```
CLPlatform[] platforms = JavaCL.listPlatforms();
for(CLPlatform p : platforms) {
    CLDevice[] newDevice = p.listAllDevices(true);
    ...
}
```

Alternatively, both `JavaCL` and `CLPlatform` provide a method called `getBestDevice`, which is my favorite method in the entire JavaCL API. By default, this searches through every connected OpenCL-compliant device to find the one with the most compute units. Then it returns a `CLDevice` object corresponding to this device.

If you'd rather determine a device's number of compute units on your own, the `CLDevice` class provides the `getMaxComputeUnits` method. There is no general `getInfo` method as there is with C++. Instead, each information parameter has its own method: `getLocalMemSize`, `getGlobalMemSize`, `getDriverVersion`, and so on. This holds true for every JavaCL class.

For example, the following code creates a `CLDevice` object for the "best" device and prints out its extension data:

```
CLDevice dev = JavaCL.getBestDevice();
for(String s: dev.getExtensions())
    System.out.println(s);
```

As shown, the `getBestDevice` and `getExtensions` methods don't require any arguments. This is a welcome change from OpenCL functions, which frequently require 5 to 10 arguments.

CONTEXTS AND COMMAND QUEUES

In addition to `getBestDevice`, JavaCL also provides `createBestContext`, which returns a `CLContext` containing the device that, by default, has the most compute units. With this method, you can create a context with a single line of code, such as the following:

```
CLContext context = JavaCL.createBestContext();
```

If you'd rather create contexts with multiple devices, you can call the `createContext` method provided by both the `JavaCL` class and the `CLPlatform` class. The full signature for this method is as follows:

```
CLContext createContext(Map<CLPlatform.ContextProperties, Object> props,
    CLDevice... devices)
```

The first argument is a `Map` whose elements match a context property with a value. As explained in chapter 2, most of these properties relate to graphics. For example, one `Map` element might combine `CLPlatform.ContextProperties.GLContext` with an OpenGL context. We'll have much more to say about OpenCL-OpenGL interoperability in chapters 15 and 16.

The second argument of `createContext` accepts a comma-separated list of `CLDevices` or an array of `CLDevice` objects. The following code shows how this works. It accesses all the devices associated with the first installed platform and uses them to form a `CLContext`:

```
CLPlatform[] platforms = JavaCL.listPlatforms();
CLDevice[] devices = platforms[0].listAllDevices(true);
CLContext context = JavaCL.createContext(null, devices);
```

Once you've created a context with `createBestContext` or `createContext`, you can create a `CLQueue` that sends commands to a given device. The `CLContext` class contains three methods that make this possible:

- `createDefaultQueue(CLDevice.QueueProperties... queueProperties)`—Returns a `CLQueue` with the given properties
- `createDefaultProfilingQueue()`—Returns a `CLQueue` configured for profiling
- `createDefaultOutOfOrderQueue()`—Returns a `CLQueue` configured for out-of-order command execution

I particularly appreciate the last two methods because they make it possible to create command queues without having to enter the constants `CL_QUEUE_PROFILING_ENABLE` and `CL_QUEUE_OUT_OF_ORDER_EXEC_MODE_ENABLE`. If you want to create a command queue without profiling or out-of-order execution, call `createDefaultQueue` with the argument set to `NULL`. The following code shows how this works:

```
CLContext context = JavaCL.createBestContext();
CLQueue queue = context.createDefaultQueue
        ((CLDevice.QueueProperties[])null);
```

Once you've created a `CLQueue`, you can access its context with `getContext` and its device with `getDevice`. This class also provides `enqueueMarker`, `enqueueBarrier`, and `enqueueWaitForEvents`, but these methods lie beyond the scope of this discussion.

PROGRAMS AND KERNELS

Before you can put a `CLQueue` to use, your host application needs to create kernels. In JavaCL, kernels are abstracted by the `CLKernel` class, and `CLKernel` objects are formed from function code inside a `CLProgram`. To create a `CLProgram`, you need to invoke one of three overloaded methods in `CLContext`:

- `createProgram(String... sourceText)`—Creates a `CLProgram` that targets every device in the context
- `createProgram(CLDevice[] devices, String... sourceText)`—Creates a `CLProgram` that targets only the selected devices
- `createProgram(Map<CLDevice, byte[]> binaries, String source)`—Creates a `CLProgram` from byte arrays

Java provides many ways to form a String from a text file, but none of them are as simple as the readFile method of JavaCL's IOUtils class. The main method in the following listing uses readFile in the process of creating a CLProgram, and then builds the program using the build method of the CLProgram class.

Listing 9.3 Creating and building a program: JavaCLProgram.java

```
public static void main(String[] args) {

    CLContext context = JavaCL.createBestContext();

    String programText = "";
    try {
        programText = IOUtils.readText(                    Create String
                    new File("root.cl"));                  from file
    } catch (IOException e) {
        e.printStackTrace();
    }

    CLProgram program =                                    Create
        context.createProgram(programText);                CLProgram
    try {                                                  Build
        program.build();                                   CLProgram
    } catch (CLBuildException e) {
        e.printStackTrace();                               Print
    }                                                  ❶   error
}
```

The printStackTrace method ❶ of the CLBuildException class is particularly interesting. It reads the program's build log and displays any compile errors that occurred. This is much simpler than the corresponding functions in C.

After a CLProgram has been compiled, the createKernels and createKernel methods make it possible to create kernels from its functions. Both of these methods build the corresponding CLProgram. The first method returns an array of CLKernels— one for each kernel function in the program. The second method accepts a function name (String) and kernel arguments, and returns a single CLKernel.

Next, we'll look at the methods in the CLKernel class that make it possible to set arguments for the kernel and send commands to a device.

9.2.4 Setting arguments and enqueuing commands

Once you have a CLKernel and a CLQueue, you can invoke the methods of CLKernel to set arguments and dispatch commands to the queue. This discussion will present the argument-configuration methods first and then examine how CLKernel's methods enqueue kernel-execution commands and data-transfer commands.

SETTING KERNEL ARGUMENTS

If you look through the JavaCL documentation, you'll see that the CLKernel class contains nineteen overloaded methods called setArg. In each case, the first argument is an int that identifies the argument's position in the kernel's parameter list. The second argument may take a number of different data types, and we'll look at the following:

- Primitive data type/primitive array—Arguments can be created from primitive values (short, int, long, float, and double) or an array of these primitives. This data is passed to the kernel by value.
- CLMem—This identifies a memory object, which can be either a CLBuffer, a CLImage2D, or a CLImage3D. This data is passed to the kernel by reference.
- CLKernel.LocalSize—This doesn't pass data to the device but tells it how much memory to allocate for the argument in its local address space.

As an example, the following code sets two arguments for a CLKernel called kernel. The first argument is an array of four ints, and the second is a CLKernel.LocalSize that tells the device to allocate 64 bytes of local memory for the kernel parameter:

```
int intArray[] = new int[]{0, 1, 2, 3};
CLKernel.CLLocalSize local = new CLKernel.CLLocalSize(64);
kernel.setArg(0, intArray);
kernel.setArg(1, local);
```

Creating memory objects is more involved. To create a CLBuffer, CLImage2D, or CLImage3D, you need to call methods of the CLContext class. We'll discuss buffer objects first.

To create a CLBuffer object, you can call create*XX*Buffer, where *XX* can be replaced by Byte, Char, Short, Int, Long, Float, or Double. This can be called in one of two ways. CLBuffers store data on the host using Java NIO buffers, and the usage of create*XX*Buffer depends on whether you've already created an NIO buffer.

> **NOTE** NIO stands for "New Input/Output," and the java.nio package contains classes that access files using memory mapping and low-level system calls. The Buffers and Channels in this package provide substantially better performance than traditional BufferedReaders and FileWriters.

If you haven't created an NIO buffer, the first usage of create*XX*Buffer requires that you identify the Buffer class you intend to use; the second usage requires that you provide the NIO buffer as an argument. This is shown in the following code, which creates two buffer objects that will be used to store floats:

```
CLBuffer<Float> buff1 =
    context.createFloatBuffer(Usage.Output, floatBuffer, true);
CLBuffer<Float> buff2 =
    context.createFloatBuffer(Usage.Output, 512);
```

There are three points to note about these two functions:

- CLBuffer is a generic type that accepts primitive data types (Byte, Char, Short, Int, Long, Float, or Double) as parameters.
- The first argument of both functions identifies the kernel's permissions with regard to reading and writing the data. Usage.Input corresponds to CL_MEM_READ_ONLY, Usage.Output corresponds to CL_MEM_WRITE_ONLY, and Usage.InputOutput corresponds to CL_MEM_READ_WRITE.
- The second argument of the second usage identifies the number of elements in the buffer. In this example, buff2 will store 512 floats.

Creating image objects is just as simple as creating buffer objects. The methods to know are `createImage2D` and `createImage3D`, and both are provided by the `CLContext` class. If you're creating an image object without initial data, the methods' signatures are as follows:

```
CLImage2D createImage2D(CLMem.Usage usage, CLImageFormat format,
    long width, long height, long rowPitch)
```

```
CLImage3D createImage3D(CLMem.Usage usage, CLImageFormat format,
    long width, long height, long depth, long rowPitch, long slicePitch)
```

The first parameter, usage, takes the same values as discussed earlier (`Usage.Input`, `Usage.Output`, `Usage.InputOutput`). The other parameters correspond to the structures and geometrical dimensions discussed in chapter 3.

Once you've created your memory objects, you can use the `setArg` method to add each to a kernel. After you've added all your kernel arguments, you're ready to dispatch a kernel-execution command to the device. We'll look at this next.

ENQUEUING KERNEL-EXECUTION COMMANDS

JavaCL makes it easy to execute kernels. The `CLKernel` class provides two methods that enqueue kernel-execution commands, and the simpler is `enqueueTask`. This requires only two arguments: a `CLQueue` and one or more `CLEvents` to form the command's wait list. The signature for this function is as follows:

```
CLEvent enqueueTask(CLQueue queue, CLEvent... waitList)
```

These arguments should look familiar, but the return value is new. The `clEnqueueTask` function in C and the `enqueueTask` function in C++ both return error codes, but JavaCL's `enqueueTask` returns a `CLEvent` that corresponds to the command's execution. This value is returned by most of JavaCL's command-enqueuing functions.

Like `enqueueTask`, the `enqueueNDRange` method enqueues a command that tells a device to execute a kernel. But in addition, this method makes it possible to configure multiple work-items and work-groups to process the kernel. The signature for this method is as follows:

```
CLEvent enqueueNDRange(CLQueue queue, int[] offsets,
    int[] globalSize, int[] localSize, CLEvent... waitList)
```

Again, this should look familiar. The `globalSize` argument sets how many work-items will be generated to execute the kernel. The `localSize` argument identifies how many work-items will be placed in each work-group.

The previous chapter presented an example index space whose global dimensions were 12 by 4 and whose local dimensions were 3 by 2. We can code this in JavaCL using the following function:

```
kernel.enqueueNDRange(queue, new int[]{12, 4}, new int[]{3, 2});
```

This function call leaves out the `offsets` parameter because JavaCL provides an overloaded version of `enqueueNDRange` that doesn't require it. As you program JavaCL, keep in mind that there are usually plenty of overloaded methods for each routine.

ENQUEUING DATA TRANSFER COMMANDS

JavaCL's data transfer routines are contained within the CLBuffer, CLImage, CLImage2D, and CLImage3D classes. We'll limit this discussion to the data transfer methods of the CLBuffer class, most of which are listed in table 9.2.

NOTE These methods correspond to the CLBuffer class in the JNA-based version of JavaCL, and do not apply to the JavaCL implementation based on BridJ.

Table 9.2 Data transfer methods of the CLBuffer class

Method	Purpose
CLEvent read(CLQueue queue, long offset, long length, Buffer buffer, boolean blocking, CLEvent... eventsToWaitFor)	Reads data from device into existing NIO buffer
Buffer read(CLQueue queue, long offset, long length, CLEvent... eventsToWaitFor)	Reads data from device into new NIO buffer
CLEvent write(CLQueue queue, long offset, long length, Buffer buffer, boolean blocking, CLEvent... eventsToWaitFor)	Transfers data from an existing NIO buffer to the device
Buffer map(CLQueue queue, CLMem.MapFlags flags, long offset, long length, CLEvent... eventsToWaitFor)	Maps a buffer object on the device to an NIO buffer on the host
CLEvent unmap(CLQueue queue, Buffer buffer, CLEvent... eventsToWaitFor)	Destroys the map between the device buffer object and the NIO buffer
CLEvent copyTo(CLQueue queue, long srcOffset, long length, CLMem destination, long destOffset, CLEvent... eventsToWaitFor)	Copies a device buffer to another memory object

Each of these data transfer methods access and store host data using NIO Buffer objects. It's important to distinguish these from regular buffer objects, which contain data on the device. Also, the signatures in table 9.2 identify the Buffer class, but in practice, you need to instantiate a specific Buffer subclass, such as IntBuffer or FloatBuffer.

The following code demonstrates how JavaCL data transfer works in practice. It sends a kernel to a device with a read-write buffer object containing 64 floats. The kernel computes the square root of each float, and the host reads and verifies the result.

Listing 9.4 Kernels and buffers: JavaCLRoot.java

```
public static final int NUM_FLOATS = 64;
public static final int NUM_ITEMS = NUM_FLOATS/4;

public static void main(String[] args) throws Exception {

    CLContext context = JavaCL.createBestContext();
    CLQueue queue = context.createDefaultQueue();
```

```
        FloatBuffer dataBuffer =
          NIOUtils.directFloats(NUM_FLOATS,              Create buffer
            context.getByteOrder());                     object
        for(int i = 0; i < NUM_FLOATS; i++) {
          dataBuffer.put(i, i * 5.0f);
        }
        CLFBuffer<Float> buff =
          context.createFloatBuffer(
            Usage.InputOutput, dataBuffer, true);

        String programText =
          IOUtils.readText(new File("root.cl"));         Create
        CLProgram program =                              program
          context.createProgram(programText);

        CLKernel kernel =                            ❶  Create
          program.createKernel("root", buff);            kernel

        CLEvent kernelEvent = kernel.enqueueNDRange(queue,
            new int[]{NUM_ITEMS}, new int[]{NUM_ITEMS});  Enqueue
        buff.read(queue, dataBuffer, true, kernelEvent);  commands

        for(int i = 0; i < NUM_FLOATS; i++)
          System.out.println(i + ": " + dataBuffer.get(i));
    }
```

The createKernel method ❶ serves three roles. It builds the CLProgram, creates the CLKernel, and makes the CLFloatBuffer the kernel's first argument.

This code creates the FloatBuffer by invoking the directFloats method of the NIOUtils class. This is one of many convenience classes provided by JavaCL, and others perform matrix processing, OpenGL interaction, and even reduction. If you intend to use JavaCL, I strongly recommend that you explore these capabilities further.

9.3 PyOpenCL

The popularity of the Python programming language has soared in recent years, and it's not hard to see why. Python is easy to learn, easy to code, and interpreters are available on all major operating systems.

Andreas Klöckner of the Courant Institute of Mathematical Sciences has extended Python's breadth of capabilities by releasing PyOpenCL. The classes and functions in this package make it possible to construct host applications with the same features as those coded in regular C. But before we delve into the internals of PyOpenCL, it's important to know how to obtain the toolset.

9.3.1 PyOpenCL installation and licensing

The main PyOpenCL site is http://mathema.tician.de/software/pyopencl, and you can download the package by scrolling down and clicking the link entitled Download PyOpenCL Here. Unlike Aparapi and JavaCL, PyOpenCL can't be immediately used once it's downloaded. You need to compile it from its source code, which is a combination of Python and C++. The compilation and installation processes depend on what operating system you're using, and you can find the latest instructions at http://wiki.tiker.net/PyOpenCL.

Andreas Klöckner has released PyOpenCL under the MIT/X Consortium License, which is the least restrictive of the licenses we've encountered in this chapter. This license allows you to "use, copy, modify, merge, publish, distribute, sublicense, and/or sell copies of the Software" without limitation. The only requirements are that you must mention PyOpenCL's copyright document in any software based on PyOpenCL.

Once you've compiled and installed PyOpenCL, you can access the pyopencl module from inside your Python scripts. The rest of this section will explain the different classes and functions provided by this module.

9.3.2 Overview of PyOpenCL development

PyOpenCL and JavaCL have a great deal in common, and both provide classes that wrap around the C data structures discussed in chapters 2 and 3. Table 9.3 lists these classes along with the pyopencl module and presents a number of their functions.

In general, a PyOpenCL script starts by accessing the pyopencl module and creating a Platform or Context object. Then it compiles a Program, creates one or more Kernels, sets kernel arguments, and dispatches kernels and other commands to a CommandQueue.

Table 9.3 Important classes of the PyOpenCL API

PyOpenCL class/module	C data structure	Important functions
pyopencl	–	get_platforms, create_some_context, enqueue_read_buffer, enqueue_write_buffer
Platform	cl_platform	info, get_info, get_devices
Device	cl_device	info, get_info
Context	cl_context	Context, info, get_info
Program	cl_program	Program, info, get_info, build, get_build_info, kernel_name, all_kernels
Kernel	cl_kernel	Kernel, info, get_info, set_arg, set_args
CommandQueue	cl_command_queue	CommandQueue, info, get_info, set_property, flush, finish
MemoryObject	cl_mem	info, get_info, release, get_host_array
Buffer	cl_mem (buffer object)	Buffer, get_sub_region, __getitem__
Image	cl_mem (image object)	Image, info, get_image_info, shape, release

9.3.3 Creating kernels with PyOpenCL

This section discusses how the PyOpenCL classes work together to form kernels, and it takes the same path as in the JavaCL discussion. We'll examine the `Platform` and `Device` classes first and the `Context` and `CommandQueue` classes second. Then we'll discuss how to compile and dispatch kernel code with the `Program` and `Kernel` classes.

PLATFORMS AND DEVICES

A `Platform` object represents an OpenCL framework installed on the host, such as Nvidia's SDK or AMD's SDK. To access the installed platforms, you need to call the `get_platforms` function of the pyopencl module. This returns a list of `Platform` objects, and you can examine the properties of each by calling `get_info`. This works like the `getInfo` function in the C++ Wrapper API and accepts a parameter that identifies the type of information being sought. For example, the following code prints the names of each platform installed on the system and their supported extensions:

```
import pyopencl
for platform in pyopencl.get_platforms():
    print("%s: %s" % (platform.get_info(pyopencl.platform_info.NAME),
                       platform.get_info(pyopencl.platform_info.EXTENSIONS)))
```

Repeating the full name of the pyopencl module can be tiresome, so the following code sets its name to cl and accomplishes the same result:

```
import pyopencl as cl
for platform in cl.get_platforms():
    print("%s: %s" % (platform.get_info(cl.platform_info.NAME),
                       platform.get_info(cl.platform_info.EXTENSIONS)))
```

As shown, the names of PyOpenCL's constants and enumerated types can be found by removing the `cl_`/`CL_` from the corresponding names in the C API. In the preceding example code, `cl_platform_info` becomes `platform_info` and `CL_NAME` becomes `NAME`. This naming convention holds true throughout PyOpenCL, so we won't discuss the `get_info` function further.

Once you've obtained a `Platform` object, you can access its connected devices with the `get_devices` function. This accepts a `device_type` parameter that can be set to `ALL`, `CPU`, `GPU`, `DEFAULT`, or `ACCELERATOR`. By default, `get_devices` sets the type parameter to `pyopencl.device_type.ALL`.

The only function provided by the `Device` class is `get_info`, but `Device` objects serve important purposes in PyOpenCL scripts. They allow you to create `Contexts` and `CommandQueues`, and we'll look at these two classes next.

CONTEXTS AND COMMANDQUEUES

A `Context` defines the collection of `Devices` that you intend to use to execute your kernels. PyOpenCL provides two ways to create `Contexts`, and the first involves calling the class's constructor. Its signature is as follows:

```
Context(devices=None, properties=None, dev_type=None)
```

If the first argument is provided, the Context will contain the specified Device objects. If the third argument is provided, the Context will contain all Devices of the given type. One of these arguments must be given to create the Context, but not both.

If you don't care how a Context is created, you can call the create_some_context function of the pyopencl module. This accepts a True/False value that allows the user to select devices for the Context. By default, create_some_context returns a Context containing the first Device of the first accessible Platform. If you only have a single OpenCL-compliant device connected to your host, this is the easiest way to obtain a Context.

After you've created a Context, you can construct CommandQueues that will send commands to Devices within the Context. The only way to construct these objects is through the class constructor, as follows:

```
CommandQueue(context, device=None, properties=None)
```

The properties argument allows you to specify whether the queue should support profiling, out-of-order execution, or both. The property names are PROFILING_ENABLE and OUT_OF_ORDER_EXEC_MODE_ENABLE, and both are provided through the class command_queue_properties. As an example, the following code creates a Context containing every Device in the first Platform, and then creates a CommandQueue with profiling enabled.

> **Listing 9.5 Creating command queues with PyOpenCL: create_queue.py**

```
import pyopencl as cl

platform = cl.get_platforms()[0]          Create
devices = platform.get_devices()          context
context = cl.Context(devices)

queue = cl.CommandQueue(context, devices[0],     Create command
    cl.command_queue_properties.PROFILING_ENABLE)   queue

dev_name = queue.get_info(cl.command_queue_info.DEVICE).\
    get_info(cl.device_info.NAME)
print("Device: %s" % (dev_name))
```

Simple, isn't it? With Python, you don't have to worry about lengthy function syntax, static typing, semicolons, or curly brackets. As you'll see next, Python's file access routines are equally easy to use.

PROGRAMS AND KERNELS

The Program class has two constructors. The first creates a Program from source text, and the second creates a Program from binary code. Their signatures are as follows:

```
Program(context, src)
Program(context, devices, binaries)
```

These serve the same roles as the clCreateProgramWithSource and clCreate-ProgramWithBinary functions in the C API. Remember that if you intend to create a Program from binary code, you must provide a binary for each target device.

The example code in this book has focused on reading source code from a file, and this is easier to do in Python than in any other language I know. All you need are the open, read, and close functions. The following code demonstrates how they're used, and then constructs a Program from the file's text:

```
program_file = open('file_name.cl', 'r')
program_text = program_file.read()
program_file.close()
program = cl.Program(context, program_text)
```

Once you've created a Program, you can compile its code with the build function. This is its signature:

```
build(options=[], devices=None)
```

For the compile options, you can use any of the options listed in table 2.7. For example, the following line builds a Program called prog for every device in the context and configures the build to respond to warnings as though they were errors:

```
prog.build("-Werror")
```

Once you've compiled a Program object, you can access the build log with the get_build_info function. This accepts a Device object and a program_build_info parameter that can be set to STATUS, OPTIONS, or LOG. For example, if you want to see the full build log for a compilation targeting a Device called dev, you could use the following code:

```
log = prog.get_build_info(dev, cl.program_build_info.LOG)
```

This statement places the text containing the build log into log. If the build completed without warning or error, log will be set to "".

There are three ways to create Kernel objects from a compiled Program. First, you can call Program.all_kernels, which returns a list containing a Kernel for every kernel function in the Program. Second, you can call the Kernel constructor, whose signature is as follows:

```
Kernel(program, name)
```

This creates a single Kernel object corresponding to the kernel function called name. The third way accomplishes the same result, but treats the function's name as an attribute of the Program object. An example will make this clear. The following two lines both create a Kernel from a function called foo:

```
k = cl.Kernel(program, 'foo')
k = program.foo
```

The following listing creates Kernels using the second and third methods. It calls the Kernel constructor to create a Kernel corresponding to the add function. Then it uses attribute lookup to create a Kernel corresponding to the multiply function.

Listing 9.6 Creating kernels with PyOpenCL: create_kernel.py

```
import pyopencl as cl

...
program_file = open('arith.cl', 'r')
program_text = program_file.read()
program = cl.Program(context, program_text)
try:                                                          Create/build
    program.build()                                          program
except:
    print("Build log:")
    print(program.get_build_info(devices[0],
        cl.program_build_info.LOG))
    raise

add_kernel = cl.Kernel(program, 'add')                       Create
mult_kernel = program.multiply                               kernels

print("Kernel Name:"),
print(mult_kernel.get_info(cl.kernel_info.FUNCTION_NAME))
program_file.close()
```

It's important to see how this code checks for errors. If the program compilation produces an error, the exception-handling routine accesses and prints the log associated with the build.

9.3.4 Setting arguments and executing kernels

After you've created a Kernel object for a function, the next step is to add arguments so that the function has data to process. PyOpenCL provides two ways to set arguments for a kernel. First, you can call setArg, whose signature is as follows:

```
setArg(self, index, arg)
```

Second, you can set arguments for a Kernel as you create it using the attribute lookup process we looked at earlier. Suppose you want to set a, b, and c as arguments of a kernel function called foo. In that case, you can create the Kernel and specify its three arguments with the following line of code:

```
program.foo(queue, global_size, local_size, a, b, c)
```

This single line creates a Kernel corresponding to foo, configures its three arguments, and then dispatches the kernel for execution with *global_size* work-items and *local_size* work-items per work-group. The fact that you can accomplish so much with one line of code is my favorite aspect of PyOpenCL.

But now two questions arise: What data types are a, b, and c? And how do you create them? The answers are somewhat involved. In PyOpenCL, a kernel argument must take one of the following forms:

- A MemoryObject, which can be instantiated as a Buffer or Image object
- A LocalMemory, which tells the device to reserve local memory for the argument

- A scalar value, such as a scalar type from the Scientific Computing Tools for Python, NumPy (`numpy.float64` or `numpy.int32`)
- An implementation of the Python buffer interface, such as `str` and `numpy.ndarray`
- A `Sampler`, which was discussed in chapter 6
- `None`, which results in a `NULL` pointer to global memory

This discussion will present the first three options, which produce arguments stored in global/constant memory, local memory, and private memory, respectively. We'll start by examining how PyOpenCL implements memory objects.

MEMORY OBJECTS

PyOpenCL provides a `MemoryObject` class that serves the same role as the `cl_mem` data structure in C. Objects of this class are used to transfer data from the host to global memory in the device. The `MemoryObject` class provides functions such as `get_info` and `get_host_array`, but there are no constructors. To transfer data between the host and device, you need its subclasses: `Image` and `Buffer`. For pixel data, create an `Image` object. Otherwise, create a `Buffer` object. The `Image` and `Buffer` constructors are as follows:

```
Buffer(context, flags, size=0, hostbuf=None)

Image(context, flags, format, shape=None, pitches=None, hostbuf=None)
```

In both constructors, the `flags` argument defines whether the memory object is read/write and how the host data should be allocated. The possible values for this argument are similar to those presented in table 3.1 without the `CL_MEM_` prefix. That is, to make the memory object write-only, you'd set flags to `WRITE_ONLY` instead of `CL_MEM_WRITE_ONLY`.

The `hostbuf` argument identifies the data that will be transferred to the device. In JavaCL, this data must be placed in a Java NIO `Buffer` object. In PyOpenCL, host data must be given as an implementation of the Python buffer interface. A common way to set host data is through an `ndarray` object, which represents an array. The `array` function is frequently used to create `ndarray`s, and the following code shows how it's used:

```
w = numpy.array([0, 1, 2, 3])
--> w = [0  1  2  3]
x = numpy.array([[0, 1], [2, 3]])
--> x = [[0  1]
         [2  3]]
y = numpy.zeros(4)
--> y = [0.  0.  0.  0.]
z = numpy.linspace(0, 6, 7)
[0.  1.  2.  3.  4.  5.  6.]
```

To set the data type of the array elements, you can follow the array specification with `astype` and a NumPy data type. These data types include `byte`, `short`, `int16/32/64`, `uint16/32/64`, and `float32/64`. This is shown in the following code:

```
x = numpy.array([0, 1, 2, 3]).astype(numpy.float32)
--> x = [0.  1.  2.  3.]
y = numpy.zeros(4).astype(numpy.uint32)
--> y = [0  0  0  0]
```

In the `Buffer` constructor, it's common to include the third argument, `size`, or the fourth argument, `hostbuf`, but not both. This is because if `hostbuf` is given, `size` will be set to the data size by default. This is shown in the following code, which forms a `Buffer` from an `ndarray` containing 1,024 `int32` values:

```
host_data = numpy.linspace(0, 1023, 1024).astype(numpy.int32)
data_buffer = cl.Buffer(context,
      numpy.memflags.READ_ONLY | numpy.memflags.COPY_HOST_PTR,
      hostBuf=host_data)
```

In the `Image` constructor, the `format` parameter requires an `ImageFormat` object to identify how the host's pixel data is structured. The `ImageFormat` constructor accepts a list containing two elements: a `channel_order` value and a `channel_type` value. The `channel_type` element has the same values as those listed in table 3.2 (without the `CL_`). Most of the `channel_order` values identify the red, green, blue, and alpha channels contained in each pixel, and possible values include `RGB`, `RGBA`, `BGRA`, `RG`, `RA`, `R`, and `A`. Others add bit padding, represented by x: `RGBx`, `RGx`, and `Rx`. The last two `channel_order` values are `INTENSITY`, which measures alpha (opacity) independent of color, and `LUMINANCE`, which is used for grayscale images.

LOCAL MEMORY AND SCALAR DATA

If you transfer a memory object to a device, its data will be stored in the device's global or constant address spaces. But in many circumstances, you may want your work-items to access data in local memory. The host can't directly read or write to this memory, but it can allocate local memory for kernel arguments. PyOpenCL provides the `LocalMemory` class for this purpose, and its constructor accepts the number of bytes to be allocated. As an example, the following code creates a `LocalMemory` object that allocates memory for 8,192 bytes. Then it makes this object the first argument of the Kernel k:

```
locmem = cl.LocalMemory(8192)
k.set_arg(0, locmem)
```

In addition to allocating local memory for kernel arguments, you can place arguments in a device's private memory by setting scalar data as the argument. The scalar data can take any of the types defined by NumPy: `int16`, `uint32`, `float64`, and so on. The following code creates an `int32` scalar called x and makes it the second argument of the kernel:

```
x = numpy.int32(30)
k.set_arg(1, x)
```

When the kernel receives the argument, x will be placed in private memory throughout the device. Each work-item will be able to read and write to its value independently.

EXECUTING KERNELS

PyOpenCL provides three ways to execute kernels:

- enqueue_task function—Executes a kernel with a single work-item
- enqueue_nd_range_kernel function—Executes a kernel with multiple work-items
- __call__ descriptor—Creates a Kernel, sets its arguments, and executes the kernel with multiple work-items

The enqueue_task and enqueue_nd_range_kernel functions closely resemble the clEnqueueTask and clEnqueueNDRangeKernel functions described in chapter 2. Their signatures are as follows:

```
enqueue_task(queue, kernel, wait_for=None)
```

```
enqueue_nd_range_kernel(queue, kernel, global_size, local_size,
    offsets=None, wait_for=None, g_times_l=True)
```

Both have a wait_for parameter that identifies a list of Event objects that form the wait list of the enqueued command. Both functions also return an Event object that can be used to monitor the completion of the kernel's execution. PyOpenCL event processing is beyond the scope of this chapter, but these Event objects perform the same roles as the cl_event structures discussed in chapter 7.

It's important to note that the global_size, local_size, and offsets parameters are given in tuples. Therefore, if your data is one-dimensional and your global size is 20, the global_size parameter must be set to (20,). This is shown in the following example, which creates and executes a kernel with 20 work-items in 5 work-groups:

```
kernel = cl.Kernel(program, 'func_name')
kernel.set_arg(0, buffer_a)
kernel.set_arg(1, buffer_b)
kernel.enqueue_nd_range_kernel(queue, kernel, (20,), (4,))
```

This example code should look friendly and familiar, but with the __call__ descriptor, you can combine these four lines into a single function call. This descriptor makes it possible to create a Kernel object and set its arguments by invoking the name of the corresponding kernel function. The full signature for the __call__ descriptor is as follows:

```
__call__(queue, global_size, local_size, *args,
          global_offset=None, wait_for=None)
```

The third parameter, args, identifies zero or more kernel arguments. They will be passed to the kernel in the order in which they're given, so there's no need to call set_arg to specify the arguments and their indices.

The __call__ descriptor simplifies the coding process, but it can be hard to understand. For example, the following line of code creates and executes the same kernel as in the preceding example code:

```
program.func_name(queue, (20,), (4,), buffer_a, buffer_b)
```

Like enqueue_task and enqueue_nd_range_kernel, this function call returns an Event corresponding to the command. This can be used to configure callback functions or to force other commands to wait.

The following code provides a more concrete example of how kernels are created and executed using the __call__ descriptor.

Listing 9.7   Executing kernels with PyOpenCL: run_kernel.py

```
import pyopencl as cl
import numpy

...
scalar = numpy.float32(5.0)
lm = cl.LocalMemory(100 * 32)
float_data = numpy.linspace(1, 100, 100)
      .astype(numpy.float32)                        Create kernel
float_buffer = cl.Buffer(context,                   arguments
      cl.mem_flags.READ_WRITE |
      cl.mem_flags.COPY_HOST_PTR,
      hostbuf=float_data)
                                                    Create/execute
program.mult(queue, (25,), (25,), scalar, float_buffer, lm)   kernel

cl.enqueue_read_buffer(queue, float_buffer, float_data).wait()

print float_data                                    Read data buffer
```

This script creates three arguments for the mult kernel: a scalar, a LocalMemory object, and a Buffer. The call to program.mult executes the kernel with 25 work-items in a single work-group. Afterward, the script reads the updated data in the read/write buffer and prints the full array.

The PyOpenCL API contains many more functions than we've discussed here, and it provides many useful capabilities for integrating graphic processing with OpenCL. If you'd like to investigate PyOpenCL further, Andreas Klöckner has written a great deal of documentation, and the PyOpenCL software package comes with a large number of useful example scripts.

9.4   Summary

This chapter has examined three markedly different ways of building OpenCL applications. Aparapi is simple to code, but it leaves out many of the capabilities you'd expect from host applications or kernels. JavaCL isn't as simple, but it lets you build host applications with all the features provided by the OpenCL 1.0 standard. PyOpenCL also enables full-featured development of host applications, but it binds OpenCL to Python instead of Java.

All Aparapi applications center on the Kernel class. Specifically, the goal of an Aparapi application is to provide code for a Kernel subclass, instantiate the subclass, and then deploy the kernel by calling its execute method. The code inside the Kernel's run method will execute on the device, but remember that the application can't access vector types or multidimensional work-items.

In contrast with Aparapi, JavaCL doesn't allow you to code kernels in Java. Instead, you can build host applications using classes that correspond to the data structures discussed in chapters 2 and 3. The methods of these classes are easy to work with, such as `createBestContext`, which creates a new `CLContext` containing the device with the most compute units. JavaCL also provides classes and methods for dealing with memory objects that access memory on the host using Java NIO `Buffer` objects. Java NIO classes provide high-efficiency data transfer, but they may be foreign to Java developers used to traditional Java IO classes.

PyOpenCL makes it possible to code host applications in Python. This toolset keeps to Python's philosophy of simplicity and concision, and a host application written in Python will generally require one-third to one-fourth the code of a similar application written in C. In particular, the `__call__` descriptor dramatically simplifies the process of creating and configuring kernels. If all other concerns were equal, I would code all of my OpenCL host applications using PyOpenCL.

When working with these tools, keep their distribution licenses in mind. Aparapi is meant for evaluation purposes only and can't be redistributed in any form for any reason. JavaCL is released under the GNU Lesser General Public License (LGPL), which means you can distribute it with any software package you like, so long as the software isn't a derivative work. PyOpenCL is released under the MIT/X Consortium License, which allows you to do whatever you want so long as you include Andreas Klöckner's copyright and the permission notice.

In the next chapter, we'll put aside third-party software development and return to C programming. We'll look into a general coding methodology for developing large-scale OpenCL applications.

General coding principles

In the preceding chapters, the example host applications have executed kernels using a single work-item. This is fine when you're learning OpenCL or testing a new application, but for production code, this is unacceptable. OpenCL's great strength is that you can execute kernels using millions or even billions of work-items, and if you're not going to put them to use, you might as well program in regular C.

Making use of all this processing power isn't easy. You need a clear understanding of how work-items and work-groups access memory, and how synchronization can be used to coordinate their operation. To reach this understanding, it helps to look at a fully optimized example application. Most of this chapter will be concerned with the process of *reduction*, or adding together elements of an array. Specifically, we're going to compute the sum of 2^{20} floating-point values using 2^{20} work-items. We'll spend some time examining the reduction algorithm, but remember that it's the *method* that's important. This example will illuminate the issues that arise when processing large amounts of data, such as memory bandwidth, memory bank conflicts, and work-group synchronization. The better you understand these issues, the better your own OpenCL applications will perform.

But before we look at reduction, it's important to discuss how the global size and local size are configured in large-scale applications. Finding the right values for these parameters will play a large role in determining your kernel's processing performance.

10.1 *Global size and local size*

One of the primary advantages of using OpenCL is that you can execute applications using thousands and thousands of threads, called work-items. The upper limit on the number of work-items you can generate is the maximum value of size_t (see SIZE_MAX in stdint.h), so it's usually a good idea to generate one for each data point you need to process. For example, if a kernel needs to sort 2^{16} integers and you want to process them using int4 vectors, set the total number of work-items to $2^{16}/4$, or 2^{14}. This total number of work-items is called the global size.

Another rule of thumb to follow when generating work-items is that the global size should be a multiple of the maximum work-group size. Chapters 3 and 4 discussed work-groups in detail, but for this chapter, there are five main points to keep in mind:

- A work-group is a collection of work-items, and each has its own numeric identifier called the group ID.
- Every work-item has two identifiers. Its global ID identifies the item among all others generated to execute the kernel. Its local ID identifies the item only among others in the same work-group.
- Each work-group has its own block of memory called local memory. For many devices, work-items can access local data much faster than they can access data in global memory.
- To conserve bandwidth, operations that access global memory are combined into one operation for the entire work-group. Therefore, it's a good idea to have work-items in a group access global memory at the same time.
- Work-items in the same work-group can be synchronized with calls to the barrier function. OpenCL doesn't provide any functions that synchronize work-items in different work-groups.

Because global memory access is so time-consuming, many kernels only access global memory twice: once to read input data into local memory, and once to write results from local memory to global memory. In this approach, all intermediate processing is performed with local memory data.

To make the best use of local memory, it's important to have as many work-items in a work-group as possible. The number of work-items in a work-group is called the local size, and OpenCL provides a straightforward method to find the maximum local size for a given kernel running on a given device. This section will explain how this method works and then show how to determine the maximum work-group size in code.

10.1.1 Finding the maximum work-group size

No matter how many work-items you generate for a kernel, the maximum number of work-items in a work-group remains the same. If your global size exceeds the maximum work-group size, OpenCL will create additional work-groups. An application may generate a nearly unlimited number of work-groups, but the number of work-groups that can execute in parallel is determined by the number of compute units on the device.

The maximum work-group size depends on two things: the resources provided by the device and the resources required by the kernel. In general, the resources that constrain work-item availability are local memory and private memory. The more memory a kernel requires, the fewer work-items will be available to execute it. Your work-items could access global/constant memory instead of local/private memory, but then memory bandwidth drops. This is an important trade-off.

Determining a kernel's resource usage can be a tedious, error-prone process. But OpenCL makes it simple by providing the `clGetKernelWorkGroupInfo` function. Its signature is as follows:

```
cl_int clGetKernelWorkGroupInfo(cl_kernel kernel, cl_device_id device,
    cl_kernel_work_group_info param_name, size_t param_value_size,
    void *param_value, size_t *param_value_size_ret)
```

This function resembles the other `clGetXXInfo` functions discussed throughout this book. It accepts a parameter name that identifies the type of information being sought and returns the data at the memory location pointed to by `param_value`. Table 10.1 lists the different parameters available for this function.

Table 10.1 Kernel work-group information parameters

Parameter name	Output type	Returned value
CL_KERNEL_WORK_GROUP_SIZE	size_t	The maximum work-group size to execute the given kernel on the given device
CL_KERNEL_PREFERRED_WORK_GROUP_SIZE_MULTIPLE	size_t	A multiple for determining work-group sizes that ensure best performance
CL_KERNEL_LOCAL_MEM_SIZE	cl_ulong	The number of bytes of local memory used by the kernel
CL_KERNEL_PRIVATE_MEM_SIZE	cl_ulong	The number of bytes of private memory used by the kernel
CL_KERNEL_COMPILE_WORK_GROUP_SIZE	size_t[3]	The work-group size set by the `reqd_work_group_size` attribute

The first parameter is the most important. If you call `clGetKernelWorkGroupInfo` with `CL_KERNEL_WORK_GROUP_SIZE`, it will give you the maximum work-group size for the specified kernel and device. The following code shows how this works:

```
size_t wg_size;
err = clGetKernelWorkGroupInfo(kernel, device, CL_KERNEL_WORK_GROUP_SIZE,
    sizeof(wg_size), &wg_size, NULL);
```

The second parameter in the table becomes helpful when you don't want to set the local size to its maximum value. This gives you a number such that, if the local size is a multiple of the number, a kernel will execute with higher performance than otherwise. For example, if the maximum local size is 1,024 and the multiple is 256, it's recommended that you set your local size to 256, 512, 768, or 1024.

The third and fourth parameters tell you how many bytes the kernel requires in local and private memory. The more you pare down the memory needed by the kernel, the lower these values will be and the more work-items you'll be able to generate to execute the kernel.

10.1.2 *Testing kernels and devices*

In the Ch10/wg_test folder, the wg_test application accepts the name of a program file and a kernel, and obtains information related to work-groups and kernel resources. Specifically, the application determines the maximum work-group size available to execute the kernel, the kernel's memory requirements, and the device's memory characteristics. The following listing presents the portion of the code that calls on `clGetKernelWorkGroupInfo` and `clGetDeviceInfo`.

> **Listing 10.1 Obtaining kernel/device information: wg_test.c (abridged)**

```
...
char device_name[48];
size_t wg_size, wg_multiple;
cl_ulong local_mem, private_usage, local_usage;
...
err = clGetDeviceInfo(device, CL_DEVICE_NAME,
    sizeof(device_name), device_name, NULL);          Obtain device
err |= clGetDeviceInfo(device, CL_DEVICE_LOCAL_MEM_SIZE,   information
    sizeof(local_mem), &local_mem, NULL);
if(err < 0) {
   perror("Couldn't obtain device information");
   exit(1);
}
...
err = clGetKernelWorkGroupInfo(kernel, device,
    CL_KERNEL_WORK_GROUP_SIZE,
    sizeof(wg_size), &wg_size, NULL);
err |= clGetKernelWorkGroupInfo(kernel, device,      Obtain kernel/work-
    CL_KERNEL_PREFERRED_WORK_GROUP_SIZE_MULTIPLE,     group information
    sizeof(wg_multiple), &wg_multiple, NULL);
err |= clGetKernelWorkGroupInfo(kernel, device,
    CL_KERNEL_LOCAL_MEM_SIZE,
```

```
        sizeof(local_usage), &local_usage, NULL);
err |= clGetKernelWorkGroupInfo(kernel, device,
    CL_KERNEL_PRIVATE_MEM_SIZE,
        sizeof(private_usage), &private_usage, NULL);
if(err < 0) {
   perror("Couldn't obtain kernel work-group size information");
   exit(1);
};
...
```

Obtain kernel/work-group information

The Ch10/wg_test folder contains a program file called test.cl, and this program defines a simple kernel called test. To test this kernel with the wg_test application, you can enter the following command:

```
wg_test blank.cl blank
```

When I execute the kernel on my AMD 5850 system, the following results are displayed:

```
For the blank kernel running on the Cypress device, the maximum work-group
    size is 256 and the work-group multiple is 64.
The kernel uses 0 bytes of local memory out of a maximum of 32768 bytes. It
    uses 0 bytes of private memory.
```

The kernel in this example performs no processing and uses no resources, so there's no way to improve its performance. But in the next section, we'll look at a more involved kernel and examine how to improve its execution speed.

10.2 *Numerical reduction*

Numerical reduction adds the elements of an array and computes a single sum. This algorithm is ideal for learning how to code large-scale OpenCL applications for three reasons:

- It's easy to understand.
- It can scale to occupy every computing resource on a device.
- It requires that work-items combine their results.

In this section, we're going to look closely at this algorithm and see how to implement it to add 2^{20} values. With a single work-item, this can be accomplished as follows:

```
sum = 0.0f;
if(get_global_id(0) == 0) {
   for(int i=0; i<1048576; i++) {
       sum += data[i];
   }
}
```

Because we demand high performance, this is completely insufficient. Next, we'll examine code that performs reduction using one work-item for each value. Then, using float4 vectors, we'll make the kernel execute even faster.

10.2.1 *OpenCL reduction*

If you look in the Ch10/reduction folder, you'll find a program file called reduction.cl that contains a kernel function called reduction_scalar. By default, the host application generates 2^{20} (1,048,576) work-items to execute this kernel. On my AMD 5850 GPU, these items are combined into 4,096 work-groups, each containing 256 work-items. On my Nvidia GTX 470 GPU, these are combined into 1,024 work-groups, each containing 1,024 work-items.

THE REDUCTION ALGORITHM

But before we look at the code, it's important to understand the overall reduction algorithm. Each work-group loads a subset of input data to local memory, adds it together, and returns the sum to the host. The host collects the values from each work-group and adds them together to obtain the final answer.

The addition procedure employed by each work-group requires $\log_2 N$ stages, where N is the number of input values and work-items. In the first stage, the N input values are added in pairs to produce $N/2$ results. The next stage adds the $N/2$ input values in pairs and produces $N/4$ results. This process continues until a single value remains. Figure 10.1 shows the full process for a work-group where $N = 8$.

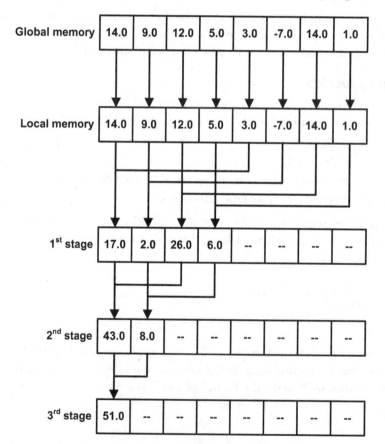

Figure 10.1
Multistage reduction in OpenCL

At the top of the figure, each work-item in the work-group reads a value from global memory and places it in local memory. But afterward, only half of the work-items are actually used in the reduction process. This supports the rule of thumb that says it's a good idea to generate a work-item for every data element.

Once the data is placed in local memory, work-items add elements x^k and $x^{k+N/2}$, and then store the results in sequence (sum 0 is stored at address 0, sum 1 is stored at address 1, and so on). This storage method reduces memory bank conflicts.

Local memory is organized into memory banks whose sizes depend on the device's architecture (there are usually 16 or 32 banks) per local memory block. The data in these banks is interleaved so that sequential 32-bit values are placed in adjacent banks. Each bank can be accessed independently, so if work-items access different banks at the same time, their read/write operations will be executed in parallel.

But if work-items attempt to access the same bank at the same time, their read/write operations will be processed serially and the kernel will wait until all the operations have finished. These memory bank conflicts can dramatically reduce the performance of an application, so it's best to avoid them at all costs.

Another reason that this reduction algorithm works well is that there's no need to use the modulo operator, %. This operator is useful when determining whether a number is odd or even, or whether it's divisible by another number. The % operator doesn't consume a great deal of time on CPUs, but it takes many cycles to process the operation on GPUs, so it's best to avoid it whenever possible.

THE REDUCTION KERNEL

Listing 10.2 presents the code that implements the reduction procedure depicted in figure 10.1. This kernel accepts the following parameters:

- data—A buffer object containing the input data: 2^{20} floats in ascending order
- partial_sums—A portion of local memory allocated to hold intermediate results
- output—A buffer object containing the output sums produced by the work-groups

Listing 10.2 Reduction using scalars: reduction.cl

```
__kernel void reduction_scalar(__global float* data,
      __local float* partial_sums, __global float* output) {

   int lid = get_local_id(0);
   int group_size = get_local_size(0);

   partial_sums[lid] = data[get_global_id(0)];          ① Read data to
   barrier(CLK_LOCAL_MEM_FENCE);                             local memory

   for(int i = group_size/2; i>0; i >>= 1) {
      if(lid < i) {
         partial_sums[lid] += partial_sums[lid + i];       Perform
      }                                                     reduction stages
      barrier(CLK_LOCAL_MEM_FENCE);
   }
}
```

```
if(lid == 0) {
    output[get_group_id(0)] = partial_sums[0];
}
}
```

Write output to global memory

Each work-item starts by transferring an element of input data to local memory ❶, and it's important to see how this works. There are 2^{20} work-items in total, one for each element in the input `data` array located in global memory. Because every global ID is unique, a work-item can read a unique element by accessing `data[get_ global_id(0)]`. In local memory, the `partial_sums` array stores one `float` for each work-item in a work-group. Within a work-group, a work-item uses its local ID instead of its global ID. This is why the work-item writes the input float from `data[get_global_id(0)]` to the local memory position `partial_sums[lid]`.

Because the work-items access local memory sequentially, memory bank conflicts are kept to a minimum. It's also worth noting that, because each work-group contains the maximum possible number of work-items, the memory bandwidth for the data transfer will reach its maximum value.

After the work-group's input data is transferred to local memory, the actual reduction starts. In the first stage, only half of the work-group's work-items take part. Each adds its corresponding element of `partial_sums` to an element half-way further in the array. The second and proceeding stages continue adding partial sums together in the manner shown in figure 10.1. After each stage, the `barrier` function forces each work-item to wait until every other work-item in the work-group has finished accessing local memory.

When the addition is finished, the work-item whose local ID equals 0 will place the final sum in global memory. More precisely, it transfers `partial_sums[0]` in local memory to `output[get_group_id(0)]` in global memory. You should have a clear understanding of the difference between `get_local_id` and `get_group_id`. The first function distinguishes a work-item from all other work-items in the work-group. The second function distinguishes a work-group from all other work-groups generated to execute the kernel.

10.2.2 *Improving reduction speed with vectors*

The code in listing 10.2 works well. It performs intermediate computation using local memory, minimizes memory bank conflicts, and distributes the work evenly among the work-items in the work-group. But there's one way you can make a significant improvement: process data in vectors instead of scalars. That is, instead of adding floats, add `float4`s.

The code in listing 10.3 shows how reduction can be implemented using vectors. For the most part, the code is similar to that in listing 10.2. But now the elements in the `data` and `partial_sums` arrays are `float4`s.

Listing 10.3   Reduction using vectors: reduction.cl

```
__kernel void reduction_vector(
    __global float4* data,                          Use vector
    __local float4* partial_sums,                   types
    __global float4* output) {

    int lid = get_local_id(0);
    int group_size = get_local_size(0);

    partial_sums[lid] = data[get_global_id(0)];
    barrier(CLK_LOCAL_MEM_FENCE);

    for(int i = group_size/2; i>0; i >>= 1) {
        if(lid < i) {
            partial_sums[lid] += partial_sums[lid + i];
        }
        barrier(CLK_LOCAL_MEM_FENCE);
    }

    if(lid == 0) {                                  Write global
        output[get_group_id(0)] = partial_sums[0];  output
    }
}
```

The host application, whose source file is Ch10/reduction/reduction.c, makes two significant changes to execute the reduction_vector kernel:

- The global size equals the number of input values divided by 4. In this example, the global size is set to $2^{20}/4 = 2^{18}$.
- The partial_sums array stores vectors instead of scalars, so it needs four times as much memory. Therefore, the host application sets the size of the allocated local memory to 4 * local_size * sizeof(float).

When you run the Ch10/reduction application, it will execute both the reduction_scalar and reduction_vector kernels. In addition to checking the results, it measures the time taken for each kernel to execute. On my system, the results are as follows:

```
reduction_scalar: Check passed.
Total time = 489031

reduction_vector: Check passed.
Total time = 136157
```

As shown, reduction completes significantly faster using vectors instead of scalars. This should make sense, because the reduction_vector kernel needs 1/4 as many work-items as the reduction_scalar kernel.

One problem with these reduction kernels is that neither actually completes the reduction operation. They provide partial sums—one for each work-group. The host can add these to obtain the final result, but in general, we want devices to complete their processing tasks without the host's assistance. This requires synchronization across work-groups, and this is the topic of the next section.

10.3   *Synchronizing work-groups*

This title is misleading. There is no `barrier` function that synchronizes work-items in different work-groups, and so long as a kernel is executing, there's no way to tell when any work-group completes its processing. Therefore, as long as a kernel continues executing, there's no way to process the results of multiple work-groups.

But once a kernel completes its execution, you can be certain that all of its work-groups have finished processing and that their results can be accessed safely. For this reason, many OpenCL applications execute *multiple kernels*—each successive kernel processes the results generated by the kernel preceding it. Launching multiple kernels can be time-consuming, but there's no getting around it. Until OpenCL devices support work-group synchronization, this is the best we can do.

To see how this works, let's look at the reduction_vector kernel in listing 10.3. This accepts 2^{18} float4 vectors and returns one float4 vector for each work-group. Instead of having the host add the output values, we're now going to continue executing the kernel until the number of output vectors falls below the local size.

Once the input can be processed with work-items in a single work-group, the host will launch another kernel to compute the final sum. This kernel is called reduction_complete:

Listing 10.4   Computing the final reduction: reduction_complete.cl

```
__kernel void reduction_complete(__global float4* data,
      __local float4* partial_sums, __global float* sum) {

   int lid = get_local_id(0);
   int group_size = get_local_size(0);

   partial_sums[lid] = data[get_local_id(0)];
   barrier(CLK_LOCAL_MEM_FENCE);

   for(int i = group_size/2; i>0; i >>= 1) {
      if(lid < i) {
         partial_sums[lid] += partial_sums[lid + i];
      }
      barrier(CLK_LOCAL_MEM_FENCE);
   }

   if(lid == 0) {
      *sum = partial_sums[0].s0 + partial_sums[0].s1 +         Compute
            partial_sums[0].s2 + partial_sums[0].s3;            final result
   }
}
```

The code in this kernel closely resembles that of reduction_vector. The only differences are that each work-item checks its local ID instead of global ID, and the final result is a float obtained by summing the elements of the final vector.

A practical example will demonstrate how reduction_vector and reduction_complete work together. On my AMD 5850 system, the host application generates 2^{18} work-items divided into 1,024 work-groups of 256 work-items each.

When reduction_vector finishes, the output contains 1,024 float4 vectors—one for each work-group.

Because 1,024 is greater than the local size, reduction_vector must be executed again. Once again, one work-item will be generated for every input vector, and on my system the 1,024 work-items are divided into 4 work-groups of 256 work-items each. The kernel's result will be an array of 4 float4 vectors.

The number of input elements (4) is now less than the local size (256), so the host application will launch reduction_complete with four work-items. The work-items add the input vectors together, and the work-item whose local ID is 0 computes the sum of the elements of the final vector.

At a high level, the computational steps used to perform reduction are similar to those used for other algorithms. Here are the three main steps:

- Work-items process data independently. No synchronization is needed.
- Work-items in the work-group process data together using local memory. Synchronization is made possible through the barrier function.
- Work-items in multiple work-groups process data together using global memory. Synchronization is made possible by launching multiple kernels.

Each successive step adds greater complexity but also greater performance. For this reason, when I code a large-scale OpenCL application, I start by executing the kernel with a single work-item. Once this works, I recode the kernel to use the work-items in a single work-group. If I can get that to work, then I recode the application to make use of multiple work-groups and multiple kernels. This isn't an easy process, but obtaining incredible performance from a fully occupied OpenCL device is worth the effort.

The next section puts aside the reduction algorithm and the grand strategy of OpenCL coding. Instead, we'll look at ten simple tricks that will improve the processing speed of your applications.

10.4 *Ten tips for high-performance kernels*

Between examining expert code and conducting my own experiments, I've gleaned ten simple methods that boost the performance of OpenCL kernels. In no particular order, here are these methods:

- *Unroll loops.* If you know in advance how many iterations will be performed by a for or while loop, you should consider coding the iterations separately. This removes the need for the comparison operations associated with the loop statements. Of course, you need to make sure that the kernel doesn't grow too large.
- *Disable processing of denormalized numbers.* As discussed in chapter 3, denormalized numbers are floating-point numbers whose values fall below the smallest regular value. They reduce the likelihood of division-by-zero operations, but their processing can take time. If division-by-zero operations aren't a concern for the kernel, the host application can set the -cl-denorms-are-zero option in clBuildProgram. This is shown in the following function call:

```
clBuildProgram(program, 0, NULL, "-cl-denorms-are-zero", NULL, NULL);
```

To disable processing of infinite values and NaNs, set the -cl-finite-math-only option. Table 2.7 lists all of the options available for compiling kernels.

- *Transfer constant primitive values to the kernel with compiler defines instead of private memory parameters.* If the host application needs to transfer a constant value to the kernel, it's better to send the value using compiler options like -DNAME=VALUE than to create a separate argument for the kernel function. For example, if you need to tell the kernel that each work-item must process 128 values, you can define the SIZE macro as follows:

```
clBuildProgram(program, 0, NULL, "-DSIZE=128", NULL, NULL);
```

Now, when the compiler builds the kernel, it will replace every incidence of SIZE with 128. No private or local memory is needed to store the constant.

- *If sharing isn't an issue, store small variable values in private memory instead of local memory.* Work-items can access private memory faster than they can access local memory. Therefore, if the kernel needs to store primitive variable data, work-items can access the data faster in private memory. But if the data needs to be shared with other work-items in the work-group, it should be stored in local memory.

- *Avoid local memory bank conflicts by accessing local memory sequentially.* Local memory is arranged into banks that are individually accessible. These banks interleave their data so that successive 32-bit elements are stored in successive banks. Therefore, if work-items access data sequentially, the read/write operations can be processed in parallel. Otherwise, if multiple work-items access the same memory bank, the memory operations will be processed serially.

- *Avoid using the modulo (%) operator.* The % operator requires a significant amount of processing time on GPUs and other OpenCL devices. If possible, try to find another method to distinguish work-items from one another.

- *Reuse private variables throughout the kernel—create macros to avoid confusion.* If a kernel uses one private variable in one section of code and another private variable in another section, the two variables can be replaced by a single variable. The problem is that, when a variable serves multiple purposes, it's confusing for the programmer to understand what's happening in code.

To fix this problem, set macros whose names correspond to the same private variable. For example, suppose the variable tmp1 should hold an exponent in one section of the kernel, a sine value in a second section, and a loop counter in another. You could code three macros as follows:

```
#define EXP tmp1
#define SINE tmp1
#define COUNT tmp1
```

With these definitions in place, you can code with EXP, SINE, and COUNT as though they were distinct variables, but private memory will only need to store a single value.

- *For multiply-and-add operations, use the* fma *function if it's available.* If the FP_FAST_FMAF macro is defined, you can compute a*b+c with greater accuracy by calling the function fma(a, b, c). The processing time for this function will be less than or equal to that of computing a*b+c.

- *Inline non-kernel functions in a program file.* The inline modifier preceding a function tells the compiler that each call to the function should be replaced with the complete function code. This is not memory efficient—if an inline function is called *N* times, the function body will be expanded *N* times—but it saves processing time by removing the context switches and stack operations associated with regular function calls.

- *Avoid branch miss penalties by coding conditional statements to be true more often than false.* Many processors predict that branch statements will return true, and they plan for this in advance by loading the address corresponding to a true result. But if the condition produces a false result, the processor must clear the processing pipeline and load instructions from a new address. This is called a *branch miss penalty*, and it can be avoided by coding if statements and similar conditional statements to produce a true result as often as possible.

These 10 guidelines can improve your kernel's performance, but be sure to profile your application to understand where the processing time is being spent. When it comes to high-performance OpenCL coding, there is no substitute for experimentation.

10.5 Summary

Coding with OpenCL is like driving a large, sixteen-wheeled truck. The principles of driving remain the same, but because there's so much cargo, you have to deal with additional concerns. The goal of this chapter has been to describe the additional concerns involved when you write OpenCL applications that process thousands, millions, or even billions of data points.

We can generate as many work-items as we like, but the size of each work-group is beyond our control—it depends on the device's resources and the kernel's resource usage. The more private and local memory the kernel requires, the fewer work-items can be placed in a work-group. The clGetKernelWorkGroupInfo function identifies the maximum work-group size for a given kernel and device, and in the interests of memory bandwidth, it's a good idea to make this size the local size parameter of clEnqueueNDRangeKernel.

Most of this chapter has been concerned with implementing reduction in OpenCL. Even though this simply adds elements of an array, coding reduction effectively for data sizes greater than one million isn't simple at all. There are memory bank issues to deal with, data transfer issues between global and local memory, and synchronization issues between work-items in the same and different work-groups.

The reduction algorithm must be performed in stages, and synchronization is needed to make sure every work-item is processing data in the same stage. This can be tricky. If the work-items are located in the same work-group, synchronization can be accomplished with the `barrier` function. If they're in different work-groups, the only way to be sure they're at the same point is to launch a new kernel.

The last part of this chapter presented ten rules of thumb to keep in mind when coding OpenCL kernels. But remember that many of these involve trade-offs. For example, unrolling loops and inlining non-kernel functions will improve processing time, but the kernel code will be larger. Similarly, treating denormalized numbers as zero will improve performance but leave you in greater danger of dividing values by zero.

In the next four chapters, we'll put aside reduction and start looking at real-world algorithms used by programmers and engineers. Chapter 11 discusses Google's MapReduce algorithm and two different ways of sorting data.

Part 2

Coding practical algorithms in OpenCL

Part 2 shows how OpenCL can be used to build applications that process vast amounts of data. Chapter 11 discusses OpenCL implementations of MapReduce, the bitonic sort, and the radix sort. Chapters 12 and 13 focus on matrix operations, including both dense matrices and sparse matrices. Chapter 14 explains how the fast Fourier transform (FFT) can be coded in OpenCL.

Reduction and sorting

11

This chapter covers

- Implementing parallel processing tasks with MapReduce and OpenCL
- Sorting data with the bitonic sort and radix sort algorithms

At long last, we're going to stop talking about OpenCL's structures and functions and start putting them to use. In particular, this chapter focuses on three practical applications of OpenCL: MapReduce, the bitonic sort, and the radix sort. These applications all use a divide-and-conquer methodology to process data in parallel, and they partition data so that each parallel process can operate independently.

The goal of MapReduce isn't to solve a particular problem, but to provide a framework for solving a class of problems that involve distributed processing. A basic MapReduce implementation consists of a mapping stage, which produces key-value pairs from input data, and a reduction stage, which processes the key-value pairs to produce output data. MapReduce is usually associated with cluster computing, but this chapter will examine how it can be executed on OpenCL-compliant hardware.

There are countless sorting algorithms available in computer science, but few are as well suited to parallel implementation as the bitonic sort and the radix sort. Both algorithms divide unsorted data into groups and then subdivide the groups further

237

for simpler processing. The bitonic sort groups elements according to how their values relate to adjacent values. The radix sort groups elements that have similar digits.

But before we discuss sorting, let's take a close look at MapReduce. Google relies on this framework for its high-speed internet data analysis, but, as you'll see, it can be applied to many other kinds of tasks.

11.1 MapReduce

Google has released many software packages for common use, from office tools like Google Docs to three-dimensional modeling applications like Google SketchUp. In contrast, MapReduce doesn't have any software directly associated with it. It's a purely theoretical framework for building distributed applications that process large-scale amounts of data. This section will explain the theory behind this framework and then describe a method of implementing MapReduce in OpenCL. The last part of this section demonstrates how this method can be applied to search for strings inside a text file.

11.1.1 Introduction to MapReduce

In 2004, Google engineers Jeffrey Dean and Sanjay Ghemawat released a research paper entitled *MapReduce: Simplified Data Processing on Large Clusters* (http://labs.google.com/papers/mapreduce.html). The paper caused a sensation in the world of cluster computing, and not just because of the theory—the concepts of mapping and reduction had long been used in the field of functional programming. The paper became famous because Google, whose meteoric $1.67 billion IPO had taken place four months prior, was divulging the technical secrets behind its success. The paper discusses both the theory of MapReduce and Google's implementation of the algorithm in its server clusters. MapReduce quickly became a topic of interest throughout high-tech corporations and academia, and that interest has continued unabated into the present.

Put simply, MapReduce is a method for processing large data sets with large numbers of processors. It doesn't focus on any particular processing task, but instead presents an approach that can be applied to multiple applications. If you're familiar with the concept of a design pattern, then you have a good idea of the role MapReduce serves in the world of parallel programming.

A MapReduce solution contains a minimum of two stages: mapping and reduction. The processors involved in the mapping stage each receive input data and produce key-value pairs. Once the mapping is finished, each processor in the reduction stage receives values corresponding to a given key. The processors performing reduction process these values and merge them together to form the output data. Figure 11.1 provides a general idea of how this works.

The keys in this diagram are all numbers, but a MapReduce key can take any data type. Remember that a key's purpose is to identify pairs that need to be reduced together. In this diagram, the pairs whose key equals 0 are sent to R0 for reduction, the pairs whose key equals 1 are sent to R1 for reduction, and so on. Note that the

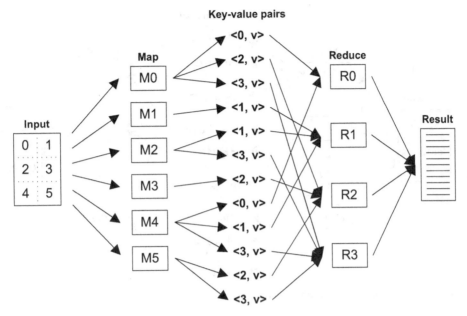

Figure 11.1 The MapReduce processing model

pairs need to be grouped by key before reduction can take place. This intermediate step is referred to by the Dean-Ghemawat paper as *combination.*

Part of MapReduce's efficiency stems from the fact that each mapping processor operates independently from every other mapping processor. The same holds true for the reduction processors. This processing independence is an important strength of MapReduce, because it means the processors don't have to wait for other tasks to complete.

An example will help clarify how MapReduce is used in practice. Suppose you have a large text document and you want to know how many times each word in the document appears. With MapReduce, you'd partition the document into equally sized chunks of text and send each chunk to a mapping processor. The mapping processors would produce key-value pairs in which the key is the word and the value is the number of times the word appears in the chunk of text. This is shown in figure 11.2.

In this example, the input data consists of a large text file, which is partitioned into multiple word groupings. The mapping processors analyze these groups independently of one another and count how many times each word appears. The words *the* and *of* have large word counts because of their high usage frequency, while *brisk* has a comparatively low word count. The map stage produces key-value pairs in which the word is the key and the word's count is the value. The figure shows each group of key-value pairs as having the same order, but this doesn't have to be the case.

The reduction processors receive the key-value pairs and sum the word counts for each word analyzed by the mapping. Once they determine the total word counts, the reduction processors merge their results into a final listing of each word and its usage count within the original document.

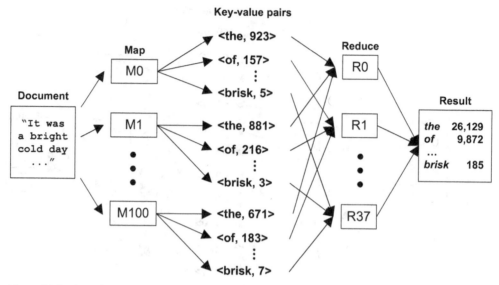

Figure 11.2   Counting words with MapReduce

In addition to counting word usage, the Dean-Ghemawat paper presents a number of other tasks that can be efficiently implemented with MapReduce:

- *Web page access*—The map stage searches through logs of HTML requests and produces key-value pairs containing URLs and the number of times they've been requested. The reduction stage adds the number of requests for each URL and merges the final results.

- *Web link relationships*—Each map processor is assigned a URL and determines how many URLs link to that URL. The mapping stage produces key-value pairs containing the target and source URLs, and the reduction stage combines these together to form a graph of web usage.

- *Inverted index*—The mapping processors analyze different documents and assemble key-value pairs matching words to document identifiers. The reduction stage takes this information and produces an inverted index that lists each word and the different documents it can be found in.

These tasks can be split easily into independent subtasks, and for this reason they're referred to as being *embarrassingly parallel.* MapReduce excels at processing embarrassingly parallel tasks, and so do most OpenCL-compliant devices, such as GPUs. Next, we'll examine how MapReduce can be implemented on OpenCL hardware.

11.1.2 *MapReduce and OpenCL*

Chapter 4 discussed the OpenCL device model, which defines address spaces within a device: global memory, constant memory, local memory, and private memory. Work-items can access local memory faster than they can access global or constant memory, so we'd like to process local data whenever possible.

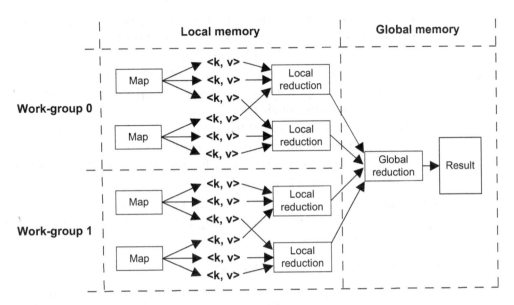

Figure 11.3 MapReduce and the OpenCL device model

Each block of local memory is specific to the work-items in a work-group. A Map-Reduce data set is much too large to be processed by a single work-group, so any MapReduce implementation will have to combine the results of multiple work-groups in global memory. Figure 11.3 shows one method of implementing mapping and reduction on an OpenCL-compliant device. It depicts two work-groups, each with two work-items.

The MapReduce implementation method presented in this figure splits the reduction stage into two substages: local reduction and global reduction. Local reduction, like the mapping stage, operates on data in local memory. Global reduction receives the results of the local reduction stages and produces a result to be sent back to the host.

There's a significant problem with this implementation. In a real MapReduce algorithm, there's no way to know in advance how many key-value pairs will be produced by the mapping stage. For this reason, MapReduce implementations commonly require dynamic memory allocation, which is provided by the C malloc function or a C++ container. But OpenCL doesn't support either of these. An OpenCL kernel needs to know in advance how much data will be processed and stored.

One solution is to combine the mapping and local reduction steps so that each work-group transfers one result to the global reduction stage. This method is considerably simpler than the ordinary MapReduce, and it may not be workable for some embarrassingly parallel algorithms. But it allows us to come up with a general five-step procedure for implementing MapReduce in OpenCL:

1   Each work-item in a work-group performs the mapping, but instead of producing key-value pairs, it also performs a portion of the local reduction stage.

2   The kernel executes a local barrier that prevents further execution until all work-items in a work-group have completed their processing.

3   In each work-group, the work-item whose local ID equals 0 reduces the work-group's output into a single result.

4   The kernel executes a global barrier that prevents further execution until all work-groups have completed their processing.

5   The work-item whose global ID equals 0 receives the result of each work-group and reduces this data to produce a final result.

The best way to understand this process is to examine and experiment with working code. Next, we'll see how this modified MapReduce implementation can be used to search for words within text.

11.1.3 *MapReduce example: searching for text*

The Dean-Ghemawat paper recommended distributed grep (global regular expression print) as one of the embarrassingly parallel tasks best suited for implementation with MapReduce. grep is a common command in Linux/Unix, and it searches through one or more files to locate every occurrence of an input string. By default, it displays every line containing the string, regardless of word boundaries.

There are many elegant algorithms available for string searching, but to demonstrate OpenCL-MapReduce as clearly as possible, our example will rely on brute force. It will search for four input strings (*that, with, have,* and *from*) using vector comparison. Figure 11.4 shows how this works.

In this figure, the four input strings are placed in a char16 vector, which is compared to another char16 containing text from a text file. The == operator compares the two vectors and places the result in a third vector. If two characters match, the corresponding byte in the third vector will be set to 0xFF. If not, the corresponding byte will be set to 0x00.

Once the comparison is complete, the work-item tests the resulting vector to determine whether one or more of the pattern words were recognized. If so, the work-item

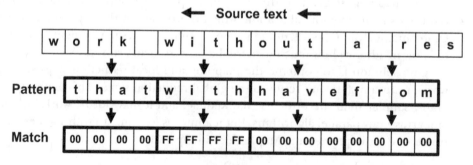

Figure 11.4 String search with vector comparison

doesn't produce key-value pairs. Instead, it atomically increments a value in local memory corresponding to the word count. That is, it performs both mapping and local reduction. Once the local reduction is completed, one work-item in every work-group atomically adds the local results to the global result.

The following listing shows how this example is implemented in code. As explained in chapter 5, the `all` function identifies whether every most significant bit (MSB) in every component of a vector is set to 1.

Listing 11.1 Implementing MapReduce in OpenCL: string_search.cl

```
__kernel void string_search(char16 pattern, __global char* text,
    int chars_per_item, __local int* local_result,
    __global int* global_result) {

    char16 text_vector, check_vector;

    local_result[0] = 0;                      Initialize
    local_result[1] = 0;                      local data
    local_result[2] = 0;
    local_result[3] = 0;                              Wait for
                                                      initialization
    barrier(CLK_LOCAL_MEM_FENCE);

    int item_offset = get_global_id(0) * chars_per_item;
                                                              Load text
    for(int i=item_offset; i<item_offset + chars_per_item; i++) {   into private
                                                                    memory
        text_vector = vload16(0, text + i);
                                               Compare text
        check_vector = text_vector == pattern;  with pattern

        if(all(check_vector.s0123))
            atomic_inc(local_result);
        if(all(check_vector.s4567))
            atomic_inc(local_result + 1);
        if(all(check_vector.s89AB))            Check word
            atomic_inc(local_result + 2);       matches
        if(all(check_vector.sCDEF))
            atomic_inc(local_result + 3);
    }
                                               Wait for check
    barrier(CLK_GLOBAL_MEM_FENCE);              completion

    if(get_local_id(0) == 0) {
        atomic_add(global_result, local_result[0]);
        atomic_add(global_result + 1, local_result[1]);   Perform final
        atomic_add(global_result + 2, local_result[2]);   reduction
        atomic_add(global_result + 3, local_result[3]);
    }
}
```

On my system, the printed output is as follows:

```
Results:
Number of occurrences of 'that': 330
Number of occurrences of 'with': 237
Number of occurrences of 'have': 110
Number of occurrences of 'from': 116
```

This exactly matches the results produced by the grep command. If you have access to GNU utilities, you can test this with the following commands:

```
grep 'that' -o Ch11/string_search/kafka.txt | wc -w
grep 'with' -o Ch11/string_search/kafka.txt | wc -w
grep 'have' -o Ch11/string_search/kafka.txt | wc -w
grep 'from' -o Ch11/string_search/kafka.txt | wc -w
```

The parameter list of string_search includes variables in global/constant memory (text and global_result), local memory (local_result), and private memory (pattern). It's important to understand how the setKernelArg function calls in string_search.c configure these parameters and their memory locations.

It's also important to understand the barrier calls in listing 11.1. These functions ensure that all memory accesses preceding the barrier are executed before any work-item can continue executing. If the barrier argument is CLK_LOCAL_MEM_FENCE, the barrier affects access to local memory. If the argument is CLK_GLOBAL_MEM_FENCE, the barrier affects the work-items' access to global memory. Chapter 7 discusses these synchronization methods in detail.

Chapter 7 also discusses atomic functions. Listing 11.1 uses two of them: atomic_inc and atomic_add. These are necessary because they ensure that the increment and addition operations will execute without interruption. Unfortunately, they don't operate on vectors, so the listing invokes them multiple times.

This example doesn't provide a formal global reduction step, but it gives a good idea of how MapReduce can be implemented efficiently in OpenCL. The rest of this chapter will examine how sorting algorithms can be implemented, and we'll start by discussing the bitonic sort.

11.2   *The bitonic sort*

Algorithms that sort data form a vital part of any programmer's repertoire, and no introductory computer science course could be complete without a discussion of bubble sorts, insertion sorts, and selection sorts. But as multicore processors gain in power and popularity, it becomes crucial to sort data using a parallelized algorithm. Some algorithms are better suited to parallel implementation than others, and the bitonic sort (also called the *bitonic merge sort*) is one of the few sorting methods that was designed to be implemented with multiple processing elements. The goal of this section is to explain how the bitonic sort works and how to implement it with OpenCL.

11.2.1   *Understanding the bitonic sort*

Most presentations of the bitonic sort proceed from start to finish, but I'd like to begin this discussion with the end goal. First, I'll explain what bitonic sequence are and how they can be sorted. Then I'll explain how to turn an unordered sequence into a bitonic sequence.

SORTING BITONIC SEQUENCES
Figure 11.5 presents three numerical sequences called *A*, *B*, and *C*.

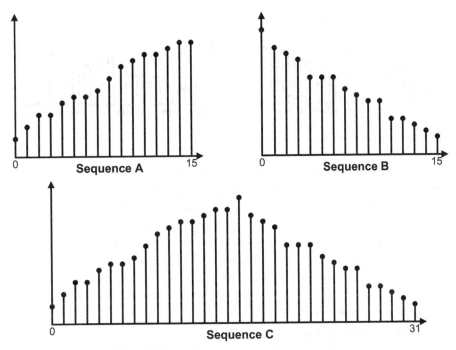

Figure 11.5 Monotonic and bitonic sets

The values of the elements in these sets don't concern us. What's important is the relationships between adjacent values. In sequence A, every element is greater than or equal to the element preceding it. For this reason, we say that sequence A is *monotonically increasing*. In sequence B, every element is less than or equal to the element preceding it, so sequence B is *monotonically decreasing*.

Sequence C is the concatenation of the elements in sequences A and B. This is not monotonic, but because it is formed of two monotonic sets, it is *bitonic*. In a bitonic set, the slope between successive pairs of elements can only change sign (greater than 0 to less than 0, or less than 0 to greater than 0) once at most.

Bitonic sets like sequence C are important to us because of an operation called the *bitonic split*. This operation consists of the following two tasks:

1. Compare each element in the lower half of the sequence (i equals 0 through $N/2 - 1$) with the corresponding element in the upper half ($i + N/2$).

2. If the element in the lower half is greater than the element in the upper half, swap the two elements.

If we perform the bitonic split on sequence C, we'll obtain the elements of sequence D, which is shown in the left side of figure 11.6. This sequence isn't bitonic, but each half of it (0 to $N/2 - 1$, $N/2 - N$) is bitonic. Further, because sequence C was bitonic, every element in the lower half of sequence D is less than or equal to the elements in its upper half. You may want to take a moment to assure yourself that this will always be the case.

Sequence D

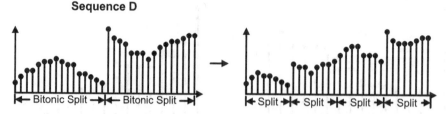

Figure 11.6   Bitonic splits

The right side of figure 11.6 shows the result of a second set of bitonic splits. As each new split is performed, the smaller elements make their way to the left while the larger elements move to the right. These bitonic splits are repeated, each time operating on sequences half the size as before. The final step takes splits with two elements each, and once this is accomplished, the elements in sequence *C* will be completely sorted.

The procedure used to sort a bitonic sequence is called the *bitonic merge*. In general, if a sequence contains *N* elements where $N = 2^k$, the bitonic merge requires k steps. Each step consists of bitonic splits, and if i runs from 1 to k, step i consists of i splits of N/i elements each.

FORMING BITONIC SEQUENCES

Now that we've discussed how to sort bitonic sequences, an important question arises: how can we convert a regular sequence into a bitonic sequence, particularly one as hill-shaped as sequence *C* in figure 11.5? This is tricky. In my opinion, the best way to understand the conversion process is to start with small sequences and progress to larger sequences.

Every two-element sequence is already bitonic, so let's look at how to make a four-element sequence bitonic. You want the first two elements to be monotonically increasing and the second two elements to be monotonically decreasing. You can accomplish this in two steps:

1   Compare the first two elements. If the first element is greater than the second, swap the two elements. This ensures that the elements are in *ascending order*.
2   Compare the second two elements. If the second element is greater than the first, swap the two elements. This ensures that the elements are in *descending order*.

As an example, suppose the sequence is {2, 1, 4, 3}. In this case, we'd swap the first two elements to place them in ascending order. We wouldn't swap the last two elements because they're already in descending order. The result would be {1, 2, 4, 3}.

Now let's make an eight-element sequence bitonic. To start, we need to make the lower half and upper half bitonic. These halves are both four-element sequences, so we can accomplish this using the steps mentioned earlier. The result is shown in figure 11.7.

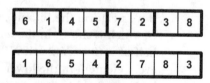

Figure 11.7   Forming bitonic halves

The lower array in figure 11.7 shows the result of comparing pairs of the original array and sorting even pairs up and odd pairs down. Both four-element halves are now bitonic, but we haven't reached our goal of a single eight-element bitonic sequence.

To make the eight-element array bitonic, we need to fully sort both four-element halves. In particular, we want the lower half to be monotonically increasing and the upper half to be monotonically decreasing. We can accomplish this using the following steps:

1 For the lower half, compare the first element and the third element, and swap them if the first is larger. Do the same for the second and fourth elements. Then compare the first and second elements, and swap them if the first is larger. Do the same for the third and fourth elements.

2 For the upper half, perform the same compare-and-swap operations as for the lower half, but reverse the sort. That is, swap elements to bring larger values toward the left, smaller values toward the right.

Figure 11.8 starts with the bottom array from figure 11.7. It sorts the lower half in ascending order and the upper half in descending order.

As shown in the figure, the result is a bitonic sequence whose lower half is monotonically increasing and whose upper half is monotonically decreasing. Because this final sequence is bitonic, we can sort its elements using the bitonic merge procedure described earlier.

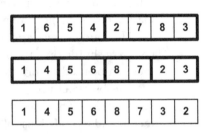

Figure 11.8 Forming a bitonic sequence

If the length of a sequence is a power of 2, then we can present a general procedure for sorting its elements with the bitonic sort:

1 Make the four-element subsequences bitonic by comparing each pair of elements. Even-numbered pairs are sorted in ascending order. Odd-numbered pairs are assorted in descending order.

2 Continue making larger bitonic subsequences (8-element, 16-element, and so on) by comparing and swapping elements in the lower half with elements in the upper half. If you remember the hill shape we're looking for, you'll know when to sort upward and when to sort downward.

3 After creating a bitonic subsequence, sort it using the bitonic merge. This isn't necessary for four-element subsequences.

This algorithm is commonly implemented using recursion, but OpenCL kernel functions can't be invoked recursively. Therefore, if we want to implement the bitonic sort with OpenCL, we need to perform the compare-and-swap operations in parallel. We'll discuss this next.

11.2.2 *Implementing the bitonic sort in OpenCL*

Coding a bitonic sort in OpenCL can be complicated, so it's a good idea to learn how to sort small datasets first and then proceed to large datasets. We'll begin by discussing how to sort four elements inside a vector and then how to sort a dataset of eight elements. With this information, we'll proceed to building a general OpenCL application to perform the bitonic sort.

SORTING FOUR ELEMENTS IN A VECTOR

The fundamental operation of the bitonic sort is to compare two elements and swap them if necessary. Many applications sort scalars with `if` statements such as the following:

```
if(x1 < x2) {
    temp = x1;
    x1 = x2;
    x2 = temp;
}
```

But OpenCL makes it possible to sort multiple values at once using vector operations. The `shuffle` function can be used to form vectors with the input elements rearranged. Then, by comparing the input vector to the shuffled vector, you can obtain a mask vector capable of rearranging the input vector's elements.

The bitonic sort application presented in this chapter relies on these shuffle-compare-shuffle operations to sort the elements in a vector, and figure 11.9 shows how they can be used to sort the elements in an `int4` in ascending order.

The bsort8.cl program file in the Ch11/bsort8 project contains a macro called `SORT_VECTOR`. This uses shuffle-compare-shuffle operations to sort the elements in a vector, and its code is as follows:

```
#define SORT_VECTOR(input, dir)   \
    comp = abs(input > shuffle(input, mask1)) ^ dir;   \
    input = shuffle(input, comp ^ swap + add1);        \
    comp = abs(input > shuffle(input, mask2)) ^ dir;   \
    input = shuffle(input, comp * 2 + add2);           \
    comp = abs(input > shuffle(input, mask1)) ^ dir;   \
    input = shuffle(input, comp + add1);               \
```

1. Shuffle the input to compare its 1st and 2nd elements, 3rd and 4th elements. Use the result to shuffle the input so that it forms a bitonic set.

2. Shuffle the input to compare its 1st and 3rd elements, 2nd and 4th elements. Use the result to shuffle the input so that high values move right, low values move left.

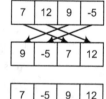

3. Shuffle the input to compare its 1st and 2nd elements, 3rd and 4th elements. Use the result to shuffle the input so that high values move right, low values move left.

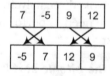

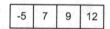

Figure 11.9 Sorting elements inside a vector

As you look at this code, remember that taking the absolute value of a vector comparison produces a vector whose elements equal 1 when the comparison is true and 0 when the comparison is false. This can be inverted by taking the exclusive-OR (^) of the result with 1.

SORTING AN EIGHT-ELEMENT SEQUENCE

Once you can arrange elements inside a vector using the bitonic sort, it's straightforward to sort elements between multiple vectors. The main operation involves comparing two vectors and swapping their elements based on the result. In bsort8.cl, this is accomplished by the macro SWAP_VECTORS, whose code is as follows:

```
#define SWAP_VECTORS(input1, input2, dir)   \
    temp = input1;                          \
    comp = (abs(input1 > input2) ^ dir) * 4 + add3;   \
    input1 = shuffle2(input1, input2, comp);   \
    input2 = shuffle2(input2, temp, comp);   \
```

This code calls shuffle2 to rearrange the elements of the input1 and input2 vectors in the order specified by dir. Chapter 5 explains how the shuffle and shuffle2 functions work.

The following code performs an eight-element bitonic sort by calling on the macros SORT_VECTOR and SWAP_VECTORS.

Listing 11.2   An eight-element bitonic sort: bsort8.cl

```
#define UP 0
#define DOWN 1

define SORT_VECTOR(input, dir)   \
    comp = abs(input > shuffle(input, mask1)) ^ dir;   \
    input = shuffle(input, comp ^ swap + add1);   \
    comp = abs(input > shuffle(input, mask2)) ^ dir;   \
    input = shuffle(input, comp * 2 + add2);   \
    comp = abs(input > shuffle(input, mask1)) ^ dir;   \
    input = shuffle(input, comp + add1);   \

#define SWAP_VECTORS(input1, input2, dir)   \
    temp = input1;   \
    comp = (abs(input1 > input2) ^ dir) * 4 + add3;   \
    input1 = shuffle2(input1, input2, comp);   \
    input2 = shuffle2(input2, temp, comp);   \

__kernel void bsort8(__global float4 *data, int dir) {

    __local float4 input1, input2, temp;
    __local uint4 comp, swap, mask1, mask2, add1, add2, add3;

    mask1 = (uint4)(1, 0, 3, 2);
    swap = (uint4)(0, 0, 1, 1);
    add1 = (uint4)(0, 0, 2, 2);
    mask2 = (uint4)(2, 3, 0, 1);
    add2 = (uint4)(0, 1, 0, 1);
    add3 = (uint4)(0, 1, 2, 3);

    input1 = data[0];
```

```
input2 = data[1];

SORT_VECTOR(input1, UP)
SORT_VECTOR(input2, DOWN)

SWAP_VECTORS(input1, input2, dir)
SORT_VECTOR(input1, dir)
SORT_VECTOR(input2, dir)

data[0] = input1;
data[1] = input2;
}
```

Form bitonic sequence

Sort bitonic sequence

This is a lot of work to sort an eight-element sequence, and I wouldn't recommend using it in time-critical applications. But you can use this kernel as a basis for coding a full bitonic sort.

A FULL BITONIC SORT

The main difficulty in coding the bitonic sort involves assigning data to work-groups. As discussed in chapter 10, clGetKernelWorkGroupInfo tells us the maximum number of work-items in a work-group for a given device and kernel. We'll call this number M. Each work-item will sort eight data points (two four-element vectors) at a time, so the number of values that can be processed by a work-group is $8M$.

Let's call N the total number of data points to be sorted. If N is less than or equal to $8M$, only one work-group is needed. But if we assume N is larger than $8M$, the number of work-groups required is $N/8M$. For example, if the maximum work-group size is 512, each work-group can process 8 * 512 = 4,096 data points. If the data set contains 1,048,576 data points, the full sort requires 1,048,576/4,096 = 256 work-groups. This chapter assumes that $N/8M$ is a power of 2.

The bitonic sort requires multiple stages to complete. In the first stage, each work-group sorts its own data. In successive stages, work-groups combine the sorted results, and the final stage sorts the entire data set with a bitonic merge. This is shown in figure 11.10, which demonstrates how eight work-items sort data.

As the algorithm progresses from stage 0 to stage 3, the bitonic sort requires that every preceding stage be processed. For the sort depicted in the figure, the proper stage order is 0, 1, 0, 2, 1, 0, 3, 2, 1, 0. The final stages implement the bitonic merge.

As discussed in chapter 7, OpenCL provides no way to synchronize work-groups except by executing new kernels. Therefore, each stage of the bitonic sort requires a

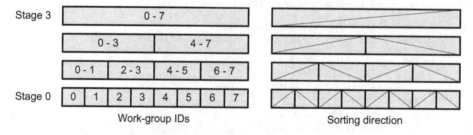

Figure 11.10 Splitting the bitonic sort among work-groups

separate kernel-execution command. The host application dispatches these commands to the device within an iteration loop, and the bsort.cl program file in the Ch12/bsort directory contains the kernel functions that work together to perform the sort:

- bsort_init—At the start of the sort, each work-item reads two vectors and sorts their components. Then the work-items in the work-group sort every data point assigned to the group.
- bsort_stage_n—This kernel performs higher stages of the bitonic sort, which form the data points into a bitonic set.
- bsort_stage_0—Each higher stage requires that every lower stage be executed. This kernel corresponds to the bottom stage of the sort.
- bsort_merge—Once the data points have been sorted into a bitonic set, this kernel places the data points in ascending or descending order.
- bsort_merge_last—This kernel performs the final sorting of the work-groups' data elements.

For example, the host application executes the following loop to perform the bitonic merge. Specifically, it iterates through a for loop and dispatches multiple commands to execute the bsort_merge function. Each kernel receives a different value for the stage parameter:

```
for(stage = num_stages; stage > 1; stage >>= 1) {
   clSetKernelArg(bsort_merge, 2, sizeof(int), &stage);
   clEnqueueNDRangeKernel(queue, bsort_merge, 1, NULL,
        &global_size, &local_size, 0, NULL, NULL);
}
clEnqueueNDRangeKernel(queue, bsort_merge_last, 1, NULL,
     &global_size, &local_size, 0, NULL, NULL);
```

After dispatching commands to execute bsort_merge, the host dispatches a command to execute bsort_merge_last. This finishes the bitonic merge and completes the sort.

Listing 11.3 presents the code for the bsort_init function. Here, each work-item in a work-group reads two float4 vectors from global memory and sorts their components, placing the sorted result in local memory. Then the work-items work together to sort all of the vectors read by the group's work-items.

Listing 11.3 A general bitonic sort: bsort.cl (abridged)

```
#define VECTOR_SORT(input, dir)                              \
   comp = abs(input > shuffle(input, mask2)) ^ dir;      \
   input = shuffle(input, comp * 2 + add2);              \
   comp = abs(input > shuffle(input, mask1)) ^ dir;      \
   input = shuffle(input, comp + add1);                  \

#define VECTOR_SWAP(in1, in2, dir)                           \
   input1 = in1; input2 = in2;                           \
   comp = (abs(input1 > input2) ^ dir) * 4 + add3;       \
   in1 = shuffle2(input1, input2, comp);                 \
   in2 = shuffle2(input2, input1, comp);                 \
```

```
__kernel void bsort_init(__global float4 *g_data,
                         __local float4 *l_data) {

   float4 input1, input2, temp;
   uint4 comp, swap, mask1, mask2, add1, add2, add3;
   uint id, dir, global_start, size, stride;

   mask1 = (uint4)(1, 0, 3, 2);
   swap = (uint4)(0, 0, 1, 1);
   add1 = (uint4)(0, 0, 2, 2);
   mask2 = (uint4)(2, 3, 0, 1);
   add2 = (uint4)(0, 1, 0, 1);
   add3 = (uint4)(0, 1, 2, 3);

   id = get_local_id(0) * 2;
   global_start = get_group_id(0) *
               get_local_size(0) * 2 + id;

   input1 = g_data[global_start];
   input2 = g_data[global_start+1];

   comp = abs(input1 > shuffle(input1, mask1));
   input1 = shuffle(input1, comp ^ swap + add1);
   comp = abs(input1 > shuffle(input1, mask2));
   input1 = shuffle(input1, comp * 2 + add2);
   comp = abs(input1 > shuffle(input1, mask1));
   input1 = shuffle(input1, comp + add1);

   comp = abs(input2 < shuffle(input2, mask1));
   input2 = shuffle(input2, comp ^ swap + add1);
   comp = abs(input2 < shuffle(input2, mask2));
   input2 = shuffle(input2, comp * 2 + add2);
   comp = abs(input2 < shuffle(input2, mask1));
   input2 = shuffle(input2, comp + add1);

   dir = get_local_id(0) % 2;
   temp = input1;
   comp = (abs(input1 > input2) ^ dir) * 4 + add3;
   input1 = shuffle2(input1, input2, comp);
   input2 = shuffle2(input2, temp, comp);

   VECTOR_SORT(input1, dir);
   VECTOR_SORT(input2, dir);
   l_data[id] = input1;
   l_data[id+1] = input2;

   for(size = 2; size < get_local_size(0);
               size <<= 1) {
      dir = get_local_id(0)/size & 1;

      for(stride = size; stride > 1; stride >>= 1) {
         barrier(CLK_LOCAL_MEM_FENCE);
         id = get_local_id(0) +
            (get_local_id(0)/stride)*stride;
         VECTOR_SWAP(l_data[id],
                     l_data[id + stride], dir)
      }

      barrier(CLK_LOCAL_MEM_FENCE);
```

Find global address

Sort first vector

Sort second vector

Swap elements

❶ **Perform upper stages**

❷ **Perform lower stages**

```
        id = get_local_id(0) * 2;
        input1 = l_data[id]; input2 = l_data[id+1];
        temp = input1;
        comp = (abs(input1 > input2) ^ dir) * 4 + add3;
        input1 = shuffle2(input1, input2, comp);
        input2 = shuffle2(input2, temp, comp);
        VECTOR_SORT(input1, dir);
        VECTOR_SORT(input2, dir);
        l_data[id]   = input1;
        l_data[id+1] = input2;
    }

    dir = get_group_id(0) % 2;
    for(stride = get_local_size(0); stride > 1;
                                    stride >>= 1) {          Perform
        barrier(CLK_LOCAL_MEM_FENCE);                        bitonic
        id = get_local_id(0) +                               merge
            (get_local_id(0)/stride)*stride;
        VECTOR_SWAP(l_data[id], l_data[id + stride], dir)
    }
    barrier(CLK_LOCAL_MEM_FENCE);

    id = get_local_id(0) * 2;
    input1 = l_data[id]; input2 = l_data[id+1];
    temp = input1;
    comp = (abs(input1 > input2) ^ dir) * 4 + add3;
    input1 = shuffle2(input1, input2, comp);
    input2 = shuffle2(input2, temp, comp);
    VECTOR_SORT(input1, dir);
    VECTOR_SORT(input2, dir);
    g_data[global_start]   = input1;
    g_data[global_start+1] = input2;
}
```

The overall structure of this code is similar to that of the bsort8 code in listing 11.2. But this code sorts every data element assigned to a work-group without regard to the work-group's size.

The nested for loop handles the main work of the sorting procedure. The outer loop ❶ performs the high stages of the sort. As each new stage is reached, the inner loop ❷ performs each of the lower stages. The outer loop index starts at 2 and doubles until it reaches half the work-group's size. With each iteration, the inner loop performs the lower stages of the sort. For example, when the outer loop index equals 8, the inner loop index proceeds from 8 to 4 to 2 to 1.

The barrier invocations are necessary to ensure that the local data will be valid for the next stage of comparing and swapping. Keep in mind that the CLK_LOCAL_ MEM_FENCE constant pertains to local memory, whereas CLK_GLOBAL_MEM_FENCE pertains to global memory.

Listing 11.3 shows that the bitonic sort lends itself well to parallelization, but it's not the only sorting algorithm for which this is true. The radix sort also provides high performance and high scalability, and this is the topic of the next section.

11.3   The radix sort

The radix sort is one of the oldest algorithms available for sorting data, but despite its age, new variations and implementations appear in research journals on a regular basis. It's particularly well suited for parallel execution, and this section will explain how it can be implemented with OpenCL. But first, this section will present the theory behind the radix sort.

11.3.1 Understanding the radix sort

Like the bitonic sort, the radix sort uses a divide-and-conquer strategy: it splits the dataset into subsets and sorts the elements in the subsets. But instead of sorting bitonic sequences, the radix sort is concerned with the digits of the elements' numeric representations. One version of the radix sort classifies numbers by examining their least-significant digits (LSDs) first while another classifies numbers by examining their most-significant digits (MSDs). In this section, we'll focus on the LSD radix sort.

The LSD radix sort places values into groups, traditionally called *buckets*, according to their least-significant digits, and then repeats the process using further significant digits. An example will make this clear. Suppose you have eight numbers presented in hexadecimal notation:

```
0x52   0xA3   0x31   0x9B   0x11   0x2B   0xC7   0xF1
```

To begin the sort, examine the least-significant digit of each element and place it in a group of values with similar digits. From small to large, the buckets are as follows:

```
0x31   0x11   0xF1   0x52   0xA3   0xC7   0x9B   0x2B
```

0x31 is placed before 0x11 because it appears earlier in the original sequence. Similarly, 0x9B comes before 0x2B.

To complete the sort, make another pass through the elements, but this time place them into buckets depending on the next least-significant digit. This produces the following sequence:

```
0x11   0x2B   0x31   0x52   0x9B   0xA3   0xC7   0xF1
```

This fully orders the sequence, because the elements had already been sorted by their least-significant digits. Note that you never have to compare elements—place each element in its proper bucket, and it will eventually reach its position in the sort. Note also that if each element contains k digits, this sort requires k passes in order to completely sort the values.

11.3.2 Implementing the radix sort with vectors

It should be clear that each step of a radix sort is essentially a shuffle: the output equals the input rearranged by digit. As discussed in chapter 5, OpenCL provides the shuffle and shuffle2 functions, which set elements in an output vector according to the indices defined by a mask. Therefore, if you can efficiently create a mask, you can rearrange a vector's elements with a single command.

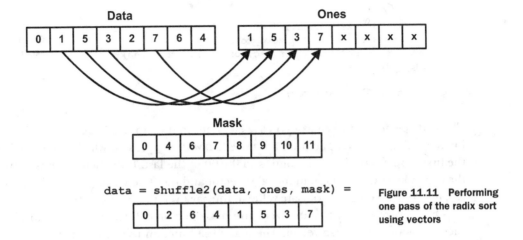

Figure 11.11 Performing one pass of the radix sort using vectors

To simplify our initial attempt at a radix sort, we'll create buckets by examining the least-significant bit of each element. If an element's least-significant bit is 1, we'll place it in a vector called Ones. Figure 11.11 shows how this works.

There's no need to create a separate vector (bucket) to hold elements that end in 0. We can leave them in the Data vector. Then we can call shuffle2 to create an output vector containing the 0-elements from the Data vector and the 1-elements from the Ones vector.

In this example, the data is contained within a ushort8 vector. Each element contains three bits, so we can completely sort this and similar vectors using three passes. The following code accomplishes this.

Listing 11.4 An eight-element radix sort: radix_sort8.cl

```
__kernel void radix_sort8(__global ushort8 *global_data) {

   typedef union {
      ushort8 vec;
      ushort array[8];
   } vec_array;

   uint one_count, zero_count;
   uint cmp_value = 1;
   vec_array mask, ones, data;

   data.vec = global_data[0];

   for(int i=0; i<3; i++) {
      zero_count = 0;
      one_count = 0;
      for(int j = 0; j < 8; j++) {
         if(data.array[j] & cmp_value)
            ones.array[one_count++] = data.array[j];        ◁──  Place element in ones vector
         else {
            mask.array[zero_count++] = j;        ◁──  Increment zero count
         }
```

```
    }
    for(int j = zero_count; j < 8; j++)
        mask.array[j] = 8 - zero_count + j;          Create sorted
    data.vec = shuffle2(data.vec, ones.vec, mask.vec);   vector
    cmp_value <<= 1;
    }
    global_data[0] = data.vec;
}
```

This code performs three passes on the elements in the input ushort8 vector. To examine the radix, the code performs a bitwise AND with cmp_value, which equals 0b001 in the first loop, 0b010 in the second, and 0b100 in the last. If the AND result is nonzero, the code places the element in the ones vector and increments one_count. If the result is 0, the code sets the appropriate value in the mask vector and increments zero_count.

Once every element is analyzed, the mask vector is further updated to identify each element in the ones vector. The shuffle2 function uses the mask vector to rearrange the data, and then the process continues again.

This procedure gets the job done, but the frequent data transfer between private and global memory takes a great deal of time. You can improve performance by operating on data stored in local memory, and you can improve performance even further by configuring multiple work-items to execute the kernel. There are many examples of high-performance radix sorts available, and both the Nvidia SDK and the AMD SDK provide examples of its implementation. Further, the Back40Computing implementation of the radix sort (available for free download at http://code.google.com/p/back40computing/) has gained renown as one of the fastest GPU-based sorting routines available.

11.4 Summary

This chapter has discussed MapReduce, the bitonic sort, and the radix sort. These important applications can be executed in parallel and can be implemented efficiently with OpenCL.

OpenCL doesn't support dynamic memory allocation, so it's difficult to code MapReduce routines that pass key-value pairs between the mapping stages and reduction stages. But you can get around this by having each mapping stage perform part of the local reduction. The word-search application presented in this chapter shows how this works. Remember to invoke the barrier command after each processing stage. This ensures that all reads/writes to memory by work-items in a work-group will be completed before further commands are executed.

The bitonic sort is one of the more complicated sorting algorithms, but it lends itself very well to parallel computation. The algorithm consists of two steps: transforming the input data into a bitonic sequence, and sorting the bitonic sequence. Both tasks require essentially the same compare-and-swap operations, and for this reason the bitonic sort is usually performed recursively. But the example code in this chapter presents a method of executing the sort in an iterative, parallel manner.

The radix sort is simpler than the bitonic sort, and it doesn't require any comparisons between elements. It examines the digits of each element, starting from the least significant to the most significant, and places the elements in buckets according to their digits.

Memory access plays an important role throughout these and similar algorithms. Global memory stores data passed to and from the host, but you need to store your data in local memory to ensure high-bandwidth access. Similarly, it's important to use barriers and similar commands to make sure work-items access memory in order.

In the next chapter, we'll put aside sorting and searching and turn to a subject more traditionally associated with high-performance computing: matrix operations.

Matrices and
QR decomposition

This chapter covers

- Implementing matrix transposition and multiplication in OpenCL
- Understanding and coding the Householder transformation
- Factoring matrices with the QR decomposition algorithm

From physics and engineering to economics and sociology, there is no getting away from matrices. These mathematical structures can represent systems of equations, statistical data, DNA sequences, and the distribution of stresses within an object. Matrices have been used to structure data for centuries, and new applications appear on a regular basis.

Just as there are many uses for matrices, there are also many different ways to analyze them. But not all matrices are easy to work with. Mathematicians frequently find it necessary to factor a disordered matrix into matrices that are easy to analyze, and then perform their operations on the factors. This factorization is conceptually similar to factoring an integer into its prime divisors or factoring a polynomial into its roots.

One of the most popular methods of factoring a matrix is called the QR decomposition. This factors a matrix into two matrices whose qualities make them simple to analyze and manipulate. The goal of this chapter is to explain the theory behind QR decomposition and show how it can be implemented with OpenCL.

There are a number of ways to compute QR decomposition, but this presentation will focus on using Householder transformations, which reflect vectors across a plane or hyperplane. But before we examine these transformations, it's important that you have a solid understanding of two fundamental matrix operations: transposition and multiplication. This chapter will present transposition first.

12.1 Matrix transposition

Taking the transpose of a matrix is one of the simplest operations in linear algebra. This section presents a brief overview of matrices, including their rows and columns, and then discusses how these rows and columns can be switched through matrix transposition. The last part of this section shows how this operation can be coded in OpenCL.

12.1.1 Introduction to matrices

A *matrix* is a rectangular arrangement of numbers. Matrices are represented graphically as a grid of numbers inside vertical bars. This is shown in figure 12.1.

In code, matrices are commonly represented by two-dimensional arrays, where the two dimensions identify the matrix's rows and columns. If a matrix has m rows and n columns, it's called an *m-by-n* matrix. If the number of rows equals the number of columns, it's called a *square matrix*.

Each row and column is a one-dimensional structure of numbers, and for this reason, we can refer to each row and column as a *vector*. These are mathematical vectors, not to be confused with the data types presented in chapter 4. We'll have much more to say about these vectors and their operations throughout this chapter.

The numbers that make up a matrix are called *elements*. Matrix notation gives each element a designation that identifies its row and column. In figure 12.1, the element c_{ij} belongs to the ith row and the jth column. If i equals j, then the element lies on an imaginary line called the matrix's *diagonal*, which runs from the upper left to the lower right.

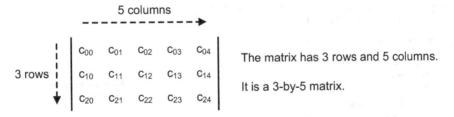

Figure 12.1 Matrix notation

Mathematicians have devised many categories for matrices, and one set of categories is based on the location of zeros within the matrix. If elements on the diagonal are nonzero and elements off the diagonal are zero, the matrix is a *diagonal matrix*. If the nonzero elements of a diagonal matrix all equal 1, the matrix is an *identity matrix*. If the elements above the diagonal, c_{ij}, equal the elements below the diagonal, c_{ji}, the matrix is a *symmetric matrix*.

If the overwhelming majority of elements are zero, the matrix is a *sparse matrix*, which the next chapter will discuss in detail. If the majority of elements, both on and off the diagonal, don't equal zero, the matrix is a *dense matrix*. This chapter focuses on dense matrices, particularly dense square matrices.

12.1.2 Theory and implementation of matrix transposition

The goal of computing a matrix's transpose is simple: to reflect each element across the diagonal so that each c_{ij} becomes c_{ji}. After a transpose, rows become columns and columns become rows. This is shown in figure 12.2, in which column 2 of the matrix becomes row 2. In text, you use ^{T} to denote a transposed matrix. For example, C^T is the transpose of the matrix C.

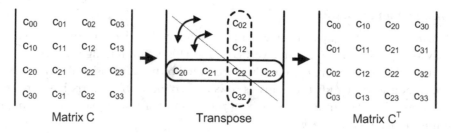

Figure 12.2 Matrix transposition

The following listing presents an in-place implementation of the transpose in OpenCL. Each work-item is assigned a block containing 16 values in 4 `float4` vectors. If a block lies on the diagonal, the work-item will swap its rows and columns. If not, the work-item will swap elements with the block across the diagonal, replacing rows with columns.

Listing 12.1 Matrix transposition: transpose.cl

```
kernel void transpose(__global float4 *g_mat,
    __local float4 *l_mat, uint size) {

  __global float4 *src, *dst;

    int col = get_global_id(0);
    int row = 0;
    while(col >= size) {            Find row/column
       col -= size--;               location
       row++;
```

```
   }
   col += row;                                    Find row/column
   size += row;                                   location

   src = g_mat + row * size * 4 + col;
   l_mat += get_local_id(0)*8;
   l_mat[0] = src[0];
   l_mat[1] = src[size];
   l_mat[2] = src[2*size];
   l_mat[3] = src[3*size];

   if(row == col) {
      src[0] = (float4)(l_mat[0].x, l_mat[1].x,
                        l_mat[2].x, l_mat[3].x);
      src[size] = (float4)(l_mat[0].y, l_mat[1].y,        Process
                           l_mat[2].y, l_mat[3].y);       block on
      src[2*size] = (float4)(l_mat[0].z, l_mat[1].z,      diagonal
                             l_mat[2].z, l_mat[3].z);
      src[3*size] = (float4)(l_mat[0].w, l_mat[1].w,
                             l_mat[2].w, l_mat[3].w);
   }
   else {
      dst = g_mat + col * size * 4 + row;
      l_mat[4] = dst[0];
      l_mat[5] = dst[size];
      l_mat[6] = dst[2*size];
      l_mat[7] = dst[3*size];

      dst[0] = (float4)(l_mat[0].x, l_mat[1].x,
                        l_mat[2].x, l_mat[3].x);
      dst[size] = (float4)(l_mat[0].y, l_mat[1].y,
                           l_mat[2].y, l_mat[3].y);
      dst[2*size] = (float4)(l_mat[0].z, l_mat[1].z,
                             l_mat[2].z, l_mat[3].z);
      dst[3*size] = (float4)(l_mat[0].w, l_mat[1].w,      Process
                             l_mat[2].w, l_mat[3].w);     block off
      src[0] = (float4)(l_mat[4].x, l_mat[5].x,           diagonal
                        l_mat[6].x, l_mat[7].x);
      src[size] = (float4)(l_mat[4].y, l_mat[5].y,
                           l_mat[6].y, l_mat[7].y);
      src[2*size] = (float4)(l_mat[4].z, l_mat[5].z,
                             l_mat[6].z, l_mat[7].z);
      src[3*size] = (float4)(l_mat[4].w, l_mat[5].w,
                             l_mat[6].w, l_mat[7].w);
   }
}
```

The host application sets the dimensionality of each work-item to 1 instead of 2, and this may seem odd at first. But as shown in figure 12.3, you don't need a work-item for every block in the matrix. You only need work items to process blocks on or above the diagonal.

The number of blocks that need to be processed is $n(n+1)/2$, where n is the number of blocks in a row. For example, a 256-by-256 matrix contains 64-by-64 blocks, so the host will generate $64(64+1)/2 = 2{,}080$ work-items to execute the kernel.

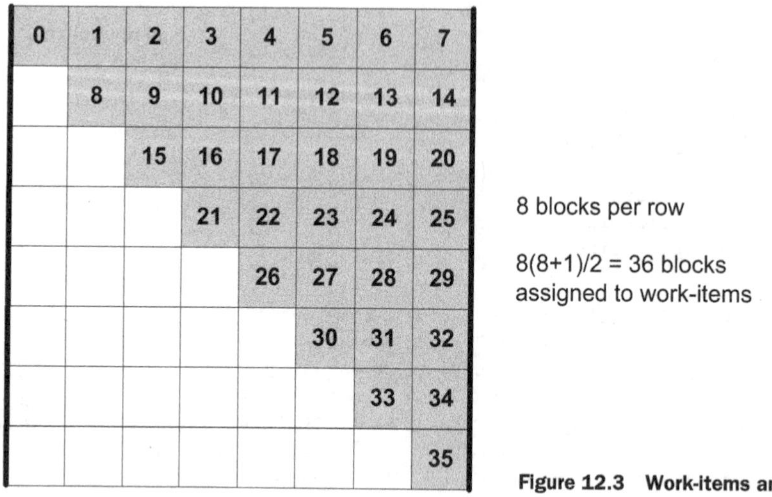

8 blocks per row

8(8+1)/2 = 36 blocks
assigned to work-items

Figure 12.3 Work-items and the transpose

Transposition is a crucial operation in linear algebra, and any professional library of matrix routines will contain a transpose routine. One important operation that makes use of the transpose is matrix multiplication, which is the topic of the next section.

12.2 *Matrix multiplication*

When a company wants to show off its new high-performance computing system, they'll frequently have it perform matrix multiplication. It's easy to see why. Matrix multiplication requires high-speed number crunching and high-speed data transfer, but few decisions. It's also a vital building block of many large-scale linear algebra routines. If a supercomputer is performing any large-scale linear algebra operation, the odds are that a great deal of its time is spent multiplying matrices.

This section presents the theory of matrix multiplication, which relies on an important vector operation called the dot product. Then we'll examine how to implement multiplication with OpenCL.

12.2.1 *The theory of matrix multiplication*

The product of two matrices, A and B, is obtained by multiplying each row of A with each column of B. This multiplication is implemented using the dot product, which was briefly discussed in chapter 5. The dot product multiplies the corresponding elements of two vectors and returns the sum of the products. For example, if vector p contains $[p_0, p_1, p_2, p_3]$ and vector q contains $[q_0, q_1, q_2, q_3]$, their dot product can be computed as follows:

$$p \cdot q = p_0 q_0 + p_1 q_1 + p_2 q_2 + p_3 q_3$$

In OpenCL, the dot product of two vectors is computed using the dot function discussed in chapter 5. This and the next chapter will make extensive use of this function.

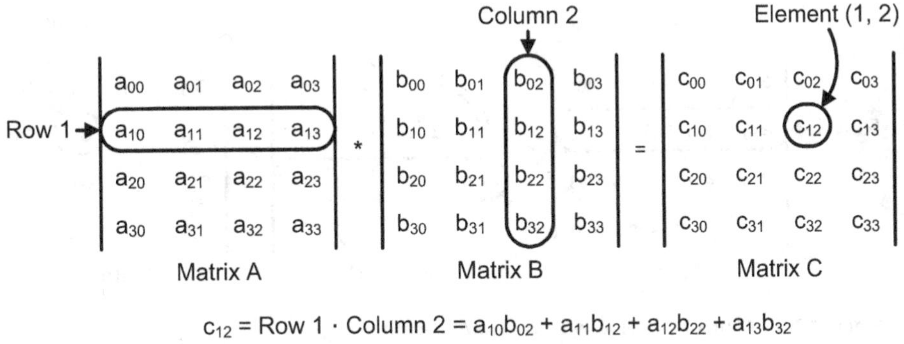

$$c_{12} = \text{Row 1} \cdot \text{Column 2} = a_{10}b_{02} + a_{11}b_{12} + a_{12}b_{22} + a_{13}b_{32}$$

Figure 12.4 Matrix multiplication

Figure 12.4 shows the matrix multiplication of two 4-by-4 matrices, A and B, and their product matrix C. The c_{12} element of the C matrix is obtained by multiplying row 1 of A and column 2 of B.

Each element in C is computed in a similar manner. In this example, the full matrix multiplication requires 16 dot products—each of the four rows of A must be multiplied by each of the four columns of B.

A and B are square matrices in this example, but nonsquare matrices can also be multiplied. But the dot product requires vectors of equal length, so the rows of the first matrix must have the same size as the columns of the second. In other words, if the first matrix has n columns, the second matrix must have n rows. Taking this a step further, if the first matrix has dimensions m by n and the second matrix has dimensions n by p, the product matrix will have dimensions m by p.

We can generalize the multiplication of rectangular matrices as follows: if matrix $C = AB$, A has dimensions m by n, and B has dimensions n by p, element c_{ij} can be computed as follows:

$$c_{ij} = \sum_{k=0}^{n-1} a_{ik}b_{kj}$$

Matrix multiplication is *not* commutative—AB does not equal BA. But matrix multiplication is *associative*: $(AB)C = A(BC)$. This property will become important later on when we look at the QR decomposition.

12.2.2 *Implementing matrix multiplication in OpenCL*

Matrix multiplication isn't hard to implement in code, but there are many details to keep in mind. The kernel needs to know the dimensions and the data types of the elements, and also how the elements are stored in memory. If the matrix data is stored in *row-major* order, the elements will be stored row by row. That is, the elements of row 0 will be followed by the elements of row 1, then row 2, and so on. If the data is stored in *column-major* order, the elements will be stored column by column. The elements of column 0 will be followed by the elements of column 1, then column 2, and so on.

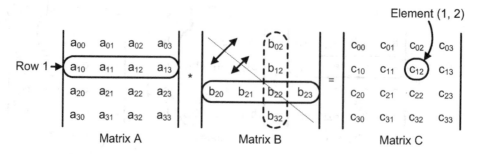

Figure 12.5   Matrix multiplication after transposition

The development kits released by Nvidia and AMD both contain OpenCL code that multiplies matrices. In both cases, the multiplication is based on scalars—input elements are multiplied one at a time. This chapter presents a different implementation. The code in the Ch12/matrix_mult project combines elements into vectors and performs the dot product with the dot function.

This presents a problem. Matrix multiplication requires dot products of rows and columns, and if the matrices are stored in row-major format (the usual format), you can't load multiple elements from a single column at a time. But you can fix this by taking the transpose of the second matrix. Figure 12.5 presents the same multiplication as in figure 12.4, but because *B* is transposed, the elements in *A* and *B* can both be accessed by row.

If you look through the matrix_mult project in the Ch12 folder, you'll see that the host application (matrix_mult.c) enqueues two kernels: one to transpose the second matrix and one to multiply the two matrices together. The following code presents the kernel that performs the actual multiplication.

NOTE   The dot products are computed with the dot function, which was briefly discussed in chapter 5.

Listing 12.2   Matrix multiplication: matrix_mult.cl

```
kernel void matrix_mult(__global float4 *a_mat,
    __global float4 *b_mat, __global float *c_mat) {

    float sum;

    int num_rows = get_global_size(0);
    int vectors_per_row = num_rows/4;

    int start = get_global_id(0) * vectors_per_row;      ┐ Find input/output
    a_mat += start;                                       │ row addresses
    c_mat += start*4;                                     ┘

    for(int i=0; i<num_rows; i++) {        ┐
        sum = 0.0f;                        │
        for(int j=0; j<vectors_per_row; j++) {   │ Multiply A row
            sum += dot(a_mat[j],                 │ by B rows
                b_mat[i*vectors_per_row + j]);   ┘
```

```
    }
    c_mat[i] = sum;
  }
}
```
↑ **Multiply A row by B rows**

This kernel doesn't access local memory because there are no intermediate results to store. This code executes quickly, but it's important to remember that it expects the second matrix, b_mat, to be in column-major order.

Matrix multiplication is an important part of many matrix operations, including QR decomposition. Another crucial subroutine in this chapter's implementation of QR decomposition is the Householder transformation, which is the topic of the next section.

12.3 *The Householder transformation*

Most discussions of vector operations include addition, subtraction, and multiplication, but vector *reflection* is also a critical operation in many algorithms. The concept is simple: given an input vector and a vector perpendicular to a surface, the goal is to find the reflection of the input vector across the surface. The procedure for computing this reflection is called the *Householder transformation*, and this section will examine this transformation in detail. But first, it's important to be familiar with the theory of vector projection.

12.3.1 *Vector projection*

The dot product of two vectors provides an idea of their relative directions. If the product is positive and large compared to the vectors' lengths, it implies that the two vectors are pointing in similar directions. If the dot product is negative, it implies that the two vectors are pointing in different directions. If the dot product is 0, it means the two vectors point at right angles to one another.

The concept of the vector projection allows you to be more precise about the similarity between two vectors. A vector projection is the portion of one vector that points in the same direction as a second vector. In figure 12.6, vector b is split into two components: a component called p, which points in the same direction as a, and q, which points in a direction orthogonal to a. It should be clear that $b = p + q$.

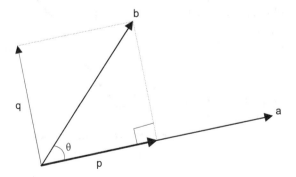

Figure 12.6   Vector projection

In this diagram, p is the vector projection of b on a. The larger p is, the more similar b is to a. Using trigonometry, you can compute the length of p as $|b|\cos\theta$. To make p point in the direction of a, you need to multiply it by a's *unit vector*. This is obtained by dividing a by its length, denoted $|a|$. The following equation shows the result of the multiplication:

$$p = |b|\cos(\theta)\frac{a}{|a|}$$

The vector projection would be easy to compute it weren't for the cosine. Thankfully, a relationship exists between the cosine of the angle between two vectors and the vectors' dot product. The proof is lengthy, but the result is as follows:

$$\cos(\theta)=\frac{a \cdot b}{|a||b|}$$

By placing this into the previous equation, you can arrive at a more workable expression for p:

$$p = |a|\frac{a \cdot b}{|a||b|}\frac{a}{|a|}= \frac{a \cdot b}{|a|}\frac{a}{|a|}= \frac{a \cdot b}{|a|^2}a$$

In general, the vector projection of vector b on vector a is expressed with the term $\text{proj}_a b$. $\text{proj}_a b$ has the same direction as a, and $b-\text{proj}_a b$ is orthogonal to a.

12.3.2 *Vector reflection*

Many algorithms in linear algebra require vector reflection, and the reason for this will become clear later in this chapter. Figure 12.7 presents a simple two-dimensional case of how this reflection works. You'll start with two vectors: x and u. u is perpendicular to M (which stands for mirror). The goal is to find x', the vector obtained by reflecting x in M. Note that, in two dimensions, M is simply a line. It's a plane in three dimensions and a hyperplane in four or more dimensions.

To find x' in terms of x and u, you need to take vector projections. Figure 12.8 shows how this works. x is split into p and q, where p is the vector projection of x on u and q is orthogonal to p. Similarly, x' is split into p' and q', where p' is the vector projection of x' on u and q' is orthogonal to p'.

Figure 12.8 makes clear the relationships between p and p' and q and q'. Because x' equals the sum of p' and q', you can compute it as shown on the next page.

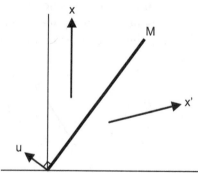

Figure 12.7   Vector reflection

$$x' = p' + q' = (-proj_u x) + (x - proj_u x)$$

$$x' = x - 2proj_u x$$

$$x' = x - 2u\frac{u \cdot x}{|u|^2}$$

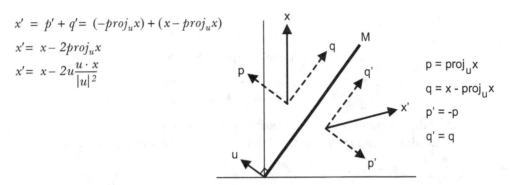

Figure 12.8   Vector reflection in terms of vector projections

This final equation gives a clear relationship between x', x, and u. This equation will help you compute the QR decomposition of a matrix. But before we discuss the decomposition algorithm, we need to come to terms with the outer product and how it can be used to form Householder matrices.

12.3.3 *Outer products and Householder matrices*

A vector can be thought of as a matrix with a single row or a single column. By default, mathematicians treat vectors as matrices with a single column, and such vectors are called *column vectors*. In contrast, transposed column vectors are considered matrices with a single row, or *row vectors*.

With this new interpretation of vectors, we can arrive at a new interpretation of the dot product. Instead of multiplying vectors, the dot product can be thought of as multiplying a 1-by-n matrix and an n-by-1 matrix. The result is a 1-by-1 matrix, better known as a *scalar*. As a result, we can refer to the dot product using matrix terminology: $a^T b$ instead of $a \bullet b$. The following equation makes this clearer:

$$a \cdot b = a^T b = \begin{bmatrix} a_0 & a_1 & a_2 & a_3 \end{bmatrix} \begin{bmatrix} b_0 \\ b_1 \\ b_2 \\ b_3 \end{bmatrix} = a_0 b_0 + a_1 b_1 + a_2 b_2 + a_3 b_3$$

Using this notation, we can arrive at a new type of product called the *outer product*. Instead of multiplying a row vector by a column vector, this product reverses the operation and computes ab^T instead of $a^T b$. Despite the similar appearance, the result of the outer product is significantly different than that produced by the dot product. The dot product multiplies a 1-by-n matrix with an n-by-1 matrix and produces a 1-by-1 matrix. The outer product multiplies an n-by-1 matrix with a 1-by-n matrix and produces an n-by-n matrix. This is shown in the following equation:

$$ab^T = \begin{bmatrix} a_0 \\ a_1 \\ a_2 \\ a_3 \end{bmatrix} \begin{bmatrix} b_0 & b_1 & b_2 & b_3 \end{bmatrix} = \begin{bmatrix} a_0b_0 & a_0b_1 & a_0b_2 & a_0b_3 \\ a_1b_0 & a_1b_1 & a_1b_2 & a_1b_3 \\ a_2b_0 & a_2b_1 & a_2b_2 & a_2b_3 \\ a_3b_0 & a_3b_1 & a_3b_2 & a_3b_3 \end{bmatrix}$$

You can use this vector-as-matrix interpretation to manipulate the equation for vector reflection. If you replace $u \bullet x$ with u^Tx, the new relationship is as follows:

$$x' = x - 2u\frac{u \cdot x}{|u|^2} = x - 2\frac{u(u^Tx)}{|u|^2}$$

As mentioned earlier, matrix multiplication is associative, so $A(BC) = (AB)C$. You can use this relationship to change $u(u^Tx)$ in the reflection equation to $(uu^T)x$. This provides the following relationship:

$$x' = x - 2\frac{u(u^Tx)}{|u|^2} = x - 2\frac{(uu^T)x}{|u|^2} = x - 2\frac{uu^T}{|u|^2}x$$

Instead of finding x' with a dot product, you now need to compute an outer product, which is more difficult. But there is a good reason to do this. If you factor the vector x out of the equation, you can arrive at the following relationship:

$$x' = \left(I - 2\frac{uu^T}{|u|^2}\right)x = Px$$

In this equation, I is the identity matrix and the term inside the parentheses is a matrix. This matrix is commonly denoted by P, and when P premultiplies a vector x, the result is the reflection of x through the hyperplane perpendicular to u. This procedure was conceived by Alston Householder; u is called the Householder vector, and P is called the Householder matrix. The reflection operation represented by P is called the Householder transformation.

When a vector is reflected twice, the result will be the vector itself. That is, $P(Px) = x$ for all x. P is its own inverse and any matrix with this property is called *involutary*.

One more point about the Householder transformation needs to be addressed. The preceding discussion explained how to find x' given x and u, but what if you start with x and x' and want to find a vector with u's direction? The answer is surprisingly simple: $u = x - x'$. Figure 12.9 presents this graphically, using the same x and x' vectors from earlier figures.

This result may not be immediately obvious, but remember that x and x' are symmetrical about M, and that u is perpendicular to M. The u vector in figure 12.9 has a different length than the u vector in previous figures, but this isn't a concern—the only requirement you have for u is that its

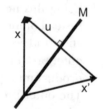

Figure 12.9 Finding the reflection vector u

direction be perpendicular to *M*. Also, the length of *u* is divided out as part of the Householder transformation.

12.3.4 *Vector reflection in OpenCL*

Implementing vector reflection in code is a straightforward process, consisting of three main steps:

1 Multiply *u* by $-\text{sqrt}(2)/|u|$.
2 Compute the matrix uu^T.
3 Add the identity matrix, *I*, to the resulting matrix.

The next listing demonstrates how this is accomplished. x_vec equals [1.0, 2.0, 3.0, 4.0] and u equals [0.0, 5.0, 0.0, 0.0]. Because u is perpendicular to the *x-z-w* hyperplane, the reflection of x_vec can be determined by inspection: [1.0, –2.0, 3.0, 4.0].

> **Listing 12.3   Vector reflection: vec_reflect.cl**

```
__kernel void vec_reflect(float4 x_vec, float4 u,
      __global float4* x_prime) {

   float4 p_mat[4];

   u *= M_SQRT2_F/length(u);

   p_mat[0] = (float4)(1.0f, 0.0f, 0.0f, 0.0f)
                 - (u * u.x);
   p_mat[1] = (float4)(0.0f, 1.0f, 0.0f, 0.0f)
                 - (u * u.y);
   p_mat[2] = (float4)(0.0f, 0.0f, 1.0f, 0.0f)
                 - (u * u.z);
   p_mat[3] = (float4)(0.0f, 0.0f, 0.0f, 1.0f)
                 - (u * u.w);

   x_prime[0].x = dot(p_mat[0], x_vec);
   x_prime[0].y = dot(p_mat[1], x_vec);
   x_prime[0].z = dot(p_mat[2], x_vec);
   x_prime[0].w = dot(p_mat[3], x_vec);
}
```

Compute Householder matrix *(annotation for the p_mat block)*

Reflect x to x' *(annotation for the dot-product block)*

If you're only interested in finding the reflection of a vector, you don't have to worry about the outer product and its matrix operations. It's much simpler to compute *x'* with the following equation:

$$x' = x - 2u\frac{u \cdot x}{|u|^2}$$

But many applications of the Householder transformation require finding both a vector's reflection and the Householder matrix corresponding to the reflection. One such application is the QR decomposition, which is the topic of the next section.

12.4   *The QR decomposition*

In linear algebra, a common task involves factoring a complex matrix into simpler matrices that are easier to analyze. This factorization is helpful when solving linear

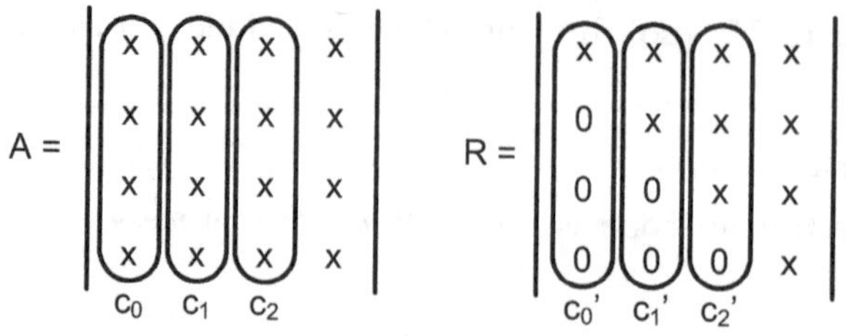

Figure 12.10   Finding the reflection vectors u_k

systems, computing determinants, or obtaining eigenvalues. One of the most popular methods of factoring a matrix is called *QR decomposition*. This operates on a rectangular matrix A and produces two matrices with interesting properties. The first matrix, denoted Q, is *orthogonal*, which means its transpose equals its inverse. The second matrix, denoted R, is upper triangular, which means every element below the main diagonal equals zero.

Before we discuss how to compute Q, let's focus our attention on R. Figure 12.10 presents the goal: to transform the columns of A (denoted c_0 through c_{k-1}) into columns of R (c_0' through c_{k-1}'), where k identifies the number of columns in A. A is square in this figure, but QR decomposition can be applied to any rectangular matrix.

Computer scientists have found many ways to convert a square matrix like A into an upper-triangular matrix like R. One of the most common and most efficient methods relies on Householder transformations. This method computes the u_k vectors needed to transform the columns of A into the columns of R. Then, once the Householder vectors are obtained, this method computes their corresponding Householder matrices and multiplies them together. This combined matrix is Q.

The steps for finding Q and R are as follows:

1 Find u_0 that reflects c_0 into c_0'.
2 Transform each column of A with the u_0 reflection.
3 Find u_1 that reflects c_1 into c_1'.
4 Transform each column of A with the u_1 reflection.
5 Construct the Householder matrix P_k for each u_k vector.
6 Repeat steps 3–5 for columns up to k–1.
7 Multiply the Householder matrices to form Q.

The rest of this section will elaborate on these steps, and we'll walk through a QR decomposition of a 4-by-4 matrix. Then we'll look at how to implement QR decomposition in OpenCL.

12.4.1 *Finding the Householder vectors and R*

You've seen how to find a Householder vector u given a vector x and its reflection x'. You can use this method to determine the u_k vectors that transform the columns c_k in figure 12.10 to their reflections c_k'. But first, you need to obtain the nonzero elements in each c_k'. This isn't difficult as long as you remember that, because x' is the reflection of x, both vectors must have the same length.

An example will show how this works. The matrix *A* has three rows and three columns. You want to find two Householder vectors, u_0 and u_1, that will transform the first two columns of A so as to make A upper triangular:

$$A = \begin{bmatrix} 13 & -17 & -10 \\ 4 & 18 & -32 \\ -16 & -8 & -24 \end{bmatrix}$$

You'll start with the leftmost column vector, which you'll call c_0. You want the reflection, c_0', to have one nonzero element on top and two zero elements below. To make sure that c_0 and c_0' have the same length, you'll set the nonzero element of c_0' equal to the length of c_0. Then you can find u_0 by subtracting c_0' from c_0. This is done as follows:

$$c_0' = \begin{bmatrix} |c_0| \\ 0 \\ 0 \end{bmatrix} = \begin{bmatrix} 21 \\ 0 \\ 0 \end{bmatrix} \qquad u_0 = c_0 - c_0' = \begin{bmatrix} 13 \\ 4 \\ -16 \end{bmatrix} - \begin{bmatrix} 21 \\ 0 \\ 0 \end{bmatrix} = \begin{bmatrix} -8 \\ 4 \\ -16 \end{bmatrix}$$

Now that you have u_0, you need to transform each column of *A* according to the reflection corresponding to u_0. You can perform these reflections using an equation presented earlier:

$$c_k' = c_k - 2u_0 \frac{u_0 \cdot c_k}{|u_0|^2}$$

This transformation gives you a new *A* matrix. As desired, the first column has two zeros beneath the nonzero element:

$$A = \begin{bmatrix} 21 & -1 & 6 \\ 0 & 10 & -40 \\ 0 & 24 & 8 \end{bmatrix}$$

Now you want to transform the second column, c_1, so that its bottom element equals zero. You can do this by setting the first element of the reflection, c_1', equal to the first element of c_1. Then, to make sure $|c_1'| = |c_1|$, you need to set the second element of c_1' equal to the length of the subvector containing the lower two elements of c_1:

$$c_1' = \begin{bmatrix} -1 \\ \sqrt{(10)^2 + (24)^2} \\ 0 \end{bmatrix} = \begin{bmatrix} -1 \\ 26 \\ 0 \end{bmatrix} \qquad u_1 = c_1 - c_1' = \begin{bmatrix} -1 \\ 10 \\ 24 \end{bmatrix} - \begin{bmatrix} -1 \\ 26 \\ 0 \end{bmatrix} = \begin{bmatrix} 0 \\ -16 \\ 24 \end{bmatrix}$$

Again, you need to transform each column of *A* according to the new reflection identified by u_1. This gives you the matrix on the following page.

It's important to note that transforming c_0 with the reflection corresponding to u_1 leaves c_0 unchanged. This is because the dot product of c_0 and u_1 equals zero. When this dot product equals zero, the reflection produces the original vector. This means you

$$A = \begin{bmatrix} 21 & -1 & 6 \\ 0 & 26 & -8 \\ 0 & 0 & -40 \end{bmatrix} = R$$

don't have to transform columns that have already been transformed—once you compute a Householder vector u_k, you only have to find reflections for columns c_k and higher.

After this last set of reflections, A is upper triangular. This transformed version of A is the R matrix generated by the QR decomposition. Next, you'll see how to use the Householder vectors u_k to create the Q matrix.

12.4.2   Finding the Householder matrices and Q

Now that you've computed the Householder vectors u_k that transform A into R, you need to find the matrix Q that serves as the inverse of this transformation. That is, you want to find Q such that $Q^{-1}A = R$, or $A = QR$.

The previous section explained how to create a Householder matrix P from a Householder vector u. The relationship is given by

$$P = I - 2\frac{uu^T}{|u|^2}$$

As discussed earlier, uu^T is an outer product that generates a square matrix. If u contains k elements, P has k rows and k columns.

In the example, you obtained R by transforming the column vectors of A with u_0's reflection first and u_1's reflection second. Therefore, R equals P_1P_0A. Because every Householder transformation is its own inverse, you can set Q equal to P_0P_1. The following equation shows how Q is computed for the example:

$$Q = P_0P_1 = \left(I - 2\frac{u_0u_0^T}{|u_0|^2} \right)\left(I - 2\frac{u_1u_1^T}{|u_1|^2} \right)$$

$$Q = \left(I - \frac{2}{336}\begin{bmatrix} 64 & -32 & 128 \\ -32 & 16 & -64 \\ 128 & -64 & 256 \end{bmatrix} \right)\left(I - \frac{2}{832}\begin{bmatrix} 0 & 0 & 0 \\ 0 & 256 & -384 \\ 0 & -384 & 576 \end{bmatrix} \right)$$

$$Q = \begin{bmatrix} 0.61905 & 0.19048 & 0.76190 \\ 0.19048 & 0.90476 & 0.38095 \\ -0.76190 & 0.38095 & 0.52381 \end{bmatrix} \cdot \begin{bmatrix} 1.0 & 0 & 0 \\ 0 & 0.38462 & 0.92308 \\ 0 & 0.92308 & -0.38462 \end{bmatrix}$$

$$Q = \begin{bmatrix} 0.61905 & -0.63004 & 0.46886 \\ 0.19048 & 0.69963 & 0.68864 \\ -0.76190 & -0.33700 & -0.55311 \end{bmatrix}$$

If you multiply this Q matrix by the R matrix computed earlier, the product will be the original A matrix. This is because $QR = (P_0P_1)(P_1P_0A) = A$.

12.4.3 *Implementing QR decomposition in OpenCL*

The qr project in the Ch12 folder computes the QR decomposition of a k-by-k matrix A, where k is set equal to 64 by default. The host application generates one work-item for every column of the matrix. These items all belong to the same work-group, so you can use the barrier command to synchronize their access to global and local memory.

Coding the QR decomposition isn't a simple process, but the main difficulty isn't computing R. Instead, the main question involves how to store and multiply the Householder matrices needed to form Q. If the matrices are large, you can't store each P_k separately. Instead, you need to initialize the Q matrix and update it as each new P_k is obtained.

For this reason, we'll split the discussion of the QR decomposition code into two parts. In the first part, we'll look at how to transform the first column of A and use it to initialize Q. In the second part, we'll examine how to transform the second through k^{th} columns of A and update Q with each new Householder matrix.

TRANSFORMING THE FIRST COLUMN AND INITIALIZING Q

The following listing presents the first part of the QR decomposition kernel. This computes the first Householder vector, u_0, needed to transform the first column into a column of an upper-triangular matrix. Then it creates the Householder matrix, P_0, from u_0 and sets Q equal to this matrix.

Listing 12.4 QR decomposition: qr.cl (part one)

```
__kernel void qr(__local float *u_vec, __global float *a_mat,
      __global float *q_mat, __global float *p_mat,
      __global float *prod_mat) {

   local float u_length_squared, dot;
   float prod, vec_length = 0.0f;

   int id = get_local_id(0);
   int num_cols = get_global_size(0);                     Load column into
                                                          local memory
   u_vec[id] = a_mat[id*num_cols];
   barrier(CLK_LOCAL_MEM_FENCE);

   if(id == 0) {
      for(int i=1; i<num_cols; i++) {
         vec_length += u_vec[i] * u_vec[i];
      }
      u_length_squared = vec_length;
      vec_length = sqrt(vec_length +                      Find lengths
                        u_vec[0] * u_vec[0]);             of vectors
      a_mat[0] = vec_length;
      u_vec[0] -= vec_length;
      u_length_squared += u_vec[0] * u_vec[0];
   }
   else {
      a_mat[id*num_cols] = 0.0f;
   }
   barrier(CLK_GLOBAL_MEM_FENCE);
```

```
for(int i=1; i<num_cols; i++) {
   dot = 0.0f;
   if(id == 0) {
      for(int j=0; j<num_cols; j++) {
         dot += a_mat[j*num_cols + i] * u_vec[j];
      }
   }
   barrier(CLK_LOCAL_MEM_FENCE);
   a_mat[id*num_cols + i] -= 2 * u_vec[id] *
      dot / u_length_squared;
}

for(int i=0; i<num_cols; i++) {
   q_mat[id*num_cols + i] = -2 * u_vec[i] *
      u_vec[id] / u_length_squared;
}
q_mat[id*num_cols + id] += 1;
barrier(CLK_GLOBAL_MEM_FENCE);
```

Transform columns of A

Initialize Q

It's important to understand how this code obtains and uses the first Householder vector, u_0. First it loads the first column of A into local memory. Then it computes the length of the vector and subtracts this length from the column's first element. This sets the local memory vector equal to u_0, and once this is obtained, the kernel uses it to transform each succeeding column of A using the following equation:

$$c_k' = c_k - 2u_0 \frac{u_0 \cdot c_k}{|u_0|^2}$$

After updating A, the kernel forms the Householder matrix P_0 from the Householder vector u_0 using the following equation:

$$P_0 = I - 2\frac{u_0 u_0^T}{|u_0|^2}$$

Once the kernel obtains P_0, it places its elements in the Q matrix. As the rest of the kernel executes, Q will multiply further Householder matrices to arrive at its final value.

TRANSFORMING SUCCESSIVE COLUMNS AND UPDATING Q

The next listing presents the second part of the QR decomposition kernel. This loops through the remaining columns of A and computes the Householder vectors needed to transform A into an upper-triangular matrix. As each Householder vector is computed, the kernel finds the corresponding Householder matrix, P_0, and uses this to update Q.

Listing 12.5   QR decomposition: qr.cl (part two)

```
...
for(int col = 1; col < num_cols-1; col++) {

   u_vec[id] = a_mat[id * num_cols + col];
   barrier(CLK_LOCAL_MEM_FENCE);

   if(id == col) {
```

```
      vec_length = 0.0f;
      for(int i = col + 1; i < num_cols; i++) {
         vec_length += u_vec[i] * u_vec[i];
      }
      u_length_squared = vec_length;
      vec_length = sqrt(vec_length + u_vec[col] * u_vec[col]);
      u_vec[col] -= vec_length;
      u_length_squared += u_vec[col] * u_vec[col];
      a_mat[col * num_cols + col] = vec_length;
   }
   else if(id > col) {
      a_mat[id * num_cols + col] = 0.0f;
   }
   barrier(CLK_GLOBAL_MEM_FENCE);

   /* Transform further columns of A */
   for(int i = col+1; i < num_cols; i++) {
      if(id == 0) {
         dot = 0.0f;
         for(int j=col; j<num_cols; j++) {
            dot += a_mat[j*num_cols + i] * u_vec[j];
         }
      }
      barrier(CLK_LOCAL_MEM_FENCE);
      if(id >= col)
         a_mat[id*num_cols + i] -= 2 * u_vec[id] *
               dot / u_length_squared;
      barrier(CLK_GLOBAL_MEM_FENCE);
   }

   if(id >= col) {
      for(int i=col; i<num_cols; i++) {
         p_mat[id*num_cols + i] = -2 * u_vec[i] *
               u_vec[id] / u_length_squared;
      }
      p_mat[id*num_cols + id] += 1;
   }
   barrier(CLK_GLOBAL_MEM_FENCE);

   /* Multiply q_mat * p_mat = prod_mat */
   for(int i=col; i<num_cols; i++) {
      prod = 0.0f;
      for(int j=col; j<num_cols; j++) {
         prod += q_mat[id*num_cols + j] *
               p_mat[j*num_cols + i];
      }
      prod_mat[id*num_cols + i] = prod;
   }
   barrier(CLK_GLOBAL_MEM_FENCE);

   /* Place the content of prod_mat in q_mat */
   for(int i=col; i<num_cols; i++) {
      q_mat[id*num_cols + i] =
            prod_mat[id*num_cols + i];
   }
   barrier(CLK_GLOBAL_MEM_FENCE);
}
```

Update the
P matrix

Place product
in prod_mat

Move prod_mat
to Q

This code iterates through the columns of A and performs most of the same tasks as the code in listing 12.4. The important difference is how Q is updated. In theory, Q is obtained with the following equation:

$$Q = P_0 P_1 P_2 \ldots P_{k-2} P_{k-1}$$

In practice, however, you can't store $k-1$ Householder matrices in computer memory. The code in listing 12.5 uses three matrices, q_mat, p_mat, and prod_mat, and updates q_mat using three steps:

1 When the kernel computes a new u_k, it sets p_mat equal to the corresponding P_k matrix.

2 The kernel computes the product of q_mat and p_mat, and places the result in prod_mat.

3 The kernel moves the elements of prod_mat to q_mat, and prepares for another multiplication.

With so much data transferred to and from global memory, this procedure is not particularly fast. But because there are only three matrices involved, this process is more memory efficient than algorithms that require $k-1$ Householder matrices.

Once the kernel finishes the last transformation of the columns of A, the result will be the upper-triangular matrix R. After the final multiplication of Householder matrices, the resulting transformation matrix will be Q. To test the decomposition, the host application multiplies Q and R and compares the result to the original values in A.

12.5 Summary

Matrix manipulation is one of the most common tasks that programmers associate with high-performance computing. This is because so many real-world matrices may have thousands or tens of thousands of elements. Matrix operations commonly involve a great deal of number crunching and data transfer, but very little decision making. For this reason, these operations are ideal for implementation with OpenCL.

This chapter has proceeded from the simplest of matrix operations to the complex. The matrix transpose doesn't perform any mathematical operations, but simply moves elements within a matrix. The example code in this chapter demonstrates how the transpose can be performed efficiently by dividing the matrix into blocks and assigning each block to a work-item.

Matrix multiplication relies on the dot product of rows and columns. More specifically, each row of the first matrix multiplies each column of the second, and the result of each dot product is a scalar. If the first matrix has dimensions n by k and the second has dimensions k by p, the product will have dimensions n by p. Vectors can be thought of as matrices—a row vector has dimensions 1 by n and a column vector has dimensions n by 1.

The Householder transformation reflects a vector across a region perpendicular to another vector. This transformation can be performed using a dot product or an outer product. Dot products are easier to compute, but when you need to combine multiple reflections, you need to use the matrices associated with the outer products.

The QR decomposition discussed in this chapter relies on Householder transformations to reflect the columns of a matrix so that they become upper-triangular. You can combine these transformations by multiplying Householder matrices to obtain the Q matrix. Once the input matrix has been transformed into upper-triangular form, it becomes the R matrix. You can test the accuracy of the decomposition by checking whether $A = QR$.

Sparse matrices 13

This chapter covers

- Accessing sparse matrix data from NIST's Matrix Market files
- Solving sparse matrix systems with the method of steepest descent
- Solving sparse matrix systems with the conjugate gradient method

The popular MATLAB toolset contains functions coded specifically to process sparse matrices, but as I used MATLAB during my college years, I never understood why. I knew that most of the elements in a sparse matrix are zero, but I didn't see why these matrices deserve special treatment. What's the big deal?

When I entered the ranks of working engineers, however, I came to understand why sparse matrices get so much attention. These matrices arise when scientists and engineers need to solve complex systems modeled using *differential equations*. These equations play a vital role in analyzing real-world dynamic systems. NASA engineers solve differential equations to put rockets into space, and financial traders solve them to gauge the volatility of stock prices. If a quantity changes over time or space, the odds are that an applied mathematician has derived differential equations to model the change.

Sparse matrices are vital in analyzing complex systems, and this chapter will present a number of methods for solving equations with sparse matrices. But before we get into the heavy math, it's important to understand the relationship between differential equations and sparse matrices. This is the topic of the first section.

13.1 Differential equations and sparse matrices

One of the most important differential equations in structural engineering is the Euler-Bernoulli equation, which relates the deflection of a beam, $w(x)$ to its supported load, q. The equation is as follows:

$$\frac{d^2}{dx^2}\left(EI\frac{d^2w}{dx^2}\right) = q$$

This equation is straightforward to solve if you're only dealing with a single beam. But if you have a complex system of interconnected elements, it becomes nearly impossible to arrive at an exact solution. For example, given the transmission tower in figure 13.1, how would you determine the deflections of its beams?

Figure 13.1 A complex assembly of beam elements

To solve the equations corresponding to a real-world system like that shown in the figure, scientists and engineers rely on a tool called *finite element analysis* (FEA). I'm not going to discuss the theory behind FEA in depth, but the basic procedure consists of five steps:

1. Divide the complex system into simple elements that are easy to analyze.
2. Obtain the differential equation or equations corresponding to each element.
3. Convert the differential equations into linear equations using an approximation method, such as the Petrov-Galerkin method or the Ritz-Galerkin method.
4. Combine the linear equations together into a matrix. This will frequently be a sparse matrix.
5. Solve the matrix to arrive at an approximate solution for the overall system.

Step 3 is particularly important. FEA approximates differential equations, which are hard to solve, using linear equations, which are easy to solve. A system like a transmission tower may contain hundreds or even thousands of these equations, but each element only connects to two or three others. Therefore, each equation will only have two or three nonzero terms. For example, if you use x_i to represent deflection and b_i to represent load, your equations might look like this:

$$a_1x_1 + a_2x_2 + a_3x_3 = b_1$$
$$a_4x_2 + a_5x_4 = b_2$$

When all the beam equations are combined together, the result is a linear system whose equations each contain a handful of terms. This system can be solved in a straightforward manner using matrix operations. In this case, the coefficients a_x are placed in matrix A, the deflection terms are placed in the vector x, and the loading terms are placed in the vector b. You can obtain each of the deflection terms within the system by solving $Ax = b$ for x.

Figure 13.2 depicts a matrix that corresponds to a structural model of a real transmission tower. The matrix size is 153 by 153, but only 10 percent (2,423) of the elements within the matrix are nonzero. These are represented by dots, and because the structural model is symmetric, the matrix itself is symmetric.

There is no clear distinction between sparse matrices and their regular, or dense, counterparts. A matrix is considered sparse if its proportion of zero-to-nonzero elements, called its *sparsity*, makes it worth our while to use processing routines specifically created for sparse matrices. This chapter will discuss two routines designed specifically to solve sparse matrix systems: the method of steepest descent and the conjugate gradient method. Both algorithms make it possible to solve linear systems represented by symmetric sparse matrices.

But before we explore how to solve these matrices, it's important to know how to access them in code. The next section explains how sparse matrices are stored and how you can read matrix elements from specially formatted text files.

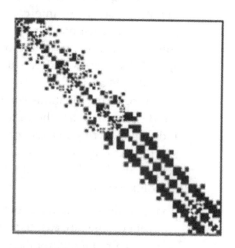

Figure 13.2   A sparse matrix corresponding to a structural model of a transmission tower

13.2   Sparse matrix storage and the Harwell-Boeing collection

Unlike the matrices from chapter 12, sparse matrices aren't stored in two-dimensional arrays. This is because sparse matrices may contain hundreds of zeros for every nonzero element. It's better to store only the nonzero elements and their locations in the matrix.

This storage method is employed by sparse matrices in the Harwell-Boeing collection, a public domain set of matrices used to model practical systems. In this section, we'll look at how to obtain these matrices and access them in code. In later sections, we'll solve the linear systems associated with these matrices.

13.2.1 Introducing the Harwell-Boeing collection

Most sparse matrices that physicists and engineers deal with are *huge*, with hundreds and thousands of rows. To see what I mean, visit the National Institute for Standards and Technology (NIST) site at http://math.nist.gov/MatrixMarket/data/Harwell-Boeing. Each link on this page identifies a set of files whose sparse matrices were generated through system analysis, from structural engineering to nuclear reactor analysis to economics and demographics. If you click on a link for a matrix, you can see how large these matrices are.

This chapter focuses on solving the BCSSTK05 matrix located in the BCSSTRUC1 set. Conveniently, this is the same 153-by-153 matrix depicted in figure 13.2. Note that the BCSSTK05 image, like the corresponding matrix file, is part of the Matrix Market repository sponsored by NIST. These resources are freely available for public use, and I'd like to thank Dr. Roland Boisvert and the other scientists in NIST's Applied and Computational Mathematics Division for making them available.

13.2.2 Accessing data in Matrix Market files

To read from a sparse matrix file in code, it's important to know how the matrix data is structured. Each sparse matrix file in NIST's Harwell-Boeing collection can be downloaded in one of two formats: the Matrix Market format and the Harwell-Boeing format. We'll focus our attention on the Matrix Market format because NIST provides C routines to read Matrix Market files.

NOTE *Harwell-Boeing* identifies both a collection of sparse matrix files and a file format. The files we'll be working with in this chapter belong to the Harwell-Boeing collection but their data is structured according to NIST's Matrix Market format. These files will be referred to as Matrix Market files.

Matrix Market filenames end with the .mtx suffix, and the file we'll be working with is bcsstk05.mtx. The information contained in this file is simple to access and consists of three parts:

- *Banner*—Identifies the matrix format and the nature of the matrix (real or complex, symmetric or general).
- *Size information*—Identifies the dimensions of the matrix and the number of nonzero elements.
- *Data*—The row, column, and value of each nonzero element in the matrix. The row-column-value format is called the *coordinate format*.

For example, the first five lines of bcsstk05.mtx are as follows:

```
%%MatrixMarket matrix coordinate real symmetric
153 153 1288
1 1   3.1431392791300e+05
4 1 -8.6857870528200e+04
5 1  5.6340240342600e+04
```

The banner states that the matrix is real and symmetric, and that its values are stored in coordinate format. The next line states that the matrix dimensions are 153 by 153 and that the file provides 1,288 nonzero values. The first nonzero value is located at row 1, column 1 and the second is located at row 4, column 1.

NOTE If a matrix is symmetric, the Matrix Market file contains only its nonzero values on the diagonal and below it. As you read these values, remember that each value below the diagonal has a corresponding value above the diagonal.

These files can be read using regular C/C++ functions, but NIST makes our lives easier by providing its own I/O routines in mmio.c. This code is public domain, and copies of this file are included in each project in the Ch13 folder. Table 13.1 lists a subset of the functions that provide information about a matrix stored in a Matrix Market file.

Table 13.1   I/O functions for analyzing Matrix Market files

Function name	Description
int mm_read_banner(FILE* f, MM_typecode *t)	Reads the banner information into t
int mm_read_mtx_crd_size(FILE* f, int *num_rows, int *num_cols, int *non_zeros)	Provides size information of a matrix stored in coordinate format (sparse matrices)
int mm_read_mtx_array_size(FILE* f, int *num_rows, int *num_cols)	Provides size information of a matrix stored in array format (dense matrices)
int mm_is_sparse(MM_typecode code)	Returns whether the matrix is sparse (1) or dense (0)
int mm_is_real(MM_typecode code)	Returns whether the matrix is real-valued (1) or complex-valued (0)
int mm_is_symmetric(MM_typecode code)	Returns whether the matrix is symmetric (1) or not symmetric (0)

These functions are easy to understand and use. The first two, mm_read_banner and mm_read_mtx_crd_size, are particularly important. The first reads the file's banner information into a MM_typecode structure, which can be used to provide information about the matrix's properties through functions like mm_is_real and mm_is_symmetric. The mm_read_mtx_crd_size returns size information for the matrix: the number of rows, the number of columns, and the number of nonzero elements.

The process of reading a sparse matrix's nonzero elements will usually take the following five steps:

1 Open the *.mtx file.
2 Read the matrix's banner information with mm_read_banner.
3 Read the matrix's size information with mm_read_mtx_crd_size.
4 Allocate memory to hold row, column, and value data.
5 Access each nonzero element of the *.mtx file with fscanf.

The following code reads data from the bcsstk05.mtx file and performs each of these five steps. Once it finishes reading the matrix values, it sorts the elements so that they're ordered by row instead of by column.

Listing 13.1   Reading a sparse matrix (read_mm.c)

```
...
void sort(int num, int *rows, int *cols, float *values) {
   int i, j, int_swap, index = 0;
   float float_swap;

   for(i=0; i<num; i++) {
      for(j=index; j<num; j++) {
         if(rows[j] == i) {
            if(j == index) {
               index++;
            }

            else if(j > index) {
               int_swap = rows[index];
               rows[index] = rows[j];
               rows[j] = int_swap;

               int_swap = cols[index];
               cols[index] = cols[j];
               cols[j] = int_swap;

               float_swap = values[index];
               values[index] = values[j];
               values[j] = float_swap;
               index++;
            }
         }
      }
   }
}

int main(int argc, char *argv[]) {

   FILE *mm_handle;
   MM_typecode code;
   int num_rows, num_cols, num_values, i;
   int *rows, *cols;
   float *values;
   double value_double;

   if ((mm_handle = fopen(MATRIX_FILE, "r")) == NULL) {      ◁─┐ Read
      perror("Couldn't open the MatrixMarket file");           │ matrix file
      exit(1);
   }
                                                              ◁─┐ Determine
   mm_read_banner(mm_handle, &code);                            │ matrix type
   if(mm_is_matrix(code))
      printf("This is a matrix.\n");
   else
      printf("This is not a matrix.\n");
   if(mm_is_sparse(code))
```

```
      printf("It is sparse, ");
   else
      printf("It is dense, ");
   if(mm_is_complex(code))
      printf("complex-valued, ");
   else
      printf("real-valued, ");
   if(mm_is_symmetric(code))
      printf("and symmetric.\n");
   else
      printf("and not symmetric.\n");

   mm_read_mtx_crd_size(mm_handle, &num_rows,              Read matrix
                    &num_cols, &num_values);               dimensions

   if(mm_is_symmetric(code) || mm_is_skew(code)
        || mm_is_hermitian(code)) {
     num_values += num_values - num_rows;
   }
   printf("It has %d rows, %d columns, and %d nonzero elements.\n",
        num_rows, num_cols, num_values);

   rows = (int*) malloc(num_values * sizeof(int));
   cols = (int*) malloc(num_values * sizeof(int));         Allocate
   values = (float*) malloc(num_values *                  memory
                        sizeof(float));

   i = 0;
   while(i < num_values) {
      fscanf(mm_handle, "%d %d %lg\n",
           &rows[i], &cols[i],                             Read nonzero
           &value_double);                                 elements
      values[i] = (float)value_double;              ◁──  ❶ Convert double
      cols[i]--;                                             to float
      rows[i]--;
      if((rows[i] != cols[i]) && (mm_is_symmetric(code) ||
           mm_is_skew(code) || mm_is_hermitian(code))) {
        i++;
        rows[i] = cols[i-1];
        cols[i] = rows[i-1];
        values[i] = values[i-1];
      }
      i++;
   }
   sort(num_values, rows, cols, values);
   fclose(mm_handle);

   free(rows);
   free(cols);
   free(values);
}
```

The nonzero values in a Matrix Market file are stored as double values. But most
OpenCL devices don't support double values, so it's a good idea to cast them to
floats, as shown in the code ❶. Also, Matrix Market row/column indices start at 1
instead of 0, so this code subtracts 1 from every index.

In addition to functions that provide information about matrices, the Matrix Market API also provides functions that create *.mtx files. The names of these functions closely resemble those in table 13.1, but `read` is replaced with `write` and `_is_` is replaced with `_set_`. For example, to write to a file, you'd use `mm_write_banner` instead of `mm_read_banner` and `mm_set_sparse` instead of `mm_is_sparse`.

At this point, you should have a solid understanding of what sparse matrices are and how to access them in code. The rest of this chapter explores different ways of solving linear systems associated with these matrices. We'll start with the method of steepest descent.

13.3 *The method of steepest descent*

Chapter 12 explained that linear systems like $Ax = B$ can be solved using QR decomposition and back-substitution. This is fine when A is small and dense, but trying to factor large, sparse matrices is a different matter. The solution process would require constructing a full matrix from the nonzero elements and operating on each of its N-by-N elements. This takes a great deal of memory and processing time.

It would be better if you could find a method that takes advantage of sparseness. That is, you want the number of floating-point operations to be dependent on the number of nonzero elements in the matrix, not on the matrix's size.

The goal of this section is to present such a method, called the method of steepest descent, or the SD method. The good news is that it relies on matrix-vector multiplication, which takes advantage of sparseness. The bad news is that SD relies on intelligent guesswork. Because this method requires a series of guesses, it's called an *iterative* method. In contrast, methods used to solve dense matrix systems are *direct* methods.

The SD method is not generally used in practical system solving, but once you understand how it works, I think you'll find it easier to understand other iterative methods, such as the conjugate gradient method presented in section 13.4. This section will discuss the theory behind SD and then show how it can be implemented in OpenCL. But first, it's important that you understand the properties of positive-definite matrices.

13.3.1 *Positive-definite matrices*

Vectors are commonly represented by arrows, and if $Ax = b$, then you can think of A as a transformation that converts an arrow called x into an arrow called b. Mathematicians frequently classify matrices by how they transform vectors, and if the two arrows have exactly the same length and direction, A is called an identity matrix.

Now suppose A transforms x so that b points in the opposite direction, or has a nonzero component that points in the opposite direction. If this is the case, then the dot product $x \cdot b$ will be negative. Similarly, if the dot product equals zero, then A has turned x so that the resulting vector points in an orthogonal direction.

Frequently, linear algebra routines require matrices that *never* flip a vector's direction or produce a vector that points in an orthogonal direction. That is, $x \cdot (Ax)$ must be positive for *all x*. If a matrix meets this requirement, we call it *positive definite*. This property will play an important role in the discussion that follows.

13.3.2 *Theory of the method of steepest descent*

Your goal is to find *x* in the equation $Ax = b$. Let's make x_0 your first guess. You can test this guess by computing Ax_0 and subtracting it from Ax. If the difference is larger than your tolerance, you'll need to make more guesses. But you can't just guess at random. You need a method that will ensure that your next guess, x_1, will be closer to *x* than x_0 was. But how?

Answering this question requires calculus. You start by obtaining a function *f* whose slope at every point *z* equals $Az - b$. Deriving this function is beyond the scope of this discussion, but the end result is as follows:

$$f(z) = \frac{1}{2}z \cdot (Az) - z \cdot b + c$$

$$f'(z) = Az - b$$

Here, $b = Ax$ and *c* is an arbitrary constant. Besides its slope, this function has a very important property. To understand it, you need to set *z* equal to two vectors $x + y$. If you assume that *A* is symmetric, you can substitute $x + y$ for *z* and arrive at the following result:

$$f(z) = f(x) + \frac{1}{2}y \cdot Ay$$

If *A* is positive-definite, the second term must be greater than zero for all *y*. Therefore, f(z) takes its minimum value when $z = x$. This is shown in figure 13.3, which depicts the graph of f(z). The figure includes both f(x) and f(x_0), where x_0 is your first guess at *x*.

The slope of f(z) equals $Az - b$, so f'(x_0) equals $Ax_0 - b$. f'(x_0) identifies the direction of the greatest rise of the function at $z = x_0$, so the direction of the greatest descent at

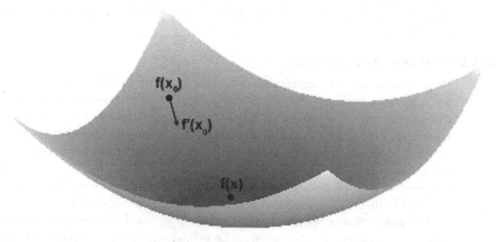

Figure 13.3   Surface plot of f(z)

$z = x_0$ is given by $-f'(x_0)$, or $b - Ax_0$. This direction is very important, and you'll call it r_0, or the residual. With this residual, you'll make your next guess in the following manner:

$$x_1 = x_0 + \alpha r_0$$

The residual vector r_0 tells you the direction you should take from x_0 to x_1. The scalar α is a parameter that varies along the line from x_0 to x_1. Because your goal is to descend, you want to choose x_1 so that $f(x_0 + \alpha r_0)$ will be less than $f(z)$ at every other point on the line. This minimum value can be found by setting $f'(z)$ equal to zero. This is given in the following equation:

$$\frac{d(f(x_0 + \alpha r_0))}{d\alpha} = f'(x_0 + \alpha_0 r_0) \cdot r_0 = 0$$

This equation uses α_0 to denote the distance from x_0 to x_1. It also states that, for $f(x_1)$ to be a minimum, $f'(x_1)$ must be orthogonal to r_0. You know that $r_1 = -f'(x_1)$, so you can state that r_0 must be orthogonal to r_1. This is shown in figure 13.4.

You know that r_1 equals $b - Ax_1$ and that it is orthogonal to r_0. With this information, you can determine α_0 in the following manner:

$$r_1 \cdot r_0 = 0$$

$$(b - Ax_1) \cdot r_0 = 0$$

$$(b - A(x_0 + \alpha_0 r0)) \cdot r_0 = 0$$

$$(b - Ax_0 - \alpha_0 Ar_0) \cdot r_0 = 0$$

$$\alpha_0 Ar_0 \cdot r_0 = (b - Ax_0) \cdot r_0$$

$$\alpha_0 = \frac{r_0 \cdot r_0}{Ar_0 \cdot r_0}$$

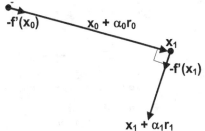

Figure 13.4   Using residuals to make further guesses

With this formula for α_0, you can arrive at your second guess, x_1. You can continue using this process to make further guesses (x_2, x_3, x_4, and so on), and test each by comparing the length of the corresponding residual, $|r_i|$, to a tolerance.

You don't have to compute $r_i = b - Ax_i$ for every guess. Instead, you can base each r_i on the preceding r_i. This is shown in the following equations:

$$r_i = b - Ax_i$$
$$r_i = b - A(x_{i-1} + \alpha_{i-1} r_{i-1}) = b - Ax_{i-1} + \alpha_{i-1} Ar_{i-1}$$
$$r_i = r_{i-1} + \alpha_{i-1} Ar_{i-1}$$

The advantage of computing r_i in this manner is that the matrix-vector product Ar_{i-1} was already computed in the process of finding α_{i-1}. Therefore, you only have to perform one matrix-vector product per iteration. If $|r_i|$ falls below a tolerance, you can stop guessing: x_i is your answer.

13.3.3 *Implementing SD in OpenCL*

While the theory behind the method of steepest descent is somewhat involved, the actual algorithm is straightforward. In coding your sparse matrix solver, you'll use the following steps:

1 Make the initial guess, x_0.
2 Compute the initial residual, $r_0 = b - Ax_0$. If you choose $x0 = [0, 0, 0, ...]$, $r0 = b$.
3 Compute the length from x_i to x_{i+1}, $\alpha_i = r_i \bullet r_i / A r_i \bullet r_i$.
4 Determine the next guess, $x_{i+1} = x_i + \alpha_i r_i$.
5 Compute the next residual, $r_{i+1} = r_i - \alpha_i A r_i$.
6 Find $|r_{i+1}|$. If this is less than your tolerance (0.01), your goal is reached.
7 Repeat steps 3 through 6.

The following code shows how these steps can be implemented in OpenCL. Here, the sparse matrix elements have been taken from the symmetric positive-definite matrix BCSSTK05. The elements of the b vector are determined at random.

Listing 13.2   Solving a sparse matrix system with the SD method (steep_desc.cl)

```
__kernel void steep_desc(int dim, int num_vals, __local float *r,
    __local float *x, __local float* A_times_r, __global int *rows,
    __global int *cols, __global float *A, __global float *b,
    __global float *result) {

   local float alpha, r_length;
   local int iteration;

   int id = get_local_id(0);
   int start_index = 0;
   int end_index = 0;
   float r_dot_r, Ar_dot_r;

   for(int i=id; i<num_vals; i++) {
      if((rows[i] == id) && (start_index == 0))
         start_index = i;
      else if((rows[i] == id+1) && (end_index == 0))  {
         end_index = i-1;
         break;
      }
      else if((i == num_vals-1) && (end_index == 0)) {
         end_index = i;
      }
   }

   r[id] = b[id];
   x[id] = 0.0f;
   barrier(CLK_LOCAL_MEM_FENCE);

   iteration = 0;
   while((iteration < 1000) && (r_length >= 0.01)) {

      A_times_r[id] = 0.0f;
      for(int i=start_index; i<=end_index; i++) {
```

Find matrix indices

Set initial guess/ residual

```
        A_times_r[id] += A[i] * r[cols[i]];
    }
    barrier(CLK_LOCAL_MEM_FENCE);

    if(id == 0) {
        r_dot_r = 0.0f;
        Ar_dot_r = 0.0f;
        for(int i=0; i<dim; i++) {
            r_dot_r += r[i] * r[i];               Compute
            Ar_dot_r += A_times_r[i] * r[i];      alpha
        }
        alpha = r_dot_r/Ar_dot_r;
    }
    barrier(CLK_LOCAL_MEM_FENCE);

    x[id] += alpha * r[id];                   Update guess/
    r[id] -= alpha * A_times_r[id];           residual
    barrier(CLK_LOCAL_MEM_FENCE);

    if(id==0) {
        r_length = sqrt(r_dot_r);
        iteration++;
    }
    barrier(CLK_LOCAL_MEM_FENCE);
}

result[0] = (float)iteration;
result[1] = r_length;
}
```

The BCSSTK05 matrix contains exceptionally large values, which means α will be very small. Because this code relies on floats instead of doubles, the lack of precision may prevent the kernel from reaching a result, x_n, sufficiently close to the theoretical answer, x. If it does produce x_n sufficiently close to x, we say that the function *converges*.

Thankfully, when it comes to solving systems represented by symmetric sparse matrices, we can do better than the SD method. The next section discusses the conjugate gradient (CG) method, which provides much faster convergence.

13.4   *The conjugate gradient method*

Like the steepest descent method, the conjugate gradient (CG) method makes a series of guesses to approximate x in $Ax = b$. Much of the theory and implementation of the CG method is similar to that for the SD method, but as you'll see, the convergence improves dramatically. This section presents how to implement this with OpenCL, but first, it's important to discuss the concepts of vector orthogonalization and conjugacy.

13.4.1 *Orthogonalization and conjugacy*

Chapter 12 discussed the dot product and vector projection, and showed how the two procedures made it possible to implement vector reflection, which is necessary for QR decomposition. Similarly, this section presents the concepts of vector orthogonalization and conjugacy, which are necessary for the CG method.

ORTHOGONALIZATION AND THE GRAM-SCHMIDT METHOD

I was once at a party where two women wore identical dresses. The second to arrive looked aghast at the first, left immediately, and returned wearing a different dress. When more women arrived, they compared their dresses to others and would probably have made similar switches if they'd worn similar dresses. In this way, all of the dresses at the party were made distinct.

The process of vector orthogonalization is similar. You start with a group of vectors, compare them in pairs, and make alterations until they're all completely different from one another. Two vectors are completely different, or orthogonal, if their dot product equals zero.

The Gram-Schmidt method orthogonalizes a set of vectors using vector projections. Vector projection was discussed in chapter 12, but as a quick review, the projection of a vector b on a vector a is the component of b that points in the direction of a. This is denoted $proj_a b$, and the equation is as follows:

$$proj_a b = \frac{a \cdot b}{|a|^2} a$$

Because $proj_a b$ has the same direction as a, $b - proj_a b$ must be orthogonal to a. Therefore, you can orthogonalize two vectors a and b by computing the projection of b on a and subtracting the projection from b.

You can continue this process for three vectors. If a third vector, c, is included in the space, the three orthogonal vectors (v_1, v_2, v_3) corresponding to (a, b, c) can be calculated as follows:

$$v_1 = a_1$$
$$v_2 = b - proj_{v1} b$$
$$v_3 = c - proj_{v1} c - proj_{v2} c$$

Note that this process projects c onto the orthogonal vectors v_1 and v_2, and not the input vectors a and b.

If there are n input vectors, $a_1...a_n$, the Gram-Schmidt process computes the nth orthogonal vector as follows:

$$v_n = a_n - \sum_{i=1}^{n-1} proj_{v_i} a_n$$

$$v_n = a_n - \sum_{i=1}^{n-1} \frac{v_i \cdot a_n}{|v_i|^2} v_1 = a_n - \sum_{i=1}^{n-1} \frac{v_i \cdot a_n}{v_1 \cdot v_1} v_i$$

The Gram-Schmidt process can produce orthogonal vectors for any number of non-orthogonal input vectors so long as the vectors are *linearly independent*. That is, no vector can be expressible as a weighted sum of the other vectors. If any vector is linearly *dependent* on the others, one of the orthogonal vectors will equal zero.

VECTOR CONJUGACY

Two vectors, p and q, are *conjugate* with respect to a matrix A if $p \bullet Aq$ equals zero. That is, two vectors are conjugate with respect to a matrix if the first vector is orthogonal to the product of the matrix and the second vector. If A is symmetric and positive-definite, then $p \bullet Aq = q \bullet Ap = 0$.

You can make a set of vectors conjugate to one another using a process similar to the Gram-Schmidt method. This is shown in the following equation:

$$v_n = a_n - \sum_{i=1}^{n-1} \frac{v_i \cdot Aa_n}{v_i \cdot Av_i} v_i$$

This relationship between vectors plays an important role in the CG method of solving sparse matrix systems.

13.4.2 *The conjugate gradient method*

The CG method has a great deal in common with the SD method, and in both cases, the goal is to make guesses, x_i, that lead from x_0 to x. Both methods use a residual vector, r_i, to judge how far the guesses are from the correct answer.

The primary difference is that, while the SD method uses r_i to set the direction from x_i to x_{i+1}, the CG method computes a new vector, p_i. The initial direction, p_0, is set equal to r_0, but each subsequent direction will be *conjugate* to the preceding direction. In equation form, this is as follows:

$$p_0 = r_0$$

$$p_i = r_i - \sum_{j=0}^{i-1} \frac{p_j \cdot Ar_i}{p_j \cdot Ap_j} p_j$$

Having chosen a direction, you can find subsequent guesses in a manner similar to that used for the SD method. The equations are as follows:

$$x_{i+1} = x_i + \alpha_i p_i$$

$$\alpha_i = \frac{r_i \cdot r_i}{p_i \cdot Ap_i}$$

The overall algorithm for using the CG method to solve a sparse matrix system requires the following eight steps:

1. Make the initial guess, x_0.
2. Compute the initial residual and direction by setting r_0 and p_0 equal to b.
3. Compute the length from x_i to x_{i+1}, $\alpha_i = r_i \bullet r_i / p_i \bullet Ap_i$.
4. Determine the next guess, $x_{i+1} = x_i + \alpha_i p_i$.
5. Compute the next residual, $r_{i+1} = r_i - \alpha_i Ap_i$.
6. Compute the next direction, $p_{i+1} = r_{i+1} + (r_{i+1} \bullet r_{i+1} / r_i \bullet r_i) \, p_i$.
7. Find $|r_{i+1}|$. If this is less than your tolerance (0.01), your goal is reached.
8. Repeat steps 3 through 7.

The following code implements these steps in OpenCL. Much of the code is similar to that of listing 13.2, but now the p_i vector identifies the direction from x_i to x_{i+1}.

Listing 13.3   Solving a sparse matrix system with the CG method (conj_grad.cl)

```
__kernel void conj_grad(int dim, int num_vals, __local float *r,
      __local float *x, __local float* A_times_p, __local float *p,
      __global int *rows, __global int *cols, __global float *A,
      __global float *b, __global float *result) {

   local float alpha, r_length, old_r_dot_r, new_r_dot_r;
   local int iteration;

   int id = get_local_id(0);
   int start_index = -1;
   int end_index = -1;
   float Ap_dot_p;

   for(int i=id; i<num_vals; i++) {
      if((rows[i] == id) && (start_index == -1))
         start_index = i;
      else if((rows[i] == id+1) && (end_index == -1)) {
         end_index = i-1;
         break;
      }
      else if((i == num_vals-1) && (end_index == -1)) {
         end_index = i;
      }
   }

   x[id] = 0.0f;
   r[id] = b[id];                                          Set initial
   p[id] = b[id];                                          guess/residual/direction
   barrier(CLK_LOCAL_MEM_FENCE);

   if(id == 0) {
      old_r_dot_r = 0.0f;
      for(int i=0; i<dim; i++) {
         old_r_dot_r += r[i] * r[i];
      }
      r_length = sqrt(old_r_dot_r);
   }
   barrier(CLK_LOCAL_MEM_FENCE);

   iteration = 0;
   while((iteration < 1000) && (r_length >= 0.01)) {

      A_times_p[id] = 0.0f;
      for(int i=start_index; i<=end_index; i++) {
         A_times_p[id] += A[i] * p[cols[i]];
      }
      barrier(CLK_LOCAL_MEM_FENCE);

      if(id == 0) {
         Ap_dot_p = 0.0f;
         for(int i=0; i<dim; i++) {
            Ap_dot_p += A_times_p[i] * p[i];
         }                                                 Compute
         alpha = old_r_dot_r/Ap_dot_p;                     alpha
      }
      barrier(CLK_LOCAL_MEM_FENCE);

      x[id] += alpha * p[id];
```

```
      r[id] -= alpha * A_times_p[id];
      barrier(CLK_LOCAL_MEM_FENCE);

      if(id == 0) {
         new_r_dot_r = 0.0f;
         for(int i=0; i<dim; i++) {
            new_r_dot_r += r[i] * r[i];
         }
         r_length = sqrt(new_r_dot_r);
      }
      barrier(CLK_LOCAL_MEM_FENCE);

      p[id] = r[id] + (new_r_dot_r/old_r_dot_r) * p[id];
      barrier(CLK_LOCAL_MEM_FENCE);

      old_r_dot_r = new_r_dot_r;

      if(id==0) {
         iteration++;
      }
      barrier(CLK_LOCAL_MEM_FENCE);
   }
   result[0] = iteration * 1.0f;
   result[1] = r_length;
}
```

Update
direction ⟵ ⌐

This code doesn't ensure that each direction vector, p_i, is conjugate to each preceding direction. Instead, it makes each new p_i conjugate to the preceding p_{i-1}. This means you don't have to store every direction vector and residual. However, each iteration requires storing two dot products of the residuals: $r_{i+1} \bullet r_{i+1}$ and $r_i \bullet r_i$.

This method converges to x much faster than the SD method, and explaining the precise reason for this improved convergence requires a great deal of mathematics. If you're interested in learning more about CG, I strongly recommend a PDF titled *An Introduction to the Conjugate Gradient Method Without the Agonizing Pain,* by Jonathan Richard Shewchuk. This can be downloaded at http://www.cs.cmu.edu/~jrs/jrspapers.html.

13.5 Summary

The applications of finite element analysis are boundless, and analysts use FEA to model such diverse systems as astrophysics, structural engineering, and the movement of pollution in the atmosphere. In each case, analysts approximate the differential equations with linear equations, and because of the many zeros, these equations are solved as sparse matrices. The goal of this chapter has been to explain what these matrices are and how they can be solved in OpenCL.

Rather than generate sparse matrices using random values, this chapter has relied on a real matrix from NIST's Harwell-Boeing collection. This 153-by-153 matrix, BCSSTK05, corresponds to the structural analysis of a transmission tower. The first section of this chapter explained how to find the characteristics of this matrix through its Matrix Market file and then read its nonzero values. With minimal modification, the example code can be used to access any matrix in the Harwell-Boeing collection or any of the other matrices in NIST's Matrix Market site, http://math.nist.gov/MatrixMarket.

Next, this chapter presented two methods of solving symmetric sparse matrix systems like BCSSTK05. Both methods are iterative, which means they make multiple guesses at the answer and then test the accuracy of each guess. The difference between the two methods is how successive guesses are made. The steepest descent (SD) method relies on a residual vector to point from one guess to the next, while the conjugate gradient (CG) method computes separate direction vectors that are conjugate to one another. As demonstrated in code, the CG method converges to the answer faster than the SD method.

The SD and CG methods are only two of many algorithms available for solving sparse matrix systems. If a system isn't symmetric, a good choice is the biconjugate gradient stabilized method, better known as BiCGSTAB. Alternatively, multigrid methods are also becoming more popular in solving systems that involve linearized differential equations. For more information on these methods, I recommend *Iterative Methods for Sparse Linear Systems* by Yousef Saad.

In the next chapter, we'll put aside matrices and start concerning ourselves with signals. The goal is to analyze time-domain signals in the frequency domain, and the best tool for the job is the fast Fourier transform (FFT).

14

Signal processing and the fast Fourier transform

This chapter covers

- The theory of frequency analysis
- Analyzing frequencies with the discrete Fourier transform
- Accelerating frequency analysis with the fast Fourier transform

Throughout the world of engineering, there is no escaping the fast Fourier transform (FFT). Cellular phones, audio players, X-ray scanners, radar receivers, and biometric scanning systems all depend on the FFT to extract frequency information from signals that vary over time and space. And in each case, speed is of the essence—the faster the frequency data is obtained, the more analysis can be performed.

The goal of this chapter is to present the theory behind the fast Fourier transform and show how it can be implemented in OpenCL. In particular, we'll focus on the Cooley-Tukey algorithm, which is the most popular of the algorithms used to compute the FFT. This requires that the size of the data set be a power of 2, but many algorithms exist for analyzing data sets of different sizes.

In my opinion, the simplest way to understand the FFT is to study the discrete Fourier transform (DFT) first, and see how this simple algorithm can be accelerated by taking advantage of the DFT's mathematical properties. But before exploring the DFT, this chapter will discuss the theory behind frequency analysis.

14.1   Introducing frequency analysis

Suppose you have a CD of a rock concert, and for some reason, your favorite song is partially obscured by high-pitched noise. It could be feedback from the amplifiers or screaming from the audience or static from the recording process, but one way or another, it ruins the song. What can you do? One solution is called *digital remastering,* which improves the sound quality of recorded media by altering the digital values. This is commonly employed to remove noise from music recorded on vinyl or other perishable media.

To understand how digital remastering works, it's important to approach the problem in a mathematical manner. Suppose the duration of the song, denoted T, is 3 minutes and 20 seconds, for a total of 200 seconds. If the song had been recorded perfectly, you'd have an infinite number of sounds during those 200 seconds. We'll denote this collection of sounds by $x(t)$, where t denotes time in seconds from $t = 0$ to $t = 199$. For example, the exact sound at $t = 60$ sec is given by $x(60)$.

Unfortunately, CDs are not perfect recordings. Most CDs are sampled at 44,100 samples per second, so the digital data representing your song contains (44,100 samples/second) * (200 seconds) = 8,820,000 samples. We'll call this sequence of samples $x[n]$, where the square brackets imply a finite number of values. In this case, n identifies the sample number instead of the time. That is, $x[4630]$ denotes the sound corresponding to the 4,630[th] sample. The time between samples, measured in seconds, is denoted Δt.

Figure 14.1 depicts the difference between perfectly sampled $x(t)$ and CD-sampled $x[n]$. The data contained in $x(t)$ and $x[n]$ both relate to time, so we'll call $x(t)$ a *time-domain signal* and $x[n]$ a *time-domain sequence.*

Returning to the problem, it should be clear that you can't remove the high-pitched noise by manipulating $x[n]$ directly. If you reduce or remove any values of $x[n]$, you'll diminish the song and noise equally. Similarly, if you amplify any values of $x[n]$, you'll increase both the song and the noise.

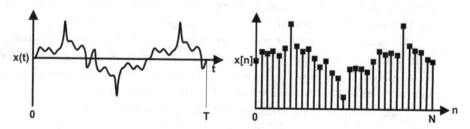

Figure 14.1   Time-domain signals: continuous and discrete

To understand how to remove noise from digital audio, you need to think of the song in terms of *frequency*. A signal's frequency tells you how often it changes during the course of a second. This is measured in Hertz, abbreviated Hz. For example, the highest string of a bass guitar vibrates nearly 98 times a second, so its frequency is 98 Hz. In general, the term *oscillation* is used to describe a signal's change over time.

In the real world, frequencies of most phenomena are spread across a range. For example, the vocal chords of the average human male vibrate between 85 and 180 Hz whereas the vocal chords of the average human female vibrate between 165 and 255 Hz.

We'll use the word *component* to identify the strength of a signal at a given frequency, and we'll denote this as $X(f)$. If a signal oscillates twelve-and-a-half times a second, its frequency component at 12.5 Hz, $X(12.5)$, will be greater than $X(f)$ at any other frequency. For a signal as complex as a song, the range of frequencies might look similar to that on the left side of figure 14.2. As shown, the frequencies corresponding to the noise (high-pitch) are on the right, while the components corresponding to the song (lower-pitch) are located toward the left.

The right side of figure 14.2 presents a finite selection of frequency components that correspond to the frequency range in $X(f)$. We'll use $X[k]$ to differentiate this set of components from the infinite set $X(f)$. Here, k is an integer that identifies the kth frequency component, so $X[26]$ returns the strength of the 26th frequency component. The frequency interval between samples, measured in Hertz, is denoted Δf.

Now we're getting close to our solution. You can't remove noise from your song by changing $x[n]$, but you can remove noise by changing $X[k]$. To do this, find the frequency components corresponding to the noise (usually toward the high end) and either diminish them or set them to zero. Similarly, if you want to amplify the bass, increase the frequency components at the lower end.

Two questions remain to be answered. First, how do you go from $x[n]$ to $X[k]$? Second, once you've modified $X[k]$, how do you convert it back to a form like $x[n]$? The answer to both questions involves the discrete Fourier transform, or DFT. This operation converts time-domain data to frequency-domain data, and the inverse DFT (IDFT) converts frequency-domain data to time-domain data. Therefore, to remove the noise from your song, you'd take the following three steps:

1 Convert $x[n]$ to $X[k]$ using the DFT.
2 Modify the frequency components of $X[k]$.
3 Convert the modified $X[k]$ to a new $x[n]$ using the IDFT.

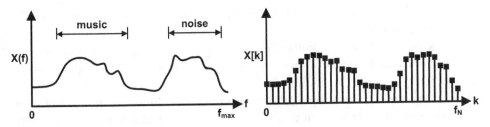

Figure 14.2 Frequency-domain signals: continuous and discrete

This process doesn't just apply to music. This type of analysis, called frequency analysis, is also used to find patterns in images, detect radar signatures from aircraft, and extract communication data from a wireless signal. In the next section, we'll look at the mathematics behind the DFT and see how to implement the algorithm in OpenCL.

14.2   *The discrete Fourier transform*

In 1822, the French physicist Joseph Fourier published *The Analytic Theory of Heat*, which presented a method of decomposing a complex mathematical function into a sum of simple functions. Over the centuries, this method has been applied to many more applications than the analysis of heat, and though Fourier focused on continuous functions, our goal is to decompose discrete signals, such as the digitized song from the previous section. We'll call these discrete signals *sequences*, and the procedure that implements Fourier's method on sequences is the discrete Fourier transform.

It's important to understand that the discrete Fourier transform (DFT) and the fast Fourier transform (FFT) both accomplish the same operation. They both convert time-domain sequences, such as the one depicted on the right-hand side of figure 14.1, into frequency-domain sequences, such as that shown on the right-hand side of figure 14.2. The FFT is faster but the DFT is easier to understand, so we'll start with this first. This section will present the mathematical theory behind the DFT, work through an example of its computation, and then show how it can be implemented in OpenCL.

But before we proceed, let's review the notation presented in the previous section.

- $x(t)$—The input signal; it contains infinite values, and t identifies time in seconds
- T—The period of the input signal, measured in seconds
- $x[n]$—The input sequence; it contains N values, and n identifies the sample index
- Δt—The time interval between $x[n]$ values, measured in seconds
- $X(f)$—The frequency response; it contains infinite values, and f identifies frequency in Hertz
- $X[k]$—The frequency sequence; it contains N values, and k identifies the frequency index
- Δf—The frequency interval between $X[k]$ values, measured in Hertz

14.2.1   *Theory behind the DFT*

One of the many operations discussed in chapter 12 is the dot product. This multiplies the corresponding components of two vectors and adds the products together. The result tells us how similar the two vectors are. A large dot product implies that the vectors point in similar directions, and a negative dot product implies that the vectors point in opposite directions.

As simple as it may seem, the dot product is the fundamental operation of the DFT. The crucial point is that if you take the dot product of $x[n]$ and a vector representing a given frequency, you'll see how similar $x[n]$ is to that frequency. More precisely, the result will tell you how often $x[n]$ oscillates with that frequency. We'll denote this second vector by $w_k[n]$, so the equation for $X[k]$ is as follows:

$$X[k] = x[n] \cdot w_k[n]$$

The DFT consists of N such dot products, and each produces a different value of $X[k]$. That is, the first dot product gives us $X[0]$, the second gives us $X[1]$, and so on.

Two questions arise. First, the DFT only computes components for N frequencies, so what frequencies should you be interested in? Second, how do you compute $w_k[n]$, the vector that represents a single frequency? Once you have answers to these questions, you'll be able to compute the dot product for $X[k]$. The following discussions will provide these answers.

FREQUENCIES OF INTEREST

The goal of the DFT is to compute $X[k]$ for a finite number of frequencies. It would be nice if you could select an arbitrary set of frequencies, but the DFT algorithm makes the selection for us. The values of the DFT's frequencies depend on the signal's period, T, and the number of samples, N.

The first frequency of interest, called the *fundamental frequency* or f_1, has a value of $1/T$. This represents a single oscillation over the course of the signal, so if a signal oscillates once during its period, f_1 will be significant. In the case of your song, $T = 200$ s, so the fundamental frequency equals $1/200 = 0.005$ Hz. This is below the human hearing range, but the DFT computes the frequency component at f_1 as $X[1] = x[n] \bullet w_1[n]$.

Further frequencies of interest, f_k, can be obtained by multiplying the fundamental frequency by k. This is expressed mathematically as

$$f_k = kf_1 = \frac{k}{T}$$

Just as f_k identifies the frequency corresponding to k oscillations in a period, f_0 identifies the frequency corresponding to no oscillations at all. This represents a frequency of 0 Hz. If a signal's value is constant over the course of its period, then it doesn't oscillate at all. In this case, $X[0]$ will be significant and components at higher frequencies will all equal 0.

For general signals, your highest frequency of interest is f_{N-1}, where N is the number of samples in $x[n]$. This gives us N frequencies of interest: f_0 through f_{N-1}. However, in some instances, you'll only need to compute components of frequencies up to $f_{N/2}$. The rationale for this will have to wait until after we examine the full DFT algorithm.

SINGLE-FREQUENCY VECTORS

For each frequency component of $x[n]$, the DFT computes the dot product of $x[n]$ and a vector that represents a single frequency. The values in these single-frequency vectors are given as *sinusoids*—the complex sums of a cosine and sine. The values of continuous sinusoids depend on frequency and time, so we'll denote them by $w_f(t)$, where f is the frequency corresponding to the sinusoid. Mathematically, $w_f(t)$ is represented with this equation:

$$w_f(t) = cos(2\pi ft) - i\,sin(2\pi ft)$$

The i in this equation represents $\sqrt{-1}$. Because $w_f(t)$ is the sum of a number multiplied by i and a number that isn't, $w_f(t)$ is a *complex number.* Complex numbers tend to make people nervous, so let's briefly review some of the basic theory:

- Each complex number, z, has a real part, denoted $Re(z)$, and an imaginary part, denoted $Im(z)$. If $z = a + bi$, $Re(z) = a$ and $Im(z) = b$.
- The conjugate of a complex number, denoted z^*, can be obtained by negating the imaginary part. If $z = a + bi$, $z^* = a - bi$.
- The modulus or magnitude of a complex number, denoted $|z|$, can be obtained by adding the squares of the real and imaginary parts. If $z = a + bi$, $|z| = sqrt(a^2 + b^2)$.
- Complex numbers can be added by adding the real parts and imaginary parts separately. If $z_1 = a + bi$ and $z_2 = c + di$, $z_1 + z_2 = (a + c) + (b + d)i$.
- Complex numbers can be multiplied in the following manner: if $z_1 = a + bi$ and $z_2 = c + di$, $z_1 z_2 = (ac - bd) + (ad + bc)i$.

The real part of $w_f(t)$ is $cos(2\pi ft)$ and the imaginary part is $-sin(2\pi ft)$. Figure 14.3 depicts both of these terms graphically. Note that the graphs of the cosine and negative sine both oscillate once from $t = 0$ to $t = T$. Therefore, these graphs present $w_f(t)$ where $f = f_1$. If you set f equal to f_2, the graphs oscillate twice, and if you set f equal to f_k, the graphs oscillate k times.

This function is helpful when you perform a continuous Fourier transform, but the DFT requires that you select a finite number of values from $w_f(t)$. For this reason, you need to rework the expression for $w_f(t)$ so that it depends only on n and k. As discussed

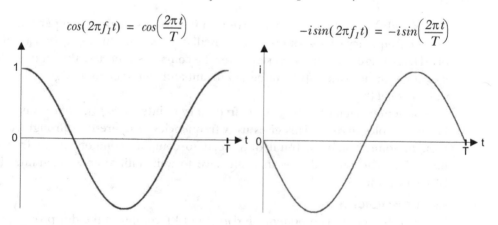

Figure 14.3   **The continuous sinusoid at the fundamental frequency**

earlier, your frequencies of interest are $f_k = k/T$, and you know that $n = \Delta t$. This gives us the following relationship:

$$w_k(t) = \cos\left(\frac{2\pi k(n\Delta t)}{T}\right) - i\sin\left(\frac{2\pi k(n\Delta t)}{T}\right)$$

One last step. You can relate the period of the signal, T, to the total number of samples, N, by noting that $T = N\Delta t$. Replacing this in the equation, you arrive at a final expression:

$$w_k(n) = \cos\left(\frac{2\pi nk}{N}\right) - i\sin\left(\frac{2\pi nk}{N}\right)$$

This gives us a vector with N values, and figure 14.4 depicts $w_k[n]$ from $n = 0$ to $N{-}1$. As with figure 14.3, this discrete sinusoid corresponds to the signal's fundamental frequency, given by $k = 1$.

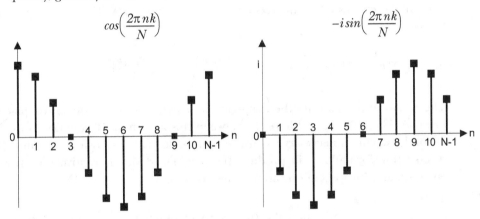

Figure 14.4 **The discrete sinusoid at the fundamental frequency**

Note that neither the cosine nor the sine returns to its starting value. Instead, they proceed from 0 to $N{-}1$. This is important to remember when computing these vectors in code. Now that you've arrived at the $w_k[n]$ vector, we can discuss the full DFT algorithm.

THE DFT AND IDFT EQUATIONS

The DFT computes the $X[k]$ vector by taking the dot product of $x[n]$ and $w_k[n]$ as k runs from 0 to $N{-}1$. This is commonly expressed using the DFT equation:

$$X[k] = x[n] \cdot w_k[n] = \sum_{n=0}^{N-1} x[n]\left(\cos\left(\frac{2\pi nk}{N}\right) - i\sin\left(\frac{2\pi nk}{N}\right)\right)$$

The relationship between $X[k]$ and $x[n]$ can also be expressed using matrix-vector multiplication. If you form the rows of a matrix W from $w_k[n]$ as k runs from 0 to $N{-}1$, the resulting matrix-vector product, $Wx = X$, can be expressed as follows:

$$
\begin{bmatrix}
w_0[0] & w_0[1] & w_0[2] & \cdots & w_0[N-1] \\
w_1[0] & w_1[1] & w_1[2] & \cdots & w_1[N-1] \\
w_2[0] & w_2[1] & w_2[2] & \cdots & w_2[N-1] \\
\cdots & \cdots & \cdots & \cdots & \cdots \\
w_{N-1}[0] & w_{N-1}[1] & w_{N-1}[2] & \cdots & w_{N-1}[N-1]
\end{bmatrix}
\begin{bmatrix}
x[0] \\
x[1] \\
x[2] \\
\cdots \\
x[N-1]
\end{bmatrix}
=
\begin{bmatrix}
X[0] \\
X[1] \\
X[2] \\
\cdots \\
X[N-1]
\end{bmatrix}
$$

This matrix, denoted W, is called the DFT matrix. If scaled properly, W is both unitary and symmetric, which means that its inverse, W^{-1}, equals its conjugate, W^*. You obtain the conjugate of a matrix by reversing the sign of every imaginary term. For the DFT, this means converting the negative imaginary sine in $w_k[n]$ into a positive imaginary sine.

This inverse matrix is important because it shows us how to compute the inverse DFT, or IDFT. The IDFT transforms frequency-domain data to time-domain data, and can be expressed in matrix-vector form as $x = W^{-1}X$. The IDFT equation is as follows:

$$
x[n] = X[k] \cdot w_k^*[n] = \frac{1}{N} \sum_{k=0}^{N-1} X[k]\left(\cos\left(\frac{2\pi nk}{N}\right) + i\sin\left(\frac{2\pi nk}{N}\right) \right)
$$

The $w_k^*[n]$ term identifies the conjugate of $w_k[n]$, in which $-i\sin(x)$ is replaced with $+i\sin(x)$. The only other difference between this and the DFT equation is the scaling factor $1/N$. This is necessary to ensure that, once $x[n]$ is transformed into $X[k]$, the inverse transformation will produce the original $x[n]$. Alternatively, both the DFT equation and IDFT equation can be scaled by $1/\sqrt{n}$.

A SIMPLE EXAMPLE

An example will clarify how the DFT works in practice. Figure 14.5 presents a time-domain signal, $x(t)$, with 16 samples. The first 6 samples form half of a triangle wave, and the other samples equal 0.

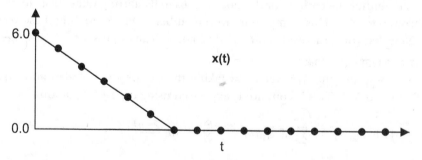

Figure 14.5 Example time-domain signal

For this example, you'll only compute four frequency components: $X[0]$, $X[1]$, $X[8]$, and $X[15]$. As discussed earlier, these components are obtained by taking the dot product of $x[n]$ and $w_k[n]$, and they are computed as follows:

$$X[0] = \sum_{n=0}^{N-1} x[n]\left(\cos\left(\frac{2\pi n(0)}{16}\right) - i\sin\left(\frac{2\pi n(0)}{16}\right)\right) = \sum_{n=0}^{N-1} x[n]$$

$$= 6.0 + 5.0 + 4.0 + 3.0 + 2.0 + 1.0 = 21.0$$

$$X[1] = \sum_{n=0}^{N-1} x[n]\left(\cos\left(\frac{2\pi n(1)}{16}\right) - i\sin\left(\frac{2\pi n(1)}{16}\right)\right) = \sum_{n=0}^{N-1} x[n]\left(\cos\left(\frac{\pi n}{8}\right) - i\sin\left(\frac{\pi n}{8}\right)\right)$$

$$= 6.0(1.0 - 0.0i) + 5.0(0.924 - 0.383i) + 4.0(0.707 - 0.707i)$$

$$+ 3.0(0.383 - 0.924i) + 2.0(0.0 - 1.0i) + 1.0(-0.383 - 0.924i)$$

$$= 14.213 - 10.439i$$

$$X[8] = \sum_{n=0}^{N-1} x[n]\left(\cos\left(\frac{2\pi n(8)}{16}\right) - i\sin\left(\frac{2\pi n(8)}{16}\right)\right) = \sum_{n=0}^{N-1} x[n]\left(\cos(\pi n) - i\sin(\pi n)\right)$$

$$= 6.0(1.0 - 0.0i) + 5.0(-1.0 - 0.0i) + 4.0(1.0 - 0.0i)$$

$$+ 3.0(-1.0 - 0.0i) + 2.0(1.0 - 0.0i) + 1.0(-1.0 - 0.0i)$$

$$= 6.0 - 5.0 + 4.0 - 3.0 + 2.0 - 1.0 = 3.0$$

$$X[15] = \sum_{n=0}^{N-1} x[n]\left(\cos\left(\frac{2\pi n(15)}{16}\right) - i\sin\left(\frac{2\pi n(15)}{16}\right)\right)$$

$$= \sum_{n=0}^{N-1} x[n]\left(\cos\left(\frac{15\pi n}{8}\right) - i\sin\left(\frac{15\pi n}{8}\right)\right)$$

$$= 6.0(1.0 - 0.0i) + 5.0(0.924 + 0.383i) + 4.0(0.707 + 0.707i)$$

$$+ 3.0(0.383 + 0.924i) + 2.0(0.0 + 1.0i) + 1.0(-0.383 + 0.924i)$$

$$= (14.213 + 10.439i)$$

Once the DFT is complete, $X[k]$ can be transformed back to $x[n]$ using the IDFT. This is just as simple to compute as the DFT. All you have to do is add the imaginary sine terms instead of subtracting them, and scale each element by $1/N$, or $1/16$ in this example.

REAL-VALUED DFT

If you look closely at the results from the DFT example, I hope you'll notice three points:

- The imaginary part of $X[0]$ equals 0
- The imaginary part of $X[8]$ equals 0
- $X[1]$ equals the conjugate of $X[15]$

If you're unfamiliar with the DFT, you might not think these points are important. But if the elements of $x[n]$ are all real-valued, then these statements will *always* hold true. In this case, you call $x[n]$ a real-valued sequence, and if $x[n]$ has N elements, you can make three general statements:

- The imaginary part of $X[0]$ always equals 0.
- The imaginary part of $X[N/2]$ always equals 0.
- For k between 1 and $(N/2)-1$, $X[k]$ always equals the conjugate of $X[N-k]$.

This last point is important because it means you don't have to compute the components $X[N/2+1]$ through $X[N-1]$. Instead, you can set $X[N-1]$ equal to the conjugate of $X[1]$, $X[N-2]$ equal to the conjugate of $X[2]$, and so on, until $X[N/2+1]$ is set to the conjugate of $X[N/2-1]$.

These properties of the real-valued DFT suggest an efficient manner for storing frequency components in memory. For $X[1]$ through $X[N/2-1]$, you'll store the real part of the frequency component followed by its imaginary part. Because $X[0]$ and $X[N/2]$ don't have imaginary parts, you'll store their real parts at the front of the sequence. This is shown in figure 14.6.

In this figure, the real part of $X[8]$ is stored second because the $X[N/2]$ component has no imaginary part. The last elements stored are the real and imaginary parts of $X[N/2-1]$.

This storage method is convenient, but it presents a problem. Because the IDFT rarely transforms real-valued data, IDFT code requires that frequency data be stored normally: $X[0]$ through $X[N-1]$ in real-imaginary pairs. Therefore, the IDFT code may need to be modified to transform data stored in this manner.

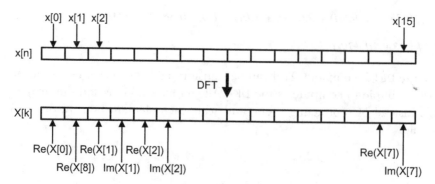

Figure 14.6   Storing frequency components of a real-valued DFT

The next section presents code for a real-valued DFT that computes only the frequency components from $X[0]$ through $X[N/2]$. It stores its results using the method depicted in figure 14.6.

14.2.2 OpenCL and the DFT

The DFT can be implemented in parallel by assigning each work-item to compute a frequency component of $x[n]$. For a real-valued DFT, only $N/2+1$ work-items are necessary, and each computes a value of $X[k]$ from $X[0]$ through $X[N/2]$.

The following listing shows how these frequency components can be computed. Each work-item constructs two `float4` vectors, `w_real` and `w_imag`, containing the cosine and sine values. Then, using the `dot` function, each updates `X_real` with the dot product of $x[n]$ and the cosine values, and `X_imag` with the dot product of $x[n]$ and the sine values. Note that the filename and function name are called *rdft* because this performs a DFT on real-valued data.

Listing 14.1 The discrete Fourier transform: rdft.cl

```
__kernel void rdft(__global float *x) {

   int N = (get_global_size(0)-1)*2;
   int num_vectors = N/4;

   float X_real = 0.0f;
   float X_imag = 0.0f;

   float4 input, arg, w_real, w_imag;
   float two_pi_k_over_N =
         2*M_PI_F*get_global_id(0)/N;

   for(int i=0; i<num_vectors; i++) {
      arg = (float4) (two_pi_k_over_N*(i*4),
                      two_pi_k_over_N*(i*4+1),        Compute
                      two_pi_k_over_N*(i*4+2),        sine/cosine
                      two_pi_k_over_N*(i*4+3));       terms
      w_real = cos(arg);
      w_imag = sin(arg);

      input = vload4(i, x);
      X_real += dot(input, w_real);       Take dot-
      X_imag -= dot(input, w_imag);       products
   }
   barrier(CLK_GLOBAL_MEM_FENCE);

   if(get_global_id(0) == 0) {
      x[0] = X_real;
   }
   else if(get_global_id(0) == get_global_size(0)-1) {
      x[1] = X_real;                                      Store results
   }                                                      in memory
   else {
      x[get_global_id(0) * 2] = X_real;
      x[get_global_id(0) * 2 + 1] = X_imag;
   }
}
```

Each work-item stores its result in memory at a location that depends on its global ID. If the item's ID is 0, it stores its real part in the first position in memory. If the item's ID is $N/2$, it stores its real part in the second position in memory. Succeeding memory locations store successive real and imaginary parts from $X[1]$ to $X[N/2-1]$.

This code is simple to understand, but by taking advantage of the DFT's properties, researchers have constructed an algorithm that obtains the same output as the DFT with fewer operations. This algorithm is called the *fast Fourier transform*, and it's the topic of the next section.

14.3   *The fast Fourier transform*

Everyone wants to crunch their numbers at high speed, but if you're a radar analyst on an aircraft or a sonar analyst on a submarine, extracting frequency information becomes a matter of life or death. If you detect the enemy before the enemy detects you, you get to shoot first.

For this and similar reasons, mathematicians have spent decades trying to improve the speed of frequency analysis, and the most popular method is the Cooley-Tukey fast Fourier transform (FFT). Researchers have devised various modifications and variations on this algorithm since its publication in 1965, but its high speed and computational simplicity have made it the reigning champion.

The goal of this section is to present this algorithm and show how it can be coded in OpenCL. This presentation will rely on intuition instead of mathematical rigor and will start with an examination of three important properties of the DFT.

14.3.1   *Three properties of the DFT*

The FFT is not simple to understand, and in my opinion, mathematical derivations tend to make the algorithm more confusing. For this reason, I prefer to approach the subject by presenting three properties of the DFT that make it possible to accelerate its processing. In order of increasing complexity, these three properties are as follows:

- *The superposition property*—If two sequences are added together, the frequency components of the sum will be the sum of the individual frequency components.
- *The shifting property*—If a sequence is shifted to the right, the resulting frequency components will equal the original frequency components multiplied by a sinusoid.
- *The stretching property*—If a signal is stretched from N to $2N$ by placing a zero after every original sample, the new frequency components $X[0]$ through $X[N-1]$ will equal the old frequency components $X[0]$ through $X[N-1]$. Further, the components $X[N]$ through $X[2N-1]$ will equal the components $X[0]$ through $X[N-1]$.

These properties may not seem interesting by themselves, but once you fully grasp them, it's straightforward to combine them in such a way as to convert the DFT to the FFT.

THE SUPERPOSITION PROPERTY

The superposition property of the Fourier transform is one of the most fundamental concepts in signal processing. Thankfully, it's also easy to understand. The frequency components of the sum of two sequences equals the sum of the individual frequency components of the sequences. That is, if $z[n] = x[n] + y[n]$, then $Z'[k] = X'[k] + Y'[k]$. Using the DFT equation, this is easy to prove:

$$z[n] = x[n] + y[n]$$

$$Z[k] = \sum_{n=0}^{N-1} z[n]\left(\cos\left(\frac{2\pi nk}{N}\right) - i\sin\left(\frac{2\pi nk}{N}\right)\right)$$

$$= \sum_{n=0}^{N-1} (x[n] + y[n])\left(\cos\left(\frac{2\pi nk}{N}\right) - i\sin\left(\frac{2\pi nk}{N}\right)\right)$$

$$= \sum_{k=0}^{N-1} x[n]\left(\cos\left(\frac{2\pi nk}{N}\right) - i\sin\left(\frac{2\pi nk}{N}\right)\right) + \sum_{k=0}^{N-1} y[n]\left(\cos\left(\frac{2\pi nk}{N}\right) - i\sin\left(\frac{2\pi nk}{N}\right)\right)$$

$$= X[k] + Y[k]$$

It can be proved in a similar manner that a scaled sequence produces scaled frequency components. That is, if the DFT transforms $x[n]$ to $X[k]$ and c is a scalar, then $cx[n]$ will be transformed to $cX[k]$.

THE SHIFTING PROPERTY

If a sequence is shifted, or delayed, in time, the real and imaginary parts of the frequency components will be multiplied by a sinusoid. More precisely, if $x'[n] = x[n-n_0]$, then $X'[k] = X[k](\cos(2\pi n_0 k/N) - i\sin(2\pi n_0 k/N))$ as k runs from 0 to $N-1$. This relationship can be derived as follows:

$$X'[k] = \left(\sum_{n-n_0=0}^{N-1} x[n-n_0]\left(\cos\left(\frac{2\pi nk}{N}\right) - i\sin\left(\frac{2\pi nk}{N}\right)\right)\right) = \sum_{n=0}^{N-1} x[n-n_0]e^{\frac{-i2\pi nk}{N}}$$

$$= \sum_{n-n_0=0}^{N-1} x[n-n_0]e^{\frac{-2\pi(n-n_0)k}{N}} e^{\frac{-i2\pi n_0 k}{N}} = X[k]e^{\frac{-i2\pi n_0 k}{N}}$$

$$= X[k]\left(\cos\left(\frac{2\pi n_0 k}{N}\right) - i\sin\left(\frac{2\pi n_0 k}{N}\right)\right)$$

Figure 14.7 depicts the relationship between $X[k]$ and $X'[k]$ graphically. The graphs on the right present only the real part of the frequency components corresponding to $x[n]$ and $x[n-3]$. In the lower right, the real part of $X'[k]$ equals the real part of $X[k]$ multiplied by $\cos(3\pi k/16)$.

Shifting a sequence changes the real and imaginary parts of its frequency components, but the overall frequency response remains unchanged. This overall response is called the *magnitude*, which is obtained by taking the square root of the squares of the real and imaginary parts. This should make sense. If you delay pressing a key on a

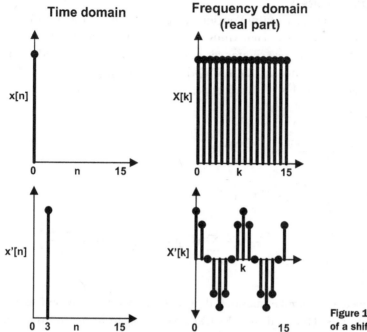

Figure 14.7   Frequency analysis of a shifted sequence

piano, the real and imaginary parts of the frequency components may change, but the overall frequency content of the signal stays the same.

THE STRETCHING PROPERTY

The term *stretching* refers to the process of placing a zero after every sample of $x[n]$, thereby doubling the size of the signal from N to $2N$. I can't think of a practical reason why anyone would want to do this, but stretching is very important theoretically: if you stretch a signal, the frequency components of the result have fascinating properties.

For example, if you stretch $x[n]$ to $x'[n]$, the new lower-frequency components, $X'[0]$ through $X'[N–1]$, will equal the old components, $X[0]$ through $X[N–1]$. Further, the upper-frequency components, $X'[N]$ through $X'[2N–1]$, have the same values as $X'[0]$ through $X'[N–1]$. Figure 14.8 presents this graphically.

In this figure, $x[n]$ is an exponentially decaying sequence with 16 samples and $x'[n]$ is a stretched version with 32 samples. The frequency components of $x'[n]$ equal those of $x[n]$ for $k = 0$ to $k = 15$. Also, the frequency components of $x'[n]$ from $k = 16$ to $k = 31$ are exactly equal to those from $k = 0$ to $k = 15$. This means that if you stretch a sequence, you don't need to compute the frequency components of the stretched sequence.

To get an intuitive feel for this property, look closely at the graph of $x'[n]$ and picture sines and cosines oscillating at frequencies f_k and f_{N+k}. You may notice that the sinusoids at both frequencies intercept the nonzero $x[n]$ elements in the same places. This means the dot product of $x[n]$ and $w_k[n]$ equals the dot product of $x[n]$ and $w_{N+k}[n]$, and therefore the frequency component $X[k]$ equals the component $X[N+k]$ for stretched sequences.

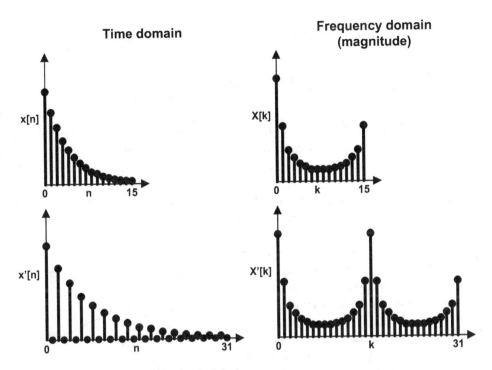

Figure 14.8 Frequency analysis of a stretched sequence

14.3.2 *Constructing the fast Fourier transform*

The merge sort algorithm compares elements two at a time, merges the two-element sorts into four-element sorts, merges the four-element sorts into eight-element sorts, and continues until the entire set is sorted. The FFT algorithm is similar in principle. It computes the frequency components of two samples at a time, merges this for four elements, then eight elements, and so on. In this manner, it computes $X[k]$ using a number of operations proportional to $N\log_2 N$, where N is the number of samples in $x[n]$. This is an improvement over the DFT, which requires a number of operations on the order of N^2.

To show how the FFT algorithm works, this discussion will walk through the frequency transformation of the four-element sequence [12.5, 6.0, –9.5, 2.0]. We'll first look at how to compute the FFT of a two-element sequence. Then, we'll derive the FFT merge process, which converts a pair of two-element FFTs into a four-element FFT. Finally, we'll look at how this merge process can be extended to transform larger sequences. After this derivation, we'll examine how the FFT's mathematical theory is implemented with high-speed OpenCL code.

THE TWO-ELEMENT FFT

The Cooley-Tukey FFT can be used to process any sequence whose size is a power of 2, and that includes sequences with only two elements. For these sequences, the FFT performs the same operation as the DFT. There are only two frequency components, $X[0]$ and $X[1]$, and they can be computed as follows:

$$X[0] = \sum_{n=0}^{1} x[n]\left(\cos\left(\frac{2\pi(0)k}{2}\right) - i\sin\left(\frac{2\pi(0)k}{2}\right) \right) = \sum_{n=0}^{1} x[n](1 - 0i) = x[0] + x[1]$$

$$X[1] = \sum_{n=0}^{1} x[n]\left(\cos\left(\frac{2\pi(1)k}{2}\right) - i\sin\left(\frac{2\pi(1)k}{2}\right) \right) = \sum_{n=0}^{1} x[n]\cos(\pi k) = x[0] - x[1]$$

It doesn't get much easier than this. The first frequency component equals the sum of $x[0]$ and $x[1]$, and the second frequency component equals the difference between them. For example, if $x[n] = [12.5, -9.5]$, $X[0] = 12.5 + (-9.5) = 3.0$ and $X[1] = 12.5 - (-9.5) = 22.0$.

Mathematicians depict this operation using figures called *butterfly diagrams*. Figure 14.9 presents the butterfly diagram corresponding to the preceding simple example.

The circles are called *nodes*, and each node returns the sum of its inputs. Both inputs arrive at the first node unchanged, so this node returns their sum, 3.0. But the −1 at the bottom of the diagram negates the lower input entering the second node, so this node returns the sum of 12.5 and −(−9.5), or 22.0.

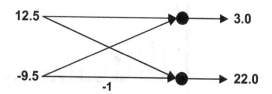

Figure 14.9   Butterfly diagram of a two-element FFT

THE FOUR-ELEMENT FFT

After the two-element operations are performed, the rest of the FFT consists of merging the results into larger and larger sequences. This can be complicated. I'll work through a simple four-element merge and then describe the general procedure.

Let's take the example sequence from the previous stage, [12.5, −9.5], and stretch it so that the resulting sequence equals [12.5, 0, −9.5, 0]. You'll call this $x[n]$. Because of the stretching property, you know that $X[k]$ equals [3.0, 22.0, 3.0, 22.0].

Let's take another sequence, [6.0, 2.0], and find its frequency components: [8.0, 4.0]. You'll stretch this sequence to produce [6.0, 0, 2.0, 0]. If you call this $y[n]$, the stretching property tells us that $Y[k]$ equals [8.0, 4.0, 8.0, 4.0]. So far, so good.

Next, let's *shift* $y[n]$ one place to the right, producing [0, 6.0, 0, 2.0]. You'll call this $y'[n]$. Because of the shifting property, you know that $Y'[k]$ equals $Y[k]$ multiplied by a sinusoid. That is, $Y'[k] = Y[k](\cos(2\pi k/4) + i\sin(2\pi k/4))$. The elements of $Y'[k]$ can be computed shown on the next page.

By these equations, $Y'[k]$ equals [8.0, −4.0i, −8.0, 4.0i]. This equals [8.0, 4.0, 8.0, 4.0] multiplied by the corresponding elements of [1, −i, −1, i].

Because of the superposition property, you know that the frequency components of a sum of sequences equals the sum of the individual frequency components. That is, if you add $x[n]$ and $y'[n]$ to form $z[n]$, $Z[k] = X[k] + Y'[k]$. In this example, adding

$$Y'[k] = Y[k]\left(cos\left(\frac{2\pi k}{4}\right) - i sin\left(\frac{2\pi k}{4}\right)\right)$$

$$Y'[0] = Y[0]\left(cos\left(\frac{2\pi(0)}{4}\right) - i sin\left(\frac{2\pi(0)}{4}\right)\right) = 8.0(1.0 - 0.0i) = 8.0$$

$$Y'[1] = Y[1]\left(cos\left(\frac{2\pi(1)}{4}\right) - i sin\left(\frac{2\pi(1)}{4}\right)\right) = 4.0(0.0 - 1.0i) = -4.0i$$

$$Y'[2] = Y[2]\left(cos\left(\frac{2\pi(2)}{4}\right) - i sin\left(\frac{2\pi(2)}{4}\right)\right) = 8.0(-1.0 - 0.0i) = -8.0$$

$$Y'[3] = Y[3]\left(cos\left(\frac{2\pi(3)}{4}\right) - i sin\left(\frac{2\pi(3)}{4}\right)\right) = 4.0(0.0 + 1.0i) = 4.0i$$

$x[n]$ and $y'[n]$ gives us $z[n] = [12.5, 6.0, -9.5, 2.0]$. Adding $X[k]$ and $Y'[k]$, you get $Z[k]$ = $[3.0, 22.0, 3.0, 22.0] + [8.0, i4.0, -8.0, -i4.0] = [11.0, 22.0 + i4.0, -5.0, 22.0 - i4.0]$.

This may seem complicated, but by stretching, shifting, and adding, you can compute the Fourier transform of $[12.5, 6.0, -9.5, 2.0]$ without performing a full DFT. The general rules for computing a four-element FFT are as follows:

1   Compute the two-element FFT of the first and third elements and the two-element FFT of the second and fourth elements.
2   Obtain the frequency components of the stretched sequences by repeating the original frequency components.
3   Multiply the frequency components of the second sequence by a sinusoid. This corresponds to shifting the sequence.
4   Add the frequency components of the first sequence to those of the second sequence.

This merge process is the heart of the FFT, and when I first encountered the algorithm, I had to work through several examples before this process made sense. I also found it helpful to trace through butterfly diagrams. Figure 14.10 presents the diagram corresponding to the full four-element example.

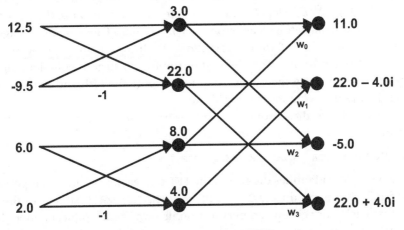

Figure 14.10   Butterfly diagram of a four-element FFT

There are two important points to note. First, the input elements are split into even/odd pairs before the processing starts. That is, this FFT processes elements $x[0]$, $x[2]$, $x[1]$, and $x[3]$ in that order. If there were eight input elements, they would be processed as follows: $x[0]$, $x[4]$, $x[2]$, $x[6]$, $x[1]$, $x[5]$, $x[3]$, $x[7]$. This rearranging is called *bit reversal* because the bits that make up an element's index must be reversed to obtain the element's position. For example, if you reverse the bits of the index 3, 0x011, you get 0x110, or 6. This means $x[3]$ takes the position that $x[6]$ would normally take in an eight-element FFT. Similarly, $x[6]$ takes the position that $x[3]$ would normally take.

It's also important to notice the w_k terms on the right side of the diagram. These identify the elements of the sinusoid used to multiply a shifted sequence. For a four-element FFT, the w_k terms equal $\cos(2\pi k/4) - i\sin(2\pi k/4)$ as k runs from 0 to 3, or $[1, -i, -1, i]$. These w_k elements scale values on the nearby lines. For example, the upward arrow from the node equaling 4.0 is multiplied by w_1, or $-i$. Therefore, the final node returns $22 - 4i$. In an eight-element FFT, w_k equals $\cos(2\pi k/8) - i\sin(2\pi k/8)$ as k runs from 0 to 7.

The process used to merge two-element FFTs into a four-element FFT can be further extended to compute FFTs of any size, as long as the size is a power of 2. In each case, the input elements are stretched, shifted, and added to form two-element FFTs, then four-element FFTs, and so on until the entire N-element FFT is computed.

Next, we'll look at how to code this algorithm in OpenCL.

14.3.3 *Implementing the FFT with OpenCL*

If a sequence contains N elements, the FFT requires $\log_2 N$ stages to compute its frequency components. The first stage computes $N/2$ two-element FFTs, the second stage merges the results to form $N/4$ four-element FFTs, and this merging continues all the way up to the final stage, which computes the N-element FFT. In general, stage k performs $N/(2*k)$ FFTs, each of whose size is $2k$.

If the FFT computation is partitioned among D work-items, and D is a power of 2 less than N, then each work-item computes the first $\log_2(N/D)$ stages of the FFT. In the final stages $(\log_2 N - \log_2(N/D) = \log_2 D)$, the work-items must synchronize their processing.

An example will make this clear. Suppose $x[n]$ contains 64 elements (6 stages) and you want to compute its FFT with 4 work-items. Each work-item will process the first $\log_2(64/4) = 4$ stages on its own. Then, after the fourth stage is complete, the work-items need to synchronize their processing to compute the fifth and sixth stages. Figure 14.11 depicts this relationship graphically.

Now let's organize these work-items into work-groups. If you take N as the total number of elements to be processed, N can be given as follows:

```
N = NUM_GROUPS * LOCAL_SIZE * ELEMENTS_PER_ITEM
```

ELEMENTS_PER_ITEM identifies the size of the FFT that each work-item can perform on its own. Similarly, the product LOCAL_SIZE * ELEMENTS_PER_ITEM tells us the size of the FFT that each work-group can perform on its own. To keep local and global synchronization to a minimum, you want to make these values as large as possible. To

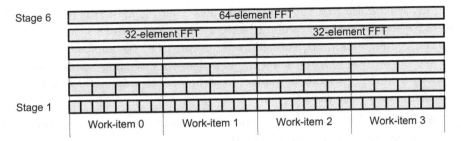

Figure 14.11 A 64-element FFT with 4 work-items

determine the maximum number of work-items in a work-group (LOCAL_SIZE), you use the clGetKernelWorkGroupInfo function presented in chapter 10.

To find the maximum number of elements that can be processed by each work-item (ELEMENTS_PER_ITEM), you need to determine how much local memory is available to each work-group. If each group can access MEM_SIZE bytes, each work-item can access MEM_SIZE/LOCAL_SIZE bytes.

To determine the size of a local memory block, you need to call clGetDeviceInfo with the CL_DEVICE_LOCAL_MEM_SIZE parameter. The following lines of code show how clGetDeviceInfo and clGetKernelWorkGroupInfo work together to tell us how much memory can be made available to each work-item:

```
size_t local_size;
cl_ulong local_mem_size, max_mem_per_item;

clGetKernelWorkGroupInfo(kernel, device, CL_KERNEL_WORK_GROUP_SIZE,
    sizeof(local_size), &local_size, NULL);

clGetDeviceInfo(device, CL_DEVICE_LOCAL_MEM_SIZE, sizeof(local_mem_size),
    &local_mem_size, NULL);

max_mem_per_item = local_mem_size/max_local_size;
```

The source code in the Ch14/fft/fft.c file uses similar function calls to find the maximum FFT that can be computed by each work-group and work-item. In this FFT, each element consists of two floats: a real value and an imaginary value.

On my target device, the maximum work-group size is 256, the local memory size is 32,768 bytes, and each float occupies 4 bytes. Therefore, each work-item can access 32,768/256 or 128 bytes. This memory can hold 128/(4*2) = 16 elements, so each item can perform a 16-element FFT on its own, and each work-group can perform a 4,096-element FFT on its own (32,768/(2*4) = 4,096).

Large-scale FFTs require multiple work-groups, and the only way to synchronize these work-groups is to execute multiple kernels. The first kernel deployed by the Ch14/fft host application, fft_init, directs each work-group to perform a separate FFT. On my system, fft_init computes one 4,096-element FFT for each work-group executing the kernel.

Next, the host application merges N-element FFTs into $2N$-element FFTs by executing the fft_stage kernel. This is called repeatedly until the entire FFT is completed.

On my system, the first `fft_stage` combines 4,096-element FFTs into 8,192-element FFTs, the second iteration combines 8,192-element FFTs into 16,384-element FFTs, and successive iterations are performed until the entire FFT is completed.

No matter how well you know the FFT algorithm, reading and writing actual FFT code is a difficult process. To explain how the `fft_init` kernel works, I'll divide the discussion into three parts:

- Each work-item loads data from global memory, computes 4-point FFTs, and stores the results in local memory.

- Each work-item continues computing larger FFTs (8-point, 16-point, and so on) until it uses all of the local memory available to it.

- The work-items in the work-group work together to compute as large an FFT as the entire local memory will support.

PART 1: LOADING DATA AND PERFORMING INITIAL FFT

The first part of `kernel_init` loads data from global memory and begins the initial stages of the FFT processing.

Listing 14.2   The fast Fourier transform, part 1: fft_init.cl

```
...
__kernel void fft_init(__global float2* g_data, __local float2* l_data,
                       uint points_per_group, uint size, int dir) {
   ...
   points_per_item = points_per_group/get_local_size(0);
   l_addr = get_local_id(0) * points_per_item;
   g_addr = get_group_id(0) * points_per_group + l_addr;

   for(i=0; i<points_per_item; i+=4) {
      index = (uint4)(g_addr, g_addr+1, g_addr+2, g_addr+3);
      mask_left = size/2;
      mask_right = 1;
      shift_pos = log2(size)-1;
      br = (index << shift_pos) & mask_left;
      br |= (index >> shift_pos) & mask_right;

      while(shift_pos > 1) {
         shift_pos -= 2;
         mask_left >>= 1;
         mask_right <<= 1;
         br |= (index << shift_pos) & mask_left;
         br |= (index >> shift_pos) & mask_right;
      }

      x1 = g_data[br.s0];
      x2 = g_data[br.s1];
      x3 = g_data[br.s2];
      x4 = g_data[br.s3];

      sum12 = x1 + x2;
      diff12 = x1 - x2;
      sum34 = x3 + x4;
      diff34 = (float2)(x3.s1 - x4.s1,
```

Bit-reverse address vector

Load global data

Perform four-element FFT

```
                              x4.s0 - x3.s0)*dir;
      l_data[l_addr] = sum12 + sum34;
      l_data[l_addr+1] = diff12 + diff34;
      l_data[l_addr+2] = sum12 - sum34;            Perform four-
      l_data[l_addr+3] = diff12 - diff34;          element FFT
      l_addr += 4;
      g_addr += 4;
   }...
```

Throughout this code, data is loaded, processed, and stored using float2 vectors, each of which contains a real float and an imaginary float. Before these vectors are loaded, however, each work-item needs to bit-reverse the input addresses. The first part of kernel_init reverses the bits of all four addresses at once. For example, if work-item 0 starts with indices [0, 1, 2, 3], the bit-reversal will return [0, 8, 4, 12].

Once the work-item obtains the bit-reversed addresses, it loads four float2 values from global memory (g_data) and performs 4-point FFTs on each group of four values. As each FFT completes, the kernel stores the result in local memory (l_data) and repeats the procedure for further groups of four elements.

The dir variable controls whether the FFT is forward (time-domain to frequency-domain) or backward (frequency-domain to time-domain). If dir is set to 1, the DFT equation will be used and the imaginary sine terms will be negative. If dir is set to –1, the IDFT equation will be used and imaginary sine terms will be positive.

PART 2: PERFORMING SUCCESSIVE STAGES OF THE FFT

After performing 4-point FFTs, each work-item will merge the results into larger FFTs. The size of the final FFT in this stage depends on how much local memory is available to each work-item. For example, if a local memory block contains LOCAL_MEM_SIZE bytes and each work-group contains 256 work-items, each work-item can access LOCAL_MEM_SIZE/256 bytes. If each complex value occupies 2 floats or 8 bytes, each work-item can perform an FFT of size LOCAL_MEM_SIZE/(256*8). That's shown in the following listing.

Listing 14.3   The fast Fourier transform, part 2: fft.cl

```
...
for(N2 = 4; N2 < points_per_item; N2 <<= 1) {
   l_addr = get_local_id(0) * points_per_item;
   for(fft_index = 0; fft_index < points_per_item; fft_index += 2*N2) {
      x1 = l_data[l_addr];
      l_data[l_addr] += l_data[l_addr + N2];
      l_data[l_addr + N2] = x1 - l_data[l_addr + N2];
      for(i=1; i<N2; i++) {
         cosine = cos(M_PI_F*i/N2);                          Compute
         sine = dir * sin(M_PI_F*i/N2);                      trigonometric terms
         wk = (float2)(l_data[l_addr+N2+i].s0*cosine +
               l_data[l_addr+N2+i].s1*sine,
               l_data[l_addr+N2+i].s1*cosine -
               l_data[l_addr+N2+i].s0*sine);
         l_data[l_addr+N2+i] =                               Compute frequency
               l_data[l_addr+i] - wk;                        components
         l_data[l_addr+i] += wk;
      }
```

```
        l_addr += 2*N2;
    }
}
barrier(CLK_LOCAL_MEM_FENCE);
...
```

This code sets N2 equal to half the length of the current FFT. The first iteration performs 8-point FFTs, so N2 is set equal to $2^3/2 = 4$. N2 doubles with each new stage until it equals the number of elements assigned to the work-item.

The code in this part consists of one outer loop and two inner loops. The outer loop corresponds to the FFT stage being computed, and the inner loops perform the FFTs needed for the stage. With each iteration of the inner loops, the work-item computes a cosine and sine value and multiplies this by the element at a distance equal to N2. This float2, called wk, is used to update two elements:

- l_data[l_addr+N2+i] = l_data[l_addr+i] – wk
- l_data[l_addr+i] = l_data[l_addr+i] + wk

When the outer loop completes, each work-item reaches a barrier and waits for the other work-items to complete their processing. Once every work-item has completed, the next part of the application starts.

PART 3: PERFORMING FINAL STAGES OF THE FFT

After the work-items complete their individual FFTs, they work together to compute larger FFTs for the entire work-group. This continues until all of the available local memory is used. For example, if a local memory block contains LOCAL_MEM_SIZE bytes and each complex value occupies 2*sizeof(float) = 8 bytes, each work-group will ultimately perform an FFT whose size is LOCAL_MEM_SIZE/8. That's shown in the following listing.

Listing 14.4   The fast Fourier transform, part 3: fft.cl

```
...
stage = 2;
for(N2 = points_per_item; N2 < points_per_group; N2 <<= 1) {
    start = (get_local_id(0) +
            (get_local_id(0)/stage)*stage) *          Assign work-
            (points_per_item/2);                       item position
    angle = start % (N2*2);
    for(i=start; i<start + points_per_item/2; i++) {
        cosine = cos(M_PI_F*angle/N2);
        sine = dir * sin(M_PI_F*angle/N2);
        wk = (float2)(l_data[N2+i].s0*cosine + l_data[N2+i].s1*sine,
                      l_data[N2+i].s1*cosine - l_data[N2+i].s0*sine);
        l_data[N2+i] = l_data[i] - wk;
        l_data[i] += wk;
        angle++;
    }
    stage <<= 1;                                        Synchronize
    barrier(CLK_LOCAL_MEM_FENCE);                       work-items
}
...
```

This code resembles the code in listing 14.3, but there are a number of important differences. First, each work-item is given a position within a larger FFT, and each processes a subset of the FFT's elements. This position is assigned with the following line of code:

```
start = (get_local_id(0) + (get_local_id(0)/stage)*stage) *
        (points_per_item/2);
```

As each work-item completes processing its subset of FFT elements, it reaches a barrier that forces it to wait for the other work-items to finish. Note that this barrier halts the work-items after *every stage*. This is because, with all the work-items working together, a new stage can't be started until the preceding stage is completely finished.

Once the `fft_init` kernel completes, the host application executes further stages of the FFT by deploying the `fft_stage` kernel. This kernel merges previous results into larger FFTs, and continues executing until the entire FFT is computed.

If the host application sets the DIRECTION macro to –1, the inverse FFT will be performed. This executes the same kernels as the forward FFT, but after the last `fft_stage` completes, the inverse FFT executes `fft_scale` to divide each result by the number of points.

14.4 Summary

Of all the mathematical algorithms discussed in this book, the FFT is my favorite. No other algorithm combines mathematical beauty with hard, practical utility. It is the most crucial algorithm in the field of signal processing, and the better you understand it, the faster your systems will execute.

The first part of this chapter discussed the topic of frequency analysis, focusing on how to remove noise from a song using digital remastering. The goal is to sample a continuous time-domain signal, $x(t)$, to produce a time-domain sequence, $x[n]$. The discrete Fourier transform (DFT) transforms $x[n]$ into a sequence containing frequency components, $X[k]$, and you can remove noise by setting unwanted frequencies to zero. Then the inverse DFT transforms the frequency components back into a time-domain signal.

The rest of the chapter explored the mathematics behind these transformations, and began with a discussion of the internals of the DFT. This simple algorithm consists of a series of dot products involving $x[n]$ and sinusoids of various frequencies. The first frequency of interest corresponds to a single oscillation over the course of the signal's period, and further frequencies are multiples of this. If a signal is real-valued, the DFT only needs to compute components for frequencies f_0 through $f_{N/2}$. The rest can be determined through symmetry.

By combining three properties of the DFT (superposition, shifting, and stretching), we can derive a better algorithm for extracting frequency data: the fast Fourier transform (FFT). This computes the DFTs of element pairs, merges the results into four-element FFTs, then eight-element FFTs, and so on. If a digital sequence contains N elements, the FFT requires $\log_2 N$ stages.

Despite its improved performance, the FFT isn't as easy to execute in parallel as the DFT. In a parallel DFT, each work-item can compute a frequency component independently, and only one synchronization point is required. In a parallel FFT, multiple synchronization points are required. Synchronization can take a great deal of time, so it may be worth your while to experiment with frequency analysis using both the DFT and the FFT.

In the next chapter, we'll put aside the purely mathematical applications of OpenCL and look at a different use of the toolset. In addition to being executed on GPUs, OpenCL kernels can interact with graphical applications. Chapter 15 introduces OpenCL's ability to accelerate OpenGL rendering.

Accelerating
OpenGL with OpenCL

Part 3 discusses OpenCL's ability to accelerate 3-D rendering applications coded in OpenGL. Chapter 15 introduces the topic of OpenGL-OpenCL interoperability and shows how to share data between OpenGL and OpenCL. Chapter 16 explains how OpenCL kernels can process image data within OpenGL textures.

15

Combining OpenCL and OpenGL

This chapter covers

- The functions needed to configure OpenGL-OpenCL interoperability
- A method for coding OpenGL-OpenCL applications
- Rendering animated models with OpenGL and OpenCL

One of OpenCL's greatest strengths is that it can accelerate applications based on OpenGL, the cross-platform API for 3-D rendering. The end goal of an OpenGL application is to compute two-dimensional arrays of numbers that correspond to pixel colors. These pixels must be computed quickly—on a high-resolution display, the application may need to compute hundreds of thousands of colors for each new frame.

> **NOTE** The content of this chapter assumes a basic familiarity with OpenGL 3.3 or above and shader development. Appendix B introduces both topics. In addition, the code in this chapter will only compile on systems that support OpenGL 3.3 or above.

Hardware-accelerated OpenGL applications rely partly on a CPU and partly on a GPU. For example, the CPU may set vertex colors and texture coordinates, and the GPU will process the CPU's data to obtain pixel colors. In a physics application, the CPU may solve the kinematic equations needed to determine a projectile's trajectory, and the GPU will transform the vertices needed to depict the object's motion.

By integrating OpenCL in an OpenGL application, you can place a greater portion of the computational load on the GPU (and similar OpenCL-compliant devices) instead of the CPU. For example, you can code kernels that initialize vertex data and solve kinematic equations without the CPU's involvement. The advantages of this are tremendous—not only is the GPU better suited for many types of mathematical operations, but this GPU-centric computing makes it unnecessary to transfer large amounts of data between the CPU and the GPU.

As discussed in appendix B, OpenGL makes it possible to code GPU routines called *shaders* that take part in the rendering process. Shaders are similar to OpenCL kernels in many respects, but kernels provide three significant advantages:

- Kernels can invoke a broader range of functions.
- Kernels can access local and private memory for high-speed data transfer.
- Kernels have synchronization routines that allow them to share data between work-items.

This third point is important to appreciate. A vertex shader can access only one vertex at a time, and a fragment shader can access only one fragment at a time. But a kernel can access all the data on a device and synchronize its processing using barriers. This makes kernels much more flexible with regard to the types of operations that can be performed on the GPU.

The disadvantage of combining OpenCL and OpenGL is that the coding process becomes much more involved. In addition to dealing with the many OpenCL data structures (contexts, programs, devices, and so on), you have to deal with OpenGL structures such as attributes, vertex buffer objects, and vertex array objects.

To simplify the coding process, this chapter presents a method of structuring code into five sequential stages. Both of the example applications in this chapter will demonstrate how this method can be put into practice. But before we get to the example code, it's important to discuss the functions that establish interoperability between OpenGL and OpenCL.

15.1   Sharing data between OpenGL and OpenCL

OpenGL applications package data using three data structures: vertex buffer objects (VBOs), texture objects, and renderbuffer objects. Similarly, OpenCL applications access data using two structures: buffer objects and image objects. The fundamental concept underlying OpenGL-OpenCL interoperability is that OpenCL memory objects can share data with OpenGL data structures. This allows kernels to process OpenGL structures as though they were regular buffer objects and image objects. Figure 15.1 depicts this graphically.

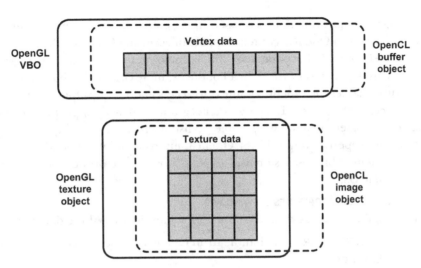

Figure 15.1 **OpenCL memory objects (buffer objects and image objects) share data with OpenGL objects (VBOs and texture objects).**

As depicted in the figure, the application doesn't transfer data between OpenCL and OpenGL data structures. They access the same data using different types of structures. After the OpenCL kernel processes the data, the OpenGL rendering process can continue normally.

To configure OpenGL-OpenCL interoperability in code, three steps must be performed in sequence:

1. Create an OpenCL context (`cl_context`) that references the current OpenGL context or share group.
2. Construct OpenCL memory objects (buffer objects and image objects) from OpenGL data objects (VBOs, texture objects, and renderbuffer objects).
3. Acquire exclusive access to the shared data for the kernel. After the kernel executes, release this access so the rendering can proceed.

This section explains the functions needed to perform these steps. They're not hard to use or understand, but they must be invoked in order to ensure interoperability.

15.1.1 *Creating the OpenCL context*

To establish interoperability between OpenCL and OpenGL, an OpenCL context must be created with a reference to an OpenGL context or share group. This context/share group serves as the bridge between the operating system and the graphical window. Once the context/share group is active, the operating system will direct all OpenGL rendering operations to its associated window.

> **NOTE** On Windows and Linux systems, the bridge between the OS and the window is called a *context*. On Mac OS systems, it's called a *share group*. In the interest of simplicity, this chapter will use the term *context* to refer to both data structures.

The clCreateContext function, discussed in chapter 2, takes center stage in this discussion. To create an OpenCL context capable of accessing OpenGL, the first step is to configure the function's first parameter, which is a pointer to a cl_context_properties structure. This has been set to NULL in all of the example code so far, but if set properly, this structure enables the OpenCL context to access and modify OpenGL data.

The cl_context_properties parameter is given as an array of property names and associated values, terminated by a 0. Table 2.5 lists each of the property names, but the names of the properties required for OpenGL interoperability depend on the host's operating system. This discussion will explain how to set properties on Windows, Linux, and Mac OS.

CONFIGURING CONTEXT PROPERTIES ON WINDOWS

On Windows, the cl_context_properties array must identify three data structures:

- CL_GL_CONTEXT_KHR—The handle to an OpenGL rendering context (HGLRC) for the X11 window
- CL_WGL_HDC_KHR—The handle to a device context (HDC) for the rendering window
- CL_CONTEXT_PLATFORM—The cl_platform structure associated with the context

You can't access the first two objects through the GL Utility Toolkit (GLUT), Qt, or any other OS-independent toolset. Instead, you need to invoke two functions from the venerable Win32 API:

- wglGetCurrentContext returns the handle to the rendering context, whose data type is given as HGLRC.
- wglGetCurrentDC returns the handle to the window's device context, whose Win32 data type is given as HDC.

These functions can be accessed through the windows.h header. The following example shows how they're used to initialize a cl_context_properties structure:

```
cl_context_properties properties[] = {
    CL_GL_CONTEXT_KHR, (cl_context_properties) wglGetCurrentContext(),
    CL_WGL_HDC_KHR, (cl_context_properties) wglGetCurrentDC(),
    CL_CONTEXT_PLATFORM, (cl_context_properties) platform,
    0};
```

The third argument is the cl_platform structure acquired through clGetPlatform. Note that the last argument of the array is always 0.

CONFIGURING CONTEXT PROPERTIES ON LINUX

The X Window System version 11, frequently called *X11*, provides the graphical interface for many operating systems including Linux. To configure a cl_context_properties structure for a system running X11, three properties must be defined:

- CL_GL_CONTEXT_KHR—The X11 rendering context (glXContext) for the window
- CL_GLX_DISPLAY_KHR—The Display object that represents the connection to an X server
- CL_CONTEXT_PLATFORM—The cl_platform structure associated with the context

The first object can be acquired by calling `glXGetCurrentContext` and the second can be acquired through `glXGetCurrentDisplay`. Both functions can be accessed through the glx.h header file, and the following code shows how they're used to initialize a `cl_context_properties` structure:

```
cl_context_properties properties[] = {
    CL_GL_CONTEXT_KHR, (cl_context_properties) glXGetCurrentContext(),
    CL_GLX_DISPLAY_KHR, (cl_context_properties) glXGetCurrentDisplay(),
    CL_CONTEXT_PLATFORM, (cl_context_properties) platform,
    0};
```

The third argument is the `cl_platform` structure acquired through `clGetPlatform`. Note that the last argument of the array is always 0.

CONFIGURING CONTEXT PROPERTIES ON MAC OS

When it comes to configuring OpenCL contexts, Mac OS is the simplest operating system to work with. The `cl_context_properties` structure needs only one property: `CL_CONTEXT_PROPERTY_USE_CGL_SHAREGROUP_APPLE`. The value associated with this property must have the data type `CGLShareGroupObj`, and it can be acquired by calling the function `CGLGetShareGroup`. This function requires a `CGLContextObj` structure, and this can be acquired by calling `CGLGetCurrentContext`. The following code shows how these functions work together:

```
CGLContextObj glContext = CGLGetCurrentContext();
CGLShareGroupObj shareGroup = CGLGetShareGroup(glContext);

cl_context_properties properties[] = {
    CL_CONTEXT_PROPERTY_USE_CGL_SHAREGROUP_APPLE,
    (cl_context_properties)shareGroup,
    0};
```

CREATING THE OPENGL-ACCESSIBLE CONTEXT

After the `cl_context_properties` structure is set, you can use it to create an OpenCL context capable of accessing OpenGL data. As discussed in chapter 2, the function needed to create an OpenCL context is `clCreateContext`. The following code shows how it can be called with a `cl_context_properties` structure called `properties`:

```
ctx = clCreateContext(properties, 1, &device, NULL, NULL, &err);
```

Once you've created a `cl_context` that supports OpenGL interoperability, you can create memory objects (buffer objects and image objects) that access OpenGL data. We'll examine this next.

15.1.2 Sharing data between OpenGL and OpenCL

To enable OpenGL-OpenCL interoperability, memory objects must be created from OpenGL data. This OpenGL data can be accessed in one of three forms:

- *Vertex buffer objects (VBOs)*—Contain vertex data such as coordinates, colors, and normal vectors
- *Texture objects*—Contain texture data in image form
- *Renderbuffer objects*—Contain pixels to be displayed

Chapter 3 explained how to create OpenCL memory objects using the `clCreate-Buffer`, `clCreateImage2D`, and `clCreateImage3D` functions. But to create memory objects capable of sharing data with OpenGL, you need to call one of four functions: `clCreateFromGLBuffer`, `clCreateFromGLTexture2D`, `clCreateFromGLTexture3D`, or `clCreateFromGLRenderbuffer`.

> **NOTE** An OpenCL memory object must be created after the corresponding OpenGL object has been created.

CREATING BUFFER OBJECTS FROM OPENGL VBOS

OpenGL applications store vertex data in vertex buffer objects, or VBOs; additional details are provided in appendix B. In a regular OpenGL application, the host creates and initializes VBOs and then transfers them to a GPU. There, the vertex shader processes the data using attributes.

By combining OpenGL and OpenCL, you can code an application that initializes VBO data on the GPU using an OpenCL kernel. This is important because vertex data no longer needs to be transferred from the CPU to the GPU.

But before a kernel can access VBO data, the host needs to create a buffer object specifically configured for the purpose. The function `clCreateFromGLBuffer` makes this possible, and its signature is as follows:

```
cl_mem clCreateFromGLBuffer(cl_context context, cl_mem_flags flags,
                            GLuint vbo_desc, cl_int *err)
```

The `context` parameter must be configured for OpenGL interoperation as described earlier. The `flags` parameter identifies the kernel's access mode, and because the kernel will usually be writing to an OpenGL VBO, this will usually be set to `CL_MEM_WRITE_ONLY`. The third parameter, `vbo_desc`, should be set to the VBO's unique identifier produced by `glGenBuffers`.

Let's look at an example. The following code creates a vertex buffer object called `vbo` and binds it to `GL_ARRAY_BUFFER`. Then it configures the VBO to hold 400 bytes and creates a buffer object, `vbo_buff`, to access its data:

```
glGenBuffers(1, &vbo);
glBindBuffer(GL_ARRAY_BUFFER, vbo);
glBufferData(GL_ARRAY_BUFFER, 400, NULL, GL_STATIC_DRAW);
vbo_buff = clCreateFromGLBuffer(ctx, CL_MEM_WRITE_ONLY, 2, &err);
```

It's important to see why the third argument of `glBufferData` is set to `NULL`. This states that the host won't transfer data to the VBO. The VBO is configured to hold 400 bytes, but this memory won't be allocated on the host. Instead, the 400 bytes will be allocated on the GPU, and the kernel will initialize the VBO data by accessing the write-only buffer object, `vbo_buff`.

Once the buffer is created, it can be accessed like a regular memory object. It can be made a kernel argument using `clSetKernelArg`, and the host can read its data with `clEnqueueReadBuffer`.

CREATING IMAGE OBJECTS FROM OPENGL TEXTURE OBJECTS AND RENDERBUFFER OBJECTS

Just as OpenGL stores vertex data in VBOs, it stores texture data in texture objects and pixel data in renderbuffer objects. And just as buffer objects can be associated with VBO data, image objects can be associated with texture/renderbuffer data. This should make sense, as applications access data in textures, renderbuffers, and image objects using two-dimensional arrays.

The process of creating an image object from OpenGL data is similar to the process of creating a buffer object. To create an image object capable of writing to texture objects, you can use the `clCreateFromGLTexture2D` and `clCreateFromGLTexture3D` functions. The signatures of these two functions are as follows:

```
cl_mem clCreateFromGLTexture2D(cl_context context, cl_mem_flags flags,
                               GLenum texture_target, GLint miplevel,
                               GLuint texture, cl_int *err)

cl_mem clCreateFromGLTexture3D(cl_context context, cl_mem_flags flags,
                               GLenum texture_target, GLint miplevel,
                               GLuint texture, cl_int *err)
```

The `texture_target` parameter accepts the name of the target to which the texture object is bound. For a two-dimensional texture, this should be set to `GL_TEXTURE_2D`. For three-dimensional textures, such as cube maps, this parameter should be set to a target such as `GL_TEXTURE_CUBE_MAP_POSITIVE_X`.

To understand the `miplevel` parameter, you need to understand how mipmaps work. Mipmaps are copies of a texture at different sizes, and OpenGL uses them to display textures at different levels of detail. Compared to the interpolation methods described in chapter 6, mipmaps provide better performance and fewer flaws in the image. Each mipmap copy corresponds to a mipmap level, and this is the value to set as the `miplevel` parameter in `clCreateFromGLTexture2D` and `clCreateFromGLTexture3D`.

Creating an image object capable of accessing a renderbuffer is simpler than creating an image object from texture data. This is because there are no mipmaps or texture targets involved. Instead, renderbuffers have `GLuint` descriptors similar to those used for VBOs. The function that creates the image object is `clCreateFromGLRenderbuffer`, and its signature is as follows:

```
cl_mem clCreateFromGLRenderbuffer(cl_context ctx, cl_mem_flags flags,
                                  GLuint renderbuffer, cl_int *err)
```

An example will show how this works. The following code creates an image object called `rend_obj` and configures it to share data with the renderbuffer whose descriptor equals 3:

```
rend_obj = clCreateFromGLRenderbuffer(ctx, CL_MEM_WRITE_ONLY, 3, &err);
```

Once you've created memory objects to share data with OpenGL objects, the next step involves synchronizing access to the data. We'll look at this next.

15.1.3 *Synchronizing access to shared data*

OpenGL and OpenCL routines can share data, but they can't access it at the same time. For example, if an OpenCL kernel is processing the shared data as a buffer object, the OpenGL vertex shader can't access the shared data as a VBO.

Synchronization between OpenGL and OpenCL is made possible through two OpenCL functions. The first is clEnqueueAcquireGLObjects, which ensures that the kernel will have exclusive access to the data. The second function is clEnqueue-ReleaseGLObjects, which allows other processes, such as the OpenGL renderer, to access the data. These functions have similar signatures:

```
int clEnqueueAcquireGLObjects(cl_command_queue queue, cl_uint num_objects,
    const cl_mem *mem_objects, cl_uint num_events_in_wait_list,
    const cl_event *event_wait_list, cl_event *event)

int clEnqueueReleaseGLObjects(cl_command_queue queue, cl_uint num_objects,
    const cl_mem *mem_objects, cl_uint num_events_in_wait_list,
    const cl_event *event_wait_list, cl_event *event)
```

Both functions operate similarly to the command-enqueuing functions discussed in chapters 3 and 6, but the third parameter is new. It accepts an array of one or more memory objects, and when clEnqueueAcquireGLObjects is called, the kernel will have exclusive access to them. When clEnqueueReleaseGLObjects is called, the kernel will give up this exclusive access.

You can think of these functions as forming a *mutex*, which was discussed in chapter 7. They serve to lock and unlock access to the memory objects defined by the mem_objects parameter.

These functions aren't hard to understand, but there are two important points to keep in mind when using them:

- Before acquiring a lock on the data, you should call glFinish to ensure that all OpenGL routines have completed their operation.
- After releasing the lock on the data, you should call clFinish to ensure that all OpenCL routines have completed their operation.

The following code shows how these functions work together to ensure that a kernel can process OpenGL data without interfering with the rendering process. In this case, the kernel proc accesses data in a buffer object called buff:

```
glFinish();
clEnqueueAcquireGLObjects(queue, 1, &buff, 0, NULL, NULL);

clEnqueueNDRangeKernel(queue, proc, 1, NULL, global_size, local_size,
    0, NULL, NULL);

clEnqueueReleaseGLObjects(queue, 1, &buff, 0, NULL, NULL);
clFinish();
```

The clFinish at the end of the code ensures that the kernel will finish its execution and that the lock will be released before further operations can commence. After clFinish completes, the vertex shader will be able to access the kernel's output.

Once the shared memory objects are created for interoperability, you may want to query the data structures to ensure they've been configured properly. This is the topic of the next section.

15.2 *Obtaining information*

The OpenCL API provides three functions that allow you to obtain information about a running OpenCL-OpenGL application. The first two functions, `clGetGLObjectInfo` and `clGetGLTextureInfo`, query the characteristics of OpenGL objects whose data is shared with OpenCL kernels. The third, `clGetGLContextInfoKHR`, provides information about an OpenGL context and its associated devices.

15.2.1 *Obtaining OpenGL object and texture information*

The `clGetGLObjectInfo` function identifies what type of OpenGL object (VBO, texture, or renderbuffer) was used to create an OpenCL memory object. Its signature is as follows:

```
cl_int clGetGLObjectInfo(cl_mem mem_obj, cl_gl_object_type *type,
   GLuint *name)
```

The first parameter, `mem_obj`, identifies the memory object created from OpenGL data. The function identifies the OpenGL data type by setting `type` equal to `CL_GL_OBJECT_BUFFER`, `CL_GL_OBJECT_TEXTURE2D`, `CL_GL_OBJECT_TEXTURE3D`, or `CL_GL_OBJECT_RENDERBUFFER`. The `name` parameter is set equal to the object's descriptor unless set to `NULL`.

As an example, suppose `mobj` is a memory object created from data inside an OpenGL object. The following code calls `clGetGLObjectInfo` to determine the type of the OpenGL object from which `mobj` was created:

```
cl_gl_object_type type;
clGetGLObjectInfo(mobj, &type, NULL);

switch(type) {
   case CL_GL_OBJECT_BUFFER:
      . . .
      break;
   case CL_GL_OBJECT_TEXTURE2D:
      . . .
      break;
}
```

If you're certain an OpenGL object is a texture, you can call `clGetGLTextureInfo` to obtain information about the texture. Like the `clGet`*XX*`Info` functions presented in chapter 2, this accepts a parameter name and returns information specific to the parameter. The signature is as follows:

```
cl_int clGetGLTextureInfo(cl_mem mem_obj, cl_gl_texture_info param_name,
   size_t value_size, void *value, size_t *param_value_size_ret)
```

The `param_name` argument can be set to either `CL_GL_TEXTURE_TARGET` or `CL_GL_MIPMAP_LEVEL`. If set to `CL_GL_TEXTURE_TARGET`, the function will identify the target to which the texture is bound, such as GL_TEXTURE_2D. If param_name is set to CL_GL_ MIPMAP_LEVEL, the function will return the texture's mipmap level.

15.2.2 *Obtaining information about the OpenGL context*

The cl_context_properties structure, discussed earlier in this section, must identify an OpenGL context to ensure OpenCL-OpenGL interoperability. The clGetGL- ContextInfoKHR function accepts a cl_context_properties structure and provides information about devices capable of supporting its context. The function's signature is as follows:

```
cl_int clGetGLContextInfoKHR(const cl_context_properties *properties,
    cl_gl_context_info param_name, size_t param_value_size,
    void *param_value, size_t *param_value_size_ret)
```

Here, param_name can be set to one of two values:

- CL_CURRENT_DEVICE_FOR_GL_CONTEXT_KHR—Returns a cl_device_id that iden- tifies the device executing the context
- CL_DEVICES_FOR_GL_CONTEXT_KHR—Returns an array of cl_device_id struc- tures that identify which devices are capable of executing the context

In both cases, the devices must be compliant with OpenCL and OpenGL. If the device running the OpenGL context is not OpenCL-compliant, clGetGLContextInfoKHR won't be able to create a cl_device_id to represent it.

The KHR at the end of the function's name shows that it's not defined in the core OpenCL API. For this reason, you can't call clGetGLContextInfoKHR directly. You need to access it through a pointer, and to obtain this pointer, you need to invoke a function called clGetExtensionFunctionAddress. The signature for this function is as follows:

```
void* clGetExtensionFunctionAddress(const char *funcname)
```

The return value of this function must be cast to a specific pointer type for the function being called. In the case of clGetGLContextInfoKHR, the pointer type defined in cl_gl.h is clGetGLContextInfoKHR_fn. For example, if you want to determine which device is executing an OpenGL context defined by props, you could call the following code:

```
cl_device_id dev;
clGetGLContextInfoKHR_fn func =
    clGetExtensionFunctionAddress("clGetGLContextInfoKHR");
func(props, CL_CURRENT_DEVICE_FOR_GL_CONTEXT_KHR,
    sizeof(cl_device_id), &dev, NULL);
```

clGetGLContextInfoKHR is useful when you don't know which device is executing the OpenGL context. But because the function isn't part of the core API, some vendors' OpenCL libraries don't support it.

At this point, you should have a solid grasp of the functions that make interopera- bility between OpenCL and OpenGL possible. In the next section, we'll look at a basic example that demonstrates how they're used.

15.3 Basic interoperability example

Interfacing OpenCL and OpenGL isn't particularly difficult, but because there are so many data structures and functions involved, it can be hard to keep your code organized. The goal of this section is to present a method for structuring OpenGL-OpenCL code that can be used in different applications. This method will be used throughout this chapter and chapter 16.

To introduce the method, this section will present an application that draws three squares in a 3-D model. This is similar to the three_squares application from appendix B, but the Ch15/basic_interop code uses an OpenCL kernel to set the coordinates and colors of the vertices. This isn't exciting as 3-D applications go, but once you see how the code works, you'll be able to extend the method to support more interesting applications.

In the basic_interop.c source file, the `main` function contains five important functions:

- `init_gl`—Initializes OpenGL operation
- `init_cl`—Initializes OpenCL operation
- `configure_shared_data`—Creates OpenGL and OpenCL data objects
- `execute_kernel`—Launches the OpenCL kernel
- `display`—Renders graphics in the window

These functions perform the bulk of the application's processing, and we'll look at each function in turn.

15.3.1 Initializing OpenGL operation

The application begins its processing by creating a GLUT window and configuring it to render OpenGL graphics. The `init_gl` function accomplishes these tasks with the following code:

```
glutInit(&argc, argv);
glutInitDisplayMode(GLUT_DOUBLE | GLUT_RGBA);
glutInitWindowSize(300, 300);
glutCreateWindow("Basic Interoperability");
glClearColor(1.0f, 1.0f, 1.0f, 1.0f);
```

These functions must be called before OpenCL functions because GLUT creates the OpenGL context needed to create an OpenCL context. If you create an OpenCL context without a running OpenGL context, it won't support interoperability.

After these GLUT functions execute, `init_gl` calls `glewInit` to check whether the application's extensions are supported. Then it calls `init_shaders` to compile the vertex shader (basic_interop.vert) and the fragment shader (basic_interop.frag). If the compilation succeeds, the shaders are attached to a program structure.

15.3.2 Initializing OpenCL operation

Chapter 2 presented the six fundamental data structures used in OpenCL applications: `cl_platform_id`, `cl_device_id`, `cl_context`, `cl_command_queue`, `cl_program`, and cl_kernel. In basic_interop.c, the init_cl function creates and configures all six of these structures.

Most of the code in init_cl is similar to that used in host applications throughout this book. The main difference is the manner in which the cl_context structure is created. The following listing presents the code.

> **Listing 15.1   Creating the OpenGL-OpenCL context: basic_interop.c (abridged)**

```
...
#ifdef MAC

CGLContextObj mac_context = CGLGetCurrentContext();
CGLShareGroupObj group = CGLGetShareGroup(mac_context);     Set properties—
cl_context_properties properties[] = {                      Mac OS
    CL_CONTEXT_PROPERTY_USE_CGL_SHAREGROUP_APPLE,
    (cl_context_properties)group, 0};

#else
#ifdef UNIX

cl_context_properties properties[] = {
    CL_GL_CONTEXT_KHR,
    (cl_context_properties)glXGetCurrentContext(),
    CL_GLX_DISPLAY_KHR,                                      Set properties—
    (cl_context_properties)glXGetCurrentDisplay(),          Linux
    CL_CONTEXT_PLATFORM,
    (cl_context_properties)platform, 0};

#else

cl_context_properties properties[] = {
    CL_GL_CONTEXT_KHR,
    (cl_context_properties)wglGetCurrentContext(),
    CL_WGL_HDC_KHR,                                          Set properties—
    (cl_context_properties)wglGetCurrentDC(),               Windows
    CL_CONTEXT_PLATFORM,
    (cl_context_properties)platform, 0};

#endif
#endif

context = clCreateContext(properties, 1, &device, NULL, NULL, &err);
```

After the context is created, the init_cl function reads the text in basic_interop.cl and compiles it. Then it creates a cl_command_queue and a cl_kernel for the basic_interop function. Once these structures are created, the OpenCL initialization is complete and the application can start creating data objects.

15.3.3 *Creating data objects*

After initialization, the main function calls configure_shared_data. This function starts by creating the vertex array objects (VAOs) and vertex buffer objects (VBOs) needed to store rendering data. For this application, the VBOs store vertex coordinates and colors, and the following code configures the first VBO:

```
glBindBuffer(GL_ARRAY_BUFFER, vbo[0]);
glBufferData(GL_ARRAY_BUFFER, 12*sizeof(GLfloat),
    NULL, GL_DYNAMIC_DRAW);
glVertexAttribPointer(0, 3, GL_FLOAT, GL_FALSE, 0, 0);
glEnableVertexAttribArray(0);
```

The third argument of glBufferData is set to NULL because the VBO will be initially empty. The VBO's data store will be allocated when it's instantiated on the GPU.

configure_shared_data creates six VBOs: three to hold coordinate data and three to hold color data. After creating these objects, the function creates six OpenCL buffer objects to access the data in the VBOs. The following code shows how this is accomplished:

```
for(i=0; i<6; i++) {
    mem_objects[i] = clCreateFromGLBuffer(context, CL_MEM_WRITE_ONLY,
        vbo[i], &err);
    clSetKernelArg(kernel, i, sizeof(cl_mem), &mem_objects[i]);
}
```

The for loop creates six buffer objects, mem_objects[i], that share data with the VBOs identified by vbo[i]. Next, the application calls clSetKernelArg to make kernel arguments out of the buffer objects. Once the arguments are set, the kernel can be executed.

15.3.4 *Executing the kernel*

In the basic_interop application, an OpenCL kernel initializes the vertex coordinates and colors inside each of the six VBOs. The kernel accesses VBO memory through buffer objects, and the following code presents the first few lines of the kernel function:

```
__kernel void basic_interop(__global float4* first_coords,
        __global float4* first_colors, __global float4* second_coords,
        __global float4* second_colors, __global float4* third_coords,
        __global float4* third_colors) {

    first_coords[0] = (float4)(-0.15f, -0.15f,  1.00f, -0.15f);
    first_coords[1] = (float4)( 0.15f,  1.00f,  0.15f,  0.15f);
    ...
}
```

The main function launches the kernel by calling execute_kernel. This acquires exclusive access to the VBO data, executes the kernel, and then releases access to the VBO data. The following code shows how it works.

Listing 15.2 Executing the kernel: basic_interop.c (abridged)

```
void execute_kernel() {

    int err;
    cl_event kernel_event;

    glFinish();
    clEnqueueAcquireGLObjects(queue,
        6, mem_objects, 0, NULL, NULL);
```
 1 Obtain data lock

```
clEnqueueTask(queue, kernel, 0, NULL, &kernel_event);

clWaitForEvents(1, &kernel_event);

clEnqueueReleaseGLObjects(queue,                        ❷  Release
    6, mem_objects, 0, NULL, NULL);                         data lock
clFinish(queue);
clReleaseEvent(kernel_event);
}
```

The clEnqueueAcquireGLObjects function ❶ ensures that the kernel can read and write to the shared data in the buffer objects. Once the kernel completes its execution, clEnqueueReleaseGLObjects ❷ allows other processes to access the shared data. Specifically, OpenGL can use the newly initialized VBO data to render graphics in the window.

15.3.5 *Rendering graphics*

The display function handles the application's graphical rendering. This function isn't called directly by main but is invoked as a callback function whenever the window needs to redraw itself.

The operation of display is straightforward. It cycles through each of the VAOs and calls glDrawArrays on each. Once the vertices are drawn, display calls glutSwapBuffers to update the pixels in the window. The following code shows how this works.

> **Listing 15.3   Rendering graphics: basic_interop.c (abridged)**

```
void display(void) {
    glClear(GL_COLOR_BUFFER_BIT | GL_DEPTH_BUFFER_BIT);

    glBindVertexArray(vao[2]);
    glDrawArrays(GL_TRIANGLE_FAN, 0, 4);

    glBindVertexArray(vao[1]);
    glDrawArrays(GL_TRIANGLE_FAN, 0, 4);

    glBindVertexArray(vao[0]);
    glDrawArrays(GL_TRIANGLE_FAN, 0, 4);

    glBindVertexArray(0);
    glutSwapBuffers();
}
```

It's important to note that display does not execute the kernel. Because the rendering is static, the VBO content only needs to be set once. In contrast, the next section explores how to code OpenGL-OpenCL applications with animated models.

15.4 *Interoperability and animation*

If a 3-D model doesn't change over time, it doesn't make a significant difference whether the rendering is performed by a GPU or a CPU. But when hundreds of thousands of pixels need to be updated with each frame, it becomes vital to perform as much processing on the GPU as possible. OpenCL can assist with this computation, and this section will demonstrate how OpenGL-OpenCL interoperability can be used to implement animation.

Specifically, the discussion will focus on drawing a sphere that spins around its vertical axis. Figure 15.2 shows what the target rendering looks like.

If you compare the code in the sphere.c source file with the code in basic_interop.c, you'll notice that the overall application structure is still the same. That is, the code contains the same five functions: init_gl, init_cl, configure_shared_data, execute_kernel, and display. But the sphere code has three significant differences:

Figure 15.2 The OpenCL kernel updates the coordinates of the sphere, and OpenGL animates the model.

- All of the vertex data is contained in a single VBO.
- The display function is called repeatedly to animate the model.
- With each call, display executes the kernel to compute new vertex coordinates.

This section will discuss each of these changes in turn. With each step, we'll examine how the code makes it possible to create and display a rotating model.

15.4.1 Specifying vertex data

The basic_interop project stores data in six VBOs, but the sphere project only needs one. This is because the model consists of a single object (the sphere) and only one color is used by the rendering. This makes the configure_shared_data function very simple. Here's the code.

Listing 15.4 Configuring the sphere's vertices: sphere.c (abridged)

```
void configure_shared_data() {

    int err;

    glGenVertexArrays(1, &vao);
    glBindVertexArray(vao);
    glGenBuffers(1, &vbo);

    glBindBuffer(GL_ARRAY_BUFFER, vbo);
    glBufferData(GL_ARRAY_BUFFER, 4 *
        NUM_VERTICES * sizeof(GLfloat),
        NULL, GL_DYNAMIC_DRAW);
    glVertexAttribPointer(0, 4, GL_FLOAT, GL_FALSE, 0, 0);
    glEnableVertexAttribArray(0);

    vertex_buffer = clCreateFromGLBuffer(context, CL_MEM_WRITE_ONLY,
```

❶ Configure VBO data

```
                     vbo, &err);
        if(err < 0) {
           perror("Couldn't create a buffer object from the VBO");
           exit(1);
        }

        err = clSetKernelArg(kernel, 0, sizeof(cl_mem), &vertex_buffer);
        err |= clSetKernelArg(kernel, 1, sizeof(float), &tick);
        if(err < 0) {
           printf("Couldn't set a kernel argument");
           exit(1);
        };
     }
```

It's important to see how the glBufferData function ❶ operates. The third argument
is NULL, so the VBO memory isn't allocated on the host—it's allocated on the GPU. Specifically, the memory occupies 4 * NUM_VERTICES * sizeof(GLfloat) bytes. By default,
NUM_VERTICES is set to 256, so the default VBO data occupies 4,096 bytes.

The VBO contains vertex coordinates for the sphere. The vertex shader in
sphere.vert receives these coordinates as attributes, and as specified by glVertex-
AttribPointer, each attribute contains four float values. The responsibility for setting these values falls to the kernel, which is executed by the display function. We'll
look at this function next.

15.4.2 *Animation and display*

To keep the sphere spinning, the display function must be called repeatedly. This is
made possible through the glutPostRedisplay function, which alerts the application
that the window needs to be redrawn. In response, display is called again. The following listing shows how the display function makes use of glutPostRedisplay.

Listing 15.5   Rendering the sphere's graphics: sphere.c (abridged)

```
void display(void) {
   glClear(GL_COLOR_BUFFER_BIT | GL_DEPTH_BUFFER_BIT);

   execute_kernel();

   glBindVertexArray(vao);                              ┐ Draw sphere
   glDrawArrays(GL_LINE_LOOP, 0, NUM_VERTICES);         ┘ vertices

   tick += 0.0001f;

   glBindVertexArray(0);
   glutSwapBuffers();                                   ┐ Redraw
   glutPostRedisplay();                                 ┘ window
}
```

After clearing the rendering state, the first step in the function's operation is to execute the kernel. The kernel sets the vertices of the sphere and the glDrawArrays function depicts these vertices in the window. glDrawArrays connects the vertices in a line
loop, which means that it draws a line from each vertex to its successor, and the last
vertex is connected to the first.

The `tick` variable is particularly important. It starts with a value of 0 and each iteration of `display` increments it by 0.0001. This new value is sent to the kernel, which uses it to change the coordinates of the sphere's vertices. This change in coordinates animates the sphere, and the increment controls how quickly the sphere rotates. The next section explains how the kernel operates.

15.4.3 Executing the kernel

To see how the kernel computes the sphere's vertices, you need to understand *spherical coordinates*. Normally, we identify points in space using rectangular coordinates (x, y, z). But for points on a sphere, it's more convenient to use (r, θ, φ):

- r—The radius of the sphere, the distance from the sphere's center to the point
- θ (theta)—The angle from the top of the sphere (the zenith) to the point
- φ (phi)—The angle along the circle perpendicular to the line connecting the sphere's center and zenith

Figure 15.3 shows how these spherical coordinates are related. The point *P* is located on the surface of a sphere whose center is *C* and whose zenith is *Z*. The coordinates of *P* are given as (r, θ, φ).

The angle θ runs from the zenith to the nadir (the lowest point on the sphere), so its angular measure runs from 0 to π radians. The angle φ runs the length of an entire circle, so its angular measure runs from 0 to 2π radians. By default, the sphere application contains 256 vertices divided into 16 longitudinal lines drawn between the zenith and the nadir. Each line contains 16 points, and each point on a line has a different value of θ.

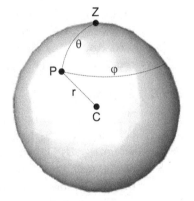

Figure 15.3 Coordinates on a sphere are given using the parameters *r*, θ, and φ.

OpenGL accepts only rectangular coordinates for its vertices, so each (r, θ, φ) triple needs to be converted into an (x, y, z) triple. Using trigonometry, this conversion can be computed as follows:

$$x = r\sin\theta\,\cos\varphi$$
$$y = r\sin\theta\,\sin\varphi$$
$$z = r\cos\theta$$

The following code shows how the kernel computes coordinates for each point on the sphere. By default, there are 256 vertices in total and the `RADIUS` value is set to 0.75.

Listing 15.6 Setting the sphere's vertices: sphere.cl

```
__kernel void sphere(__global float4* vertices, float tick) {

    int longitude = get_global_id(0)/16;
    int latitude = get_global_id(0) % 16;
```

```
float sign = -2.0f * (longitude % 2) + 1.0f;        Compute spherical
float phi = 2.0f * M_PI_F * longitude/16 + tick;     coordinates
float theta = M_PI_F * latitude/16;

vertices[get_global_id(0)].x =
   RADIUS * sin(theta) * cos(phi);
vertices[get_global_id(0)].y =
   RADIUS * sign * cos(theta);                        Set vertex
vertices[get_global_id(0)].z =                        coordinates
   RADIUS * sin(theta) * sin(phi);
vertices[get_global_id(0)].w = 1.0f;
}
```

This kernel processes vertices as float4 vectors instead of float3 vectors. OpenCL supports float3 vectors, but on every system I've tested, float3 arrays are stored internally as float4 arrays. This is why the kernel sets a value for the fourth vector component.

The vertices are divided into lines of 16 vertices each—the first sixteen vertices form the first line, the second sixteen vertices form the second line, and so on. The points in a line all have the same value of φ, and the tick variable, incremented by the display function, increases this value. As φ increases, the lines rotate counterclockwise around the vertical axis. If you change the code so that tick is decremented by the display function, the lines will rotate clockwise around the axis.

15.5   Summary

When it comes to cross-platform 3-D rendering, OpenGL has little competition. You can find it used frequently in games, scientific visualization, and computer-aided design (CAD). The fact that this rendering can be accelerated with OpenCL is, in my opinion, OpenCL's most important benefit. The goal of this chapter is to show how this acceleration works in code.

The central concept is data sharing. OpenGL and OpenCL don't transfer data between themselves—they read and write to the same memory. To make this sharing possible, applications create OpenCL memory objects from OpenGL objects. More precisely, the host application creates buffer objects from VBOs and image objects from textures and renderbuffer objects.

An OpenCL kernel can process these shared objects as though they were regular buffer objects and image objects, but only after it has obtained exclusive access to the memory. The clEnqueueAcquireGLObjects function acquires this exclusive access, and clEnqueueReleaseGLObjects releases it. Once clEnqueueReleaseGLObjects completes, the data can be processed normally by the OpenGL rendering pipeline.

This chapter presented two examples of OpenGL-OpenCL interoperability. The first, basic_interop, executes an OpenCL kernel that initializes the vertex coordinates and colors in a static OpenGL rendering. The structure of the basic_interop.c code presents an approach that can be used to organize general OpenGL-OpenCL applications. This consists of five stages: initializing OpenGL operation, initializing OpenCL operation, configuring shared data, executing the kernel, and displaying the drawing.

The second application uses the same code structure to display an animated sphere. The animation is accomplished by executing the kernel repeatedly, each time with an updated value of the vertices' angles. With each iteration, the kernel computes different vertex coordinates and the model rotates around its axis.

The examples in this chapter have used OpenCL to access data in OpenGL VBOs, but kernels can also be used to process textures. High-speed texture processing is an important topic in the world of games and graphics, and the next chapter will discuss how OpenCL can be used to accelerate this operation.

Textures and renderbuffers

In 1992, the computer game *Wolfenstein 3D* started a revolution and launched the genre known as the *first-person shooter* or *FPS*. Since its release, the basic elements of FPS gameplay haven't changed: keystrokes move the character, mouse motion sets the character's direction, and mouse clicks fire the character's weapon.

The graphics, on the other hand, have changed dramatically. Instead of pixelated bad guys who look and move like LEGO men, monsters in modern games are rendered with such incredible detail that you can see every scale, scowl, and razor-sharp claw.

These visual improvements are made possible by *textures*. An OpenGL texture is an image that the renderer stretches or shrinks to cover a surface (see appendix B for a full discussion of real-time rendering with OpenGL). Simple applications apply textures to a model and don't make any changes, but for high-quality special effects, applications use advanced image processing techniques to update the texture in real time. One prominent use for this is lighting. For example, a game developer may want the alien's skin to change its appearance depending on whether it is being viewed by day, by night, or by night-vision goggles.

These special effects demand high-speed image processing, and this is an important advantage of OpenCL-OpenGL interoperability. Instead of having the CPU process textures, an OpenCL kernel on the GPU can process the texture's data before it's used by the renderer. This chapter will demonstrate how this works, and the primary focus is image filtering. An OpenCL kernel can accentuate or minimize details within an image, but before we get into the code, it's important to become familiar with the mathematical operations that make image filtering possible.

16.1 Image filtering

Professional image-editing applications, such as Adobe Photoshop and the GNU Image Manipulation Program (GIMP), provide tools that add effects to images such as blurring, sharpening, and embossing. These effects are accomplished using image filters. The theory behind these filters is involved, but the underlying mathematical operations are easy to understand. The filtering process computes a series of two-dimensional dot products and makes each product a pixel in the output image.

> **NOTE** The filtering method discussed in this section is called *spatial filtering*. In contrast, *frequency filtering* uses a two-dimensional version of the fast Fourier transform (FFT) discussed in chapter 14.

As explained in chapter 12, a one-dimensional dot product accepts two input vectors and returns the sum of the products of their corresponding elements. If p and q are vectors, their dot product is calculated as follows:

$$p \cdot q = p_0 q_0 + p_1 q_1 + p_2 q_2 + p_3 q_3$$

Similar in principle, a two-dimensional dot product accepts two matrices and returns the sum of the products of their corresponding elements. For example, suppose A and B are two 3-by-3 matrices whose elements are as follows:

$$A = \begin{bmatrix} a_{00} & a_{01} & a_{02} \\ a_{10} & a_{11} & a_{12} \\ a_{20} & a_{21} & a_{22} \end{bmatrix} \qquad B = \begin{bmatrix} b_{00} & b_{01} & b_{02} \\ b_{10} & b_{11} & b_{12} \\ b_{20} & b_{21} & b_{22} \end{bmatrix}$$

The two-dimensional dot product of A and B can be computed with the following equation:

$$\begin{aligned} A \cdot B = {} & a_{00} b_{00} + a_{01} b_{01} + a_{02} b_{02} + a_{10} b_{10} + a_{11} b_{11} + a_{12} b_{12} \\ & + a_{20} b_{20} + a_{21} b_{21} + a_{22} b_{22} \end{aligned}$$

Image filtering treats an image as a matrix of values and computes a two-dimensional dot product for each pixel in the image. In general, the goal is to draw attention to or away from differences between adjacent pixels.

Figure 16.1 The high-frequency noise in this image needs to be filtered.

The second matrix in the product is called (confusingly enough) a *kernel*. The values of the kernel determine what effect the filter will have on the image. An example will show how this works. Figure 16.1 presents an input image with noise.

The noise in this image can modeled as unwanted variation between pixels. You can reduce this variation by replacing each pixel with the average of the pixel's color and those of the pixels surrounding it. To perform this operation, you'll represent the image as a matrix called M, and you'll use M_{ij} to refer to the pixel at row i and column j. The filtered pixel can be obtained as follows:

$$M_{ij}[out] = \frac{\begin{bmatrix} M_{i-1,j-1} & +M_{i,j-1} & +M_{i+1,j-1} \\ +M_{i-1,j} & +M_{i,j} & +M_{i+1,j} \\ +M_{i-1,j+1} & +M_{i(i,j+1)} & +M_{i+1,j+1} \end{bmatrix}}{9}$$

This operation can also be performed by taking the dot product of these nine image pixels with a kernel, K_{Box}, whose elements are as follows:

$$K_{Box} = \frac{\begin{bmatrix} 1 & 1 & 1 \\ 1 & 1 & 1 \\ 1 & 1 & 1 \end{bmatrix}}{9} \qquad\qquad Filter = K_{Box} \cdot M$$

This dot product must be performed for each pixel in the input image. Once this is done, the resulting image will have the same size as the original. Because the elements of K_{Box} add to 1, the result will also have the same average brightness. Figure 16.2 shows what the filtered image looks like.

Figure 16.2 The box filter removes noise by blurring adjacent pixels.

This filter, called a *box filter* or *mean filter*, has removed much of the noise in the original image by averaging neighboring pixels. But it has also removed a significant amount of detail that isn't noise. You can do better. The rest of this section will present three other types of filters commonly used to process textures: the Gaussian blur, sharpening, and embossing.

16.1.1 The Gaussian blur

When it comes to removing noise, the Gaussian blur generally gives better results than the box filter. The term *Gaussian* refers to a specific function that, in one dimension, produces the frequently encountered bell curve. Figure 16.3 shows what the Gaussian function looks like in two dimensions.

To implement this function as a kernel, you need to approximate its values in a 3*3 matrix. The following matrix presents one possible kernel:

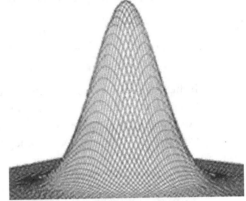

Figure 16.3 The Gaussian blur removes noise using this two-dimensional Gaussian function.

$$K_{Gaussian} = \frac{\begin{bmatrix} 1 & 2 & 1 \\ 2 & 4 & 2 \\ 1 & 2 & 1 \end{bmatrix}}{16}$$

Filtering with this kernel produces a blurring effect similar to that of the box filter, but it gives priority to the central pixel and the pixels adjacent to it. This means that the filtered image keeps more of the differences between one pixel and the next. Figure 16.4 shows what the result looks like.

As shown, the Gaussian blur serves as a compromise between the unfiltered image and the deep blurring effect produced by the box filter. It's important to note that the kernel used for this filter is only one possible implementation of the Gaussian blur. The values in the kernel can be modified to produce more or less blurring.

Figure 16.4 The Gaussian blur doesn't remove as much noise as the box filter, but doesn't take away as much detail either.

16.1.2 Image sharpening

In contrast to the box filter and Gaussian blur, which reduce the difference between pixels, a sharpening filter accentuates the difference. Instead of adding values of neighboring pixels, the sharpening filter subtracts them from the central pixel. An example sharpening kernel is shown here:

$$K_{sharpening} = \begin{bmatrix} -1 & -1 & -1 \\ -1 & 9 & -1 \\ -1 & -1 & -1 \end{bmatrix}$$

If the central pixel has the same value as those around it, the resulting pixel's value will be equal to that of the original. But if the central pixel has a greater value than its neighbors, the filtered value will be significantly magnified. This is shown in figure 16.5, which depicts the sharpened image on the right.

Figure 16.5 The sharpening filter accentuates detail within an image.

A sharpening filter magnifies noise along with other details in the image. Therefore, it's a good idea to apply a blurring filter, such as the Gaussian filter, before sharpening the features of an image.

16.1.3 Image embossing

Embossing enhances the features of an image so that surfaces appear to be cast in relief. This is similar to sharpening, but embossing increases brightness in one direction and reduces brightness in another. One implementation of an embossing filter is as follows:

$$K_{Emboss} = \frac{\begin{bmatrix} -2 & -1 & 0 \\ -1 & 1 & 1 \\ 0 & 1 & 2 \end{bmatrix}}{2}$$

Because of the directional sharpening, the resulting figure appears to reflect light as though it had been engraved in metal. This effect is depicted on the right side of figure 16.6.

Figure 16.6 An embossing filter makes an image look as though it's been engraved in metal.

The overall gray color is produced because the kernel values sum to 0.5. Similarly, the overall color will be white if the kernel elements add to 1 and black if they add to 0. Therefore, with the right values, the kernel can affect the brightness of an image in addition to sharpening or blurring its features.

At this point, you should have a basic understanding of spatial filtering and the manner in which kernels can be used to filter images. The next section shows how to implement this process with OpenCL and display the results in an OpenGL rendering.

16.2 *Filtering textures with OpenCL*

Coding an OpenCL kernel to perform image sharpening doesn't present significant difficulty—all that's needed are a series of two-dimensional dot products. But coding the host application to integrate OpenCL's data structures with OpenGL's texture processing takes careful effort. An example of this can be found in the Ch16/texture_filter/texture_filter.c source file.

The texture_filter application reads the image in the input.png file, filters the image with a sharpening filter, and displays the result as a texture. The goal of this section is to explain how this process works. Throughout this discussion, you'll rely on the same five functions discussed in the last chapter: init_gl, init_cl, configure_shared_data, execute_kernel, and display.

16.2.1 *The init_gl function*

The init_gl function initializes the GLUT window and the overall operation of OpenGL. Then it continues the initialization process by invoking three functions:

- init_buffers—Creates one VBO containing vertex coordinates and one containing texture coordinates
- init_textures—Creates and configures a texture object to hold pixel data
- init_shaders—Compiles the vertex shader (texture_filter.vert) and fragment shader (texture_filter.frag)

It's important to note that init_textures doesn't set pixel data for the texture object. That is, it doesn't call glTexImage2D. The texture's image data will be set later on by the OpenCL kernel.

16.2.2 *The init_cl function*

The init_cl function creates the primary OpenCL data structures used by the application: platform, device, context, program, command queue, and kernel. In texture_filter.c, this function also reads in pixels from the input image (input.png) and creates a two-dimensional image object to hold them. This is shown in the following code:

```
read_image_data(TEXTURE_FILE, &tex_pixels, &width, &height);

png_format.image_channel_order = CL_R;
png_format.image_channel_data_type = CL_UNSIGNED_INT8;
```

```
in_texture = clCreateImage2D(context,
        CL_MEM_READ_ONLY | CL_MEM_COPY_HOST_PTR,
        &png_format, width, height, 0, (void*)tex_pixels, &err);
```

The pixels read from the image are formatted in grayscale. More precisely, each pixel has a single component, and this component is given as an unsigned char. Once the kernel reads these pixels, it will apply the sharpening filter to accentuate detail in the image.

16.2.3   *The configure_shared_data function*

No matter which SDK I use, I get a CL_INVALID_IMAGE_FORMAT_DESCRIPTOR error when I attempt to create an image object from a texture object by invoking clCreateFromGLTexture2D. To get around this error, I've found it helpful to employ an intermediate storage mechanism called a *pixel buffer object*, or *PBO*. A PBO can hold data for a texture so that, when glTexImage2D is called, the texture's image data is read from the PBO.

PBOs have a lot in common with vertex buffer objects (VBOs), discussed in appendix B. Both object types store OpenGL data and both use the same functions for creation (glGenBuffers), binding (glBindBuffer), and associating data (glBufferData). Most importantly, VBOs and PBOs can both be used with clCreateFromGLBuffer to create shared OpenGL buffer objects. This function is central to OpenGL-OpenCL interoperability, and chapter 15 explains its usage in detail.

The following listing presents the full code of the configure_shared_data function in texture_filter.c. It creates the PBO, uses it to create a buffer object, and then makes the buffer object an argument of the kernel.

Listing 16.1   Configuring shared data: texture_filter.c (abridged)

```
void configure_shared_data() {

    int err;

    glGenBuffers(1, &pbo);
    glBindBuffer(GL_ARRAY_BUFFER, pbo);
    glBufferData(GL_ARRAY_BUFFER,                    Configure
                width*height*sizeof(char),           PBO
            NULL, GL_STATIC_DRAW);
    glBindBuffer(GL_ARRAY_BUFFER, 0);

    out_buffer = clCreateFromGLBuffer(context,       Create shared
                CL_MEM_WRITE_ONLY, pbo, &err);       buffer object
    if(err < 0) {
        perror("Couldn't create a buffer object from the PBO");
        exit(1);
    }

    err = clSetKernelArg(kernel, 1, sizeof(cl_mem), &out_buffer);
    if(err < 0) {
        printf("Couldn't set a kernel argument");
        exit(1);
    };
}
```

The `glBufferData` function sets the size of the data to be stored by the PBO, but not the data itself. More precisely, the PBO's size is given (`width*height*sizeof(char)`) and the actual data is set to `NULL`. This is because the PBO's data store is shared with the buffer object `out_buffer`. This holds the kernel's output, and after the kernel finishes executing, the PBO will be able to access the output data as if it had been set with `glBufferData`.

16.2.4 *The execute_kernel function*

After the application creates the kernel and sets its arguments, it calls `execute_kernel` to deploy the kernel function, `texture_filter`, to the device. The host application generates one work-item for each pixel in the input image, and this is accomplished in the following code:

```
global_size[0] = width;
global_size[1] = height;
clEnqueueNDRangeKernel(queue, kernel, 2, NULL, global_size, NULL,
    0, NULL, &kernel_event);
```

The following listing presents the kernel code. The first argument is an image object containing the input pixels. The second argument contains the filtered results.

Listing 16.2   Applying the sharpening filter: texture_filter.cl

```
__constant sampler_t sampler = CLK_NORMALIZED_COORDS_FALSE |
    CLK_ADDRESS_CLAMP_TO_EDGE | CLK_FILTER_NEAREST;

__kernel void texture_filter(read_only image2d_t src_image,
                        __global uchar* dst_buffer) {

    int k[9] = {-1, -1, -1, -1, 9, -1, -1, -1, -1};        ◀── ❶ Set filter kernel

    int x = get_global_id(0);
    int y = get_global_id(1);

    int pixel =
     k[0] * read_imageui(src_image, sampler,
            (int2)(x-1, y-1)).s0 +
     k[1] * read_imageui(src_image, sampler,
            (int2)(x,   y-1)).s0 +
     k[2] * read_imageui(src_image, sampler,
            (int2)(x+1, y-1)).s0 +
     k[3] * read_imageui(src_image, sampler,
            (int2)(x-1, y)).s0 +
     k[4] * read_imageui(src_image, sampler,          Compute dot
            (int2)(x,   y)).s0 +                       product
     k[5] * read_imageui(src_image, sampler,
            (int2)(x+1, y)).s0 +
     k[6] * read_imageui(src_image, sampler,
            (int2)(x-1, y+1)).s0 +
     k[7] * read_imageui(src_image, sampler,
            (int2)(x,   y+1)).s0 +
     k[8] * read_imageui(src_image, sampler,
            (int2)(x+1, y+1)).s0;

    dst_buffer[y*get_global_size(0) + x] =             ❷ Assign
        (uchar)clamp(pixel, 0, 255);                      output pixel
}
```

The filtering kernel used by the function ❶ contains the same coefficients as used by the sharpening kernel discussed earlier. The function uses these values to perform dot products of nine elements each. The results are initially stored as signed integers, but the last line of the function ❷ casts the output value to an unsigned char and invokes the clamp function to constrain the output value to fall between 0 and 255.

Once the kernel completes its processing, the host application releases the shared output data for use by the OpenGL renderer. The following code shows how the shared data in the PBO is used to set the data inside the application's texture:

```
glBindBuffer(GL_PIXEL_UNPACK_BUFFER, pbo);
glTexImage2D(GL_TEXTURE_2D, 0, GL_LUMINANCE, width, height,
      0, GL_LUMINANCE, GL_UNSIGNED_BYTE, 0);
glActiveTexture(GL_TEXTURE0);
```

The first line binds pbo to the GL_PIXEL_UNPACK_BUFFER target. This target makes pbo a pixel buffer object, and once the binding is set, any function that would normally read from CPU memory will now read from the PBO. Therefore, the glTexImage2D function obtains its image data from the bound PBO, and the pixels are formatted according to the function's parameters: GL_LUMINANCE specifies that each pixel contains one component, and GL_UNSIGNED_BYTE specifies that each component has a single byte. Once this function is called, the texture can be applied to an OpenGL surface normally.

16.2.5 The display function

The display function is called every time the OpenGL window needs to redraw itself. Because the model contains only one vertex array object and one texture, the code for this function is easy to understand:

```
void display(void) {
    glClear(GL_COLOR_BUFFER_BIT);
    glBindVertexArray(vao);
    glBindTexture(GL_TEXTURE_2D, texture);
    glDrawArrays(GL_TRIANGLE_FAN, 0, 4);
    glBindVertexArray(0);
    glutSwapBuffers();
}
```

Figure 16.7 presents the final result. As shown, the sharpening filter accentuates detail within the image.

The filter's purpose can be changed easily by modifying the values of the kernel matrix. For better results, the number of values can be changed from 3 by 3 to 5 by 5 or 7 by 7. This spatial filtering can also be performed in the fragment shader instead of an OpenCL kernel.

Figure 16.7 The OpenCL kernel sharpens the image by computing a series of two-dimensional dot products.

But for complex texture processing algorithms, it's generally better to employ OpenCL kernels because of their local memory access and broader range of functions.

16.3 *Summary*

High-speed texture processing is a vital component of modern graphical applications, and this chapter has shown how to filter OpenGL textures with OpenCL. The primary algorithm under discussion is spatial filtering, which computes a two-dimensional dot product for each input pixel.

This chapter has concentrated on three types of spatial filters. The Gaussian blur removes noise by taking a weighted average of the input pixel and the pixels surrounding it. The sharpening filter accentuates detail by subtracting the values of neighboring pixels from the central pixel. An embossing filter sharpens in one direction and blurs in another, thereby producing an image that appears to have been engraved in metal.

Accessing texture objects with OpenCL can be problematic because the function `clCreateFromGLTexture2D` isn't fully supported. Therefore, there's no way to create an image object directly from OpenGL textures. Instead, you can use pixel buffer objects (PBOs). OpenGL applications rely on PBOs for improved data transfer between the CPU and GPU, but they're important for OpenGL-OpenCL interoperability because you can create buffer objects from PBOs with `clCreateFromGLBuffer`. Then, once the PBO is bound to the `GL_PIXEL_UNPACK_BUFFER` target, it can be used to set image data within a texture.

OpenCL and OpenGL are both powerful toolsets, but no one has ever called them simple. Getting the two to work together is one of the most complex programming tasks I can think of, and because I can't think of a harder topic related to OpenCL, this will be the last chapter of the book. Next, appendix A discusses the process of installing OpenCL on Windows, Linux, and Mac OS systems.

appendix A:
Installing and using a software development kit

There's no getting around it. If you want to build an application based on OpenCL, you need to install a software development kit (SDK). These are freely available as web downloads, but depending on your operating system and hardware vendor, they can be confusing to work with. The goal of this appendix is to help alleviate this confusion. Specifically, this appendix will explain how to obtain, install, and use an SDK capable of running on your system. But first, let's look at OpenCL SDKs in general.

A.1 Understanding OpenCL SDKs

At the time of this writing, the two most popular OpenCL SDKs are the ones released by AMD and Nvidia. The AMD SDK is called the Accelerated Parallel Processing (APP) SDK and the Nvidia SDK is called the GPU Computing SDK. Both companies have released different versions for different operating systems.

Before you install an SDK, there are two points you should be clear on. First, you should know the precise make and model of the hardware you intend to program, and whether it supports OpenCL. Second, you should have a basic understanding of which files in the SDK are important.

A.1.1 Checking device compliance

Which SDK you need depends on your operating system and the nature of your hardware. For example, if you want to build applications to run on your GPU, you need to know whether your graphics card was produced by AMD or Nvidia. You also need to know the model of the graphics card, such as a Radeon 5850 or a GTX 470.

To find this information, do one of the following:

- On Windows, open the Control Panel, open the Device Manager, and open the entry for Display Adapters.
- On Linux, open a terminal and execute the command `lspci`. If you see anything called ATI, AMD, or Radeon, your graphics card is AMD-based. If you see Nvidia, your card is based on Nvidia hardware.
- On a Mac, open the Apple menu and select the About This Mac entry. Click the More Info button and click Graphics/Displays in the left pane. Remember the value of the field entitled Chipset Model. This will identify your graphics card.

Once you've identified your target hardware, you need to make sure it's OpenCL-compliant. If you have Nvidia hardware installed, you can verify its compliance at http://developer.nvidia.com/cuda-gpus. For AMD hardware, go to the website http://developer.amd.com/sdks/AMDAPPSDK/pages/DriverCompatibility.aspx. Find the table called System Requirements and make sure your operating system and hardware are supported.

A.1.2 OpenCL header files and libraries

Before you can build any C/C++ application, you need the right header files and the right libraries. The header files declare constants, data structures, and functions, and libraries contain the functions' executable code. Most OpenCL applications only need a single header file: cl.h. On Windows and Linux, cl.h is located in a directory called CL. On Mac OS systems, it can be found in a directory called OpenCL.

The subject of OpenCL libraries is more complicated on Windows and Linux, but not for Mac OS users. On Mac OS systems, this library is a Mach-O file called OpenCL, and it comes with every version of Mac OS X from 10.6 onward. As long as you use -framework OpenCL in your makefile, the compiler will find the cl.h header file and the OpenCL library.

Both AMD and Nvidia provide libraries called OpenCL (OpenCL.dll on Windows, libOpenCL.so on Linux). In addition, both vendors' platforms on Windows and Linux support the cl_khr_icd extension. This means they provide a second library called an *installable client driver*, or ICD. The ICD serves as the interface to the OpenCL-compliant devices. Figure A.1 shows this relationship.

When you build an OpenCL application, you have to tell the linker how to access the primary OpenCL library, which is called libOpenCL.so on Linux systems and OpenCL.dll on Windows. But you don't have to identify the name or location of the ICD. This is important, because it means you can distribute your application without knowing anything about the user's vendor-specific hardware.

At runtime, however, the application must be able to access the ICDs. On Linux systems, the names of the ICDs are provided in text files inside the /etc/OpenCL/vendors folder. On Windows, the vendor-specific libraries are identified in the registry. When an SDK installs, it accesses the registry key HKEY_LOCAL_MACHINE\SOFTWARE\Khronos\OpenCL\Vendors. This is shown in figure A.2.

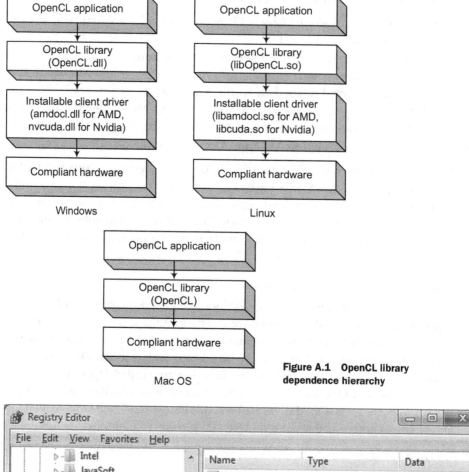

Figure A.1   OpenCL library dependence hierarchy

Figure A.2   Identifying the installable client drivers on Windows

When an OpenCL application executes on Windows or Linux, it looks through the ICD names and loads the corresponding library files as they're needed. For this reason, the ICD libraries must be placed in a location where the linker can find them. As shown in table A.1, this location depends on the vendor and the operating system.

Table A.1 Default locations of installable client drivers

Operating system	Nvidia	AMD
Windows	C:\Windows\system or C:\Windows\system32	C:\Windows\system or C:\Windows\system32
Linux	/usr/lib or /usr/lib64	Defined by the LD_LIBRARY_PATH environment variable

At this point, you should know which development kit you need and the SDK files that make OpenCL development possible. The following sections provide platform-specific instructions for your operating system and hardware vendor.

NOTE These instructions are valid for SDKs based on OpenCL 1.1. They may not apply to future versions.

A.2 OpenCL on Windows

AMD and Nvidia make it easy for Windows users to build OpenCL applications—all you have to do is download and run a couple of executables. This section explains how this is accomplished, and after the SDK is installed, how to build the SDK's example projects.

NOTE These instructions assume that you have Visual Studio installed. Appendix C explains OpenCL development using the freely available Minimalist GNU for Windows (MinGW).

A.2.1 Windows installation with an AMD graphics card

On Windows, AMD provides its OpenCL implementation as part of its Accelerated Parallel Processing (APP) toolset. Installing this is a straightforward process, and the following instructions will make this clear:

1 Update your system with the latest AMD driver and Catalyst tool. You can download new drivers at http://support.amd.com/us/gpudownload.

2 Open a browser and go to http://developer.amd.com/sdks/AMDAPPSDK/downloads. This is the primary website for AMD OpenCL support.

3 Scroll down to the Downloads section. Download the SDK installer that corresponds to your system. On my 64-bit Windows 7 system, the file is called amd-app-sdk-v2.5-Windows-64.exe.

4 Execute the installer, which will extract the SDK files to your system. Click the Unzip button on the right.

5 AMD's Catalyst Install Manager should appear, but if it doesn't, execute the Setup.exe file in the directory containing the extracted SDK files. The Catalyst Manager will ask which language it should use. Select a language, and click Next.

6 The following page asks whether you'd prefer the Express or Custom installation. I recommend the Custom installation. Click Next, and make sure that any component containing the word *Developer* is selected. Click Next again.

7 Read the end-user license agreement. Click Accept and then Next.

8 Click through the next series of pages to complete the installation of the AMD APP SDK. When the Catalyst dialog box says Installation complete, click Finish.

Once the installation is complete, you should check your environment variables to see where AMD placed its SDK files. On Windows, you can find these variables by right-clicking Computer or My Computer and selecting Properties. In the system dialog box, click Advanced system settings on the left. When the System Properties dialog box appears, click the button entitled Environment Variables.

The Environment Variables dialog box lists two types of variables: variables that apply to the current user (user variables) and variables that apply to all users (system variables). This is shown in figure A.3.

If you look through the system variables, you'll find two variables set by AMD during the SDK installation process:

- AMDAPPSDKROOT—Identifies the directory containing the primary SDK files. On my 64-bit Windows 7 system, this is C:\Program Files (x86)\AMD APP.

- AMDAPPSDKSAMPLESROOT—Identifies the directory containing the SDK's sample projects. On my Windows 7 system, this is C:\User\<name>\Documents\AMD APP.

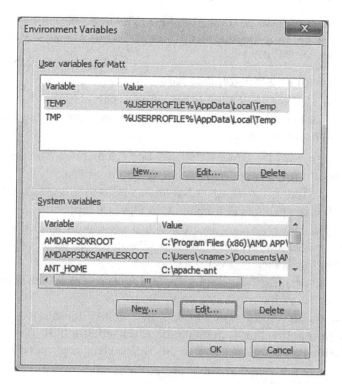

Figure A.3 Checking AMD environment variables on Windows 7

A.2.2   *Building Windows applications with an AMD graphics card*

Once you've verified that the environment variables have been created, I recommend that you explore their directories. The $(AMDAPPSDKSAMPLESROOT)\samples\opencl directory is particularly interesting. It contains a number of example projects that perform operations ranging from sorting to financial modeling.

If you have Visual Studio, you can build these example projects with little effort. Double-click the *.sln file that corresponds to your version of Visual Studio. Then, inside Visual Studio, use F7 to compile all the projects at once. The build of the simpledx10 project may fail if you don't have Direct3D installed, but the other projects should compile without error.

You can create a working application easily by modifying the code in one of these sample projects. But if you want to code an OpenCL application from scratch, there are two points to keep in mind:

- The OpenCL headers, such as cl.h, are located in $(AMDAPPSDKROOT)\include\CL.
- To access the OpenCL DLL, link against the import library OpenCL.lib in the $(AMDAPPSDKROOT)\lib\[x86|x86_64] folder.

As you progress in building OpenCL applications for AMD hardware, you may want to use AMD's SDKUtil library, whose utility functions serve a number of purposes, including file access and output of formatted text. The source code for the SDKUtil library can be found in $(AMDAPPSDKSAMPLESROOT)\samples\opencl\SDKUtil, and the header files can be found in the directory $(AMDAPPSDKSAMPLESROOT)\samples\opencl\SDKUtil\include.

A.2.3   *Windows installation with an Nvidia graphics card*

On Windows, Nvidia provides its OpenCL implementation as part of its GPU Computing SDK. Installing this toolkit is a straightforward process that involves downloading and running two executables. The following instructions show how this works:

1 To obtain the latest Nvidia driver, go to www.nvidia.com/page/drivers.html. Download the executable file that corresponds to your version of Windows and graphics card. Install the driver by launching the executable.

2 After the latest driver is installed, go to http://developer.nvidia.com/cuda-downloads and click the link for the latest CUDA Toolkit. On the following page, scroll down and find the table that lists downloads for Windows.

3 Click the link for the GPU Computing SDK and download this file to your system. On my computer, this file is called gpucomputingsdk_4.0.19_win_64.exe.

4 Execute the GPU Computing SDK file. Register your installation and choose a setup type and a location for the SDK files. Click Install and wait for the installer to finish.

Once the installation is complete, you should check your environment variables to see where Nvidia placed the SDK's files. On Windows, you can find these variables by

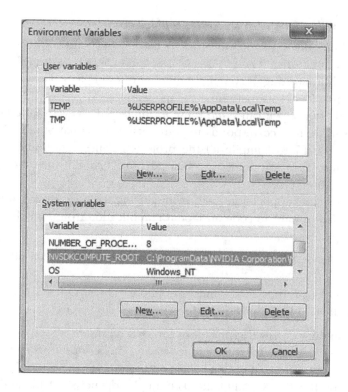

Figure A.4   Checking Nvidia's environment variable on Windows 7

right-clicking Computer or My Computer and selecting Properties. In the system dialog box, click Advanced System Settings on the left. When the System Properties dialog box appears, click Environment Variables.

The Environment Variables dialog box lists two types of variables: variables that apply to the current user (user variables) and variables that apply to all users (system variables). This is shown in figure A.4.

If you look through the system variables, you'll find the NVSDKCOMPUTE_ROOT variable, which identifies where the GPU Computing SDK has been installed. On my 64-bit Windows 7 system, the SDK can be found at C:\ProgramData\NVIDIA Corporation\NVIDIA GPU Computing SDK 4.0.

> **NOTE** If the current Windows driver on Nvidia's main page doesn't support the capabilities you're interested in, you may want to install the development driver from the CUDA Toolkit page. But I recommend the current driver (version 280.26) because it supports OpenCL 1.1 whereas the development driver (version 270.81) doesn't.

A.2.4 *Building Windows applications with an Nvidia graphics card*

I recommend that you look through the NVSDKCOMPUTE_ROOT directory and pay particular attention to the OpenCL subdirectory, which contains the files needed to build OpenCL applications. In addition, the $(NVSDKCOMPUTE_ROOT)\OpenCL\src directory contains a number of example projects that perform operations ranging from adding vectors to generating pseudo-random numbers.

If you have Visual Studio installed, you can build these example projects with little effort. In the $(NVSDKCOMPUTE_ROOT)\OpenCL\src directory, double-click the *.sln file that corresponds to your version of Visual Studio. Then, inside Visual Studio, use F7 to compile the solution. The builds of oclSimpleD3D10Texture and oclSimpleD3D9Texture may fail if you don't have Direct3D installed, but all of the other projects should compile without error. After the build, you can run the sample executables in the OpenCL\bin\win[32|64]\Release directory.

You can create your own applications easily by modifying the code in any of these sample projects. But if you want to code an OpenCL application from scratch, there are two points to remember:

- The OpenCL headers, including cl.h and cl_ext.h, are located in the $(NVSDKCOMPUTE_ROOT)\OpenCL\common\inc\CL folder.
- To access the OpenCL DLL, link against the import library OpenCL.lib in the $(NVSDKCOMPUTE_ROOT)\OpenCL\common\lib\[Win32|x64] folder.

As you progress in building OpenCL applications for Nvidia hardware, you may want to use Nvidia's oclUtils library, whose utility functions serve a number of purposes, including image formatting and querying your device. The oclUtils header file can be found in $(NVSDKCOMPUTE_ROOT)\OpenCL\common\inc and the library itself can be found in $(NVSDKCOMPUTE_ROOT)\OpenCL\common\lib.

A.3 OpenCL on Linux

AMD and Nvidia both support OpenCL development on Linux, but the installation process is more involved than it is on Windows. A common source of confusion involves the libraries. The main OpenCL library, libOpenCL.so, must be identified in your makefiles. But the proprietary libraries, such as libamdocl64.so and libcuda.so, don't need to be identified. These libraries, called *installable client drivers* or ICDs, are accessed automatically through text files in the /etc/OpenCL/vendors directory.

A.3.1 Linux installation with an AMD graphics card

AMD's implementation of OpenCL is provided as part of the APP SDK. Before you install the SDK, you should make sure your graphics driver is current and that you have the latest version of AMD Catalyst. At the time of this writing, AMD's Linux driver is called fglrx, and you can detect proper installation using the command fglrxinfo.

NOTE Don't be alarmed if the driver doesn't install correctly the first time. A web search will reveal tips and workarounds that others have used to get past the problem. I strongly recommend the Phoronix website at www.phoronix.com.

Once you've installed the latest AMD driver for Linux, perform the following steps to install the OpenCL SDK:

1 Open a browser, and go to http://developer.amd.com/sdks/AMDAPPSDK/ downloads. This is the primary website for AMD OpenCL support.

2 Select the SDK archive that corresponds to your system. On my 64-bit system, the file is called APP-AMD-SDK-v2.5-lnx64.tgz.

3 Decompress the SDK archive and launch the installation script, Install-AMD-APP.sh. On my system, this is done with the following command:

```
sudo sh Install-AMD-APP.sh
```

4 This script will extract the SDK files to your system and the default installation directory is /opt/AMDAPP. The script will also set an environment variable that identifies the installation directory (AMDAPPSDKROOT) and update the LD_LIBRARY_PATH variable so that the linker can find the required library.

5 Reboot your computer to complete the installation. To verify that the environment variable has been set correctly, enter the following command:

```
echo $AMDAPPSDKROOT
```

If you finished these steps with no errors, congratulations! You have successfully installed the AMD APP SDK on Linux. To make sure everything works, change to the top-level SDK directory, which should contain directories called bin, docs, include, lib, make, and samples. Then change to the samples directory.

Execute make to build the example applications. If the build procedure concludes without error and the executables run without error, you can be confident that everything is installed correctly. Otherwise, you may need to re-install the driver or the SDK itself.

A.3.2   *Linux installation with an Nvidia graphics card*

Installing OpenCL on a Linux system with Nvidia hardware is a straightforward process. Work through the following instructions, and you should have no difficulty:

1 To obtain the latest Nvidia driver, go to www.nvidia.com/page/drivers.html. Download the driver that corresponds to your operating system and graphics card.

2 Nvidia drivers can only be installed when the X server isn't running. To halt the X server, use the following command (replace gdm with kdm if you use KDE):

```
sudo /etc/init.d/gdm stop
```

3 Get to a command line with Ctrl-Alt-F1. Then log in and uninstall any existing Nvidia drivers with the following command:

```
sudo nvidia-uninstall
```

4 Change to the directory containing the SDK files you downloaded from Nvidia. Install the Linux driver with the sh command. On my system, this is done with this command:

```
sudo sh NVIDIA-Linux-x86_64-280.13.run
```

5 Accept the Nvidia license and accept all optional installations and modifications. Once the driver is installed, you may want to restart your system (sudo reboot).

6 Once the installation completes, the next step is to obtain Nvidia's GPU Computing SDK. Go to http://developer.nvidia.com/cuda-downloads and click the link for the latest CUDA Toolkit.

7 On the next page, scroll down and find the table that lists Linux downloads. Click the link for the GPU Computing SDK and download the file (gpucomputingsdk_x.y.z_linux.run) to your system.

8 Install the GPU Computing SDK with the sh command. On my system, this is done with this command:

```
sudo sh gpucomputingsdk_4.0.17_linux.run
```

9 Select a directory to install the SDK. Don't be concerned if the installer asks for the location of the CUDA Toolkit. It isn't necessary for OpenCL development.

10 When the installation completes, open the .bashrc configuration file in your home directory and export an environment variable called NVSDKCOMPUTE_ROOT. This will be used by makefiles to identify where Nvidia's libraries and include files are located. On my system, I've installed the SDK to /opt/nvsdk, so this is done as follows:

```
export NVSDKCOMPUTE_ROOT=/opt/nvsdk
```

11 Add a line in .bashrc to update the PATH variable so that it includes the SDK directory. On my system, this looks like the following:

```
export PATH=$NVSDKCOMPUTE_ROOT/bin:$PATH
```

12 Make this environment variable active with the following command:

```
source ~/.bashrc
```

NOTE If the current Linux driver on Nvidia's main page doesn't support the capabilities you're interested in, you may want to install the development driver from the CUDA Toolkit page. But I recommend the current driver (version 280.13) because it supports OpenCL 1.1 whereas the development driver (version 270.41) doesn't.

A.3.3 *Building OpenCL applications for Linux*

Once you've completed the full installation process on Linux, you're ready to start coding and executing applications. Functions intended for the host can be written in regular C and C++, while functions intended for auxiliary devices are written using OpenCL constructs. Files containing kernel functions commonly take the *.cl suffix.

To understand the Linux build process, it's a good idea to look at the makefiles in this book's example code. Makefiles in later chapters include graphic libraries such as libGL.so, but the makefile in Ch1/matvec includes only the basic OpenCL library, libOpenCL.so. The following listing shows the Linux-specific portion of the makefile.

Listing A.1 Linux processing in an OpenCL makefile

```
LIBS=-lOpenCL
ifeq ($(PROC_TYPE),)
    CFLAGS+=-m32                                    Set Linux
else                                               flags
    CFLAGS+=-m64
endif

ifdef AMDAPPSDKROOT
    INC_DIRS=. $(AMDAPPSDKROOT)/include
    ifeq ($(PROC_TYPE),)
        LIB_DIRS=$(AMDAPPSDKROOT)/lib/x86          Set AMD-
    else                                           specific flags
        LIB_DIRS=$(AMDAPPSDKROOT)/lib/x86_64
    endif
else

ifdef NVSDKCOMPUTE_ROOT                             Set Nvidia-
    INC_DIRS=. $(NVSDKCOMPUTE_ROOT)/OpenCL/common/inc    specific flags
endif
```

This makefile adds the -lOpenCL and -m32/-m64 flags to all Linux-based builds, but the INC_DIRS and LIB_DIRS macros are determined by the SDK vendor. If the AMDAPPSDKROOT variable is set, then the makefile assumes you intend to use AMD's tools. In this case, INC_DIRS is set to $AMDAPPSDKROOT/include and LIB_DIRS is set to one of the two directories under $AMDAPPSDKROOT/lib.

If the NVSDKCOMPUTE_ROOT variable is set and the AMDAPPSDKROOT variable isn't, the makefile assumes you want to use Nvidia's files in the build. In this case, INC_DIRS is set to $CUDA/OpenCL/common/inc. The LIB_DIRS variable doesn't need to be set because Nvidia places libOpenCL.so in the /usr/lib and /usr/lib64 directories, which is where the linker looks automatically.

If you intend to build applications on a Linux system that includes AMD and Nvidia hardware, you can set AMDAPPSDKROOT, NVSDKCOMPUTE_ROOT, or both. It doesn't matter which vendor's cl.h header or libOpenCL.so library is used. What's important is that your applications can access the correct ICD. If you receive a CL_PLATFORM_NOT_FOUND_KHR error or code -1001, you need to check the files in the /etc/OpenCL/vendors directory. If none of these files identify the ICD library you need, you may have to create a new file or modify an existing one.

A.4 *OpenCL on Mac OS*

If you're running Mac OS X 10.6 or later, you're in luck. You already have OpenCL installed, and you can find the framework files at /System/Library/Frameworks/OpenCL.framework. In particular, the OpenCL library can be found in the framework's Libraries/OpenCL folder. But there's no need to access it directly. As long as you include the -framework OpenCL option in your compilation step, the compiler will know where to find it.

The example code in this book is divided into projects, and each project contains a makefile that checks the operating system and sets the build parameters accordingly. The build process is simple: change to a directory containing a make-file and run make.

To understand the build process on Mac OS systems, it's a good idea to examine one of the makefiles. In each case, the makefile identifies the operating system by call-ing uname -s and converting the result to uppercase. If the output string contains DARWIN, the makefile sets the CFLAGS, INCLUDE_DIRS, and LIBS macros to Mac-specific values. This is shown in the following listing, taken from the makefile in Ch1/matvec.

Listing A.2 Building OpenCL applications for Mac OS

```
OS = $(shell uname -s 2>/dev/null                       Check for
          | tr [:lower:] [:upper:])                      Mac OS
DARWIN = $(strip $(findstring DARWIN, $(OS)))

ifneq ($(DARWIN),)
   CFLAGS += -DMAC
   LIBS=-framework OpenCL

   ifeq ($(PROC_TYPE),)                                  Set Mac OS flags
      CFLAGS+=-arch i386
   else
      CFLAGS+=-arch x86_64
   endif
else
```

The -framework OpenCL flag includes the cl.h header file, but there's a subtle point to keep in mind. The OpenCL framework places cl.h in a folder called OpenCL, whereas Windows and Linux systems place cl.h in a folder called CL. This can produce prob-lems if you intend to compile code on multiple operating systems. For this reason, you'll see the following comparison throughout the host code in this book:

```
#ifdef MAC
#include <OpenCL/cl.h>
#else
#include <CL/cl.h>
#endif
```

This ensures that the cl.h header file will be accessible whether you compile your application on Windows, Linux, or Mac OS systems.

A.5   *Summary*

Whether you're building software or hardware, the first order of business is to know your tools. In the case of OpenCL development, the tools are conveniently provided through freely available SDKs. The more time you spend understanding how these SDKs work, the less time you'll spend dealing with strange linking and compiling errors.

To make use of AMD's and Nvidia's SDKs, you need to understand the OpenCL library hierarchy. Every OpenCL application needs to link to a library containing OpenCL's standard functions. This library is called OpenCL.dll on Windows, libOpenCL.so on Linux, and OpenCL on Mac OS systems. If your development process uses makefiles, your makefile must identify the name and location of the OpenCL library.

But you don't have to identify the vendor-specific libraries that interface with the vendor's hardware. The SDK makes these libraries, installable client drivers (ICDs), available so that the OpenCL runtime can find them. In Windows, the SDK adds registry entries identifying the ICDs' names. In Linux, the ICDs are identified by text files in the /etc/OpenCL/vendors directory.

The majority of this appendix has centered on obtaining and installing SDKs for different operating systems and hardware. In each case, I've recommended that you examine and compile the SDK's example projects. This will make sure that your build tools are working properly and that your environment variables are correctly set. In addition, as you look through the vendor's projects, you'll have a better idea of how OpenCL applications are coded and compiled.

appendix B:
Real-time
rendering with OpenGL

The names resemble each other, but OpenCL and OpenGL serve very different purposes. While OpenCL is used for general computation, OpenGL (Open Graphics Language) is concerned with rendering 3-D graphics. By rendering, I mean that OpenGL accepts a model composed of three-dimensional figures and produces a two-dimensional array of pixels that can be drawn in a window. This rendering executes in a loop, and if the properties of the figures change, the renderer will update the drawing. Figure B.1 provides an example of a static rendering.

All the pixels in this figure have colors, but it would be tedious to set each color separately. Instead, the application defines three-dimensional points, called *vertices*, and routines to be invoked during the rendering, called *shaders*. As the application runs, the shaders process the vertices and draw the pixels in the window.

Despite their different purposes, OpenGL applications operate similarly to OpenCL applications. As explained throughout this book, an OpenCL application consists of two parts: a host application and a kernel. The host application initializes input data, packages it, and sends it to a device. The kernel processes the data as it executes on the device.

OpenGL applications work in much the same way. The host application initializes input data, packages it, and sends it to a GPU, which processes the data using shader routines. Shaders have a lot in common with OpenCL kernels, but instead of general-purpose processing, their sole concern is graphics. Further, shaders

Figure B.1 A simple OpenGL rendering

only run on GPUs, and instead of sending output back to the host application, the GPU uses the output to display pixels on a screen. OpenGL version 4.1 supports five different types of shaders, but only two of them are required: a vertex shader and a fragment shader. This is shown in figure B.2, which compares the operation of OpenCL and OpenGL applications.

> **NOTE** In addition to vertex shaders and pixel shaders, the OpenGL 4.1 spec also defines geometry shaders, tessellation control shaders, and tessellation evaluation shaders.

OpenGL is a vast topic, and for a full discussion of the API, I recommend *The OpenGL SuperBible* by Richard S. Wright et al. In contrast, the humble goal of this appendix is to provide you with enough background to enable you to code simple 3-D applications. The discussion will follow the right side of figure B.2. We'll examine how the host packages data first and then look at how to code vertex and fragment shaders. Then we'll see how the OpenGL Utility Toolkit (GLUT) creates windows that OpenGL applications can draw on.

But before getting into OpenGL and GLUT coding, it's important to have the required libraries and header files. Therefore, the first section will cover OpenGL installation.

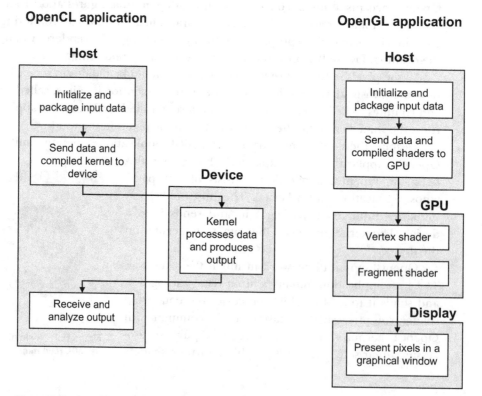

Figure B.2 OpenCL and basic OpenGL operation

B.1 Installing OpenGL

To compile the example code in this appendix, you need three packages:

- *OpenGL 3.3 or higher*—Needed to build OpenGL applications
- *GLUT*—Creates the underlying window for OpenGL applications
- *OpenGL Extension Wrangler Library (GLEW)*—Simplifies dealing with OpenGL extensions

It's likely that you already have one or more of these installed on your system. To check, look through the files in your OpenCL installation directory. In particular, look for the header files gl.h, glu.h, glut.h, and glew.h, and libraries with similar names. If you find these files on your system, you're all set.

If not, these packages are free to download and are available for multiple operating systems. This section will explain how to obtain and install these tools for computers running Windows, Linux, and Mac OS.

NOTE Before proceeding, it's important to make sure your graphics drivers are up to date.

B.1.1 OpenGL installation on Windows

Since Windows 98, the OpenGL library is installed on Windows systems by default. If you look through your primary system directory (C:\Windows\System32 or C:\Windows\System), you should find a library called opengl.dll or opengl32.dll. This is the library you need when you build OpenGL applications.

Modern versions of Visual Studio provide header files for OpenGL development. The precise location may change from version to version, but my Visual Studio 2010 system stores gl.h and glu.h at C:\Program Files\Microsoft SDKs\Windows\v7.0A\include\GL.

If you don't have GLUT installed, you can download it freely from the internet. The main site of the freeglut project is http://freeglut.sourceforge.net/index.php, and you can find binaries for Windows at www.transmissionzero.co.uk/software/freeglut-devel. Once you've downloaded and decompressed the archive, place the header files and libraries where they will be discovered by the compiler. The DLLs should be placed in your primary system directory.

The last step involves installing the GLEW package. The primary website for this is http://glew.sourceforge.net, and you can download Windows-specific binaries from this site. Again, place the header files and libraries where the compiler will find them.

B.1.2 OpenGL installation on Linux

On Linux, OpenGL is easy to install using packaging tools such as apt-get or rpm. The following command installs the required OpenGL headers, gl.h and glu.h:

```
sudo apt-get install mesa-common-dev libglu1-mesa-dev
```

Installing GLUT is just as easy. The following command installs the freeglut package (version 3), which contains the header file (glut.h) and library (libglut.so) needed to compile GLUT-based applications:

```
sudo apt-get install freeglut3 freeglut3-dev
```

Finally, if you can't find glew.h or libglew.so on your system, you can install the GLEW package with the following command:

```
sudo apt-get install libglew-dev
```

To test the installation, run glxinfo on the command line. You should receive a great deal of data concerning the supported OpenGL version and the capabilities available on your system.

B.1.3 OpenGL installation on Mac OS

Mac OS already provides frameworks for OpenGL and GLUT, so there's no need to download these separately. But you will need to install GLEW, and this means compiling it from source. To obtain the GLEW source code, go to http://glew.sourceforge .net and click the download link entitled TGZ.

Once you've downloaded and decompressed the GLEW archive, go to a command terminal. Change to the directory containing the GLEW source code and enter the following commands:

```
make
sudo make install
```

This will place the header file in /usr/include/GL and the library file in /usr/lib. Note that the GLUT header files are in a directory called GLUT, not GL.

Once you've installed the required files for OpenGL, GLUT, and GLEW, you'll be able to access C/C++ functions for OpenGL rendering. In the next section, we'll begin our examination of these functions by seeing how to code applications that execute on the host.

B.2   OpenGL development on the host

As discussed in chapter 3, an OpenCL application sends data from a host to a device using structures called memory objects. It makes these memory objects arguments of the kernel using setKernelArg, and once the kernel completes its execution, the host can read its output using a function like clEnqueueReadBuffer or clEnqueueReadImage.

In OpenGL, host applications have much more to do. At the very least, they need to perform four steps:

1 Place vertex data in vertex buffer objects (VBOs).
2 Make vertex data accessible to the shaders by configuring vertex attributes.
3 Compile shader code and load the shader executables onto the GPU.
4 Launch the rendering process.

This section will present each of these four steps and the functions needed to perform them.

B.2.1 *Placing data in vertex buffer objects (VBOs)*

When creating a 3-D model in OpenGL, the first step is to define the vertex data. Vertex data includes coordinates in three-dimensional space, and colors, normal vectors, texture coordinates, and any other data that may change from vertex to vertex.

In the interests of efficiency, it's best to define data for multiple vertices at once. For example, the three_squares application that we'll build in this appendix provides coordinates and colors for four vertices at a time. The following code sets the coordinates and colors of the vertices in the first square:

```
GLfloat first_coords[] = {-0.15f, -0.15f, 1.0f,
                          -0.15f,  0.15f, 1.0f,
                           0.15f,  0.15f, 1.0f,
                           0.15f, -0.15f, 1.0f};
GLfloat first_colors[] = {0.0f,  0.0f, 0.0f,
                          0.25f, 0.0f, 0.0f,
                          0.50f, 0.0f, 0.0f,
                          0.75f, 0.0f, 0.0f};
```

Note that this data is given using normalized values, which run from 0.0 to 1.0. For example, the color of the third vertex in the square is given by (0.50, 0.0, 0.0). If each channel is given as an 8-bit integer, this would correspond to (128, 0, 0), or a red color with medium intensity.

To store vertex data, you need to create a vertex buffer object or VBO. Like OpenCL buffer objects, VBOs make it possible to transfer data from the host to a device, specifically a GPU. But VBOs are slightly more complicated to work with. To see what I mean, look at table B.1, which lists the OpenGL functions related to VBOs.

NOTE OpenGL buffer objects can store many different types of data besides vertex data, such as pixel data and texture data. But the usage of buffer objects in this appendix will be limited to VBOs.

Table B.1 Functions related to vertex buffer objects (VBOs)

Function	Purpose
void glGenBuffers(GLsizei num, GLuint* descriptors)	Creates buffer objects and initializes an array of num descriptors
GLboolean glIsBuffer(GLuint desc)	Identifies whether the descriptor corresponds to a buffer object
void glBindBuffer(GLenum target, GLuint descriptor)	Makes the buffer object active
void glBufferData(GLenum target, GLsizeiptr size, const GLvoid* data, GLenum usage)	Associates the buffer with data
void glDeleteBuffers(GLsizei num, const GLuint* descriptors)	Deletes buffer objects identified by the descriptors

Don't be concerned about the new data types. OpenGL has its own system-independent types that serve the same roles as OpenCL's types. The GLuint type identifies an unsigned integer and GLsizei corresponds to size_t. When specific constants are needed to identify an enumerated type, GLenum is used.

The first function in the table creates one or more VBOs by initializing the memory referenced by the descriptors parameter. These VBO descriptors, like file descriptors on GNU systems, are unsigned integers.

As an example, the following code declares an unsigned integer to serve as a VBO descriptor and then calls glGenBuffers to create a buffer object:

```
GLuint vbo;
glGenBuffers(1, &vbo);
```

A VBO can't be immediately used after it's created. It needs to be made *active*. If a VBO is active, future OpenGL functions that read or write VBO data will access it instead of other VBOs. The process of making a VBO active is called *binding*, and the function to use is glBindBuffer. The following code makes vbo the active vertex buffer object:

```
glBindBuffer(GL_ARRAY_BUFFER, vbo);
```

The first parameter identifies a target, which tells OpenGL how the buffer data will be used. An OpenGL VBO can be bound to one of many possible targets including GL_ARRAY_BUFFER, GL_ELEMENT_ARRAY_BUFFER, GL_PIXEL_PACK_BUFFER, and GL_PIXEL_UNPACK_BUFFER. Only one buffer object can be bound to a target at any time.

Once a VBO is made active, it can be associated with vertex data using glBufferData. The signature for this function is as follows:

```
void glBufferData(GLenum  target, GLsizeiptr  size, const GLvoid* data,
                  GLenum  usage);
```

The last argument identifies how the data will be accessed. This can be set to one of the values listed in table B.2.

Table B.2 Access parameter values in glBindBuffer

Parameter value	Meaning
GL_STATIC_DRAW	Data is meant for drawing—it will be modified once and used frequently.
GL_STATIC_READ	Data is meant to be read from the renderer—it will be modified once and used frequently.
GL_STATIC_COPY	Data is meant to be read and written—it will be modified once and used frequently.
GL_DYNAMIC_DRAW	Data is meant for drawing—it will be modified repeatedly and used frequently.
GL_DYNAMIC_READ	Data is meant to be read from the renderer—it will be modified repeatedly and used frequently.
GL_DYNAMIC_COPY	Data is meant to be read and written—it will be modified repeatedly and used frequently.

Table B.2 Access parameter values in `glBindBuffer` (continued)

Parameter value	Meaning
GL_STREAM_DRAW	Data is meant for drawing—it will be modified once and used a few times.
GL_STREAM_READ	Data is meant to be read from the renderer—it will be modified once and used a few times.
GL_STREAM_COPY	Data is meant to be read and written—it will be modified once and used a few times.

These parameters provide storage hints for the renderer—they tell the renderer how and how often the data will be accessed. Our renderings in this appendix will be *static*, so we'll call `glBufferData` with `GL_STATIC_DRAW`. The following code associates the active VBO with the `first_coords` array defined earlier:

```
glBufferData(GL_ARRAY_BUFFER, 12*sizeof(GLfloat), first_coords,
             GL_STATIC_DRAW);
```

This code buffers the twelve `float`s in the `first_coords` array and tells the renderer that the data will be accessed frequently. After this function is called, all operations that affect the active VBO will access the values in `first_coords`.

After an application finishes using a VBO, it can unbind the VBO from the target by calling `glBindBuffer` with the descriptor set to 0. When the VBO is no longer needed, the application can deallocate its memory with `glDeleteBuffers`, which accepts the same parameters as `glGenBuffers`.

The following code presents the lifecycle of a trivial VBO:

```
GLuint vbo;
float vertex_data[12] = {-0.5, -0.5, 0.0, -0.5, 0.5, 0.0,
                          0.5, 0.5, 0.0, 0.5, -0.5, 0.0};
glGenBuffers(1, &vbo);
glBindBuffer(GL_ARRAY_BUFFER, vbo);
glBufferData(GL_ARRAY_BUFFER, 12*sizeof(GLfloat), vertex_data,
             GL_STATIC_DRAW);
glBindBuffer(GL_ARRAY_BUFFER, 0);
glDeleteBuffers(1, &vbo);
```

To be useful, the VBO needs to be transferred to the GPU, where it will be processed by a shader. But before a shader can access the VBO's data, the application needs to create attributes. Attributes specify the format of the VBO's data, and we'll look at this next.

B.2.2 Configuring vertex attributes

Vertex attributes identify properties of data within VBOs, such as the data's type, the number of elements, and whether the values are given in normalized form. Once these attributes are set, the data can be sent to shaders executing on the GPU.

Vertex array objects (VAOs) store the associations between attributes and VBOs. In general, OpenGL applications create one VAO for every independent object in the rendering. Table B.3 lists the functions needed to create and configure these bindings.

Table B.3 Functions related to vertex array objects (VAOs) and attributes

Function	Purpose
void glGenVertexArrays(GLsizei num, GLuint *descriptors)	Creates VAOs and initializes an array of descriptors
void glBindVertexArray(GLuint descriptor)	Makes the VAO active

void glVertexAttribPointer(GLuint index,
    GLint size, GLenum type,
    GLboolean normalized,
    GLsizei stride,
    const GLvoid* pointer)
	Sets the organization of the vertex array data

void glEnableVertexAttribArray (GLuint index)	Makes the vertex array active
void glDrawArrays(GLenum mode, GLint first, GLsizei count)	Draws data associated with the vertex array
void glDisableVertexAttribArray (GLuint index)	Makes the vertex array inactive
void glDeleteVertexArrays(GLsizei n, const GLuint* arrays);	Deletes and deallocates vertex array objects

The first two functions, glGenVertexArrays and glBindVertexArray, work like glGenBuffers and glBindBuffer. glGenVertexArrays creates one or more VAOs and initializes an array of unique descriptors. Once a VAO descriptor has been created, the VAO can be made active by calling glBindVertexArray with its descriptor. This is shown in the following code:

```
unsigned int vao;
glGenVertexArrays(1, &vao);
glBindVertexArray(vao);
```

The most important function in table B.3 is glVertexAttribPointer. This accepts properties related to the data in the active VBO: number of elements, type, normalization, and byte width between successive data elements. These attributes make it possible for the shader to interpret the data in the VBO.

The function's first parameter, index, serves a similar purpose to the index parameter of OpenCL's setKernelArg—it identifies the order of the attribute among all attributes passed to the shader. For example, if an attribute's index value is set to 0, it will be the first attribute accessed by the shader.

After attributes have been set for VBO data, glEnableVertexAttribArray places the vertex attribute array in the enabled state. This ensures that the attribute will be passed to the shader when it starts processing. This function accepts a value corresponding to the index value of glVertexAttribPointer. The following code shows how it's used:

```
glVertexAttribPointer(0, 12, GL_FLOAT, GL_FALSE, 0, 0);
glEnableVertexAttribArray(0);
```

Here, the vertex attribute array with index 0 provides information about the data in the active VBO. Specifically, it states that the VBO data contains twelve non-normalized floats with no stride between them. The last parameter is set to 0, so the data corresponding to the attribute array begins at the start of the VBO's data store.

Once the VBOs and VAOs have been configured for host data, the data is ready to be delivered to shaders. But before any shader executable can process data, it needs to be loaded onto the GPU. This is the topic of the following discussion.

B.2.3 *Compiling and deploying shaders*

In OpenCL, a host application reads kernel functions into char arrays, compiles them, and deploys them to the device. In OpenGL, the process is similar—the host application reads shader code, compiles it, and transfers the binary to the GPU.

More precisely, the process of deploying OpenGL shaders consists of five main steps:

1. Create shader objects and associate them with code.
2. Compile each of the shader objects.
3. Create a program object and attach the shader objects.
4. Link the program to form a GPU executable.
5. Deploy the executable to the GPU.

Table B.4 lists the functions that make this possible. Note that shader objects and program objects are identified by GLuint descriptors.

Table B.4 Functions that compile and deploy shaders

Function	Purpose
GLuint glCreateShader(GLenum shaderType)	Creates a shader object with the given type
void glShaderSource(GLuint shader, GLsizei count, const GLchar** string, const GLint* length)	Sets the source code for a shader object
void glCompileShader(GLuint shader)	Compiles the source code for a shader object
void glGetShaderiv(GLuint shader, GLenum pname, GLint* params)	Obtains information regarding a shader object
void glGetShaderInfoLog(GLuint shader, GLsizei maxLength, GLsizei* length, GLchar* infoLog)	Returns the log containing information about a shader's compilation
GLuint glCreateProgram()	Creates an empty program object

Table B.4   Functions that compile and deploy shaders (*continued*)

Function	Purpose
void glBindAttribLocation(GLuint program, GLuint index, const GLchar* name)	Assigns a variable name to a given attribute
void glAttachShader(GLuint program, GLuint shader)	Attaches a shader object to a program object
void glLinkProgram(GLuint program)	Create an executable from a program object
void glUseProgram(GLuint program)	Makes the program object active
void glDeleteProgram(GLuint program)	Deallocates a program object
void glDetachShader(GLuint shader, GLuint program)	Detaches a shader object from a program object
void glDeleteShader(GLuint shader)	Deletes and deallocates a shader object

Every OpenGL application requires a vertex shader and a fragment shader, so each of the first four functions must be called twice. To create the shader objects, you'd use code similar to the following:

```
GLuint vs, fs;
vs = glCreateShader(GL_VERTEX_SHADER);
fs = glCreateShader(GL_FRAGMENT_SHADER);
```

Unlike glGenBuffers and glGenVertexArrays, glCreateShader returns only a single descriptor. This is because an application can only have one shader for each shader type. An application can only have one vertex shader and one fragment shader.

Once the shader structures are created, the next step is to associate them with source code. Suppose the vertex shader source text is in the vs_chars array and the fragment shader source text is in the fs_chars array. The application can associate the source code with the shader by calling glShaderSource. The following code shows how this works:

```
glShaderSource(vs, 1, (const char**)&vs_chars, &vs_length);
glShaderSource(fs, 1, (const char**)&fs_chars, &fs_length);
```

In this code, vs_length is the number of chars in the vs_chars array and fs_length is the number of chars in the fs_chars array. Once the source code is loaded, the shaders can be compiled with the following function calls:

```
glCompileShader(vs);
glCompileShader(fs);
```

The glCompileShader function returns void, so it doesn't provide any notification if the compilation fails. To obtain information about the compilation, you need to call another function called glGetShaderiv. Like getProgramBuildInfo in OpenCL, this function returns data corresponding to a parameter. If the parameter is set to GL_COMPILE_STATUS, the function will return GL_TRUE if the compilation succeeded and GL_FALSE if it failed.

If a shader fails to compile, you need to examine the build log, and obtaining this involves two steps. First, find the size of the build log by invoking glGetShaderiv with GL_INFO_LOG_LENGTH. Then call getShaderInfoLog to read the log. This is shown in the following code.

Listing B.1 Compiling shaders and checking the build log: three_squares.c

```
...
void compile_shader(GLint shader) {

    GLint success;
    GLsizei log_size;
    GLchar *log;

    glCompileShader(shader);                              Check build
    glGetShaderiv(shader, GL_COMPILE_STATUS, &success);   status
    if (!success) {
        glGetShaderiv(shader, GL_INFO_LOG_LENGTH,         Find log
                      &log_size);                          size
        log = (char*) malloc(log_size+1);
        log[log_size] = '\0';
        glGetShaderInfoLog(shader, log_size+1,            Read
                           NULL, log);                     log
        printf("%s\n", log);
        free(log);
        exit(1);
    }
}
...
```

Once the shaders have been compiled successfully, the application needs to link them together within a new type of structure called a *program*. Programs are created with the glCreateProgram function, and the following code shows how it works:

```
Gluint prog = glCreateProgram();
```

Next, the vertex attributes must be associated with variable names that will be used by the shader. As discussed earlier, each attribute is given a unique index by the glVertexAttribPointer function, and the goal of glBindAttribLocation is to match each index to a name. For example, the following code matches the attribute whose index equals 0 with the name in_coords:

```
glBindAttribLocation(prog, 0, "in_coords");
```

This must be called for every attribute to be processed by the vertex shader. Then the shaders must be attached to the program using glAttachShader. The following code attaches the vertex shader vs and the fragment shader fs to the program prog:

```
glAttachShader(prog, vs);
glAttachShader(prog, fs);
```

We're almost done. Once the attributes are associated with names and the shaders are attached to the program, the program can be linked and installed with the following code:

```
glLinkProgram(prog);
glUseProgram(prog);
```

After these functions execute, the shaders attached to the program will be deployed to the GPU. The GPU will execute them when it comes time to render graphics.

Next, we'll look at how the host gets the rendering process started.

B.2.4   *Launching the rendering process*

So far, this section has discussed how to package vertex data and deploy shaders to the GPU. Once these steps are accomplished, the only task remaining is to start the rendering. The glDrawArrays function makes this possible, and its signature is as follows:

```
void glDrawArrays(GLenum mode, GLint start_index, GLsizei num_indices);
```

The first parameter, mode, tells the renderer what shapes to form from the model's vertices. These shapes are called *primitives*, and table B.5 lists the different parameters that specify what primitives should be drawn.

Table B.5   Drawing modes that identify primitives

Mode	Primitive
GL_POINTS	A series of individual points.
GL_LINES	Each pair of vertices forms a separate line.
GL_LINE_STRIP	Each vertex is connected to its successive vertex.
GL_LINE_LOOP	Each vertex is connected to its successive vertex, with the last vertex connected back to the first.
GL_LINES_ADJACENCY	Similar to GL_LINES, but each endpoint has an adjacent vertex that can be accessed by a geometry shader.
GL_LINE_STRIP_ADJACENCY	Similar to GL_LINE_STRIP but each endpoint has an adjacent vertex that can be accessed by a geometry shader.
GL_TRIANGLES	Each set of three vertices forms a separate triangle.
GL_TRIANGLE_STRIP	Forms a triangle with the first three vertices—each succeeding vertex forms a triangle with the two preceding it.
GL_TRIANGLE_FAN	Forms a triangle with the first three vertices—each succeeding two vertices form a triangle with the first vertex.
GL_TRIANGLES_ADJACENCY	Similar to GL_TRIANGLES, but each endpoint has an adjacent vertex that can be accessed by a geometry shader.
GL_TRIANGLE_STRIP_ADJACENCY	Similar to GL_TRIANGLE_STRIP, but each endpoint has an adjacent vertex that can be accessed by a geometry shader.
GL_PATCHES	A disordered group of vertices—the arrangement is determined by a tessellation control shader.

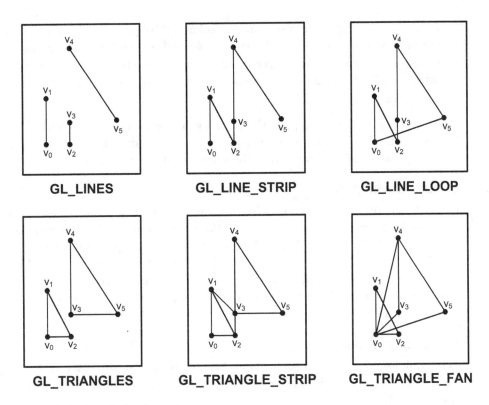

Figure B.3   OpenGL drawing modes

In effect, these drawing modes tell OpenGL how to connect the dots (vertices) whose attributes are stored within the active array. Figure B.3 depicts six of the different drawing modes.

The simplest drawing modes are GL_POINTS, GL_LINES, and GL_TRIANGLES. When these modes are set, each primitive is drawn separately, without connections to others. That is, if GL_LINES is set, each pair of vertices is drawn as a separate line. If GL_TRIANGLES is set, each triple of vertices forms a separate triangle.

The GL_LINE_STRIP and GL_TRIANGLE_STRIP modes create interconnected primitives from each successive vertex. If GL_LINE_STRIP is set, the renderer draws a line from the first vertex to the second, third, fourth, and so on. If GL_TRIANGLE_STRIP is set, then each successive vertex forms a triangle with the two vertices preceding it. For example, if there are four vertices, v_0 to v_3, this mode will cause two triangles to be drawn: v_0-v_1-v_2 and v_1-v_2-v_3.

Five of the drawing modes become useful when optional shaders are inserted in the rendering pipeline. The four modes involving adjacency, such as GL_LINES_ADJACENCY, require that a geometry shader process adjacent vertices. Similarly, the GL_PATCHES mode can only be specified when a tessellation control shader is available to establish order among the vertices.

Once the drawing mode is set, the second and third parameters of `glDrawArrays` determine which vertices will be drawn. The second parameter identifies the starting index, and the third parameter specifies the number of vertices. For example, the following code tells the renderer to draw six vertices as separate triangles:

```
glDrawArrays(GL_TRIANGLES, 0, 5);
```

As far as host programming goes, `glDrawArrays` is the last function you need to know. But OpenGL applications also require that you code routines to execute on the GPU. These functions, called *shaders*, form the subject of the next section.

B.3   Shader development

OpenGL supports a number of different types of shaders, but they're all coded with the same language: the OpenGL Shading Language, or GLSL. If you understand how to code OpenCL kernels, coding with GLSL won't present significant difficulty.

This section will provide an overview of OpenGL shader development. First we'll look at the data types and functions that shaders can access. Then we'll examine the two types of shaders required by all modern OpenGL applications: vertex shaders and fragment shaders.

B.3.1   Introduction to shader coding

In my opinion, the best way for an OpenCL programmer to understand shaders is to see how they compare with kernels. Table B.6 presents a list of similarities and differences between the two.

Table B.6   Shader code and kernel code—similarities and differences

Similarities	Differences
Shaders and kernels must be implemented as C functions that return void.	Shader functions must be called `main`. Kernels can take any name, but must be preceded by the `__kernel` modifier.
Shaders and kernels process data in vectors and provide mathematical operators for vectors.	Shaders support matrix data types. Kernels don't.
Shaders and kernels are math-oriented—there are no strings, no pointers, and no access to stdio.h or similar routines from the C Standard Library.	Shaders have built-in variables, some of which must receive values. Kernels don't have built-in variables.
Shaders and kernels can execute functions that closely resemble those in traditional math.h.	OpenCL variables have modifiers that identify where they're stored on the device.

The fundamental difference between kernels and shaders is that, while a kernel can serve any purpose, each shader in an OpenGL application has a specific role to play. At the very least, an OpenGL application must have one shader to process vertices and one to process fragments.

Regardless of the type, each shader consists of a C function called `main`. The following code presents a simple generic shader that sets an output vector variable, `out_vec`, equal to twice the value of an input vector variable, `in_vec`:

```
in vec4 in_vec;
out vec4 out_vec;

void main(void) {
    out_vec = in_vec * 2;
}
```

This gives an idea of how shaders are structured. The `main` function doesn't accept or return any parameters—it operates on variables declared outside the function.

DATA TYPES AND MODIFIERS

Dealing with data is one of the most interesting aspects of shader coding. While OpenCL kernels support operations on scalars and vectors, shaders support operations on scalars, vectors, and matrices. Table B.7 presents an abridged set of the data types available.

Table B.7 Shader data types (not including samplers)

Data Type	Content
`bool, int, uint, float, double`	Scalars—Boolean, integer, unsigned integer, float, and double
`bvec2, bvec3, bvec4`	Vectors containing Boolean values
`ivec2, ivec3, ivec4`	Vectors containing signed integers
`uvec2, uvec3, uvec4`	Vectors containing unsigned integers
`vec2, vec3, vec4`	Vectors containing float values
`dvec2, dvec3, dvec4`	Vectors containing double-precision values
`mat2, mat3, mat4`	Square matrices containing float values
`mat2x3, mat2x4, mat3x2, mat3x4, mat4x2, mat4x3`	Rectangular matrices containing float values
`dmat2, dmat3, dmat4`	Square matrices containing float values
`dmat2x3, dmat2x4, dmat3x2, dmat3x4, dmat4x2, dmat4x3`	Rectangular matrices containing float values

Vectors in shader code closely resemble vectors in OpenCL kernels. They're initialized in the same way and it's easy to repeat a single value throughout a vector. For example, the following lines of code both initialize a `float` vector whose four components equal 3.0:

```
vec4 v = (vec4)(3.0, 3.0, 3.0, 3.0);
vec4 v = (vec4)(3.0);
```

To access vector components, GLSL relies on the same dot-suffix method as that discussed in chapter 4. Some of the GLSL suffixes, however, are new:

- x, y, z, w—Identify coordinate elements or vector components
- r, g, b, a—Identify channels of a pixel's color
- s, t, p, q—Identify elements of texture coordinates

For example, if vec1 and vec2 both contain four elements, you can set vec2 equal to the reverse of vec1 with either of the following lines of code:

```
vec2 = vec1.wzyx
vec2 = vec1.abgr
```

Coding with matrices is similar to coding with vectors, but there's one important point to keep in mind: *the elements need to be given in column-major order.* This means that elements must be given one column at a time. For example, suppose you wanted to initialize an ivec4 called v with the following data:

$$v = \begin{bmatrix} 1 & 2 & 3 & 4 \\ 5 & 6 & 7 & 8 \\ 9 & 10 & 11 & 12 \\ 13 & 14 & 15 & 16 \end{bmatrix}$$

To initialize this matrix in a shader function, you could use the following code:

```
ivec4 v = (ivec4)(1, 5, 9, 13, 2, 6, 10, 14, 3, 7, 11, 15, 4, 8, 12, 16);
```

OPERATORS AND FUNCTIONS

The shader operators and functions defined in the GLSL standard serve the same roles as the OpenCL operators and functions described in chapter 5. The basic arithmetic operators are available (+, -, *, and /) and can be used with scalars, vectors, and matrices.

The vector functions available for shaders also closely resemble the functions presented in chapter 5. In particular, most of the shader functions for comparison, exponentiation, trigonometry, and geometry have the same names and usages as those used in OpenCL kernels. For example, if you want to set vector *c* equal to the dot product of vectors *a* and *b*, you'd use the following code:

```
c = dot(a, b);
```

The main difference between shader functions and kernels is that GLSL's functions operate on matrices. GLSL also provides functions specifically for matrix operations, and table B.8 lists each of them.

Table B.8   Matrix functions available in shaders

Shader function	Purpose
mat matrixCompMult(mat x, mat y)	Multiplies input matrices component-wise
mat outerProduct(vec x, vec y)	Returns the outer product of two vectors
mat transpose(mat x)	Returns the transpose of a matrix

Table B.8 Matrix functions available in shaders *(continued)*

Shader function	Purpose
`float determinant(mat x)`	Returns the determinant of a square matrix
`mat inverse(mat x)`	Returns the inverse of a square matrix

It's important to understand the difference between the `matrixCompMult` function in table B.8 and the matrix multiplication discussed in chapter 12. Regular matrix multiplication computes the dot products of the rows of the first matrix and the columns of the second. Therefore, the multiplication of an *m*-by-*n* matrix and an *n*-by-*p* matrix will produce an *m*-by-*p* matrix. In a shader, this operation is performed using the * operator.

In contrast, the `matrixCompMult` function doesn't compute dot products. It multiplies each element of the first matrix by the corresponding element of the second matrix and places the product in the corresponding position of the result. That is, it performs a two-dimensional set of scalar multiplications. Note that, to use `matrix-CompMult`, both input matrices must have the same size.

Chapter 12 explained the theory behind the outer product and the transpose operations, which GLSL implements with the `outerProduct` and `transpose` functions. The last two functions, `determinant` and `inverse`, only operate on square matrices. `determinant` returns a single `float` that serves as a matrix's characteristic value. In two dimensions, the determinant gives the area of the region bounded by the two vectors that form the matrix. In three dimensions, the determinant gives the volume of the region bounded by the three vectors that form the matrix.

The last function, `inverse`, returns the inverse of a square matrix. For example, if *A*, *B*, and *C* are matrices, and $AB = C$, then $B = A^{-1}C$, where A^{-1} is the inverse of *A*. In code, you can compute the inverse as follows:

```
a_inverse = inverse(a);
```

The GLSL specification provides a full description of the operators and functions available for shaders. This can be freely downloaded from www.opengl.org/documentation/glsl/.

B.3.2 Vertex shaders

The first of the two required shaders in an OpenGL application is the vertex shader. This runs on the GPU and executes once for every vertex in the model. This shader receives the attributes defined by the host application, such as coordinates, colors, texture coordinates, and normal vectors.

A vertex shader can't add or remove vertices from the model, but it can change the vertices' attributes, such as their coordinates or colors. It may seem odd to change these attributes immediately after the host initialized them, but there are good reasons for this. If you want the renderer to present the model from a given angle, the vertex shader can update the vertices' coordinates. Similarly, to change the way an object in the model reflects light, the vertex shader can change the vertices' normal vectors.

A vertex shader must set the position of each vertex it processes. More precisely, every vertex shader needs to provide a value for a built-in variable called gl_Position. This is a vec4, so the shader needs to provide four components for each position.

An example will help explain how this works. Suppose the host application creates an attribute called in_location that identifies vertex coordinates within a VBO. In this case, a simple vertex shader would look like the following:

```
in vec4 in_location;

void main(void) {
    gl_Position = in_location;
}
```

This shader sets the position of each vertex equal to the in_location attribute set by the host application. This may seem trivial, but without this, the renderer won't know which attribute corresponds to the vertex's position.

Most vertex shaders perform more work than setting output coordinates equal to input coordinates. In many cases, vertex shaders use matrix-vector multiplication to update vertices' positions. As explained in chapter 12, the multiplication of an *n*-element vector by an *n*-by-*n* matrix will produce a second *n*-element vector. If coded correctly, a matrix can be used to rotate, move, or scale vertices in a model. These operations are collectively called *transformations*, and their corresponding matrices are called *transformation matrices*.

For example, the AppB/three_squares application creates a model and rotates it so that the squares can be viewed from a specific viewpoint. This rotation is accomplished by the vertex shader, whose code is contained in the AppB/three_squares/three_squares.vert source file. Here's what this code looks like.

Listing B.2 Vertex shader: three_squares.vert

```
in   vec3 in_coords;                                      Vertex
in   vec3 in_color;                                       attributes
out  vec3 new_color;

void main(void) {

    new_color = in_color;
    mat3x3 rot_matrix = mat3x3(0.707, 0.641, -0.299,
                              -0.707, 0.641, -0.299,      Rotation
                              -0.000, 0.423,  0.906);      matrix
    vec3 coords = rot_matrix * in_coords;
    gl_Position = vec4(coords, 1.0);
}
```

Here, the host application provides the vertex shader with two attributes for each incoming vertex. The in_coords attribute identifies the position of the vertex, and in_color identifies the color of the vertex. The shader creates a 3-by-3 matrix called rot_matrix and multiplies it by the vertex's coordinates, thereby transforming the vertex's position.

The host application associates the color attribute with the name `in_color`. The vertex shader receives this attribute but doesn't modify its value. Instead, it creates another `vec3` variable called `new_color` and passes this to the next stage. In this simple application, the next stage is the fragment shader, which we'll look at next.

B.3.3 *Fragment shaders*

After the vertex shader completes its processing, the OpenGL renderer combines vertices into primitives such as points, lines, or polygons. Afterward, OpenGL will convert these three-dimensional figures into two-dimensional shapes composed of pixels. This conversion process is called *rasterization.*

But the pixels produced by rasterization aren't necessarily the final pixels displayed by the renderer. Instead, OpenGL refers to these preliminary pixels as *fragments.* The primary goal of a fragment shader is to accept the fragment colors produced by rasterization and determine the pixel colors in the final display.

Just as the vertex shader executes once for each vertex in the model, the fragment shader executes once for each fragment. The shader can't change a fragment's position or access other fragments, but it can serve the following five functions:

- Apply texture data
- Configure lighting—the ambient, diffuse, and specular components of reflected light
- Set the fragment's depth
- Perform bump-mapping—add roughness to an image
- Add other effects such as fog and shadow

In the three_squares application, the only purpose of the fragment shader is to set the fragment's output color. This is very easy. If the fragment shader only contains one output variable, the fragment's color will be set to this value. This is shown in the following code.

> **Listing B.3   Fragment shader: three_squares.frag**

```
in  vec3 new_color;
out vec4 out_color;

void main(void) {
    vec3 tmp_color = new_color + vec3(0.25f, 0.25f, 0.25f);
    out_color = vec4(tmp_color, 1.0);
}
```

`out_color` is the only variable declared with the `out` modifier, so the renderer will set the fragment's color to its value. The input variable, `new_color`, corresponds to the output variable (`new_color`) of the vertex shader. As shown in listing B.3, this variable contains the color attribute defined by the host application.

The vertex shader passes `new_color` to the fragment shader, but the value of the color may not be the same as the color attribute defined on the host. This is because pixel colors may be interpolated before reaching the fragment shader (chapter 6 discusses interpolation in detail). The fragment shader can't perform interpolation itself because it can't access colors of other fragments.

At this point, we've examined OpenGL host applications, vertex shaders, and fragment shaders. We're almost ready to render a 3-D model, but there's one last step: we need to form a window to provide the rendering canvas. The next section will explain how this works.

B.4   Creating the OpenGL window with GLUT

Figuratively speaking, you might say that OpenGL paints the picture and GLUT forms the frame and canvas. Technically speaking, GLUT creates the window that OpenGL uses to render graphics. GLUT isn't the only toolset that provides this capability, and both Qt and GTK allow you to create full-featured GUIs with OpenGL. But in my opinion, GLUT is the easiest for newcomers to use. The goal of this section is to present its functions and show how they work together to form canvases for OpenGL.

B.4.1   Configuring and creating a window

The first steps in any GLUT-based application are to load the GLUT runtime, configure window properties, and then create a data structure to represent the window. Table B.9 lists six functions that initialize GLUT windows.

Table B.9   GLUT initialization functions

Function	Purpose
void glutInit(int* argc, char** argv)	Launches the GLUT runtime
void glutInitWindowSize(int w, int h)	Sets the window's width and height
void glutInitWindowPosition(int x, int y)	Sets the coordinates of the window's initial position
void glutFullScreen()	Configures the window to occupy the entire screen
void glutInitDisplayMode(uint mode)	Sets the window's display mode, which identifies pixel format and color buffering
int glutCreateWindow(char* title)	Creates a window with the given title, returns a numeric descriptor for the window

Of these functions, glutInit must be called first. glutCreateWindow is usually called after all other GLUT configuration functions have been called.

The most important of the configuration functions is glutInitDisplayMode, which configures properties related to the window's pixel content and display characteristics. It accepts a single parameter that can be set to one of the constants in table B.10 or an OR'ed combination thereof.

Table B.10 GLUT display modes

Display mode constant	Configuration property
GLUT_RGB, GLUT_RGBA, GLUT_INDEX, or GLUT_LUMINANCE	Sets the channel format used for pixels within the window
GLUT_SINGLE or GLUT_DOUBLE	Sets whether the window uses single-buffering or double-buffering
GLUT_ACCUM, GLUT_ALPHA, GLUT_DEPTH, or GLUT_STENCIL	Identifies buffers to store data related to OpenGL buffering
GLUT_MULTISAMPLE	Enables full-screen anti-aliasing

The GLUT_RGB and GLUT_SINGLE modes are enabled by default. But throughout this book, the example OpenGL code will set the display mode to GLUT_RGB | GLUT_DOUBLE under the assumption that modern hardware can handle double-buffered graphics. As an example, the following code creates a 500-by-150-pixel window at the location $(0, 0)$:

```
glutInit(&argc, argv);
glutInitWindowSize(500, 150);
glutInitWindowPosition(0, 0);
glutInitDisplayMode(GLUT_RGB | GLUT_DOUBLE);
int window = glutCreateWindow("Title");
```

This code creates the data structure that GLUT uses internally to represent the window, but it doesn't actually display a new window. Before we can get to that, we need to set up event handling.

B.4.2 Event handling

Event handling is an important concern when coding graphical user interfaces (GUIs). You need a way to tell the application how to respond to mouseovers, mouse clicks, keystrokes, resizing events, and every other kind of external stimulus an application can receive. GLUT makes this simple by providing event-handling functions that accept pointers to functions called *callback functions*, which respond to the corresponding events. Table B.11 lists a subset of these functions and the events they respond to.

Table B.11 GLUT event-handling functions

Function	Event
void glutDisplayFunc(void(*func)(void))	Window display
void glutMouseFunc(void(*func) (int button, int state, int x, int y))	Mouse click or release at the given coordinates
void glutReshapeFunc(void(*func) (int width, int height))	Resizing of the GLUT window

Table B.11   GLUT event-handling functions (*continued*)

Function	Event
void glutKeyboardFunc(void(*func) (unsigned char key, int x, int y))	Keystroke
void glutVisibilityFunc(void(*func) (int state))	Change in the window's visibility status
void glutTimerFunc(unsigned int ms_time, void(*func)(int value), value)	Passage of the specified amount of time
void glutIdleFunc(void (*func) (void))	Called when events aren't being received

The callback function identified by glutDisplayFunc tells the window how to display itself. For this reason, it's the only callback registration function that *must* be implemented in a GLUT application. To see how it works, let's suppose you have a function called display, as follows:

```
void display() {
   . . .
}
```

The following code ensures that GLUT will call this function when it needs to redraw the pixels in the window:

```
glutDisplayFunc(&display);
```

As a further example, the following code creates a function that receives reshaping events and then registers it as a GLUT callback function:

```
void reshape(int width, int height) {
   . . .
}
```

```
glutReshapeFunc(&reshape);
```

In both of these examples, the name of the callback function is taken from the name of the corresponding GLUT registration function. This convention makes coding easier, and it is employed throughout this appendix as well as chapters 15 and 16.

B.4.3   Displaying a window

After you've initialized the window and registered its event-handling routines, you're ready to display the window on the user's screen. The function that makes this possible is glutMainLoop, which doesn't accept any parameters or return any values. It starts the GLUT processing cycle that receives events and invokes their callback functions as needed. The loop continues until the GLUT application terminates.

The following code shows how GLUT applications call glutMainLoop and many of the other functions discussed so far. This registers two callback functions—one that executes when the window draws its pixels, and one that responds to resizing events.

Listing B.4 Simple GLUT application: glut_intro.c

```c
#define FREEGLUT_STATIC
#include <GL/freeglut.h>
#include <stdio.h>

void reshape(int width, int height) {
    printf("New dimensions: %d %d\n", width, height);
}

void display() {
    glClear(GL_COLOR_BUFFER_BIT);
    printf("Displaying the window\n");
    glutSwapBuffers();
}

int main(int argc, char **argv) {

    glutInit(&argc, argv);
    glutInitDisplayMode(GLUT_RGB | GLUT_DOUBLE);    Initialize
    glutInitWindowSize(500, 150);                   window
    glutInitWindowPosition(200, 100);               structure
    glutCreateWindow("Introducing GLUT");

    glutDisplayFunc(display);       Set event
    glutReshapeFunc(reshape);       handling

    glClearColor(1.0, 1.0, 1.0, 1.0);    Start
    glutMainLoop();                 ←──   GLUT loop
    return 0;
}
```

When this code is compiled and executed, the result will be a 500-by-150-pixel window, such as the one shown in figure B.4.

When the window first appears, GLUT will invoke the reshape call-

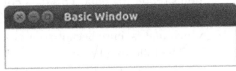

Figure B.4 Example GLUT window

back function first and the display callback function second. These functions will be called again whenever the window is resized. This is shown by the following output:

```
New dimensions: 500 150
Displaying the window
New dimensions: 468 133
Displaying the window
New dimensions: 413 130
Displaying the window
New dimensions: 334 130
Displaying the window
New dimensions: 280 127
Displaying the window
```

The callback functions that handle display and resizing events will play particularly important roles in the discussion that follows. As we add OpenGL-specific code to these functions, we'll see the content of the window become much more interesting.

B.5   Combining OpenGL and GLUT

To make a GLUT window capable of displaying OpenGL graphics, three steps are required:

1 Code the initialization process to specify vertex data and compile and deploy shaders.
2 Set GLUT's resize callback to invoke glViewport, which will tell the OpenGL renderer how large the display canvas is.
3 Set GLUT's display callback to invoke glDrawArrays, which will render the 3-D model in the GLUT window.

These steps are straightforward, as long as you remember when each GLUT function is called. For example, the resize callback is called whenever the window is resized. The display callback is called whenever the window needs to draw itself. This section will discuss each of these three steps.

B.5.1   GLUT/OpenGL initialization

If you compare the code in AppB/three_squares/three_squares.c and the code in listing B.4, you'll see that the main function in three_squares.c calls two additional functions: init_buffers and init_shaders. These functions handle the OpenGL initialization tasks for the application.

INITIALIZING OPENGL BUFFERS

The goal of init_buffers is to create the VAOs and VBOs needed to store the application's rendering data. This data consists of six VBOs—three containing vertex coordinates and three containing vertex colors. Each VBO contains data for four vertices, which makes sense because our goal is to render three squares.

The following listing presents the code that defines and configures vertex data for the first square. The first_coords array contains the coordinates for the square's vertices, and the first_colors array contains coordinates for the square's colors.

> **Listing B.5   Setting VBOs to hold rendering data: three_squares.c**

```
. . .
GLfloat first_coords[] = {-0.15f, -0.15f,  1.0f,
                          -0.15f,  0.15f,  1.0f,
                           0.15f,  0.15f,  1.0f,
                           0.15f, -0.15f,  1.0f};
GLfloat first_colors[] = {0.0f,  0.0f,  0.0f,
                          0.25f,  0.0f,  0.0f,
                          0.50f,  0.0f,  0.0f,
                          0.75f,  0.0f,  0.0f};
. . .
void init_buffers(void) {

   glGenVertexArrays(3, vao);

   glGenBuffers(6, vbo);                    ❶ Create six
                                              VBOs
   glBindVertexArray(vao[0]);
```

❶ Create six VBOs

```
glBindBuffer(GL_ARRAY_BUFFER, vbo[0]);
glBufferData(GL_ARRAY_BUFFER, 12*sizeof(GLfloat),      Configure
        first_coords, GL_STATIC_DRAW);                 first VBO
glVertexAttribPointer(0, 3, GL_FLOAT,
                      GL_FALSE, 0, 0);
glEnableVertexAttribArray(0);

glBindBuffer(GL_ARRAY_BUFFER, vbo[1]);
glBufferData(GL_ARRAY_BUFFER, 12*sizeof(GLfloat),      Configure
        first_colors, GL_STATIC_DRAW);                 second VBO
glVertexAttribPointer(1, 3, GL_FLOAT,
                      GL_FALSE, 0, 0);
glEnableVertexAttribArray(1);
...
```

Six data arrays are needed in total, so the application creates six VBOs by calling `glGenBuffers` ❶. Then it configures each VBO by making it active, buffering the data, and creating an attribute for the data. The `glEnableVertexAttribArray` function stores the attribute and the corresponding data within the active VAO.

DEPLOYING SHADERS

The second initialization function, `init_shaders`, implements the shader deployment process described earlier. The following listing presents this function in full.

> **Listing B.6   Initializing shaders to process rendering data: three_squares.c**

```
void init_shaders(void) {

    GLuint vs, fs, prog;
    char *vs_source, *fs_source;
    GLint vs_length, fs_length;

    vs = glCreateShader(GL_VERTEX_SHADER);          Create
    fs = glCreateShader(GL_FRAGMENT_SHADER);        shaders

    vs_source = read_file(VERTEX_SHADER, &vs_length);
    fs_source = read_file(FRAGMENT_SHADER, &fs_length);

    glShaderSource(vs, 1, (const char**)&vs_source, &vs_length);
    glShaderSource(fs, 1, (const char**)&fs_source, &fs_length);

    compile_shader(vs);                             Compile
    compile_shader(fs);                             shaders

    prog = glCreateProgram();

    glBindAttribLocation(prog, 0, "in_coords");
    glBindAttribLocation(prog, 1, "in_color");

    glAttachShader(prog, vs);
    glAttachShader(prog, fs);

    glLinkProgram(prog);                            Deploy
    glUseProgram(prog);                             program
}
```

The functions used in this code are the same as those presented in table B.4. Note that, because the application requires two shaders, many functions are called twice.

The shaders are compiled with `compile_shader`, which isn't an OpenGL function. This compiles the argument and outputs the build log if the compilation fails. Its code is given in listing B.1.

The last function invoked in listing B.6 is `glUseProgram`, which installs the linked program object on the GPU. There's no need to call `glDeleteProgram` because the program will be deallocated at the application's conclusion.

B.5.2 Setting the viewport

To render a scene, OpenGL needs to know the size and location of the canvas region. This is provided by `glViewport`, whose signature is as follows:

```
void glViewport(GLint x, GLint y, GLsizei width, GLsizei height)
```

The operation of this function is straightforward. The x and y parameters identify the upper-left position of the region, and `width` and `height` identify the size. If a user moves or resizes the GLUT window, the viewport needs to be updated. Therefore, the `resize` callback function calls `glViewport` in the following manner:

```
void reshape(int w, int h) {
    glViewport(0, 0, (GLsizei)w, (GLsizei)h);
}
```

Here, the x and y parameters identify the region's location in the GLUT window's client area, not the absolute location within the screen.

B.5.3 Rendering the model

As described in the preceding section, the GLUT window calls the `display` callback every time it needs to redraw its content. The OpenGL function `glDrawArrays` launches the rendering process, so it makes sense that the `display` callback should invoke `glDrawArrays`. This is precisely how OpenGL rendering is accomplished with GLUT. The following listing presents the full code of the `display` callback.

Listing B.7   Rendering the model: three_squares.c

```
void display(void) {
    glClear(GL_COLOR_BUFFER_BIT | GL_DEPTH_BUFFER_BIT);

    glBindVertexArray(vao[2]);                      Draw
    glDrawArrays(GL_TRIANGLE_FAN, 0, 4);            first VAO

    glBindVertexArray(vao[1]);                      Draw
    glDrawArrays(GL_TRIANGLE_FAN, 0, 4);            second VAO

    glBindVertexArray(vao[0]);                      Draw
    glDrawArrays(GL_TRIANGLE_FAN, 0, 4);            third VAO

    glBindVertexArray(0);
    glutSwapBuffers();
}
```

Here, `glDrawArrays` is called three times—once for each vertex array object configured in the init_buffers function. This draws each of the three squares of the model. Figure B.5 shows what the result looks like.

The first line of code deserves explanation. OpenGL stores state information using a series of buffers. The color buffer stores the colors of each pixel in the display, and the depth buffer, also called the z-buffer, stores a depth value for each pixel. The `glClear` function resets buffers to their default configurations, so the `glClear` function in listing B.7 resets both the color buffer and the depth buffer.

Figure B.5   The three squares rendering

This code sets the colors of the model's vertices using basic RGB values, but we can do better. Professional game developers prefer to add detail to every surface in a design, and to make this possible, they rely on textures.

B.6   Adding texture

Textures make it possible to associate image data with the surfaces of a model. If you think of OpenGL vertices as forming a skeleton, then textures form the skin. Figure B.6 shows how this works. The texture_squares application creates textures from the three images on the left and uses them to cover the squares.

Working with OpenGL textures is like putting up wallpaper. In both cases, blank surfaces are made more appealing through the application of decorative images. The corners of the pattern must be carefully matched to the corners of the surface. It's also important to make sure that the pattern is oriented correctly as it's applied.

But textures are easier to work with than wallpaper because there's no need to do any measuring. OpenGL will stretch or shrink the texture as needed to fit the space. Also, if a texture needs to be minimized, you can tell OpenGL to use miniaturized versions of the texture called *mipmaps*.

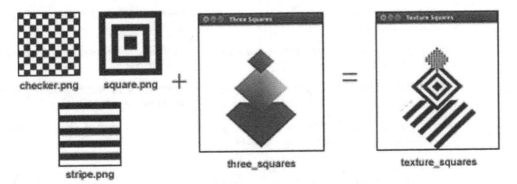

Figure B.6   Covering model surfaces with textures

The goal of this section is to explain how to convert image data into two-dimensional textures and apply the textures to surfaces in a model. There are three steps involved:

1 In the host application, create a texture object and configure it with data from an image file.
2 In the vertex shader, match the texture's coordinates to vertices of the model.
3 In the fragment shader, set the output color equal to the texture color.

After discussing the functions needed to implement these steps, we'll look at the texture_squares application, which converts the images on the left of figure B.6 into textures and uses them to form the rendering on the right.

B.6.1   Creating textures in the host application

The process of initializing textures in OpenGL is similar to that of initializing VBOs. There are four steps:

1 Create one or more descriptors to represent the textures.
2 Make a texture active.
3 Set characteristics of the active texture.
4 Associate the active texture with data.

Table B.12 lists the functions needed to implement these steps. As with VBOs, texture descriptors are given as GLuints.

The first two functions, glGenTextures and glBindTexture, operate like the glGenBuffers and glBindBuffer functions discussed earlier. The first creates one or

Table B.12   Functions related to textures

Function	Purpose
void glGenTextures(GLsizei num, GLuint* descriptors)	Creates texture objects and initializes an array of descriptors
void glBindTexture(GLenum target, GLuint descriptor)	Makes the texture object active for a given target
void glPixelStorei(GLenum param_name, GLint param)	Identifies characteristics about how the pixel data is stored
void glTexParameteri(GLenum target, GLenum param_name, GLint param)	Identifies characteristics about how the texture should be used
void glTexImage2D(GLenum target, GLint level, GLint internalformat, GLsizei width, GLsizei height, GLint border, GLenum format, GLenum type, const GLvoid* data);	Associates image data with the texture
void glDeleteTextures(GLsizei num, const GLuint* descriptors)	Deletes texture objects identified by the descriptors

more texture objects, and the second makes a texture active by binding it to a target. This discussion is focused on forming textures from two-dimensional images, so the target of interest is `GL_TEXTURE_2D`.

The `glPixelStorei` and `glTexParameteri` functions both provide OpenGL with information about the texture. The first identifies how the texture's pixels are stored in memory. To create a texture from uncompressed data, the parameter name should be `GL_UNPACK_ALIGNMENT` and the value should be the byte alignment of each pixel row. For example, the following code specifies that the pixel rows are stored at 1-byte boundaries:

```
glPixelStorei(GL_UNPACK_ALIGNMENT, 1);
```

The parameters accepted by `glTexParameteri` are more involved and tell OpenGL how the texture should be displayed in the rendering. Table B.13 lists six of the parameter names accepted by `glTexParameteri` and the nature of the information they provide.

Table B.13 **Texture parameters (abridged)**

Parameter	Information
`GL_TEXTURE_MIN_FILTER`	Defines the interpolation method used for minimization
`GL_TEXTURE_MAG_FILTER`	Defines the interpolation method used for enlargement
`GL_TEXTURE_MIN_LOD`	Identifies the texture's lowest mipmap level
`GL_TEXTURE_MAX_LOD`	Identifies the texture's highest mipmap level
`GL_TEXTURE_WRAP_S`	Configures how the texture should be displayed in the s-direction at coordinates beyond its dimensions
`GL_TEXTURE_WRAP_T`	Configures how the texture should be displayed in the t-direction at coordinates beyond its dimensions

One of the main purposes of `glTexParameteri` is to specify how the active texture should be displayed when the viewer zooms in or out. If the texture needs to be enlarged, the first parameter in the table identifies which interpolation method should be employed. The parameter value can be set to `GL_NEAREST` for nearest-neighbor interpolation or `GL_LINEAR` for bilinear interpolation. Chapter 6 discusses both methods in detail.

If a texture needs to be minimized, there are more options available. In addition to nearest-neighbor and bilinear interpolation, the minimization can make use of mipmaps. A mipmap is a smaller version of the original texture image, and its dimensions are scaled by 1/2, 1/4, 1/8, and so on. Mipmaps make it possible for OpenGL to display textures at reduced size without the processing burden and potential error associated with interpolation.

Each mipmap has a level, and the higher the level, the smaller the size. For example, if the user zooms out of a scene, the mipmap level used may increase from 2 to 3 to 4.

The GL_TEXTURE_MIN_LOD and GL_TEXTURE_MAX_LOD identify the lowest and largest mipmap levels available.

The last two parameters in the table relate to texture coordinates. Before OpenGL can apply a texture to a model's surface, the application must match the texture's coordinates to vertex coordinates. For two-dimensional textures, the coordinates are given in (*s*, *t*) pairs. This is shown in figure B.7.

The responsibility for creating the correspondence between these coordinates falls to the vertex shader, and this will be discussed shortly. For now, it's important to know that the GL_TEXTURE_WRAP_S and GL_TEXTURE_WRAP_T

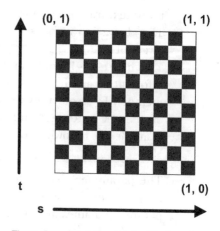

Figure B.7 Texture coordinates for a two-dimensional image

parameters tell OpenGL what to display when the texture coordinates go beyond the minimum and maximum. Both parameters accept the same five values: GL_CLAMP, GL_CLAMP_TO_BORDER, GL_CLAMP_TO_EDGE, GL_MIRRORED_REPEAT, and GL_REPEAT. Chapter 6 discusses these values and figure 6.1 shows how the resulting textures are displayed.

As an example, the following code creates a texture and makes it active. Then it calls glTexParameteri to tell OpenGL that bilinear interpolation should be used for enlargement and minimization. Also, pixels at coordinates beyond the texture should be repetitions of the texture's pixels:

```
glGenTextures(1, &texture);
glBindTexture(GL_TEXTURE_2D, texture);
glPixelStorei(GL_UNPACK_ALIGNMENT, 1);
glTexParameteri(GL_TEXTURE_2D, GL_TEXTURE_WRAP_S, GL_REPEAT);
glTexParameteri(GL_TEXTURE_2D, GL_TEXTURE_WRAP_T, GL_REPEAT);
glTexParameteri(GL_TEXTURE_2D, GL_TEXTURE_MAG_FILTER, GL_LINEAR);
glTexParameteri(GL_TEXTURE_2D, GL_TEXTURE_MIN_FILTER, GL_LINEAR);
```

After the texture is created and its characteristics are set, glTexImage2D can be used to associate the texture with pixel data. This serves a purpose similar to glBufferData, but in addition to the data dimensions, glTexImage2D also needs to know how the pixels in the texture, called *texels*, are organized. Table B.12 lists all the arguments of this function; three important arguments are as follows:

- internalformat identifies the number of components in each texel. Example values include GL_RGBA8, GL_RGBA16, GL_RGB8, GL_RGB16, GL_ALPHA8, GL_ALPHA16, GL_LUMINANCE8, and GL_LUMINANCE16.
- format identifies the properties of individual texels. Example values include GL_RGBA, GL_RGB, GL_ALPHA, and GL_LUMINANCE.
- type sets the data type of each component. Example values include GL_FLOAT, GL_INT, GL_UNSIGNED_BYTE, and GL_SHORT.

As an example, the following code associates a two-dimensional texture with a 60*40 array of texels called `tex_data`. Each texel in `tex_data` is composed of RGB components, and each component is given as an unsigned byte:

```
glTexImage2D(GL_TEXTURE_2D, 0, GL_RGB8, 60, 40, 0, GL_RGB,
             GL_UNSIGNED_BYTE, tex_data[i]);
```

`glTexImage2D` is the last of the functions that need to be called to configure a texture. Once this is accomplished, the next step involves matching the coordinates of the texture to vertices in the model. This matching process is called *texture mapping*, and it will be discussed next.

B.6.2   *Texture mapping in the vertex shader*

As explained in section B.3, the vertex shader sets the coordinates of a vertex by initializing a built-in variable called `gl_Position`. The vertex shader can also access a built-in variable called `gl_TexCoord`. This variable represents an array of textures, and when an element of this array is set equal to an array of coordinates, those texture coordinates will be matched to the vertex being processed by the shader.

Each element of `gl_TexCoord` can be set to a vector containing four coordinates, but for two-dimensional textures, only the first two coordinates need to be set. As an example, the following code sets the (s, t) components of `gl_TexCoord[0]` equal to $(3, 4)$:

```
gl_TexCoord[0].st = vec2(3, 4);
```

In general, vertex shaders determine texture coordinates using one of two methods. First, a shader may compute texture coordinates based on the coordinates of the vertex being processed. In the following line of code, the shader sets the texture coordinates (s, t) equal to the (x, y) coordinates of the vertex:

```
gl_TexCoord[0].st = gl_Position(x, y);
```

Second, the shader can access texture coordinates through input attributes. As explained earlier, attributes identify specific portions of VBO data. For example, the following code initializes the vertex coordinates of the first square (`first_coords`) and the coordinates of the texture (`tex_coords`) used to cover the square:

```
GLfloat first_coords[] = {-0.15f, -0.15f, 1.0f,
                          -0.15f,  0.15f, 1.0f,
                           0.15f,  0.15f, 1.0f,
                           0.15f, -0.15f, 1.0f};
GLfloat tex_coords[] = {0.0f, 0.0f,
                        0.0f, 1.0f,
                        1.0f, 1.0f,
                        1.0f, 0.0f};
```

The attribute corresponding to the `tex_coords` data is called `in_texcoords`, and the following listing shows how the vertex shader accesses these coordinates and sets them equal to the `gl_TexCoord[0]` output.

Listing B.8   Simple texture mapping: texture_squares.vert

```
in  vec3 in_coords;
in  vec2 in_texcoords;

void main(void) {

    gl_TexCoord[0].st = in_texcoords;                          ⟵  Assign texture
    mat3x3 rot_matrix = mat3x3(0.707, 0.641, -0.299,              coordinates
                              -0.707, 0.641, -0.299,
                              -0.000, 0.423,  0.906);
    vec3 coords = rot_matrix * in_coords;
    gl_Position = vec4(coords, 1.0);
}
```

This code listing closely resembles listing B.2, but in addition to setting the location of each vertex in the model, it also matches the vertex with a texture coordinate. Once this is done, the fragment shader will be able to access the texture's color values.

B.6.3 *Applying textures in the fragment shader*

Just as the vertex shader can access a built-in output variable called gl_TexCoord, the fragment shader can access a built-in input variable called gl_TexCoord. In both cases, the variable represents an array of textures, and each element of the array contains texture coordinates.

The texture function makes it possible to access the color at a given location in the texture. This can be called in a number of different situations, but for a simple two-dimensional texture, its signature is as follows:

```
vec4/ivec4/uvec4 texture(sampler2D sampler, vec2 coords)
```

The first argument is a *sampler*, which serves a purpose similar to the sampler_t structures discussed in chapter 6. It identifies which interpolation method should be used for the texture and how to display the texture when coordinates go beyond the texture's borders.

For basic sampling, you don't have to configure a custom sampler. A fragment shader can access a built-in sampler as a *uniform*. Uniforms are similar to attributes in that shaders can access them as input. But uniforms are constant—they don't change from pixel to pixel or from fragment to fragment. Further, attributes can only be accessed by vertex shaders, not fragment shaders.

The following listing presents the code for the fragment shader in the texture_squares application. It calls texture with the default sampler2D to obtain the texel color at the coordinates identified by gl_TexCoord. Then it sets the fragment's output color, new_color, equal to the texel color.

Listing B.9   Texture application: texture_squares.frag

```
uniform sampler2D tex;
out vec4 new_color;

void main() {
```

```
        vec3 color = vec3(texture(tex, gl_TexCoord[0].st));    ◁──┐ Obtain
        new_color = vec4(color, 1.0);                              │ texel color
}
```

The code for the host application (texture_squares.c) closely resembles the code presented in the previous section (three_squares.c). The primary difference is that the main function in texture_squares.c calls a function called init_textures to create textures from image data. This function creates VBOs to hold texture coordinates for each of the three squares. There are no VBOs to hold vertex colors.

When the host application executes, it creates the window and sends the VBO data (vertex coordinates and texture coordinates) to the vertex shader and the fragment shader. The vertex shader maps the texture coordinates to the vertex, and the fragment shader sets the output color to that of the texture. Once the three textures have been applied to the three squares, the result is what you saw on the right side of figure B.6.

B.7   Summary

The principles underlying OpenGL development aren't significantly different from those underlying OpenCL development. In both cases, the host application initializes the data and the device processes it. The primary difference, of course, is that OpenGL data is graphics-oriented and the device uses the processed data to draw pixels on a screen.

An OpenGL host application has four main tasks to accomplish. First, it has to create vertex buffer objects (VBOs) from vertex data. Then, it has to form attributes that identify the format and content of the VBO data. Shaders process this data, but before they can execute, the host needs to compile the shader code and deploy the linked program to the device. The last responsibility of the host is to launch the rendering process.

Once the rendering starts, the shaders running on the GPU handle the data processing. The vertex shader receives the attributes from the host and determines the final location of each incoming vertex. The fragment shader determines the final color of each pixel drawn in the display. Both shaders are coded in the OpenGL Shading Language, or GLSL. GLSL bears a number of similarities to OpenCL's kernel language, and both languages provide vector data types and mathematical functions to operate on the vectors.

The GL Utility Toolkit, or GLUT, creates windows capable of displaying the rendering produced by OpenGL. GLUT doesn't provide as many features as professional toolkits like Qt or GTK, but it's easy to learn and use. After you call the functions to initialize the window, you can tell GLUT which functions should respond to events. To configure GLUT to work with OpenGL, the resize callback function should call OpenGL's glViewport function. The display callback function should call glDrawArrays.

Textures make it possible to add detail to the rendering. A texture's pixels, texels, are used to cover a surface of the model. Coding with textures consists of three steps. First, the host application creates texture objects and defines the texels of each. Then, the vertex shader matches the texture coordinates with vertices. Last, the fragment shader accesses the texture to determine which color to set as output.

OpenGL is a complicated toolset, and it takes time to understand how the different data structures work together to render graphics. I strongly recommend that you analyze the code in this appendix and other example code to understand what the functions do and why they're needed. Then, once you have a basic understanding of the API, you should experiment with your own graphical applications. The learning curve is steep, but I find it particularly rewarding to create a three-dimensional world and see it rendered on a computer screen.

Appendix C doesn't present any new APIs or functions to learn. Instead, we'll look at an open source set of tools capable of compiling and linking applications on Windows. The toolset is called the *Minimal GNU for Windows,* or *MinGW.* If you're already familiar with GNU development, I'm sure you'll find it easy to use.

appendix C:
The minimalist GNU for
Windows and OpenCL

Microsoft's Visual Studio is a popular tool for coding and compiling Windows applications, but throughout academia and commercial supercomputing, you'll see a greater focus on GNU (GNU's Not Unix) build tools such as gcc (GNU Compiler Collection). These tools are installed automatically on Mac OS and Linux, but Windows users can only access them by installing special packages.

Two such packages are Cygwin or MinGW (the Minimalist GNU for Windows). Cygwin gives you a wide range of GNU-based applications, whereas MinGW provides only the essential GNU tools needed to compile C/C++ code. The goal of this appendix is to show how to install MinGW, how to configure its build process using makefiles, and how to use MinGW to build OpenCL-based applications.

Mac OS and Linux developers may find MinGW helpful because it makes it possible to build native Windows applications without Windows. But this discussion is directed toward Windows users who want to access GNU build tools without installing Linux or buying a Mac. Therefore, the first topic discusses how to install MinGW on the Windows operating system.

C.1 Installing MinGW on Windows

There are two ways to install MinGW on Windows. You can use a text-based installer called mingw-get or run an automated graphical installer called mingw-get-inst. Both are easy to work with, but the automated installer is particularly well suited for Windows users. These instructions will focus on the graphical installer. Specifically, we'll examine how to run the installer and add new capabilities to the MinGW installation.

C.1.1   *Obtaining and running the graphical installer*

To get MinGW running on your system, follow these steps:

1   Open a browser, and go to www.mingw.org. This is the primary site for the MinGW project.

2   Find the Navigation menu on the left, and open the About entry. Click the link entitled Downloads. This opens a site in SourceForge.net, which hosts files related to open source projects.

3   Click the Files link. This should be located in a horizontal series of links under the project title.

4   Download an executable called mingw-get-inst-*num*.exe, where *num* is the current version. This will download the automated graphical installer to your system.

5   After the download is complete, double-click the executable. This will open a graphical wizard whose first page welcomes you to MinGW.

6   Click Next in the welcome page and, assuming you have sufficient privileges, click Next in the Administrator Install page.

7   The next page asks whether you'd like to download the most recent repository catalogue. This is usually a good idea, so select the radio button entitled Download Latest Repository Catalogues and click Next.

8   Accept the GNU public license. This states that MinGW is free and that if you distribute MinGW as part of a larger package, the package must be free as well.

9   Select a directory on your system where you'd like to install MinGW. This chapter assumes you've chosen the C:\MinGW folder. Do not install MinGW in a directory whose name contains spaces.

10   Click Next. Select the location of the program's shortcuts and click Next.

11   The next page asks which components you'd like to install. The C Compiler option is chosen by default, but I strongly recommend that you also select the C++ Compiler option and the MSYS Basic System option as well. This is shown in figure C.1.

12   Click Next and Install. The installer will open a command window and download the required files. Then it will install them into the directory you've chosen. Click Finish to end the installation process.

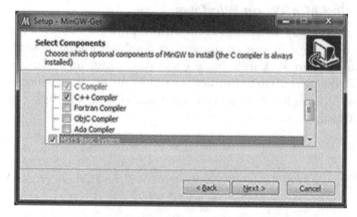

Figure C.1   Selecting components for the MinGW installation

Congratulations! You're now the proud owner of a world-class set of tools for compiling and linking C/C++ applications for Windows. But before you continue, I recommend that you do two things. First, update your PATH environment variable to point to MinGW's executables. Second, open the MinGW installation directory and look through the new files and folders.

SETTING THE PATH VARIABLE

Before you start using the tools, you should make sure they can be accessed from the command line. This means adding the C:\MinGW\bin directory to your PATH environment variable. There are two main ways to access environment variables in Windows:

- *Classic view (XP, Vista)*—Open the Start menu and the Control Panel. Select the System entry and Advanced System Settings. At the bottom of the dialog box, click the Environment Variables button.
- *Modern view (Vista, 7)*—Open the Start menu and the Control Panel. Click the System and Security option. Click System and then click Advanced System Settings on the left. At the bottom of the dialog box, click the Environment Variables button.

The resulting dialog box should look similar to the one displayed in figure C.2.

Under the System Variables heading, scroll down and double-click the Path variable. Add C:\MinGW\bin to the directories that Windows will search when you execute a command from the command line, and remember to separate the directory from the others with a semicolon.

Once you've updated the PATH variable, I recommend that you open a command interpreter (cmd.exe) and attempt to execute the command gcc. If you get the message gcc: no input files, you've succeeded. MinGW is installed properly and you've set the environment variable correctly.

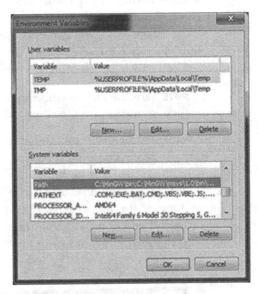

Figure C.2　Setting environment variables

If you receive a message saying that gcc is not recognized as an internal or external command, the environment variable wasn't set correctly. This error may also occur if the terminal was opened before the environment variable was set. In this case, restart the terminal and try again.

EXPLORING MINGW

It's a good idea to open the installation directory (C:\MinGW by default) and look through your new files. There are many subdirectories, but the following four are particularly important:

- *bin*—Contains executables (mingw32-make, mingw32-gcc, mingw32-g++)
- *include*—Contains headers needed to build *nix applications
- *lib*—Contains libraries needed to build *nix applications
- *msys*—Contains files that create a Unix-like shell

The bin directory contains mingw32-make and mingw32-gcc executables, whose functions closely resemble those of regular make and gcc. For mingw32-make, the name change is important to distinguish the utility from a common Windows make utility, which relies on MSCVRT.dll. For mingw32-gcc, the name implies that the build process is a cross-compilation—from Unix to Windows.

The last subdirectory mentioned, msys, stands for *minimal system*, which refers to a Unix-like shell from which you can enter Unix-based commands. We'll look at this next.

C.1.2   *Installing new tools in MinGW*

If you open the top-level msys directory and its version subdirectory (1.0 on my system), you'll find a batch script called msys.bat. If you've installed MinGW correctly, double-clicking this file will bring up a command window with the title MINGW32. This is shown in figure C.3.

At this prompt, you can enter regular Unix commands like ls, rm, mkdir, and mv, and you can even access make. But MSYS doesn't provide a full Unix shell—it just makes it easy to access MinGW's capabilities in a Unix-like manner.

> **NOTE**   For the sake of convenience, you can create a shortcut for msys.bat and then set msys.ico as the shortcut's icon.

If you enter the pwd command at the prompt, MSYS will tell you the name of the directory you're in. This should be /home/*user*, where *user* identifies your account on your computer. This is your home directory. The root directory, identified as /, corresponds to the msys directory in the MinGW installation.

One of the most useful commands to know is mingw-get, which allows you to download additional capabilities and install them into MinGW. For example, if you want to execute Perl scripts in MSYS, enter the following command:

```
mingw-get install msys-perl
```

Figure C.3   The
MSYS window

You can also use this command to add Java or Fortran development, or to access the GNU debugger (gdb). Alternatively, instead of invoking `mingw-get`, you can run executables like mingw32-gcc, which compile code into executables. The next section discusses this important topic.

C.2   Building MinGW executables

Now that you've installed MinGW, you're ready to start creating applications. This section will explain the process of building Windows executables with MinGW and will focus on the gcc compiler and the different ways to control its operation. But first, let's verify the MinGW installation by coding and building a simple program.

C.2.1   Building Hello World! with MinGW

Before you start building large-scale MinGW applications, it's a good idea to test the build tools with a simple executable. To start, we'll look at the procedure for compiling the venerable hello.c source file.

> **Listing C.1   Testing the MinGW toolchain: hello.c**

```
#include <stdio.h>

main() {
    printf("Hello, world!\n");
}
```

If you place the source code for this chapter in your MSYS home directory (C:\MinGW\msys\1.0\home*name*), you can compile this code easily. Change to the hello directory and enter the following command:

```
mingw32-gcc -o hello hello.c
```

This should produce an executable called hello.exe. To test that this is a valid Windows application, use the `file` command:

```
file hello.exe
```

The `file` command will verify that this executable follows the PE32 format, which is used by all 32-bit Windows executables. To run the executable, just enter the full name on the command line.

> **NOTE** If you're interested in using MinGW for 64-bit builds, the site to visit is http://sourceforge.net/projects/mingw-w64. The 64-bit build tools must be compiled from source code, so the installation procedure is complex.

C.2.2   The GNU compiler

mingw32-gcc is a MinGW-specific variant of the famous gcc compiler. gcc is one of the great success stories of open source computing, as it not only provides world-class performance but has also been ported to hundreds of processor platforms. Whether you're developing code for a tiny embedded system or a cluster of supercomputers, it's likely that someone has created a gcc port to compile and build your applications. And best of all, gcc is *free*.

The gcc executable runs from the command line, and its operation is constrained through *options* like -o, -L, and -d. Some ports of gcc provide special options for compiling and linking executables, but for most builds, every flavor of gcc relies on the same basic set. Table C.1 lists these options and the purposes they serve.

Table C.1   Basic options of the gcc compiler

Option	Purpose
-o filename	Stores output (executable, library, object file) in file named filename
-Werror	Reports warnings as errors
-Wall	Reports additional warnings
-w	Suppresses warnings
-I dir	Searches for included files in the dir directory
-L dir	Searches for libraries in the dir directory
-llib	Links the library lib into the build
-g	Produces debugging information during the build
-v	Displays all commands executed during the build
-O0/-O1/-O2/-O3	Uses optimization capabilities during the build (0—least optimization, 3—most optimization)
-E	Preprocesses the file, but doesn't compile
-S	Preprocesses and compiles the file, but doesn't assemble
-c	Compiles and assembles, but doesn't link

The -g option incorporates debugging data into the executable, which can be read by gdb (GNU debugger) as it steps through the executable's code. For a full discussion of gdb's usage and command syntax, visit the gdb website at www.gnu.org/software/gdb/.

When you call a command like mingw32-gcc -o hello hello.c, the mingw32-gcc executable does more than just compile hello.c. It calls on other GNU tools to perform the full build. In most builds like this one, the full process consists of four steps:

1   *Preprocessing*—The preprocessor modifies the source code according to *preprocessor directives*, such as #include, #ifdef, and #pragma statements.
2   *Compilation*—The compiler parses the source code and compiles the source into assembly language that targets the desired processor.
3   *Assembly*—The assembler converts assembly language to machine code, which is placed into an object file.
4   *Linking*—The linker reads in object code, either in object files or libraries, and produces the final result of the build.

gcc performs all of these steps by default, but you can change this by using the last three options in the table: -E, -S, and -c. The first option tells gcc to preprocess the source code, but to go no further. To see how this works, add this to the earlier command:

```
mingw32-gcc -E -o hello.y hello.c
```

The -o option tells gcc to place its output in hello.y, and because of the -E option, this output will contain the preprocessed code from hello.c. If you open hello.y, you'll see that gcc has replaced the #include <stdio.h> statement with the content of the stdio.h header. Similarly, you can see the assembly language generated by the compiler with the following command:

```
mingw32-gcc -S -o hello.s hello.c
```

The last option, -c, tells the compiler to produce an object file, frequently given the suffix *.o. These files contain machine code, but they're not executables. Instead, these files can be included in other builds, and gcc will link them into the final executable. I'll have much more to say about object files and linking in a later section, but for now, it's important to discuss the topic of GNU makefiles.

C.3   *Makefiles*

I don't know about you, but I don't like to type commands like mingw32-gcc every time I want to build an application. Instead, I prefer to write scripts that store the information needed to run the build. Then, rather than type lengthy build commands on the command line, I can just execute the script. This makes life much easier.

GNU build scripts are called *makefiles*, and they're executed by a utility called make. When you run make on a GNU command line, it searches for a file called Makefile in the current directory. If it finds the file, it runs the file's commands and executes the build. To change any aspect of the build, just alter the text in Makefile and run make again.

If you want to see what a real-world makefile looks like, open the GNU folder in this book's example code and look through the project files. Except for chapter 9, each chapter's projects contain makefiles capable of building OpenCL executables.

Writing makefiles is a vital task in GNU development, and this section will discuss the structure of a makefile and the syntax of the build script. Then we'll look at an example MinGW project that includes a makefile.

C.3.1   *Structure of a GNU makefile*

GNU makefiles have a unique syntax that can take a significant amount of time to learn fully. But the fundamentals are simple to understand, and once you've learned the basics, you can write scripts for all but the most complex of projects.

Most simple makefiles consist of four types of statements:

- *Dependency statements*—Statements that identify a file to be created (target) and the files needed for its creation (dependencies)
- *Shell statements*—The commands that tell make how to build a target
- *Comments*—Text on a line following # are ignored by the make utility
- *Macro declarations*—Text substitution statements that serve the same purpose as #define directives in C code

The first two types of statements combine to form *rules*, which tell the make utility how to construct a specific target. Rules form the heart of a makefile, and once you understand how they work, you'll be well on your way to writing scripts of your own.

MAKEFILE RULES

At the very least, a cooking recipe consists of three parts: the name of the dish to be cooked, the ingredients, and the steps needed to convert the ingredients into the final dish. Makefile rules have the same structure. A rule starts by identifying the name of the target and the files required for its creation, called *dependency files* or just *dependencies*. Then it lists the precise steps needed to create the file.

For example, suppose you want the make utility to build a target called output.o from files called input.c and input.h. If the build process consists of three steps, your makefile rule might take the following shape:

```
output.o: input.c input.h
    step 1
    step 2
    step 3
```

More generally, the structure of a makefile rule is as follows:

```
target_file: dependency_files
    shell statements...
```

The first line of the rule is called the dependency statement. It consists of the name of the target followed by a colon and the names of the dependency files. If the target file already exists, the make utility checks the dependencies' timestamps to find out if any have changed more recently than the target. If any dependency files are more current than the target, the make utility reruns the build. Otherwise, make will tell you that the target is up to date.

If make can't find a dependency file, it searches for a rule that will build the file. In this manner, a single build step may involve multiple rules. For example, suppose the first three rules of a makefile are as follows:

```
ab: cd.o fg.o
    echo "1!"
    mingw32-gcc -o ab cd.o fg.o

fg.o: fg.c fg.h
    echo "2!"
    mingw32-gcc -c -o fg.o fg.c fg.h

cd.o: cd.c cd.h
    echo "3!"
    mingw32-gcc -c -o cd.o cd.c cd.h
```

If you execute make without arguments, the utility will process only the first rule of a makefile. Here, the target of the first rule is ab, which requires the object files cd.o and fg.o. If make can't find these files, it looks for rules that will tell it how to construct them.

cd.o is the first missing dependency, so make searches for a rule that defines how to build this file. cd.o is the target of the third rule, so make processes this *before* it completes the processing of the first rule. During the processing, make executes both commands under the dependency statement: it echoes 3! on the command line and then compiles cd.c into cd.o.

After compiling cd.o, make searches for the second missing dependency, fg.o. The second rule specifies how to build this object file, so make processes the rule, echoing 2! and compiling cd.c into cd.o.

Once the dependencies are created, make completes the processing of the first rule. It echoes 1! to standard output and completes the build of the target. Note that, if the make utility finds cd.o and fg.o at the start, the second and third rules won't be processed at all.

These three rules contain shell statements that tell make what actions to perform when processing the rule. Any GNU shell statements can be inserted here, from echo to ls (list directory contents) to pwd (print working directory). But the most common shell statements in a makefile are those that call on gcc to build the target. In a MinGW makefile, a shell statement would call mingw32-gcc to form the target file from its dependencies.

> **NOTE** The whitespace preceding each shell statement *must* be a single tab character, not one or more spaces. If you get an error related to a missing separator, it's likely that the problem involves improper indentation.

In addition to shell statements that build files, makefiles also find commands that delete files with the rm command. These commands are commonly part of a rule whose target's name is clean, and we'll discuss targets like this shortly.

COMMENTS

Makefile comments are easy to understand. Text following the # character on the same line will be ignored by the make utility. This is demonstrated in the following rule declaration:

```
# Build the cd.o object file from cd.c and cd.h
cd.o: cd.c cd.h
    echo "3!"        # Print 3! to standard output
    mingw32-gcc -c -o cd.o cd.c cd.h
```

Note that makefiles only support single-line comments. There are no multiline comment delimiters similar to /* and */ in C/C++ development.

MACROS

Macros in makefiles are similar to string variables in C/C++ code. Once a macro is set equal to a text value, the make utility will replace the macro with its value throughout the script. More specifically, when you set a macro's value with a statement like NAME=VALUE, make will replace $(NAME) with VALUE.

Macros are frequently declared at the start of the makefile and identify tools and options used in the build. For example, the following macros identify the C compiler and the flags used during its compilation:

```
CC = mingw32-gcc
CFLAGS = -Wall -g
```

With these macros set, it becomes easier to configure a build within a rule declaration. For example, the following rule uses these macros to create a target called foo from bar.c and baz.c:

```
foo: bar.c baz.c
    $(CC) $(CFLAGS) -o foo bar.c baz.c
```

Macros not only save time when it comes to writing rules, but they also make it easier to manage changes. For example, suppose you want to optimize your compilation by adding the -O3 option and removing the -g. Rather than rewrite every rule in the script, you only need to change the CFLAGS macro once.

For added convenience, GNU provides special macros that correspond to file-names. These are called *automatic variables*, and table C.2 lists four common variables and their values.

Table C.2   Automatic variables

Macro	Value
$@	The name of the rule's target
$^	Dependency names, separated by spaces
$<	The first dependency
$?	Dependencies more current than the target

The $@ and $^ variables are particularly useful because they make it unnecessary to enter the names of the target file and its dependencies. For example, suppose you were trying to compile bar.c and baz.c with a rule such as this:

```
foo: bar.c baz.c
    $(CC) $(CFLAGS) -o foo bar.c baz.c
```

With automatic variables, you can replace that rule with this:

```
foo: bar.c baz.c
    $(CC) $(CFLAGS) -o $@ $^
```

This usage not only saves time but adds generality—you can copy and paste the same build command into multiple rules without regard to the names of the target or its dependencies. If you look through the makefiles in the GNU folder, you'll see that every build command specifies its target and dependencies using $@ and $^.

C.3.2   *Targets and phony targets*

As mentioned earlier, if you enter make on a command line with no arguments, the make utility will process only the first rule in the makefile. But if you follow make with the name of a target, the utility will process whichever rule constructs that target. Returning to the earlier example, if you enter make cd.o, make will process the third rule because its target is cd.o.

In most rules, the target is a file, such as an executable, library, or object file. But GNU also allows *phony targets*, which are targets that don't correspond to files. Phony targets make it possible to do two things:

- Process multiple unrelated rules with one call to make.
- Execute commands that don't relate to a real target.

The first purpose becomes important when a makefile builds a set of target files, and you want to build all of them with a single make command. For example, suppose a makefile contains rules to build three library files: lib1, lib2, and lib3. Normally, you'd have to build them with separate commands: make lib1, make lib2, and make lib3. But if you make the library files dependencies of a phony target, then make will build the libraries whenever make is executed with the phony target. Here's an example:

```
all: lib1 lib2 lib3
```

The all target isn't a file, but this doesn't matter to the make utility. If you execute make all, the utility will search for lib1, lib2, and lib3. If it can't find them, it will process whatever rules are needed to build the three missing dependencies.

NOTE Rules called all are frequently used in makefiles, and many installation instructions of GNU-based projects require that you enter make all at the command line.

The second usage of phony targets becomes helpful when you want to execute shell statements that have nothing to do with building a file. These targets are commonly used to execute a command that accesses a makefile's macros. For example, suppose you want to delete a target identified by $(TARGET) and all of the object files (*.o) in the directory. In this case, you could code the following rule:

```
clean:
    rm $(TARGET) *.o
```

If a makefile contains this rule, the command make clean will execute the rm statement, deleting $(TARGET) and any object files in the directory. It's interesting to note the difference between this rule and the previous one. The rule that builds all has three dependencies but no shell statements to be executed. The rule that builds clean has a shell statement to be executed, but no dependencies.

NOTE Makefile rules are flexible with regard to dependencies and shell statements, but one rule holds firm—every shell statement must be preceded by a tab character, and only a tab character.

Before the make utility processes a rule, it checks to see if the target exists. A conflict may arise if a file exists with the same name as a phony target. For example, if you run make clean in a directory containing a file called clean, make may decide that the target is up to date, and not bother executing the rule's shell statement.

To remove potential conflicts, the make utility recognizes the .PHONY target. All dependencies of this target will be understood to be phony targets. The following rule uses .PHONY to tell the make utility that clean is a phony target:

```
.PHONY: clean
```

With this rule in place, the make utility won't search for a file called clean when make clean is called. Instead, the utility will always execute the shell statements defined by the rule.

C.3.3   Simple example makefile

In the AppC directory, the folder called simple contains four files: src1.c, src2.c, simple.c, and Makefile. The src1.c file defines a function called hello1 and the src2.c file defines a function called hello2. The main function in the simple.c file calls hello1 and hello2, which print text to standard output.

To build an executable from src1.c, src2.c, and simple.c, src1.c and src2.c must be compiled into object files src1.o and src2.o. Then, after main.c is compiled, the object code can be linked into the final executable. The following listing presents the makefile that the project uses to perform the build.

Listing C.2   A simple makefile

```
PROJ=simple
CC=mingw32-gcc                         Macro
CFLAGS=-std=c99 -Wall                  declarations

$(PROJ): $(PROJ).c src1.o src2.o
    $(CC) $(CFLAGS) -o $@ $^

src1.o: src1.c
    $(CC) $(CFLAGS) -c -o $@ $^

src2.o: src2.c
    $(CC) $(CFLAGS) -c -o $@ $^

.PHONY: clean
                                       Phony
clean:                                 targets
    rm $(PROJ).exe *.o
```

This script sets the PROJ macro equal to the name of the project, simple. This is also used as the name of the first target. When the make utility attempts to build this target for the first time, it looks for the dependencies src1.o and src2.o. To build these object files, make processes the next two rules.

There's still much more to learn about makefiles, and if you're interested, you can find full documentation at www.gnu.org/software/make/manual/html_node/index.html. But if you understand rules, macros, and phony targets, you'll have no trouble writing scripts for the majority of builds you encounter. This includes OpenCL builds, which is the topic of the next section.

C.4   *Building OpenCL applications*

So far, this chapter's MinGW examples have assumed that all the required dependency files are in the working directory. But in many instances, such as in building OpenCL applications, you'll need to access files in many different folders. gcc accepts two options that identify additional directories:

- -I—Identifies a directory containing source files to be included in the build
- -L—Identifies a directory containing libraries to be included in the build

These two options are important in OpenCL development because, on Windows, every build needs to access a header file called CL/cl.h and a library called either OpenCL.dll or OpenCL.lib. Conveniently, both Nvidia and AMD set an environment variable that defines where their development files are located. At the time of this writing, Nvidia's variable is NVSDKCOMPUTE_ROOT and AMD's variable is AMDAPPSDKROOT.

An operating system's environment variables can be accessed in a makefile as macros, and the following listing shows how this works.

Listing C.3   A makefile for Windows OpenCL compilation

```
PROJ=platform_ext_test
CC=mingw32-gcc
CFLAGS=-std=c99 -Wall
LIB=-lOpenCL

ifdef AMDAPPSDKROOT                                      Check AMD
    INC_DIRS="$(AMDAPPSDKROOT)include"                   installation
    LIB_DIRS="$(AMDAPPSDKROOT)lib\x86"
else

ifdef NVSDKCOMPUTE_ROOT
    INC_DIRS=
        "$(NVSDKCOMPUTE_ROOT)\OpenCL\common\inc"         Check Nvidia
    LIB_DIRS=                                            installation
        "$(NVSDKCOMPUTE_ROOT)\OpenCL\common\lib\Win32"
endif

endif

$(PROJ): $(PROJ).c
    $(CC) $(CFLAGS) -o $@ $^ -I$(INC_DIRS) -L$(LIB_DIRS) $(LIB)

.PHONY: clean

clean:
    rm $(PROJ).exe
```

This script checks AMD's environment variable first, and if it has a non-null value, it sets INC_DIRS equal to the directory containing CL/cl.h and LIB_DIRS equal to the directory containing the OpenCL library. If AMD's environment variable isn't set, the script checks for Nvidia's environment variable and looks for the same directories. It's important to see that, regardless of whether the SDK comes from Nvidia or AMD, only one rule performs the build.

> **NOTE**   If a developer has installed SDKs from both AMD and Nvidia, this makefile will target only the AMD installation. Therefore, if you intend to distribute this makefile, you may want to create separate rules for separate installations, and have developers enter `make amd` or `make nvidia` as needed.

In contrast to `-L`, which identifies library directories, the `-l` option identifies the specific names of libraries to be included in the build. The file's suffix doesn't have to be provided. This is helpful for OpenCL builds because, on Windows, the OpenCL library name can be either OpenCL.lib or OpenCL.dll. Because the `LIB` macro is set to `-lOpenCL`, make will recognize either library and link it into the build process if it finds them.

One last point must be mentioned. On many GNU systems, it doesn't matter where you place the library definition in the shell statement. But in MinGW development, the library must be positioned somewhere after the target. Just to be safe, I place my libraries at the end of the build command, and that's why the `LIB` macro follows the rest of the macros in the build.

C.5   *Summary*

I once worked with a programmer who looked down on GNU tools, believing them to be inferior because they were open source. He couldn't have been more wrong. Thousands of developers have spent decades improving these tools, and thanks to their labor, anyone with a PC and an internet connection can build world-class software.

MinGW makes it possible for Windows users to access these tools, enabling them to build C/C++ applications without Microsoft's Visual Studio. This appendix discussed how to obtain and install MinGW, and then call on its mingw32-gcc compiler to build applications. Options make it possible to control the compiler's operation and specify precisely which tasks should be performed.

One of the unique characteristics of GNU development is the syntax of its build scripts, makefiles. Makefiles consist of rules that define files to be built (targets), files required for the build (dependencies), and a series of shell statements to be executed. By default, the `make` utility executes the first rule in a makefile, but if `make` is called with the name of a target, the corresponding rule will be processed.

With the right makefile, it's straightforward to run MinGW builds for OpenCL applications. The only hard part is identifying the location of the CL/cl.h header and the OpenCL library. The key is to rely on the environment variables created by the SDKs during their installation. By using these in a makefile, you can access the OpenCL header and library even if you're not certain which SDK has been installed.

appendix D:
OpenCL on mobile devices

Each new generation of mobile devices provides more capabilities than the last, and it's only a matter of time before high-performance embedded computing becomes a serious priority. A great deal of this performance will be provided by the devices' GPUs, so it's important to understand how OpenCL operates on handheld and mobile devices.

Chapter 10 of the OpenCL 1.1 standard defines the OpenCL Embedded Profile. This is the criteria that embedded devices must meet to be considered OpenCL-compliant. These requirements are a subset of the rules that apply to desktop systems, so there's nothing significantly new or different to learn. But when you're porting OpenCL code to run on a tablet computer or smart phone, it's crucial to know which capabilities are available and which aren't.

First, OpenCL provides a macro that kernels can check to see if the target implements the embedded profile: `__EMBEDDED_PROFILE__`. If this macro is set to 1, the kernel can only access an abridged set of OpenCL capabilities. Otherwise, the kernel can access all the capabilities defined by the full profile.

The differences between the embedded profile and the full profile fall into two main categories: numerical processing and image processing. This appendix discusses both, and we'll start by examining how embedded OpenCL processes numbers.

D.1 Numerical processing

For the most part, OpenCL numerical operations can be executed on an embedded device without any change. In both the embedded profile and the full profile, 64-bit values are optional but 32-bit values (int and float) are required. Other characteristics of number processing on embedded devices are as follows:

- All of the built-in numerical functions defined for the full profile must be available for embedded devices. But the required accuracy for embedded operations may be reduced. Section 9.10.8 of the OpenCL 1.1 standard defines the minimum accuracy for embedded operations.

- Embedded devices must be able to convert between numeric data types, but when normalized values (0.0 to 1.0) are converted to regular floating-point values, the accuracy may be reduced.

- Embedded devices must support rounding to zero (`CL_FP_ROUND_TO_ZERO`) or rounding to nearest even (`CL_FP_ROUND_TO_NEAREST`). If rounding to nearest even is supported, it must be the default rounding method. Chapter 4 discusses these and other rounding methods.

- If the `CL_FP_INF_NAN` parameter isn't set and an operation produces an infinite value or not-a-number (NaN), the embedded profile doesn't place any restriction on the output value. That is, +inf, -inf, and NaN values are implementation-defined.

- With one exception, denormalized numbers on embedded devices must be processed similarly to denormalized values on full-profile devices. The exception is that, when calling `vstore_half` and `vload_half`, denormalized values of the `half` data type may be set to 0.

- Atomic functions are optional for embedded devices. To check for their availability, the extension names used on embedded devices are the same as on full-profile devices. For example, on 32-bit systems, the atomic extension names are as follows:

```
cl_khr_global_int32_base_atomics
cl_khr_global_int32_extended_atomics
cl_khr_local_int32_base_atomics
cl_khr_global_int32_extended_atomics
```

As shown here, nearly all numeric operations available for the full profile will be available on embedded devices. But accuracy may be reduced and irregular values such as infinite values and denormalized values may not be processed at all.

In addition to supporting numerical operations, the embedded profile supports all operations related to programs, kernels, and buffer objects. But when it comes to image objects, operations on embedded devices are limited in comparison with full-profile devices. The next section explores this in detail.

D.2   Image processing

Chapter 6 discusses image objects and the manner in which they're processed on full-profile devices. The OpenCL embedded profile also supports image objects, but only under certain constraints:

- If the data channel type is set to `CL_FLOAT` or `CL_HALF_FLOAT`, samplers must be configured to use nearest-neighbor interpolation with the `CL_FILTER_NEAREST` setting. Otherwise, the values returned by `read_imagef` are undefined.

- Embedded devices do not have to support three-dimensional image objects. To check whether support is available, examine the CL_DEVICE_IMAGE3D_MAX_WIDTH, CL_DEVICE_IMAGE3D_MAX_HEIGHT, and CL_DEVICE_IMAGE3D_MAX_DEPTH parameters. If these all equal 0, the device does not support three-dimensional images.

- Samplers can be set to any of the available addressing modes (CL_ADDRESS_NONE, CL_ADDRESS_CLAMP, CL_ADDRESS_CLAMP_TO_EDGE, CL_ADDRESS_REPEAT, and CL_ADDRESS_MIRRORED_REPEAT). For embedded devices, the minimum number of available samplers is 8.

- The required minimum number of channels available for image data is 4, and the only required value for image_channel_order is CL_RGBA.

- Embedded devices do not support every value for the image_channel_data_type. The only values that must be supported are CL_UNORM_INT8, CL_UNORM_INT16, CL_SIGNED_INT8, CL_SIGNED_INT16, CL_SIGNED_INT32, CL_UNSIGNED_INT8, CL_UNSIGNED_INT16, CL_UNSIGNED_INT32, CL_HALF_FLOAT, and CL_FLOAT.

In most cases, any OpenCL code that processes images will run on embedded devices. But as shown by this list, embedded devices don't support all image types or all pixel formats.

D.3 Summary

The world of embedded software development is growing by leaps and bounds, and as mobile devices gain more graphical computing power, the need for OpenCL programmers will rise accordingly. Remember that nearly all of the major players in embedded processor development—Intel, AMD, ARM, and Nvidia—belong to the OpenCL Working Group.

The good news is that for embedded OpenCL you don't have to learn any new data structures or functions. But if numerical accuracy is a concern, you should look over the limitations imposed by the embedded profile. In particular, if you need to process irregular values—inf, NaN, or denormalized values—you may need to rewrite your code specifically to recognize them.

Embedded devices support image processing to a limited extent. The standard doesn't require devices to support three-dimensional image objects or samplers that filter images using bilinear interpolation. Also, the only required channel order is CL_RGBA, so traditional RGB and grayscale images may not be supported.

index